AMERICA
RELIGIONS AND RELIGION

Fourth Edition

Catherine L. Albanese
University of California, Santa Barbara

Australia • Brazil • Canada • Mexico • Singapore • Spain • United Kingdom • United States

THOMSON
WADSWORTH™

America: Religions and Religion, Fourth Edition
Catherine L. Albanese

Publisher/Executive Editor: *Holly J. Allen*
Acquisitions Editor: *Steve Wainwright*
Assistant Editor: *Barbara Hillaker*
Editorial Assistant: *Gina Kessler*
Technology Project Manager: *Julie Aguilar*
Marketing Manager: *Worth Hawes*
Marketing Assistant: *Alexandra Tran*
Marketing Communications Manager: *Stacey Purviance*
Project Manager, Editorial Production: *Megan E. Hansen*
Creative Director: *Rob Hugel*
Executive Art Director: *Maria Epes*
Print Buyer: *Karen Hunt*
Permissions Editor: *Bob Kauser*
Production Service: *Winifred S. Sanchez, Interactive Composition Corporation*
Copy Editor: *Tami Taliaferro*
Cover Designer: *Yvo Riezebos*
Cover Image: *Peabody Museum, Harvard University, Photo 33-54-10/1536 T1394*
Compositor: *Interactive Composition Corporation*
Printer: *Thomson West*

Printed in the United States of America
1 2 3 4 5 6 7 09 08 07 06

Thomson Higher Education
10 Davis Drive
Belmont, CA 94002-3098
USA

Library of Congress Control Number: 2006926967

Student Edition: ISBN 0-534-62739-0

To the memory of my grandfather,
Frank S. Spiziri (1878–1958), one among the many

CONTENTS

Preface to the First and Second Editions

Americans during their formative years were a people in movement through space. . . . This is the mighty saga of the outward acts, told and retold until it has overshadowed and suppressed the equally vital, but more somber, story of the inner experience. Americans have so presented to view and celebrated the external and material side of their pilgrims' progress that they have tended to conceal even from themselves the inner, spiritual pilgrimage, with its more subtle dimensions and profound depths.

Sidney E. Mead, The Lively Experiment, *pp. 7–8*

So wrote Sidney Mead in his classic work as he explored the space, time, and religion of the American people. There was a "one story" to be celebrated, an epic tale of triumph written, as Mead said, "with cosmic quill." Yet in the midst of the heroic narrative, inner experience remained unexplored, even by the doers of the mighty deeds.

Mead knew then, and we know now, that not all of these Americans were alike. Over and over again, we have grown familiar with clichés about the fact and experience of pluralism in the United States. To be plural means to be more than one, to be many. To be a pluralistic land means to be one country made up of many peoples and many religious faiths. Yet when we look at America's history books—and more to the point here, America's religious history books—we find that they generally tell one major story, incorporating the separate stories of many peoples into a single story line arranged chronologically. The one story is the "mighty saga of the outward acts," as Mead so clearly saw. For if you tell the one story of America, perforce, it will center on the history-makers, the Anglo-Saxon and Protestant majority—and perhaps those most like them—who dominated the continent and its culture into the later twentieth century. To keep the story line going, you will focus on exemplary deeds and overall achievements while looking only briefly, if at all, at the deeper, more hidden dimension of spirituality.

There is surely a point to such single-line storytelling, for it conveys the idea of a common culture shared by all Americans. At its best, it binds many diverse peoples into one political community, one nation. It does so by picking up the threads of their separate stories and showing how the many encounter and assimilate with the dominant group, always to form part of the one continuous narrative. However, to face up to the implications of pluralism means to recognize that it is problematic to recite, even if artfully and inclusively, one story before exploring the realities of the many stories. Like it or not, to do so suppresses the distinctive identities of the many peoples who count themselves part of the American venture. True, some accounting of their presence can be and, in contemporary versions, usually is expressed through the single story plot. Still, the inner and spiritual stories of these diverse peoples are swept away into the march of mainstream American history. Telling merely one story, without first telling many stories, is possible only at a considerable cost—that of losing touch with the richness and texture of American pluralism.

This book arises from a conviction that the cost is too high. Standing within the pluralistic experiment, the book tells, first, not one but many stories. Only thereafter does it search for the tentative oneness amidst the manyness of the United States. Moreover, it seeks to tell a different kind of story by viewing religious history as a complex recital that leads to the inner world of the human spirit and imagination. In other words, the text deals with two kinds of events.

First are the simple, clear-cut, and short-term events with which most history usually deals. Where useful and available, dates will be noted and leaders named; new organizations and popular configurations will be recorded and outer achievements marked. Second, and just as important for the history of religions, are inner events of consciousness that find outer expression in religious settings. Unlike the names and dates of a more politically oriented history, these sets of events are not neat, tidy, and easily comprehended in conventional historical summaries. Most of the time, they unfold gradually, over centuries. To borrow—and modify—an idea from the French historian Fernand Braudel, they are events of "long duration." Such long-term events do not have sharp and precise edges, like a frame around a battle painting of the Civil War. Rather, these events are grasped as emerging out of the experience of people, vocalized and expressed through sacred story and ritual, everyday behavior, and sometimes institutions. Hence, this book tries to follow the pathways from outer expression to inner experience. It assumes that the inner stories are immensely significant in American religious history.

In keeping with the goal of relating the religious stories of the many and the one, the text is concerned with popular religion, the religion of the people. It aims to explore each religious world from the point of view of its entire community. For that reason, issues of more concern to leaders than to other participants—governance and politics, for example—are downplayed, although they are not wholly ignored. For the same reason, considering the many stories before the single story has added significance. Although ordinary people are aware of pluralism, they usually do not choose to confront it head on. Rather, they live in their own separate centers of religious meaning constructed from an inherited past and a necessary present.

However, the book also recognizes that people *do* live out their particular religious histories within the larger society—in an ultimately public space that involves other groups of people. Therefore, a general sociological framework forms a kind of horizon for the text. Although problems exist with any typology of religious groups, the framework of this book is based mostly on conventional understandings of them. More important, the book implicitly works from ideas derived from the sociology of knowledge. When, for example, Americans are called strangers in the land, the background of the social setting for their experience is never far away in the text. The social reasons why Americans know what they know are seen as important to the religious question. Finally, in the formulation of its basic theme the book has profited from anthropological insights concerning the importance of boundaries. As social spaces where two peoples or two realities meet, boundaries assume monumental importance in America. They are discussed further in the Introduction, and, in this context, so is the understanding of religion that governs the text.

As background for this discussion, it is assumed that definitions of religion can be divided into three types: substantive, functional, and formal. *Substantive* definitions of religion focus on the inner core, essence, or nature of religion and define it by this thing-in-itself. They tend to emphasize a relationship with a higher being or beings (God or the Gods) and to be favored by theologians and philosophers. *Functional* definitions of religion emphasize the effects of religion in actual life. They stress the systems of meaning-making that religion provides and how it helps people deal with the ills, insecurities, and catastrophes of living. Functional definitions are favored by scholars in the social sciences. Lastly, *formal* definitions of religion look for typically religious forms gleaned from the comparative study of religions and find the presence of religion where such forms can be identified. Religious forms include sacred stories, rituals, moral codes, and communities; and formal definitions of religion tend to be favored by historians of religions. Since this book is not a theoretical work, in the strict sense it does not define religion. But it does describe religion working from the discipline of the history of religions, and so its understanding of religion is formal. Because the book is as much about "plain" religious history and is likewise open to sociological and anthropological categories, its understanding is also functional.

The order of chapters in Part One is mostly historical, as the Introduction explains. The first six chapters introduce the early cast of characters—Native Americans, Jews (who arrived with Christopher Columbus), Catholics, Protestants (in two chapters), and African Americans—more or less in the order of their appearance. The following chapters trace new religious developments in the chronological order in which they became significant. The chapter on regional religion focuses on a religious culture of long duration—that of Southern Appalachia. A major function of the chapter is to introduce the concept of regional religion as a fruitful way to study a religious people, but the chapter also views an emphasis on regionalism in religion as part of a distinctly modern "moment" in American religious history. Seeing the inward-turning growth of religious regionalism juxtaposed to the cultural stretch toward religions of the East tells us more than seeing either of these two phenomena alone. Similarly, a final chapter in this section views two contemporary religious movements together. Looking at conservative Protestantism and New Age religion in concert throws important light on American religion in the present as a cultural system.

Like that of Appalachia, other case studies are included in many of the chapters. The criterion for their selection has tended to be intrinsic religious interest more than the numerical size of the group. Indeed, if the text were to operate on the numerical principle in Part One, most of the material would be about Protestants, with a section on Catholics and a brief mention of African Americans, Jews, and other groups close in size. From the viewpoint of an interest in religious forms and meanings, however, counting people is not the best approach to the study of religion in America. More than that, such an approach may be exceedingly deceptive since, of necessity, it favors those religions whose members build strong, enduring organizations that keep conventional written records. Many religions in nineteenth- and twentieth-century America were structurally too diffuse for such endeavors and, besides, were ideologically alienated from these kinds of concerns regarding number. Yet their presence in our culture may be far greater than we would at first suspect. For example, we will see that this is true for metaphysical traditions like New Thought and for Asian disciplines like yoga.

In contrast to Part One, Part Two examines the "one story" of religion in America and therefore uses a more topical approach. The one story here has three aspects, and a pedagogic logic suggests that the sequence move from the most clearly recognizable and familiar face of religion to its less noticed manifestations. Within the chapters, the narrative runs from past to present when that is possible. However, dominating movement in short-term events is the continuing presence of the long-term event that is the one religion of America. From the seventeenth century, the basic structure of that religion was, in rough form, present. So the text aims to trace the elements of structure, form, and content according to methods that, it is hoped, will disclose something of the religious nature of America. A concluding chapter, which deals with the one religion and the many religions of America, works historically within a thematic framework. It surveys the history of the relationships among the many and the one as, again, a long-term event.

Notes are avoided throughout the book in order not to burden the beginning student. At the end of each chapter, however, is a short and selective bibliography that serves two purposes. First, it suggests sources to the student for further and more extensive discussion of material in the preceding chapter. Second, it indicates, in a general but not exhaustive way, sources that the text itself reflects. As a rule, new terms are explained when used initially. Biblical quotations are from the King James

Version for historical reasons. Any reference to God or the Gods in the text is capitalized because the book acknowledges the truth of all of the Gods in the power that they hold in people's lives. The past tense is generally employed throughout the text as well. This does not in itself imply that religious beliefs and practices discussed have fallen into disuse but rather that they are events of long duration begun, in most cases, before our time. The present tense is used only sparingly for contemporary religious phenomena.

In its goal of bringing to readers a faithful report of the many religious people in America, the book has profited from the insights of many individuals. If writing this work has taught me anything, it has brought home how much scholarship is a community affair. Charles H. Long introduced me to the distinction between ordinary and extraordinary religion on which subsequent chapters rest. Martin E. Marty influenced me with his own wide interest in questions of pluralism. Numerous friends and colleagues knowledgeable in specific traditions read and criticized, with painstaking care, earlier drafts of sections of the text. For their advice and encouragement in doing so for the first edition, I thank Jonathan M. Butler, Theodore Chamberlain, Jay P. Dolan, Robert S. Ellwood, Jr., Eric L. Friedland, Sam D. Gill, Philip Gleason, Stephen Gottschalk, Richard A. Humphrey, Charles H. Long, Alfonso Ortiz (now deceased), Sharon Welch Patton, Albert J. Raboteau, Frank E. Reynolds, Ernest R. Sandeen (now deceased), Jan Shipps, Jane S. Weeks, Rose Wendel, and Ronald M. White. In addition, I owe other debts to the scholars who read the entire first-edition text and made helpful suggestions for its improvement. For these good offices, I thank Sandra Sizer Frankiel, Martin E. Marty, Robert S. Michaelsen, Frank E. Reynolds, the late Ernest R. Sandeen, J. Benton White, and Peter W. Williams. I thank, too, Sidney E. Mead, who granted me permission to quote from *The Lively Experiment* and ably criticized this preface. For the second edition, I thank for their reading and comments Kay Alexander, Katharine L. Dvoràk, Stephen Gottschalk, Richard L. Hoch, Laurie Maffly-Kipp, Robert S. Michaelsen, Timothy Miller, Carlton T. Mitchell, Grant Wacker, and J. Benton White. All of these people have enlightened and assisted me in many ways, but I hasten to add that I alone am responsible for any remaining errors and omissions. I am also responsible for the interpretive stance the text reflects.

The Liberal Arts College of Wright State University was tremendously supportive of the first edition, allowing me to rearrange and lighten my teaching schedule in order to have the spring quarter of 1979 free for research and writing, and extending a research grant to me to aid in manuscript preparation. That assistance brought me Virginia Blakelock, whose helpfulness extended far beyond the excellence of her typing. Patricia A. Schwab and Veda D. Horton in the Religion Department also assisted generously with the typing. David L. Barr, my colleague at the time in the department, was an invaluable consultant on points concerning biblical matters, and all of my colleagues cheered and supported me. Dean Eugene B. Cantelupe and his office assumed the financial burden for my seemingly endless photocopying requests; Margaret Roach of the university library prepared the original index; and Stephen Haas and others also at the library rendered many services.

For the second edition, Gregor Goethals offered helpful suggestions for illustrations, for which I remain grateful. I am grateful, too, to Lynne Williamson, who, several years ago and in another context, introduced me to the Algonkian copper gorget whose representation appears on the cover and elsewhere in this book. For use of the photograph itself, I thank the Peabody Museum of Harvard University, and—as important—I thank the anonymous Algonkian artist of long ago whose elegant and eloquent artifact I have borrowed in its representation. Meanwhile, I owe a continuing debt to Sheryl Fullerton, former Religion Editor at Wadsworth, for the help, support, and encouragement that have made both first and second editions possible. And I thank my new friends at Wadsworth, Jerilyn Emori and Cynthia Schultz, who have patiently worked with a seemingly eternally tardy author in the production of the second-edition text.

My present colleagues at the University of California, Santa Barbara, have also supported and encouraged me as I worked to produce this new edition, and I remain grateful for the intellectual climate they have created in my world. I also owe a debt of a different order to the multitalented photocopying machine in Santa Barbara's Department of Religious Studies. And I acknowledge the many students there and elsewhere over the years who have responded to material in the first edition and so helped to shape the changes resulting here.

Finally, to my parents, Louis and Theresa Albanese, who were my earliest teachers, I owe debts still larger. It was they who gave me my first understanding of the vitality of a community of one people against the backdrop of pluralism. And that is also why I have chosen to dedicate this book to an ancestor whom I remember dearly and whose memory I cherish.

Preface to the Third Edition

For this new edition, I have focused my efforts mainly in two areas. First, I have updated chapters to include significant developments since the second edition was published. Thus, the third edition contains new material on a variety of topics and themes, with probably the largest amount on the Branch Davidians, Heaven's Gate, the Christian Coalition, Promise Keepers, *Star Trek*, and the Grateful Dead. There are, of course, other additional materials—on Native Americans and the law, on Latinos and especially Mexican Americans, on liberal Protestant women in the Re-Imagining Conference and Community, on Afro-Caribbean religions in the United States, on liberal churches in Appalachia, on the evangelical Sojourners Community, and on the Peoples Temple and Jonestown—to name a few. With an aim of keeping the text approximately the same length as it was in its second edition, it has been at least challenging to decide what to include and what to leave out—and what to strike to make room for new inclusions.

Second, however, I have rethought terminology—and, therefore, interpretation—in a series of instances. Most important has been a revisionary look at the term *syncretism* and its replacement by more inclusive language regarding religious combinativeness. My own discomfort with "syncretism" has been expressed more fully in the essay "Exchanging Selves, Exchanging Souls," which I contributed to Thomas A. Tweed's *Retelling U.S. Religious History* (Berkeley: University of California Press, 1997). In brief, *syncretism* comes trailing cultural baggage from New Testament studies, where it has been used to distinguish between the pure religion of Christianity and the adulterated and religiously inferior forms created by varieties of non-Christians who combined elements from different traditions. Even the neutralization of the term in later historical contexts leaves the inference that some religions syncretize and others do not. Such a judgment is arguably simplistic in any historical setting. It is especially so in the United States, where the contact of diverse religious people has been an everyday affair and where all traditions—even the dominant Protestant one—have undergone profound changes because of their proximity to one another and their mutual experience in the land. Faced with this interpretive problem, I have been instructed by concepts and terms employed by my colleague Allan G. Grapard in his book *The Protocol of the Gods: A Study of the Kasuga Cult in Japanese History* (Berkeley: University of California Press, 1992). Grapard's careful discussion there of *combinative* religion alerted me to the importance of religious combination in the United States. Hence, in this new edition, I stress contact and combination among *all* religious peoples—those who were, and continue to be, dominant and those who have played the role of cultural "others." I talk, therefore, about "combinativeness" and "combinationism," not about "syncretism."

On another front, I have introduced language about "spiritual practice groups" in a series of chapters. This is because I believe that the older sociological concept of the "cult" has become too deeply problematic; in the context of media usage and a trail of negative connotations, it obscures more than it reveals. The spiritual practice groups need to be noticed for their (usually small) size, their newness, their distinctive forms of religious behavior (hence, "spiritual practice"), and their openness to charismatic leadership and ongoing "revelation." All of that acknowledged, there are huge differences in religious orientation among different spiritual practice groups, so that lumping them together leads to faulty constructions of each and all of them. With that assessment, I have consciously worked to *de*construct the notion of "cultic" commonality. Thus, I have introduced materials about groups like the Peace Mission Movement, the Nation of Islam, the Branch Davidians, Heaven's Gate, the Healthy-Happy-Holy Association, Transcendental Meditation, and numerous other groups in the religious families in which they are most at home. My hope is that this heuristic strategy will bring more light than heat to the discussion of religious creativity, its promises, and its pitfalls outside the major orthodoxies of our society.

Other language changes will be noticeable to the careful reader. While I invoke "America" for the traditional, looser, and more visionary associations it conveys, more often, for precision, I talk about the "United States." I have also employed terms like "New World" and "frontier" more sparingly than before because of the Euro-centric trappings they carry. Whose New World? And whose frontier? These are significant questions in a society in which pluralism is no longer merely one characteristic but the very substance of the structure and frame.

As in previous editions, my debts are large. Wadsworth provided wonderful and supportive third-edition editors in Peter S. Adams and Greg Hubit. They made the often tedious tasks of book production as easy as these things can be. Meanwhile, this edition will go to press with a Web page and capabilities for students to engage in virtual activities that I myself am just beginning to fathom. All of this is, as I like to say, above my intellectual level. Hence, I acknowledge the work of Richard J. Callahan and Sarah McFarland Taylor in creating the Web site for this book and, as I also like to say, feeding it well. I thank them, too, for their splendid research assistance and for their continual urging that I take on the Grateful Dead. It has turned out that other students with whom I have worked had been as interested in the Dead. My discussion of them would have been immensely poorer without material from the dissertation-in-progress of Robin Sylvan to guide me. It would have been much poorer, likewise, without a seminar paper by Robert L. Hertenstein, which argued the case for the Dead as a form of nature religion, and a conference paper for the American Academy of Religion by Oren Baruch Stier, which explored the Deadhead community online. I have already noted my debt to Allan Grapard in dealing with religious combination. On that score, I have a related debt, too, to Christel Manning, whose insightful master's thesis a number of years ago alerted me to the usefulness of applying ideas about religious combinativeness in an American context. Meanwhile, Wade Clark Roof has helped me with recent statistics regarding Islam, and Grant Wacker with the same regarding pentecostalism. Norman Girardot has kept me posted on the latest developments in the ongoing saga of Elvis Presley. Michael McClymond has assured me of the good health of a series of conservative Protestants who are getting up in years, and more generally Sylvelin Edgerton, in the Davidson Library, has found the obituaries of others who have passed on. A series of undergraduates over the years have managed to tell me what they thought of the book, and their comments have helped me more than they know. Finally, my parents, now in their eighties, continue to express their enthusiasm and support for my work. The text that follows is my way to say "Thank you!"

Preface to the Fourth Edition

This edition is what I fondly term my "slash-and-burn" contribution to the discipline. I have shortened and simplified to meet the needs of a new generation of students and new kinds of courses. I have eliminated a chapter, conflated three others, added a section on the Jehovah's Witnesses to one chapter, and updated throughout. Themes of pluralism and postpluralism stand out more strongly. Pluralism here stands for religious people living side by side—sometimes in conflict, other times with tolerance and respect, and still other times with cooperation for mutual goals and benefit. Postpluralism means religious combination—the spiritual expression of the habit all humans have of copying from one another, sometimes consciously and sometimes unaware.

Throughout the text, I have used boldface to help students notice key concepts, people, and events. I have also moved the (shortened and updated) bibliographies to the end with a view to making them easier to consult. Two new graphs—homegrown and a little bit hokey—accompany the text. For helping me to create them and for general research assistance, I am grateful to Aaron Gross. Others who have helped me on various phases of this project deserve thanks, too. Among them are Juan Campo, Julianne Cordero-Lamb, Gaston Espinosa, Gregory Johnson, Michael McNally, Marc Mullinax, Father Jack Clark Robinson, Ann Taves, and David White. Students in my Introduction to American Religion course have helped me more than they know. So have countless others with a word, an idea, or an observation that started me thinking in different ways. So, also, have the many reviewers who took Wadsworth seriously when the company asked for comments and provided lucid critiques of my earlier work. I remain profoundly grateful to all of them, and I hasten to add that any problems that remain are my own. Barbara Hillaker at Wadsworth has been a continuing help in the revision process. My biggest debt, though, is to Steve Wainwright for his magnificent patience, his willingness to tackle computer glitches that I could not solve, and his general resolve to do everything possible to streamline the revision process. I hope that he and others are pleased with the results!

An Elephant in the Dark

There is a story that both Buddhists and some Muslims claim as their own. It is about a group of blind men who had never before encountered an elephant. Each of the men felt the elephant and later described the experience. Some, who had felt the head of the animal, claimed that an elephant was like a pot. Others, who had felt an ear, claimed that an elephant was like a harvest basket used to separate grain. Still others had touched a tusk, and they announced that an elephant was part of a plow, while yet another group that had patted the trunk thought an elephant was a plow, whole and complete. The moral of the story, of course, goes beyond elephants. Each individual tries to fathom life's meaning from a place of personal darkness. Each describes the part of life experienced, and none can speak about the whole. The lesson is to accept the fact of human limitation with humility and the fact of life's complexity with awe. Nobody will ever know the whole story, because life's vastness far exceeds our senses or our ability to understand.

What does all of this have to do with religious history in the United States? In this study, we will in some sense be like blind people trying to feel an elephant. First, there will be so much elephant to feel: there will be so many American religions to explore. Our nation has been home to many native religions, grown new ones, and accepted others from abroad. Second, we will be feeling our religious elephant in the dark. We will be in the dark because even as we try to study American religious history, the meaning of the term *religion* is itself open to question. Staring long and hard at what we call religion tends to dissolve its boundaries. Scholars have become less certain about what should count as religion. Do belief systems without a God or Gods—like some forms of Buddhism—count? Do political ideologies? Do symbolic practices—like some neopagan rituals—in which participants acknowledge no objective existence for the Goddess count, too? Given the ambiguity, this study of American religious history must reflect it. In other words, the task will in some ways be like trying to see an elephant in the dark. Initially, we will need to understand what we mean by religion. After progress is made in that study, it will be easier to find and make sense of United States religions and religious history.

Both of these tasks—trying to understand what religion means and trying to understand specific religious systems in history—are the work of fields of study called, respectively, comparative religions and religious history. This text is a study of religion in the United States from the perspectives of comparative religions and of general religious history. The text will be asking three questions in the following pages. First, what is religious about American religious history? Second, what is American about American religious history? Third, what continues and what changes in the course of American religious history? We begin with the task of trying to understand, in a general sense, what we mean by religion.

Defining Religion

From the viewpoint of common sense, every one knows what religion is. It is one of those obvious realities that we have either grown up practicing or observing others practice. Everyone knows what religion is—that is, until someone tries to define it. In the act of defining, religion seems to slip away.

We might want to limit religion to a relationship that humans consider themselves to have had with God or the Gods, while another person might ask if atheists were religious. We might want to call religion a way of living, an ethical system such as Confucius taught, but somebody could counter that all people have had some way of living and many of these ways were not, in any recognizable sense, religions. We might say that religion had to do with a quality of experience, a powerful feeling that people have had. Yet a few in the group would be sure to suggest that the most powerful experience they could remember at a religious service on many a Saturday or Sunday morning was being lost in a daydream. Still again, we might venture that religion was the thing in life a person was most ultimately concerned about, but one sarcastic member of our group would be sure to ask if that meant racehorses or the lottery.

Why is it that so common a feature of human life proves so baffling? What is it about religion that eludes our grasp? A definition, says *Webster's Third New International Dictionary*, is an "act of determining or settling." It is "the action or the power of making definite and clear or of bringing into sharp relief." Definition, in fact, comes from the Latin word *finis*, which means an end or limit—a boundary. A definition tells us where some reality ends; it separates the world into what is and what is not that reality.

Given that emphasis on boundary, there is a special reason why religion eludes definition. Religion cannot be defined very easily because it thrives both within and outside of boundaries. It crosses the boundaries that definitions want to set because, paradoxically, it, too, concerns boundaries. The boundaries of religion, however, are different from the logical boundaries of good definitions. In the end, religion is a feature that encompasses all of human life. It exists in organized and informal versions, among rich and poor, with thisworldly and otherworldly orientations, and so forth. So it is difficult if not impossible to define religion. It may therefore be more fruitful to think not of defining religion but, instead, of trying to describe it. To describe something is to say what it generally looks like and how it usually works. It is not to say what its innermost realities are, and it is not to say definitely what separates these realities from every other object in the world. Still, describing a thing can tell us much about what it is. Looking at the past and present appearances of religion can tell us what functions and forms go along with it. Learning to recognize these functions and forms helps us know when we are looking at religion. Hence, in what follows, we will not so much try to define religion as to describe it.

Religion and Boundaries

What we know about various religions suggests that they arose to deal with boundaries. For many peoples, physical boundaries that marked the limits of the territory of another group were frightening. They divided land that was safe, the source of nurture and sustenance, from land that was alien and unfriendly, the home of hostile spirits and strange or warring peoples. So it was that any exchanges conducted across these boundaries were stressful and that people strengthened themselves for these exchanges through the use of ritual. In the formula of word and act, people at a dangerous place in the physical landscape could call on special help; they could ease their encounter with whatever was alien. This assistance seemed to come from the unknown, from forces that went beyond ordinary life. In other words, alien land and people were countered by a second form of "otherness," more powerful than the first. By enlisting the help of this new "other power," life could go on as intended. The "other" force that saved a difficult situation was called religious. And the rituals through which other power or powers were contacted were religious rituals.

But territorial boundaries were only one kind of border with which people dealt. There were also the limits of their own bodies, the boundaries of skin that separated each person in a group from every other person. Crossing the boundary of one's body could not be avoided: it happened every day in the simple acts of eating and drinking, of defecating, or of having sexual intercourse. It occurred even when words passed from one person to the next. Thus, rituals like prayer before a solemn speech or meeting grew up around these exchanges of language. In many cultures, prayer also accompanied the taking of food and drink. Similarly, the products of human bodies at their boundaries—hair, spittle, nail parings, feces—were considered dangerous or helpful, depending on circumstances. In a number of cultures, people feared that an enemy who found strands of their hair or their nail parings could bring evil upon their persons. Hair and nail parings, along with other "boundary" products of the body became focuses for ritual. Religious specialists learned to use them in ceremonies, and people stood in awe of these products of their bodies.

Finally, there were the temporal boundaries in the life cycle that any person passed through. In experiencing birth, puberty, marriage, and death, a person crossed the border between one form of life, which was known and secure, and a new kind of life, which was often somewhat fearful. So there were rites that would ease the passage across the boundaries from one stage in the life cycle to another. In our own society, many engage in ceremonies of baptism for infants and Bar or Bat Mitzvahs and confirmation rites at adolescence. Marriage brings its solemnities, and at death, both wakes and funerals form the usual rites of passing.

This concern for boundaries has been apparent throughout the history of human societies. Borders continued to be places invested with religious significance—for example, by the imposing, birdlike *garudas* at the entrances of Hindu temples or the equally arresting gargoyles at the outside corners of medieval Christian cathedrals. These signs and boundary markers warned all comers that they were crossing a frontier into a sacred precinct. They effectively divided one world from another. Even in the realm of language, religious or theological discourse has aimed to speak about the unspeakable. It has been "limit" language, language that pushes to the edge of human knowledge and tries to talk about what goes beyond. Death, judgment, heaven, hell—these were critical events for the Christian theology that so many Americans have historically held. They were also words to cross the boundary of the known world, attempts to make sense of mysterious realities from a different world.

Like these many Christians, all Americans participate in a long tradition of mixing boundary questions with religious questions. Thus, for Americans as others, religion concerns the way to locate oneself in space through holy places and sacred rites as boundary markers. It concerns, too, the way to locate oneself in time through origin stories or theological traditions that also express boundaries. But location is always social. It concerns one's place among other human beings, and it means staking a claim on the landscape of identity.

The internal landscape of identity provides a new territory in which boundaries become important. By searching for identity and finding it, individuals metaphorically establish inner boundaries, discover through testing who they are not, and begin to affirm who they are. In the process, each individual finds that these personal boundaries overlap with those of others, so that there can be a free process of exchange. Religion through the ages has tried to answer the continuing human question, "Who am I?" More particularly, religious writers of our times have made much of the issue of identity, since today's world has given people many choices about the boundaries of the inner space they will occupy. In more traditional societies, most people grew up in a culture that took outer and inner worlds for granted, with ancient and prescribed rules for living. But in a mobile society this picture of fixed space disappears. The presence of many possibilities for finding an inner world of one's own means that many decisions have to be made.

Hence, in our era, identity has become a problem in a way that it was not during much of the past.

Two Kinds of Religion

The preoccupation with boundaries that comes with the search for identity points to an important fact: people are concerned not just about how to cross boundaries but also about how to live well within them. Finding one's identity means finding the inner space and social space within which it is possible to thrive. And so, if religion is about boundaries, it is not just about crossing them but, as in the question of identity, about respecting them, too. Therefore, learning to live well within boundaries and learning how to cross them safely give rise to two kinds of religion. The first kind is **ordinary religion**—the religion that is more or less synonymous with culture. Ordinary religion shows people how to live well within boundaries. The second is **extraordinary religion**—the religion that helps people to transcend, or move beyond, their everyday culture and concerns. Extraordinary religion grows at the borders of life as we know it and seeks to cross over. In the West, extraordinary religion helps people to contact God.

Ordinary religion, as the scholar Joachim Wach said, is the trunk of the tree of culture. It is the source of distinguishable cultural forms and the background out of which the norms arise that guide us in our everyday lives. Yet ordinary religion resists precise definition. The reason is that it is the taken-for-granted reality that we all assume, the statements and actions that make up our picture of the way the world is, the things we do not have to think about or would not dream of arguing over because they are so obvious. Ordinary religion puts its premium on the things that are ever present and (mostly) unconsciously revered within everyday life. So this kind of religion can reveal itself in intuitive statements and vague sayings about the meaning of life: "Whatever will be, will be"; "It is better to give than to receive"; "Every cloud has its silver lining"; and the like. This kind of religion is better at being implicit than explicit.

In a more specific sense, ordinary religion can reveal itself in the many customs and folkways that are part of a culture: expected ways of greeting people; wedding etiquette concerning clothes, manners, and obligations; habits of diet; and holiday behavior, to mention a few. Each of these, if examined, can tell worlds about the main values of a society. Each is a concrete expression of the ways in which people are accustomed to think and act. As such, each is a boundary marker that helps people to locate themselves. For example, a bridal gown suggests the traditional values of the importance of marriage and family. The distinctiveness of wedding attire speaks for how significant such values still are, for how strongly the bride—and the culture—uses the institution of marriage to mark social space. In another expression, ordinary religion can reveal itself in what today is often called "spirituality." Here ordinary religion takes a somewhat more self-conscious form, and the role of a subculture and smaller group may become important. The point, though, is that for a form of spirituality to be an instance of ordinary religion, it must concern itself with living well *in this world*, not in another.

To sum up, ordinary religion tends to be at home with the way things are. It functions as the (usually unexamined) religion of a community as community. Because it is about living well within boundaries, it values the social distinctions that define life in the community and respects the social roles that people play. It honors the ranks that they hold and the general institutions of government, education, family, and recreation to which they assent. When it becomes self-aware as "spirituality," it is still a version of spirituality that concerns way of life and regular social pattern. Thus, ordinary religion is the religion that reinforces the bonds between members of a society, that provides social "glue" to make people cohere.

By contrast, extraordinary religion is, as the term literally announces, extra ordinary, *outside the ordinary circle of society*. Indeed, extraordinary religion involves an encounter with some form of difference, whether natural or supernatural. It is specific and usually easily recognizable as religion. Thus, if ordinary religion is diffused throughout culture, extraordinary religion is condensed—present in clear and strongly identified forms that stand out from their background. Extraordinary religion encourages a special language that also distinguishes it, and its sense of going beyond the boundaries often finds expression in universal statements. The special language of extraordinary religion maps a landscape that people have not clearly seen. It gives people names for the unknown and then provides access to a world beyond. It assures people that the "other" world does touch this one but is never merely the same as it. In Christianity, for example, language of God, grace, and salvation posits realities beyond the material world. Moreover, extraordinary religion often encourages religious activity not only on the part of the community as a whole but also on the part of individuals. Here, then, are forms of "spirituality" that, unlike the spirituality of ordinary religion, challenge believers to pass into unknown territory. Mystics and prophets are the heroes and heroines of extraordinary religion.

Even so, we call this religion extraordinary not because it is hard to find or to express but because it concerns itself with what is extraordinary in our day-to-day existence. It may involve ecstasy, but it may also involve a simple Sunday morning church service. The point is that people in some symbolic way voice their concern with going beyond boundaries to the "other" side. Such concern is what makes the religion extraordinary, and as we will see, such concern is what makes it visible and easy to find.

As we move through the religious landscape of the United States, we will find that here, as elsewhere, ordinary and extraordinary religion are often difficult to separate. In fact, in traditional societies the two are often closely blended, and people use the same or similar symbols to express both everyday and nonordinary concerns. For instance, in Judaism the most repeated ritual of extraordinary religion has been the Sabbath meal, a weekly family observance that joins a formal framework of prayer and blessings to ordinary conversation and enjoyment around the dinner table. And those who speak of spirituality in the present-day United States often blend ordinary with extraordinary religious concerns. Spirituality may guide office behavior (ordinary), but it may also govern meditation practice in which an experience of universal oneness occurs (extraordinary).

One sign of religious difference in the West has been the increasing separation of extraordinary from ordinary religion. As we will notice, Protestantism, more than any other religious movement, tried to make a clear distinction between the two. However, even with this Protestant goal and even with the overall Protestant character of the United States, there have been numerous examples of the fusion of ordinary and extraordinary religion. Sometimes, as in the Jewish example of the Sabbath meal, people have tried to make the extraordinary world easy and familiar by setting it in the midst of ordinary reality. At other times, people have become so involved in the extraordinary claims of an "other" world that they have drawn everything possible along with them. For example, in some of the new religious movements of our time, people make radical breaks with their former lives to embrace total commitment to extraordinary concerns.

Components of a Religious System

Both ordinary and extraordinary religion exist as **religious systems**; that is, they are composed of parts related to other parts, which together form a whole. For convenience, we can think of these parts as the four Cs: creed, code, cultus, and community. These four terms, taken together, name the related symbols that make up a religious system. Each of them, therefore, is present in both ordinary and extraordinary religion.

First, religion is expressed in **creeds**, or explanations about the meaning of human life. Such creeds take various forms, from highly developed theologies and sacred stories of origin to informal oral traditions and opinions that surface in casual conversation. Second, religion is expressed in **codes**, which are rules that govern everyday behavior. These may take the form of moral and ethical systems, but they may also be the customs that have become acceptable in a society. Third, religion is expressed in **cultuses**, which are rituals to act out the understandings expressed in creeds and codes. Such cultuses are not to be confused with small and intense religious groups sometimes pejoratively called cults (a term this text does not use). Rather, ritual cultuses, with their formal and repeated character, reinforce creeds and codes in complete religious systems.

Finally, religion is expressed in **communities**, groups of people either formally or informally bound together by the creed, code, and cultus they share. In ordinary religion, such communities tend to be ethnic or cultural (South Asian Indians, African Americans, Polish people), uniting those who share a common land, history, and language. In extraordinary religion, such communities, especially in the West, have tended to be identified with formal institutions (Catholic, Methodist, Adventist). They are designated in terms of their social organization as churches, denominations, sects, or smaller spiritual-practice groups.

The Ladder of Fortune. This Currier & Ives lithograph from 1875 provides a useful illustration of ordinary religion. The print lists virtues to aid the ambitious who seek business success. Prints such as this hung on the walls of family dwellings and were also used in Sunday schools.

In the chapters that follow, we will learn more about each of these forms of extraordinary religious community. For now, let it be clear that these descriptive terms reflect the level and kind of organization in the different groups. **Churches** (which in our sense include non-Christian groups) are the most broadly inclusive, and **denominations** are more or less inclusive. Meanwhile, **sects** and, finally,

spiritual-practice groups, at the other end of the spectrum, are the most exclusive and so have the fewest members. Similarly, churches are the most accommodating to the rest of culture and the least demanding of their members, while sects and spiritual-practice groups make the most radical demands on members. Churches are most at home in settings in which there is a national religion; and therefore, properly speaking, foreign-born churches have become denominations—voluntary communities of believers—in the United States. Here, separation of church and state has meant that there can be no official national religion.

We learn from the components of a religious system that religious beliefs—ideas—are only one part of a religion. Code, cultus, and community all tell of concrete ways in which religion is acted out. More than a form of belief, religion is a matter of practice, an *action system*. Body and emotions play as large a role in a living religion as philosophical concepts. Perhaps, in fact, they play a larger role. Of course, there are connections between all parts of a religious system. Religious practice in code, cultus, and community organization expresses the ideas of the religious creed. Similarly, the religious creed provides an intellectual rationale for why people act in the religious ways that they do. Mind and body are both necessary to human religious life, and they are always interconnected.

A *Short Description of Religion*

So far, we have noticed that the story of religion has been one about how to deal with boundaries. We have seen that in ordinary religion people learn how to live well within the boundaries of their world and that in extraordinary religion they learn to cross them to reach a different, or "other," world. We have found that in both of these kinds of religion people have followed a systematic path in expressing their religion through creeds, codes, cultuses, and communities.

It is time now to sum all of this up in a short descriptive statement (some might call it a "working definition") to guide us as we explore religious history in the United States. **Religion** here can be seen as *a system of symbols (creed, code, cultus) by means of which people (a community) locate themselves in the world with reference to both ordinary and extraordinary powers, meanings, and values.* Locating oneself means taking note of where the boundaries are and placing oneself in relation to them. This may mean placing oneself carefully within the boundaries, out on the frontier, or some of each. The point is that the process goes on continually wherever people are. From this perspective, while many people live without Gods, nobody lives without religion. Moreover, many people absorb seemingly contradictory elements and live comfortably in more than one religious system. This is at least part of what many are expressing when they self-consciously reject the term *religion* and speak instead of being spiritual. For the purposes of this text, they are practicing religion.

Describing religion in this way will be helpful to us later, because it gives priority to understanding religion concretely. It does not tell us what the substance, or core, of religion is, but it tells us how religion works (to deal with boundaries), and it tells us what forms (creed, code, cultus, community) it takes. Describing religion in this way also avoids making religious ideas the most important part of religion. As we will see in our study of the United States, for many people religion was not so much thought about as acted out. By contrast, the problem with many attempts to define religion has been that, in one way or another, they have fallen into the trap of making the specific content of people's ideas essential to the meaning of religion. That is, definitions of religion have often ended by assuming that religion had to be about the Gods, a world beyond, or sacredness. Body and emotions, wrongly, became second to the self-conscious contents of the mind—contents expressed in a special language considered to be religious.

Finally, describing religion this way leaves aside the question of evaluating religion, but it is also clear that making intellectual sense of religion can help in the evaluation process. Generally speaking, religion deals with boundaries in **restorative** or **transformative** ways. **Restorative religion** works to bring back a sense of order and safety, of tranquility and peace, when these seem eroded. So it keeps people on tracks they find comfortable, whether in ordinary or extraordinary places. **Transformative religion** functions to change things. The changes may be **constructive**, enhancing life. Or they may be **destructive**, negating life as most people understand it. Asking questions and making judgments about religion are human tasks that need to be performed.

Finding American Religion

We have been pursuing the meaning of the term *religion*, but so far we have paid little attention to the United States. Now it is time to reflect more on *American* religion and what is religious about it. (The phrase "American religion" is here used as shorthand for religion within the political boundaries of the United States, and the expressions "Americans" and sometimes "in America" are used to refer to the nation's people and territory simply for convenience.)

Many Religions and One Religion

American religious history, in this text, is the paradoxical story of the manyness of religions and the oneness of religion. The **manyness of religions** means religious pluralism and postpluralism. It refers to the distinct religions of the many peoples in the United States and their continuing religious creations and alterations. Conversely, the **oneness of religion** means the religious unity among Americans. It refers to the dominant public cluster of organizations, ideas, and moral values that have characterized this country. We begin, therefore, with a short examination of religious manyness and oneness in America.

Religious manyness is so much at the center of this story that, if it did not smack of irreverence, the earlier elephant analogy might be expanded to call America a religious "zoo," a menagerie of many religious animals of sometimes altogether different species and sometimes hybrids. Each of these is a form of extraordinary religion. But each has also included generous portions of ordinary religion, coming from the cultural roots of an extraordinary religion wherever it originated. Thus, the many religions have repeatedly introduced novelty into the existing situation, and they have done so both historically and geographically.

Historically, each new native or immigrant group brought an added element. Other people had to take account of a new religious group and make room for it. Moreover, other Americans had to find a way to include it in the script and operating instructions that governed religious liberty. Geographically, as different areas of the United States became home to diverse peoples, a particular group might give the life and style of the area a regional flavor that was, in fact, a religious flavor from the group. For example, the Amish left an indelible impression on the life of Lancaster County, Pennsylvania, as did the Hopi Indians on northeastern Arizona and Jewish immigrants on parts of Los Angeles.

Further, each group in the country changed through time. More important, each people changed by, in, and through its relationships with the mainstream that gave to the nation its public religious "oneness." So we need to take account of the interaction of the many with the one (public) center in which the many were shaped by the one. We will see, too, as the study progresses, that the mainstream (the one) was shaped by the many and, also, that the many were shaped by their mutual condition of being different and by their contacts and exchanges with one another. If every religion was about boundaries, the story of religion in the United States was doubly so. Perhaps this is the reason why European observers in the nineteenth century reported that the United States seemed more religious than any other nation. Newcomers who might formerly have taken religion for granted, and not have been actively involved, in America might practice their inherited faith with self-conscious deliberateness.

Meanwhile, the religion of oneness supplied a continuing theme. This was the impulse toward the collapse of boundaries (again) between peoples to transform them all into partisans of the center. Although the Catholic tradition has been strong in both the West and Southwest, historically this religion of oneness has been mostly Protestant, Anglo-Saxon, and white. It has, however, picked up many fellow travelers along the way, especially among Northern European immigrants. New realities and events have made their impressions on it, but it nonetheless is still present even though its Protestantism has shown signs of declining.

This religion of oneness inherits the concerns of extraordinary religion from that Protestant heritage. But it is, above all, the ordinary religion of American culture, which comes through the media, the public-school system, government communications, and commercial networks. In both its ordinary and extraordinary forms, it has historically been the religion of a kind of "ruling" elite among Americans—those who through their background, education, and leadership roles have controlled the main carriers of culture. This ruling elite, whether it has intended to or not, has shaped the mainstream of American culture.

To cite but one example, for several centuries the influence of the elite dominated textbooks used in schools. Far and away the earliest and most striking Euro-American attempts at public education were made in seventeenth-century New England. There the plans for each new town required inclusion of a schoolhouse. As each came into existence, it needed books, and they came at first from overseas and then from American authors. These texts affirmed the theological beliefs of Puritans regarding Adam's sin and the grace of God (extraordinary religion). More significantly in the long run, they also included observations about human behavior and success as, for instance, in classics like Aesop's fables (ordinary religion). It was natural that when other communities sought to establish schools, they looked to New England for books or at least for models of how to write them. Then in the nineteenth century, when the common-school movement spread across the United States demanding free public schools for all, again there was a search for adequate texts. And again the models came from New England. Thus, it is not surprising that millions of American schoolchildren learned far more about Puritanism in New England than, say, about the Moravian or Cherokee Indian religions in Georgia.

Historically, sheer numbers were on the side of the religion of oneness. Many people, especially among the early immigrants to the nation, embodied its values. Therefore, from another point of view the religion of oneness has been not so much the religion of a ruling elite as that of a democratic majority. It has contained the beliefs and moral judgments that made their greatest mark on the early American community because they were shared by the largest single group of people. It has reflected, in short, the public face of the nation. At the same time, geographically, the religion of oneness means the ways of looking at religion and the styles of religious behavior that are generally present throughout the country. Even in places where the religion of oneness is now relatively unimportant, it frequently commands the public media. In other words, even though Catholics and Indians predominate in the Southwest and even though African Americans make up the majority in some inner cities, that picture is not clearly reflected in the dominant image of religion in America.

More about Boundaries

Like the meaning of religion itself, the meaning of religion in America is linked to the question of boundaries. Earlier in the discussion of boundaries, we viewed the issue of identity as a problem of setting up and respecting inner ones. This internal process, however, has external and social results; that is, we tend to act out our inner beliefs. Whether religion is ordinary or extraordinary, as we have already seen, it is expressed in communities. From this perspective, the many religions and one religion are engaged in a dispute concerning boundaries. The many religions, each of them distinct, want to draw clear boundaries between themselves and others. The clearer the boundaries, the tighter and more cohesive the religious group becomes—a fact that we noticed in the brief treatment of the differences among religious groups ranging from churches to spiritual-practice groups. Meanwhile, the one religion tries to include everyone and to draw one great boundary around the whole. In its quest for unity, it aims to lessen the diversity that separate boundaries help to guarantee. To complicate matters further, people keep changing religiously as they borrow ideas and practices from members of other religions.

All of these boundaries and boundary-crossings are social: they concern problems about the relationships among people in ordinary life. In contrast, the boundaries of extraordinary religion go beyond social arrangements: they present people with the goal of crossing into a sacred and otherworldly domain. Thus, the quarrel over boundaries between the many religions and the one religion helps us especially to understand what is *American* about American religion. But the goal of crossing worldly boundaries in extraordinary religion emphasizes what is *religious* about American religion.

A Short Tour of American Religious History in the Text

The text that follows is divided into four parts. The first three concern manyness, and the last oneness. The approach is historical and also topical. Part One contains a series of chapters on what might be called the "original cast"—those groups whose presence together created the initial mix of religious and ethnic traditions that marked America. We start with the religions of Native Americans, the peoples who originally dwelled in the land, and then turn to the major European religions that came to these shores. Beginning with the Jews who came first with Christopher Columbus, we continue with the Spanish and French Catholics who were early present and the other national groups of Catholics who followed them. Then, in two chapters, the text looks to Protestants, who arrived as English colonists and thereafter dominated the political and religious history of the country. Finally, for the original cast, the text turns to African Americans. Present from the early seventeenth century, they became a prime early example of the blending of an indigenous heritage with American experience and Protestant Christianity.

Part Two considers the historical effects of the American environment on religious creativity. In two chapters we examine a number of distinctive "newmade" religions that arose, mostly in the nineteenth century. We see, therefore, what happened religiously during a middle period in American history. At this time new religious sects and communes absorbed social tensions and transformed them—into original solutions to problems that plagued people in a world that seemed to grow ever less friendly. In the metaphysical traditions, which are treated next, we see people deal with these issues by turning not to sectarian communities where ethnic bonds could be cultivated but instead to other homesteads in their minds. By turning within, people sought a safe haven as the United States continually changed.

Part Three picks up the story and stories at the end of the nineteenth century, when Asians began to immigrate in greater numbers, bringing their religions with them. At the same time, some non-Asian Americans were attracted to aspects of these religions. So, for both groups, a pattern of cultural stretching and expansiveness became more visible. Now, especially, the manyness of new religious movements led to a non-Protestant revival for many Americans. But there was also a countering "contraction," and we explore that, too, as new Asian immigrants looked inward to their own communities and other Americans expressed their anxiety and even hostility toward Asian presence. Then, in the second chapter in Part Three, the theme of cultural stretching and retreat—and of American religious history—becomes a way to look at the last few decades. As pluralism increased, religious trends from an expansive "new spirituality" to the consolidating conservatism of others made themselves felt in the nation's life.

Part Four leaves the narrative histories of many religious groups to look more closely—in one long chapter—at what they have in common. First, we acknowledge the power of the Protestant mainstream and its historic decisions about religion. We discover how separation of church and state transformed every religious society into a voluntary organization, leading, in turn, to religious activism and competition. We find, too, how concerns about activity led to increasing moralism. We gain a sense of how intellectual difficulties in religious thought were avoided in order to appeal to the greatest audience of active people and also a sense of how revivalism emerged to cultivate religious feeling.

Second, we follow the ways that Protestantism blended with civil religion, the religion of the nation-state, in which the idea of America itself became a center for religious worship. With a strong presence in American religious history, civil religion became especially visible at the time of the nation's wars. More recently, it has surfaced as a continuing theme in the War on Terror after September 11, 2001.

Third, thinking about civil religion opens out to reflecting on the larger cultural religion of the United States. Civil religion in one way was a form of this religion, but civil religion was also deliberately shaped by legislators and government leaders. In the less self-conscious forms of cultural religion, people themselves created an ordinary religion to express the specifically American ways in which they found meaning in life, and we track some important examples. In a concluding chapter, we examine some of the relationships between manyness and oneness—relationships of contact and encounter in which there were many conflicts, but in which people also influenced one another and many religious combinations occurred. We cast a glance backward on what we have seen throughout the text.

In Overview

This text joins a study of American religious history to insights gained from the more general study of comparative religions. In it, one task is to understand what makes something religious. Although it has proved extremely difficult for scholars to say completely, we have seen that the question of boundaries is important. Here, boundaries are both external and internal; they are also both social boundaries between different groups and boundaries between this world and one thought to go beyond it. These two kinds of boundaries correspond roughly to two kinds of religion. The first of these, **ordinary religion** (concerned with social boundaries), is what we normally refer to as culture. The second, **extraordinary religion** (concerned with boundaries to a world or worlds beyond), tries to reach beyond culture to encounter an "other" dimension to life, such as the God or Gods a people claims. Both ordinary and extraordinary religion express themselves as religious systems. As such, both contain **creeds** (belief systems), **codes** (norms for behavior), and **cultuses** (ritual actions), which combine to give a **community** a language for naming and expressing various powers, meanings, and values in life.

When we apply this understanding to the United States, we find that it is complicated by the historical importance of social boundaries in this country and by the other changes that history has brought. Mostly related to ordinary religion, social boundaries have worked to establish a **"one" religion** that has been historically dominant because of its share of population, power in government and supporting institutions, and public prestige. The social boundaries also indicate the presence of **many religions**, the expressions of various groups of people. In the chapters that follow, we deal with both the many religions and the "one" religion.

Studying American religions and religion in this way is aiming for a good deal. And we have to admit at the outset that we will only partially succeed. Sometimes, factual records will be lacking, and more times the elusive records of people's experiences will defy recovery. Sometimes, the subtleties of response will all but prevent a refined analysis (further elephants? further darkness?). But the "messiness" of the materials is not an excuse for refusing to make sense of them. It is in this spirit that we need to go forward. We begin at the beginning, therefore, with the religions of Native Americans.

Ellis Island, 1907. New York's Ellis Island was the main port of entry for European immigrants at the beginning of the twentieth century.

Part One

MANYNESS: THE ORIGINAL CAST

From the first, a central feature of American history was the manyness of American religions. Religious **pluralism**, in which separate religions exist side by side and maintain their differences, was present with the aboriginal inhabitants. So was religious **postpluralism**, in which religions consciously or unconsciously borrow from one another and blend ideas and practices. Native Americans were organized in separate nations, and each nation possessed its distinctive religion. They also shared many basic ideas and ceremonial practices. Jews, Roman Catholics, and Protestants added to the manyness in America as they immigrated. They brought not only external differences with one another but, besides, internal divisions within each group because of the different ways they lived out their given religions. Yet they, too, were influenced by one another's beliefs and practices, and they grew more alike as time passed. Similarly, African Americans added to the complexity with religious constructions of their own—constructions that built not only on their past but also on what they found in America.

Native Americans—American Indians—were the first human inhabitants of the Americas. For centuries, in separate nations, they developed their own cultures without serious interruption by Europeans or others. But by the late fifteenth century that situation began to change, and by the seventeenth century Europeans had arrived to stay. The sixteenth century saw Spanish Catholics and their missionaries in Florida and New Mexico, while the seventeenth century brought French Jesuit missionaries south of the St. Lawrence River. Meanwhile, Jews of mostly Portuguese origin were settled in Brazil until wartime circumstance forced them to flee in 1654—many to the Dutch colony of New Amsterdam that would later become New York. By this time, English Protestants of broadly Puritan leanings had dug in on the Eastern seaboard, and African Americans were supplying forced labor to Atlantic Coast English masters.

Five religious groups, broadly conceived, were now present in what would become the United States. Native Americans had been joined by Jews, Roman Catholics, English Protestants, and African Americans. Throughout the eighteenth century, this original religious "cast" would occupy the stage of American history, largely unchallenged by other religious players. Already, though, the diversity was impressive, with significant differences, especially, among Native Americans, English Protestants, and African Americans, all inherited from their respective pasts. And already, changes were afoot, and new religious combinations could be seen.

Chapter 1

Original Manyness: Tradition and Change among Native Americans

Nicholas Black Elk was a famed holy man among the Oglala, who are probably now the best known of the Sioux nations of the Upper Midwest. In the 1930s and 1940s, his words and descriptions of Oglala religious ceremony and his role in preserving it came to public attention through the writings of others. It also became clear that Nicholas Black Elk had been a leader in bringing religious innovation to the Oglala. He became convinced that the Ghost Dance—which had come from the Paiute nation much further to the west—would save his people as whites were encroaching on them at the end of the nineteenth century. Already, then, he was endorsing both his own native religion and a blended religion that took its roots from another Indian nation. Besides these, though, Black Elk was a Roman Catholic, and a Roman Catholic catechist teaching others at that.

Black Elk was not unusual in his willingness to use different religious practices at the same time. Native Americans, along with many other ethnic minorities in the United States, have been adept at preserving their difference and borrowing from others as needed or desired. Today they enjoy a new vigor as they demonstrate that their cultures have endured and grown in the face of the dominant Euro-American mainstream. In fact, in law courts, in public demonstrations, and in academic life, Native Americans have signaled militancy. Central to these manifestations of cultural strength has been Native American religious life. American Indians are reclaiming sacred places and practices—and they are also expressing their solidarity with an international network of indigenous rights activism allied to essentially religious claims. Meanwhile, record numbers of them are Christians and charting new paths for what it means to be native and Christian.

Tradition, of course, came first, and we start there. The resiliency of Native American religious traditions in the midst of the political battles of our times is already a clue to something that is apparent again and again. For Indians, traditionally, ordinary religion—the cultural religion within boundaries—and extraordinary religion—the clear attempt to reach beyond them—have been fused. Indian nations typically had no word for religion because they did not separate the ordinary details of living from their sacred ceremonies. They saw their beliefs and activities as part of the same whole.

Native American Diversity

From one point of view, neither Nicholas Black Elk nor any other Native American can stand for all American Indians. About 550 different Indian societies and distinct languages have been identified in North America, and even perhaps a half century ago, about 150 Native American languages were still being used north of the Rio Grande River. Indian languages have been divided into five major groups, a fact that, in itself, suggests the diversity of Indian cultures. Algonkian, Hokan-Sioux, Uto-Aztecan, Athabascan, and Penutian—the five language stocks—are profoundly different from one another, as different, say, as Italian is from Japanese. And if we include Alaska, a sixth language family, the Eskimo-Aleut, brings still more difference.

Just as languages expressed the diversity of the Indians, so did the geographical areas in which Native Americans lived and so did their cultural characteristics. Some were hunter-gatherers, others were agriculturalists, and still others were various combinations of the two. Some societies were highly organized, while others were loosely knit. Some seemed to absorb elements from the cultures of their neighbors, but others remained more isolated. Some gave prominence to women in kinship organization and in actual responsibility. Others were, as anthropologists say, patrilineal (taking their rights from the man's side of the family) and patrilocal (living after marriage in the man's household, or village/band). Basketry, pottery, and weaving flourished among many groups, but in others, if they existed, they were not too important. Indian peoples erected shelters in various styles, sizes, and materials. Some Native Americans were warlike, and others fought only with great reluctance, regarding the slaughter of another human being as a form of pollution.

In such a picture of manyness, it seems fair to ask if there were as many Native American religions as there were Native American languages and cultures. The question, however, already betrays a Euro-American way of seeing and organizing things. By contrast, Native Americans fused the ordinary and the extraordinary, so that culture was tradition was religion. Thus, one of the strongest points of cultural collision between Indians and whites was in their understanding of what whites called religion. Indians thought that every people had its own sacred stories and rituals on which its world was based. Euro-American Christians argued that their religion was the universal truth for all. Even though in mission practice they spread the values of European culture along with Christianity, in theory at least, they thought Christianity went beyond culture. Indians, in other words, would hardly ride a country circuit to win converts whom they could not adopt wholesale into their communities. But on their side, Euro-Americans saw converting the "heathen" as one of the reasons they should settle the North American continent.

Common Characteristics in Religion

Although there were as many Native American religions as there were Indian national groups and societies, looking at their common characteristics is helpful when we want to see the contrast with Euro-American religions. Because so much of the later discussion will deal with Euro-American religions, it is important to look at these shared elements in Indian religions. It will be important later also to have some sense of the differences among them and the changes they all experienced.

In general, Native Americans have possessed a strong sense of relationship with what they hold sacred. They have seen their sacred realities as very closely linked to their daily existence. Whereas Euro-Americans conceived of space as a three-level universe with God, human beings, and nature on different levels, Native Americans have thought of a world to which they were bound by ties of kinship. There were beings like the Grandfathers who were Thunder Beings, Grandmother Spider, and the Corn Mother. There were animals who took on human form such as Coyote the Trickster or sacred birds or sacred buffalo. There were gifted human beings such as **shamans**—holy people who, as sacred healers, mystics, and magicians in one, were said to fly like birds and talk to animals. The world, in short, has been a huge extended family network, with the Indians existing as younger, less gifted brothers and sisters among their more venerable relations.

When it comes to the dimension of time, Indians have seen themselves as connected to sacred events that occurred before the coming of the present world. These events, shrouded for them in mystery, were the acts of creation that had caused the world and themselves to be. For Native Americans, these events have been enduring models on which life should be based. All events, in fact, have been of a piece, and history has been considered sacred. For example, when Edmund Nequatewa, a twentieth-century Hopi, attempted to describe Hopi truth for outsiders (in his book *Truth of a Hopi*), he began with Birdmen in the original Hopi underworld and included the twentieth-century founding of the village of Hotevilla. Traditional account and recent event were collapsed because, just as Indian space existed as one whole, so, too, did Indian time.

In such a world—in which ideas of kinship with sacred beings have flourished and tradition has been as real as clashes with the government of the United States—the material world was, above all, holy. While Euro-Americans in their religions tend to separate material from spiritual things and to exalt the spiritual, Native Americans have expressed in many ways their sense of the sacredness of matter. The distinction between natural and supernatural worlds, an easy shorthand for describing Euro-American religions, is forced and strained when applied to the traditional religions of Native Americans. Indians have seen awesome and mysterious power at work in every portion of nature. It has been, for them, personal power, and the forces of the universe could be named as relatives. But it has never or hardly ever been abstract power that was separate from nature. Sacred beings, for example, have been conceived as animal and plant guardians who, in pacts long ago, pledged the bodies of their species as food for Indian peoples. Thus, Native Americans evolved elaborate rules of courtesy for hunting or planting, apologizing to the spirits of the life forms they took, offering first "fruits" to these spirits, and being careful to use every portion of what they killed.

Native Americans have also thought of their personal inner worlds as sacred. For them, dreams have revealed holy, hidden things that often would not be known in other ways. For example, the Iroquois had their dream-guessing rite in which individuals presented themselves to the tribal council so that personal dreams could be interpreted. On the Plains, leaders of the hunt were men who prayed for months and had dreams they believed were significant. And sometimes, for native peoples, the free soul traveled in dreams to distant places to learn, while at other times dreams brought visions from guardian spirits.

Meanwhile, bridging the space between inner and outer, the name of an Indian person should indicate his or her kinship with the natural world and also tell something of inner essence. For many Native Americans, names were traditionally changed as significant deeds and happenings etched new marks in their character. So there could be Black Hawk, or Afraid of Horses, or White Rabbit, or Moves from Your Sight Little Red Star. Colors were important here, for each of the four directions had its color, which brought with it certain qualities. The red of the north might be the color of wisdom, while the white of the south might be thought to give innocence and trust.

Changing a name, however, has been only one form of a process that traditional Native Americans have seen all around them. Transformation was almost, in European terms, a law, and Indian lore has been filled with accounts of animal–human changes. **Trickster figures** such as Hare or Raven or Coyote were shapeshifters who could assume any form they chose in the midst of their adventures. They have been seen as beings of creative power who helped to put the present world in order. At the same time, they seem to embody a principle of disorder that continually disturbs the regular workings of society.

The "hero" of the Winnebago Trickster cycle, for example, violated the first rule of a warrior: that he must keep himself away from women, who possessed an alien power capable of interfering with the warrior's power. Trickster, in other words, could change from world maker (he was creator) to world breaker (he was violator) and back again. He could also shift from the sly, cunning creature who could outwit Bear or Coyote to the fool who fought himself because his right arm and left arm did not know that they belonged to each other and who burned his own anus to punish it for not standing guard while he slept. He was male, yet he became female, married a chief's son, and bore him three little boys. Most of the time, as a male he carried his penis around in a box with him and did not quite know how to treat it. Yet when Chipmunk managed to gnaw most of it up, Trickster used the pieces to make potatoes, artichokes, ground-beans, and rice for the people.

Trickster seemed to live without boundaries, and yet his creative work put boundaries in place. He posed the major issue for Native American religions directly. Continuity and discontinuity, identity and transformation were statements about boundaries. Indians seemed to be saying that the frameworks that bound them together were all-important. At the same time, they were admitting how fragile and, indeed, fictive these frameworks were. Belief in transformations implied a world that was made of one substance and also implied forms that were always disappearing. Trickster figures continually reminded Indian people of these ideas.

Traditionally, Native Americans highlighted the importance of transformation in their ceremonies. Many societies had sacred clowns who were at once funny and frightening. They could do foolish things, such as dressing themselves backwards and acting in a backward and upside-down manner. They could embarrass others by sexual joking or mimicking, and they could tease mercilessly. Yet they were very serious figures, such as the Sioux clown, or *heyoka,* who assumed his calling because of his sense of visionary power that came from a Thunder Being. Sometimes clowns brought retribution to the people, like the Fool Dancers of the Kwakiutl, who threw stones, or the False Faces of the Iroquois, who sprayed hot cinders. Indeed, clowns were to ritual what Tricksters were to cycles of traditional story. By turning the standing order inside out, they pointed to the fragility of boundaries and the necessity, sometimes felt, to destroy them. Creative disorder, they seemed to be saying, could and would regenerate the order on which religion and society depended.

Often, in ceremonies, masked dancers carried transformation further still as they impersonated different Gods and guardian spirits and sometimes, in the course of the dance, felt they became the figure they impersonated. In the Pueblo villages of the Southwest, according to tradition, the *Kachinas* came from the mountains to perform on ritual occasions during the year through the male dancers who assumed their forms. Meanwhile, in hunter societies, people believed that shamans changed diseases into material objects that could be sucked out of their patients. Special dreams became ceremonies by being acted out. Sacred stories became history, and history was changed into sacred stories. Native American religions proclaimed the deceptiveness of appearances. For them, this ordinary world touched another, and sacredness was never far away.

Living in such a world, Native Americans believed their task was to bring themselves into harmony with it. For them, the harmony conferred power in the hunt, in the field, in war, or in government. The solemn recitation of origin narratives became one characteristic way to come into harmony with beginnings. Other rituals also provided ways for Indian believers to harmonize with a larger sacred world. The sweat lodge, a sun dance, or a sacred game of ball all were examples. Often, in such ceremonies and even in everyday tasks, Indians were preoccupied with the directional points. For example, four—for the four directions—was a privileged number that appeared frequently in story and legend as well as in ceremony. The number five was privileged as well, for it added the center to the four corners. So, too, number seven added a vertical dimension: there was the highest point; the lowest; and the center where the person stood. Understood in this way, religion became a centering process in which Native Americans learned to maintain harmony by living equidistant from all the boundaries.

Standing in the middle with the six directions at equal points, the Native American described a three-dimensional circle. It was like the circles traced by vegetation or the circles that figured so frequently in ceremonies and also in the construction of dwelling places. Circles were sacred for Indians because they reflected and imitated shapes they saw in the natural world. To be in harmony meant to live as part of the circle, or the medicine wheel, of this world. Thus, in their religions, Native American peoples were living out their own versions of the ancient idea of **correspondence**. Their societies were understood to be small-scale replicas of a larger reality that surrounded them. By looking at the picture as painted on the larger canvas of the natural world, they believed they could better comprehend life's meaning and appropriate work. Because they saw themselves as made of the same stuff as the natural and sacred world, the boundaries could always be easily crossed. Yet because the natural and sacred world was seen as one of centers, circumferences, and directions, Native Americans could plant themselves securely in their corresponding middle place, which was the ordinary world.

By contrast, Euro-Americans tended to see the world in more separately defined ways. God, they believed, had caused the world to be, and his law governed its movements. In that sense, he could be said to dwell within it. Yet for them he also far transcended it. Meanwhile, his human creatures had increased the separation between God and the world by their fall in the Garden of Eden. In this understanding, sin had entered the world, and it had affected not just human beings but all of nature. For Euro-Americans, the world had become a three-level affair. God tried to control human beings, and human beings tried to control nature. If there was rebellion in both cases, it only emphasized the fact that the one creation had been, in the Euro-American view, pulled apart.

Differences in Native American Religious Traditions

For the most part, we have been viewing Native American religious traditions in terms of what they have had in common. But there were also important differences among them, even if this survey can only briefly touch on them. To give some sense of the range, though, we take up briefly the religions of the distinctive cultures of the Oglala and the Hopi. The first is a Sioux hunter-gatherer society of the Plains, and the second is an agricultural Pueblo culture from the Southwest.

The Oglala

The **Oglala**, who were victims of the United States military in the Wounded Knee Massacre of 1890, are perhaps the best-known single American Indian society. They were one of the thirty-one or so Indian nations who in the nineteenth century roamed the prairies of North America between the Mississippi River and the Rocky Mountains, setting up temporary camps and moving them as the seasons changed and they pursued the buffalo. More specifically, the Oglala belonged to the Teton division of the Seven Fireplaces of the Sioux family. They dwelled in the western portion of Sioux territory and, along with other nations of the Teton Sioux, spoke Lakota.

Like other Tetons, the Oglala had originated in what is now the state of Minnesota and had come onto the Plains, where in about 1750 they obtained horses, an event that changed their fortunes and led to their wealth and fame as buffalo hunters. With horses they no longer had to travel and hunt on foot, carrying their belongings on their backs or with their dog travoys. Ironically, the horses had come from whites—from the Spanish of the Southwest from whom the animals had strayed or been stolen or traded. Thus, the beginning and end of the flowering of their culture were linked to Euro-Americans. But in this heyday of their fortunes, the religion of the Oglala reflected the centrality of the buffalo and taught the values of Native American hunters. Like American Indian religions in general, it blended ordinary with extraordinary.

The traditional account of the Oglala's origin, like that of many another Indian people, concerns their emergence from the earth—in this case through the intrigues of a Trickster figure, Inktomi the Spider. Through a wolf, Inktomi wooed the people with food and clothing until a few came to the upper world to investigate its virtues. Here, Inktomi plied them with more gifts and promised them youth, so that they returned to the people in the world below with glowing tales. Although an old chief and an old woman warned of cold wind and the need for hunting, some still came to the upper world. The results were not what they hoped but, instead, pain and misery. The children cried for food while Inktomi laughed. Yet all was not lost, for they met Old Man and Old Woman, who taught them to hunt, clothe themselves, and make tipis. Oglala life had begun.

This is but one of a cycle of sacred stories that explain the origins of things. What is important here is that this particular sacred story tells of *Oglala* beginnings. It is about a specific people, not about the world in general. Like all sacred accounts, this story is true in the sense that it tells the meaning of existence in the world as the Oglala knew it. We are a people of the earth, the story is saying, and although creation was a kind of trick that was played on us (we did not really know what it meant to be born; we did not really have any choice), still we have learned to take care of ourselves. Our life goes on.

The origins of life, however, concerned not only physical existence. There were origins, too, for the rituals that acted out the meaning of being Oglala. So tradition explained the gift of a **sacred pipe** to the people. **White Buffalo Calf**

Woman—a sacred woman in white buckskin with a bundle on her back—approached two warriors with her gift, but only one survived (the other had wrong thoughts). Later, the story told, she entered the Oglala camp and presented the pipe to the chief. "With this sacred pipe," she said, "you will walk upon the Earth; for the Earth is your Grandmother and Mother and She is sacred." Since before the beginning of the nineteenth century, the pipe has figured in the rituals of the Oglala—the sign of their felt bond to one another and to the earth. According to the tradition, the pipe accompanied the gift of ritual. For the mysterious woman also offered the people a round stone containing seven inscribed circles, each of the circles representing a rite that they would receive. After she had taught them the first—a ceremony meant to keep spirits of the dead—she walked away, turning into a buffalo calf as she did.

The White Buffalo Calf Woman of the traditional story gave the Oglala a ceremonial repertoire, with the sacred pipe at its center, for the expression of all their religious needs. Thus, in the first rite of **ghost keeping**, the Oglala have been able to deal more easily with death. The soul, or spirit, of a deceased person, it was believed, could be kept for a period of time ranging from six months to two or more years. Elaborate ceremonies surrounded the making and keeping of a ghost bundle, including a lock of hair from the dead person. Members of the family observed ritual taboos, and a special dwelling was built for the bundle. When the day arrived on which they intended to release the spirit, the ceremonies were equally elaborate.

The other rituals of the Oglala have included the sweat lodge ceremony, the vision quest, the sun dance, the "making of relatives," the girl's puberty ritual, and a sacred ball game. Each of them has been characterized by minute prescriptions for word and gesture, hinging always on the use of the directional points. Each ritual, in other words, locates the Oglala in a world of meaning by a centering process with regard to space. In the **sweat lodge** ritual, for instance, rules governed the construction of the lodge, the use of space within it, and the roles that those who participated played. The leader had to move sunwise as he entered the lodge. There were seven heated stones (a sacred number) at first, and prayers had to be offered over them before more stones could be added. Later, after the door was sealed, the ritual went forward with attention to the four directions as various gestures and actions were performed.

In the **vision quest**—performed alone on a sacred hill away from the camp, usually for the first time in adolescence—men, and sometimes women, sought a vision in which guardian spirits would reveal their relationship to the seeker and bestow the knowledge/power desired. The ritual was conducted under the guidance of a holy person and involved the smoking of a sacred pipe, preliminary purifications in the sweat lodge, fasting, and prayer. Once the seeker reached the sacred hill, there was the same attention to directions we have previously seen: four saplings formed poles at the four directions, and the seeker traced a cross by returning to the center from each of the four. Even though the seeker might be alone for one to four days, the vision quest thus began in community. The holy person who guided the quest embodied the spiritual wisdom of the Oglala as a people. When at last the seeker believed that the vision had been granted and returned, he (or she) related the experience in the presence of others and listened as the holy person and guide interpreted its meaning. If there was a place for the individual in Oglala religion, it was a place that was very carefully circumscribed. The gift of the seven rites was conceived as a gift to all the people.

The communal character of Oglala religion was especially evident in the **sun dance**. The only ritual that occurred at a special time of year, the sun dance took place in the early summer after the buffalo "harvest." Often it was an intertribal affair involving a huge encampment in which many people came together. The ritual extended over four days, and each day had its proper ritual tasks, its formal and necessary ceremonies. A lodge was constructed, a cottonwood tree selected and trimmed according to prescription to form the sacred pole at the center, and the pole painted and decorated with symbolic offerings, among them reminders of the buffalo. In a dance that followed, warriors in their finest attire circled the pole, running to each of the directions to flatten the ground and symbolically "killing" the images of a man and a buffalo at the pole. But the culmination was the actual dance around the pole that gave the lengthy rite its name. The dancers were literally bound to the sacred center, attached by thongs to the pole. They performed either gazing at the sun from morning until night or with skewers digging into their flesh. Under their leader they danced themselves into an ecstasy of sacrifice until they fell exhausted or the flesh was pulled from their bodies and they were released. They fasted for the duration of the dance, demonstrating in this hunting version of a first-fruits festival that, in return for the gift of life they acknowledged, they would offer themselves.

Similarly, the remaining rituals of the Oglala did not stint in their prescriptions for careful and symbolically elaborate ceremonial behavior. The "making of relatives" was designed to unite two people to each other in a bond considered closer than that between relatives, committing them to die for each other, if necessary. The puberty ritual for girls, the buffalo ceremony, was performed at first menstruation with the intention of placing young women in the care of the sacred buffalo and of securing for them a relationship with White Buffalo Calf Woman. At their menstrual periods thereafter, women lived temporarily alone, a practice common among Native Americans, who believed that women possessed a power that, if it came into contact with that of the hunter-warriors, could damage it. The religious power seen in women figured in the seventh rite of the Oglala as well. In a ritual that perhaps symbolized the game of life, a young girl threw out a ball to people standing at the four directions. The ball stood for knowledge, and the people trying to catch it were struggling, said the Oglala, to free themselves from ignorance.

The ball used in the seventh rite, like so many of the objects that were part of the rituals, was considered **wakan**, or holy. Wakan was a quality thought to be possessed by the elements such as thunder and lightning, by the animals or plants, sometimes by human beings, and sometimes even by objects. For the Oglala, wakan was that dimension of reality that caused transformation. It was the mysterious force that surrounded them in the world the sacred buffalo had given, and in its culminating aspect it was **Wakantanka**, sometimes equated with the God of Christianity and Judaism. However, Native Americans tend to see sacredness as a quality suffusing all things and to personify their Gods ambiguously so that at the same time they both are and are not separate from the natural world. Euro-Americans tend toward more precision—and separation—in their concept of the supernatural. Finally, if any being was wakan among the Oglala, it was the buffalo. Sacred story and ritual together demonstrated how central the buffalo traditionally was. Oglala religion, like Oglala life, revolved around the being from which, or whom, they drew all of their sustenance—economic, in buffalo meat, hide, and even teeth, but even more, spiritual. The buffalo gave the Oglala a center and an identity. If they were people of the earth, it was because they were people of the buffalo.

The people of the buffalo traveled a long path from 1700 to the twenty-first century. Despite the advances of a Euro-American culture that threatened to take away their lands and livelihood, the Oglala have maintained their identity. No longer depending for their survival on hunters and warriors, present-day Oglala survive as a people because of their religion. The pipe is still an Oglala means of prayer, and prayer today, as in the past, is addressed to Wakantanka. Sweat lodge, vision quest, and sun dance all continue, and in the contemporary Oglala community there is a strong reawakening of religious traditionalism. A **reclamation movement**—for the return of lands, artifacts, and the remains of ancestors—is linked to the resurgence of tradition, and so is a new **indigenous rights activism**. Meanwhile, traditional religious practices have been joined by others: for some people, the peyote religion, which, in a communion ritual, sees and uses the plant as a sacred power person (see the section later in this chapter); for a few, traces of the Ghost Dance (see the same discussion); and for most, Christianity. Usually, contemporary Oglala belong to one or another Christian denomination, and many traditionalist leaders, like the earlier Nicholas Black Elk, see no conflict between Christian adherence and the older ways. By staying in touch with their religious past, the Oglala have also adapted to change.

The Hopi

A much different group of Native Americans from the Oglala, the **Hopi** are numbered among the Pueblo, or "village," Indians of the American Southwest, so named because they have dwelled together in adobe and stone apartment villages. River, or eastern, Pueblo peoples, the Tanoans and the Keresans, settled along the Rio Grande in what is now the state of New Mexico. To the west, in the desert, lay the country of the Zuni (New Mexico) and the Hopi (Arizona). Life in the desert proved to favor cultural continuity, for, with greater isolation from Spanish, Mexican, and Anglo-American conquerors than their eastern cousins, the Hopi for most of their history remained largely untouched by Christianity.

Hopi origins are veiled in mystery. Some scholarship has suggested that their ancestors came into the Southwest over 2,000 years ago. They dug pits in the floors of caves to store their food and eventually began to live in pit houses in the caves or out in the open. Other scholars say that the Hopi came from the California desert to their present-day land from about the years 500 to 700. The Hopi themselves tell of crossing the ocean on rafts or of emerging from the earth. What is clear, though, is that from about 900 to 1300, their culture reached its heights. This was the era of cliff dwellings, carved into the sides of mountains at places that were easy to defend, and of apartment terraces, villages that are still characteristic of the Pueblo peoples. Old **Oraibi**, the ancient ceremonial village of the Hopi, dates back to this time.

In their past, the Hopi combined farming with hunting and gathering, particularly when their crops failed. But hunting and gathering gradually declined, and the Hopi continued to be farmers, growing crops of corn, beans, and squash. They considered tilling the soil a man's job, but social organization revolved around women, with communities organized in matrilineal clans. In the villages, it was clear that ritual life centered on the men, and the **kivas** there were sacred pit houses where the various clans conducted rituals from which women were excluded. Yet, although women had been barred from participation in kiva rites, Hopi tradition reflected the prominence of female symbolism. The Hopi had emerged from the womb of Mother Earth, their most sacred stories told them, and the kiva itself, essentially a large hole dug in the earth, was a forceful reminder. Sacred origin stories named women as creators. In one from Oraibi, two Hard Being women (deities of hard objects such as shells, corals, turquoise, and beads) created birds, animals, a woman, and a man.

In another well-known story of their origins, the people enjoyed a good life in the world below until evil entered into their hearts, sexual excesses grew, and so did hatred and quarreling. In their plight the chiefs tried to find an escape, and they fashioned a Pawaokaya bird, singing over him to give him life. Meanwhile, the chiefs planted a pine tree and a reed beside it to reach the hole into the upper world. The bird flew in circles around the two "ladders," found the opening but nothing else, and returned exhausted. So, according to the story, the chiefs made a hummingbird and then a hawk who, in turn, repeated the search and also came back unsuccessful and exhausted. Finally, the chiefs created Motsni, who flew through to the upper world, found the site of present-day Oraibi, and also encountered Skeleton. When he heard Motsni's tale, Skeleton explained that he was living in poverty but that the people were welcome to join him. So they came, emerging from their plant ladders to the world above. Later, aided by Spider Woman, they fashioned a symbol that turned into the moon and another that became the sun. The people had begun to make their way. They were also given the gift of corn, and small though the gift was, with it the Hopi were also given an identity. After a series of migrations, the clans arrived at their villages, and life, as the Hopi knew it, began. To help them remember, in each sacred kiva of the Hopi was a **sipapu**, a hole intended as an opening to the world below. Most times covered by a stone, it was opened at the initiation ceremonies at the end of the year with the belief that the dead could leave the womb of Earth to participate.

Blending folk memory and folk philosophy, the Hopi narrative fused history with interpretation. Emergence from the earth was historical truth for the Hopi, if their ancestors dwelled in the pit houses that were echoed in the kivas. Similarly, matrilineal organization must have existed for a long time, for it was said that in the beginning the Hard Being women (deities) had created a woman first and then a man. This order of creation was a model for customs in Hopi society by which women owned their houses and household goods and, in a sense, their children, who derived their clan kinship from their mothers. Finally, Skeleton and the small gift of corn suggest the precariousness of life in the desert growing subsistence crops. Yet, as with the Oglala, the truth of Hopi tradition did not depend on historical memory. Its statement of identity made their account true, for in telling who they were, the Hopi were also telling what meaning and significance they attached to their lives. Like the Oglala, the Hopi were saying that they were people of the earth.

Unlike the Plains people, however, Hopis were clearly saying through their religion that they were farmers. While the Oglala possessed only one calendric ritual in the sun dance, for the Hopi every rite depended on the cycle of the seasons. Desire for harmony with nature, in their case, was expressed in ritual harmony with its changing seasons: transformation, so central for all Native Americans, here meant following the movements of the natural world through cyclic time. The motivating force behind the calendar of rites was the ever-present need for water to make crops grow in this desert region. Once again, as for the Oglala, religion and everyday economic need were not strangers. Just as the buffalo was central for the Oglala, water was primary for the Hopi. In both cases, ordinary religion and extraordinary religion were traditionally fused. Rituals were ways for maintaining the boundaries so that life could be lived within the safe fences of economic and social organization. Rituals were also ways to cross over these boundaries and experience what these Native Americans felt as the power of the sacred.

In general, the rites of the Hopi year possessed certain common features. True, each ceremony was conducted by one or more hereditary chiefs and clans. At its most basic level, therefore, it might be appropriate to talk about the religions of the Hopi: each clan had its specific area of religious responsibility and thus its particular religious lesson and action to teach. Yet all the ceremonies aimed at the production of rain for fertility and growth. All utilized, as well, similar ritual techniques: the offering of prayer sticks, the building of an altar of sacred objects, the sprinkling of corn as medicine to lead to the transformations of nature that the people desired, the recitation of the emergence story, verbal forms of prayer, attention to the four directions, and the use of song and dance. Finally, the ceremonies usually followed a similar time pattern with eight days of preparation and then eight days of secret rites culminating in a public dance on the ninth day. With a full calendar of annual ceremonies, traditional Hopi spent roughly one-third to one-half of the year in the *work* of ritual.

The major division in the ceremonial year was—and still is—between the Kachina rituals from December through July and the non-Kachina ones from August through November. Here the word *Kachina* might refer to any one of three different phenomena in Hopi society. **Kachinas**, first, have been thought to be spiritual beings. Inner and invisible forms, they are understood to give a spiritual dimension to outer and physical existence. They have not been considered Gods in the Euro-American sense but have been honored as spirits—of the dead; of minerals, plants, and animals; even of the planets. They are said to be intermediaries from the sacred world who, during the second half of the year, dwell in the San Francisco peaks on the outer edge of Hopi country (the border, once more) and visit the Hopi villages during the first half when the Kachina rituals have been held. Well over 250 in number (some say as many as 600 have been known), the Kachinas were traditionally never worshiped but rather looked upon as friends and endowed with a variety of human qualities. New ones were continually appearing as old ones were forgotten, so that the catalog of Kachina spirits was fluid and variable. So, too, were their personalities, ranging from benevolent, kindly spirits to others who inspired fear by their whippings to punish offenders in Hopi society.

Second, Kachinas are also the male dancers who, during the Kachina ceremonies, impersonate both male and female Kachinas. Wearing masks that represent particular Kachinas and are thought to confer sacred power, the performers have sought to dance themselves into a state in which they felt that they became the Kachinas they impersonated. Third, Kachinas are the exquisitely carved dolls that the Kachina dancers give to Hopi children during the ceremonies to teach them about the Kachina beings. Made in traditional and highly stylized patterns from cottonwood roots, the Kachina dolls have not been toys in the modern American sense, but neither are they sacred objects. Rather, they have perhaps been "show" objects in the Hopi home, reminding all, and especially the children, of the spirit Kachinas the dolls represent. Beings, dancers, and dolls, all the Kachinas point to the extraordinary reality that for the Hopi lay behind the ordinary world.

By now it should be evident that Kachina ceremonies have been those in which Kachina dancers impersonated the spirit Kachinas, and the spirit Kachinas were believed to manifest themselves. The Hopi thought that the dual calendar (Kachina/non-Kachina) was necessary because they believed that, in the world below this one, life corresponded to arrangements in Hopi society. Thus, whatever rituals occurred during the first part of the year above were replicated during the second half in the world below. The Kachinas had to be elsewhere in the summer and fall: this was why they could not dance in the village plazas with the Hopi.

These Kachina rituals continue to endure and in recent times have received new attention. But earlier, with greater contacts with whites and Christian ways, erosions in the ceremonial life of the villages began to occur. At the same time, witchcraft grew with the spread of anxiety. Beliefs in negative forms of witchcraft and sorcery had, indeed, long been part of Hopi life. The traditional account of the emergence, in its complete form, spoke of the presence of sorcery both in the world below and above. But as time passed, witches and sorcerers seemed to multiply everywhere, and fear and dissension struck at the heart of Hopi society. Old prophecies came to be associated with the contemporary presence of whites and the beginning of a time of purification.

Crow Mother Kachina. Kachina doll representing the Crow Mother, known as the mother of the Hu Kachinas. At the February Powamu, or bean dance, the Crow Mother appeared through the performance of a male Hopi dancer.

From 1862 on, Mormons, with their accounts of Indian descent from the tribes of Israel (see Chapter 7), became the most successful missionaries to the Hopi. It was not necessary, though, to abandon Hopi tradition and ceremony in order to embrace Mormonism or to follow other Christian denominations. Like Nicholas Black Elk and other Oglala, a Hopi could participate in traditional religion and new (Christian) religion at the same time. In fact, from 1870 on there was no avoiding the cultural presence of the United States. Religious and cultural compartmentalization became a continuing feature of Hopi life, with "blocks" of thinking and acting that remained traditionally Hopi and other "blocks" that accommodated the alien culture and its Christian religion. Like the religion of the Oglala, Hopi religion has sought to preserve and protect the ordinary even as it has linked believers to the extraordinary. In fact, new prophecies from Hopi traditionalists in the twentieth century and after have looked to the changes that befell Hopi society as part of larger changes ahead for America and have predicted a "purification day" to come. Like the Oglala, the Hopi see the religious future in terms of present change and also through the lens of their own particular past. And what is true for the Oglala and Hopi is true for all. Each Native American nation has its traditions of origin, its ceremonial cycle, and its identity as "the people" cherished by sacred powers allied to nature and cherishing them in return.

Change in Native American Traditions

The Oglala and Hopi maintained traditional ways and yet changed, and so did other Native Americans. Even a return to tradition has had new meaning as Indians have used their religious past to support their identity in contemporary times. For example, in 1990 the **Native American Graves Protection and Repatriation Act (NAGPRA)** became law, providing a legal framework for the repatriation of human remains and some cultural artifacts from certain institutions receiving federal support. Native Americans needed to show "cultural affiliation" or "lineal descent" in order to repatriate what they desired. Or they could base their claims on the authority of "traditional religious leaders." Thus, religious tradition took on a new and politicized role. But—perhaps surprisingly—not all Native Americans held similar views about what should be done. In one case among the Cheyenne in 1997, for example, some Cheyenne wanted human remains to *stay* at the Smithsonian Institution in Washington, D.C., instead of being repatriated. Ceremonial concerns were uppermost in the dispute. These same ceremonial concerns are clear, too, in the new National Museum of the American Indian, which opened at the Smithsonian in 2004. Here Native American people represent themselves, and objects are treated with regard for their layers of spiritual meaning that go beyond historical or aesthetic considerations. Meanwhile, claims to **sovereignty** in land disputes have relied in a number of cases on traditional religious practice and belief regarding particular tracts of land.

In addition to this self-conscious turn toward tradition, general Native American responses to new cultural forces have been threefold. First, Native Americans might keep up the practices of their traditional religions but add to them elements derived from Christianity. Second, Native Americans might turn to a variety of new religious practices and movements. Third, Native Americans might be converted to various denominational forms of Christianity, either working to maintain their traditional religion alongside the new or renouncing the old, at least on the surface, in favor of the new. In all cases, though, forms of religious **combination**, either clear or subtle, ruled the day. Indian people used elements at hand to create religious responses that filled their contemporary needs.

Clear forms of religious combination occurred in those regions that were missionized by Spanish Catholic priests, that is, in the Southwest and California. In the Rio Grande Pueblos of New Mexico, for example, after the initial period of encounter from 1540, there was little or no contact with Catholic priests in the late eighteenth century and through most of the nineteenth. Thus, the Pueblos for a period of about 150 years were free to modify Catholic rituals to serve Native American ends. The results were ceremonial calendars in the various pueblos that for the most part were based on traditional Native American beliefs and practices. But added to them were Catholic ceremonies meant to satisfy Pueblo needs. There was little interest in Jesus or the Virgin, in heaven and hell, or in the Christian understanding of God. Yet a saint's day became an occasion for festivity, and Holy Week and Christmas, while not historical commemorations of events in the life of Jesus, were times for prayer. Similarly, the Roman Catholic All Souls' Day provided an opportunity to honor departed ancestors with gifts.

Perhaps the most prominent example of new religious practice was the **Ghost Dance**, which swept the Plains in the late nineteenth century. When the old religions seemed to fail as the whites pushed the Indians out of their lands, new religious prophets arose to proclaim rites and ceremonies that would bring the power to end white ascendancy and to restore the Indians to harmony with the earth and themselves. Among these new religious prophets was a Paiute Indian from Nevada named Jack Wilson, or **Wovoka**. He claimed to have died twice and to have seen God. Thereafter, he began to predict that the earth and whites would be destroyed by flood and that the Indians should perform the ceremony of their ancient round dance so that the flood would wash under them and they would survive. Then, predicted Wovoka, the earth would spring to life in a new creation, and the Indians would be reunited with their dead ancestors and dwell together in plenty.

The Ghost Dance, as it was called, spread rapidly among other Native American peoples as delegations from various Indian nations came to learn the ceremony. Indians who practiced the dance claimed to be reunited with deceased relatives and to feel empowered by tokens—like a piece of meat or a feather—they received from the spirit world. But the Ghost Dance had stark repercussions among the Oglala, who—with Nicholas Black Elk's encouragement—reshaped the dance to suit themselves. They began to wear ghost shirts as they danced—long white garments that, decorated with red-colored symbols and eagle feathers, they believed were bulletproof. This conviction contributed to their deaths at Wounded Knee. The Oglala, wearing their ghost shirts, thought they could not be harmed by the bullets of the United States Seventh Cavalry.

Other new religious movements among American Indians fared better. For example, the nineteenth-century Seneca religion led by the prophet **Handsome Lake** (d. 1815) resulted in the enduring organization of **Gaiwiio**, the Old Way of Handsome Lake. Indeed, even during his lifetime the religion of Handsome Lake spread from the Seneca to all the Nations of the Iroquois. Based on claims of visions, Handsome Lake preached the imminent destruction of the world, the reality of sin, and a need for salvation. Later he added an emphasis on moral reform. Beginning in the 1840s, the Code of Handsome Lake combined a traditional account of the late prophet's visionary experience and teaching with both ritual prescriptions for a longhouse (the traditional Iroquois structure) church and moral guidance that underscored the sacredness of the family. In our own time, numerous reservation Iroquois follow the Code of Handsome Lake.

In our own time, too, **peyote religion** flourishes in the **Native American Church** and also independently. A pan-Indian movement, peyotism grew beginning in the second half of the nineteenth century and spread northward onto the Plains. By the early years of the new century, it was carried across the Mississippi River eastward by Native Americans who lived on Oklahoma reservations. Peyote religion now exists from the Plains cultures of the Sioux to the reservations of the Navajo and Pueblo peoples. It has become the most widespread among contemporary Indian religions. The **Peyote Way**, as it is often called, centers on a communion ritual in which believers eat some form of the peyote cactus (*Lophophora williamsii*) in a ceremony usually lasting all night. There are prayer, song, meditation, sacramental consumption of peyote, and—when the communicant is said to be favored by the spirit power of the plant—extraordinary visual and auditory experiences. Communicants say that peyote heals and gives knowledge, and they are also aware of the Christian elements in their religion. But they have actively *used* Christianity to express their own religious vision, and so in their combinatory religion they have strongly bent Christian material to Native American beliefs and values.

The Christian elements in peyote religion point to the fact that the new religious practices and movements discussed here all contain Christian elements. What makes them different from the combinative style of the earlier Pueblo example, though, is the presence of a new vision, even if shaped from older materials. It is a vision borne by the authority of a strong leader or leaders who proclaim a distinctive teaching that transforms foreign material more thoroughly in native directions. It is also marked by organizational commitment, and, most importantly, by the introduction of a ceremony or ceremonies that use elements from traditional Indian rituals while integrating the new or borrowed elements.

Different from these forms of religious combination is a third, more subtle one, when Native Americans have turned in a more direct way toward Christianity. **Denominational Christianity** sprang up in various forms with the first presence of Euro-American Christians who sought to convert the Indians to Christianity. The Spanish and French brought their priests, and the English sent Protestant missionaries. So there were "praying Indians" in colonial New England towns, while later, in California, Franciscan missionaries created mission communities of Christian Indians. Throughout the nineteenth century, with the development of the reservation system, knowledge of Christianity spread among the Indians. Today it would be difficult to find a reservation without the presence of one or more Christian churches.

Take, for example, the **Eastern Cherokee**, who live on the Qualla Boundary Reservation in western North Carolina. In the early nineteenth century the

Cherokee lived across a series of southern states, and Christian missionary work began among them in 1801 with a Moravian center and school. Soon the Presbyterians came, and later the Cherokee allowed Baptists, Methodists, and Congregationalists. When the federal government forced most of the Cherokee Nation to resettle west of the Mississippi in 1838, a small remnant escaped the deportation to remain in the East. Many of them were Baptists and Methodists, and eventually the Baptists won the most adherents among these Eastern Cherokee. In keeping with the mid-twentieth-century Baptist message throughout the South, it was fundamentalist Christianity that the Eastern Cherokee were taught. Predominating themes were human sinfulness and the need to believe in salvation through Jesus to escape the torments of hell. The Cherokee attended services and listened to the preaching.

But there was more to this Cherokee adherence to Christianity than first meets the eye. The Cherokee could relate to the Christian message of kinship and love because, in their clans and extended families, they already felt they experienced both. Similarly, they could relate to the message of guilt and the need for atonement because in their traditional religion the quest for a rebalancing through purity had been an important theme. The ritual of baptism, so central to the Baptist form of Christianity, echoed, for the Cherokee, their traditional cold baths in streams, the ceremony they knew as "going to water." Observers of Cherokee worshipers in the later twentieth century reported that, unlike Southern whites, they sat impassively through sermons and revivals and that men sometimes dozed as a preacher reached the emotional heights of his sermon. At death, Cherokee mourners have been reported as keeping to their traditional pre-Christian funeral ceremony. Given this and similar evidence, it is clear that Cherokee Christianity has actually been a blending of Christian and traditional themes. The Cherokee, like other Native American peoples, turn to Christianity in terms of prior beliefs and practices that make the new religion plausible. After conversion, worshipers shape the Christianity to their own requirements.

At the same time, Indian Christians have been vigorous in their commitment to the new ways, even as they have worked to assert native control over them. A key example in our time is the Catholic Native Americans who participate in annual **Kateri Tekakwitha Conferences** and smaller **Kateri circles**. Named for Blessed Kateri Tekakwitha, a seventeenth-century Mohawk convert to Catholicism who is now a candidate for sainthood in the Catholic church, the Kateri conferences and movement signal the strength of Catholicism in native circles. Native leadership is important to the conferences, as are native languages, musical instruments, and prayer instruments (such as eagle staffs, feathers, sacred pipes, incense for smudging, and the like). Vestments display native designs, and native ritual traditions are honored. This practice of **inculturation**—the inclusion of native symbols and rituals in official church services—has apparently been successful. In the early twenty-first century, about 12 percent of Native Americans have identified themselves as Catholics—nearly 500,000 people. The Kateri movement remains perhaps the largest recent religious expression of Indian people.

Kateri Tekakwitha Conferences, with their Catholicism, fare well in gaining general cultural understanding and acceptance by non-Indian Americans. But Native American religions have not always enjoyed such acceptance and respect. The story of the Ghost Dance tells that. So does a history of repression of Native American ceremonies by the federal government until very recently. It was only in 1978 that the nation saw the passage of the **American Indian Religious Freedom Act**, in which Congress resolved that "it shall be the policy of the United States to protect and preserve for American Indians their inherent right of freedom to believe, express, and exercise [their] traditional religions." Even after that, Indian tradition did not prevail in white America. A series of court challenges by Indian peoples invoked the congressional resolution to little avail.

In these court cases, it is land that typically has been at stake. For Native Americans, this means sacred sites associated with traditional religious beliefs and ceremonies. In the case of *Lyng v. Northwest Indian Cemetery Protective Association*, for example, the United States Supreme Court in 1988 decided against Native American plaintiffs. The United States Forest Service proposed to build a paved road between Gaston and Orleans, California (the "G-O Road"), to be used for logging and other commercial and recreational purposes. This road was to cross land in the Six Rivers National Forest and to pass through an area considered highly sacred by Yurok, Karok, and Tolowa Indians. The Indians argued that centrally important ceremonies required that religious leaders have access to the "high country" and that the proposed road would violate the undisturbed sacredness of the space. The Indians won their case in United States District Court, but the Supreme Court reversed the decision.

However, it was not legal contention over a sacred site that finally brought Indian religious difference and its right to exist to national attention. Rather, it was the practice of Indian peyotism, a Supreme Court case regarding it, and a new federal law thereafter. Indian peyotism became the focus of mainstream public concern in 1990 when a case involving the ceremonial practice made its way to the United States Supreme Court. Two members of the Native American Church in Douglas County, Oregon, had been discharged from their substance abuse counseling positions because of their peyotism. Alfred Smith and Galen Black were subsequently denied unemployment benefits by the state of Oregon. They appealed at the state level and won their cases in light of the "free exercise" clause of the United States Constitution's Bill of Rights. They had eaten peyote sacramentally; they ought not to have been refused unemployment compensation for misconduct, said the Oregon Supreme Court. The *Smith* case eventually was appealed to the United States Supreme Court twice, and on the second appeal, in *Oregon v. Smith*, the Court held that a valid—and neutral—state law could be enforced even if that law conflicted with the practice of religion. The free exercise right of an individual did not, according to the Court, exempt the person from a general law.

Non-Indian religious leaders from a broad coalition of groups read the *Smith* decision as a threat. Some sixty-eight organizations, diverse in their theology, their religious practice, and their politics, joined forces in the wake of the Supreme Court case. Their efforts temporarily succeeded in 1993 when Congress passed the **Religious Freedom Restoration Act**, a law that insisted on a "compelling" government interest before the state could intrude on religious activity. The government, said the law, must find the "least restrictive means" to its own ends when those ends came into conflict with religion. Four years later, in 1997, the Supreme Court responded. In a historic decision, the Court struck down the Religious Freedom Restoration Act. The Congress had exceeded its powers, the Supreme Court decision said. This time, though, the lower court test case on which the justices ruled had not concerned peyote.

Whether the Religious Freedom Restoration Act was constitutional or not, among Indian peoples peyotism—and other Native American religious practices—continue to flourish. With or without national attention and support, American Indians are creating and combining elements in their own religious responses to the times. Their understanding of sacred space and their political will to express their views and to work to achieve their goals are likely to continue for the foreseeable future.

In Overview

Native American religious traditions have been diverse, but Indians have held many things in common. Their sense of **continuity with the sacred world** has been expressed in beliefs regarding kinship with nature and in traditional sacred stories that reflect no break between the events of creation and the ordinary history of the people. For American Indians, the outer, **material world** has been holy, and so, too, has the **inner world of dreams**. Moving between the different worlds has meant that boundaries can be breached and **transformations** are important. Holy beings have been seen as shapeshifters, able to assume new form or change the world around them. Living in **harmony with the natural world** has been the great religious requirement, for Indians have thought that the human world should correspond with the natural one.

Among the **Oglala** of the North American Plains and the **Hopi** of the Southwest, different versions of Native American religion gave ordinary and extraordinary meaning to existence. Like Indian societies in general, both collapsed ordinary and extraordinary religion into one. At the same time, the Oglala, a hunter-gatherer society, and the Hopi, an agricultural people, are case studies in diversity. Their respective traditions show us how American Indian religion really means American Indian religions. Still further, American Indians experienced religious change, especially after the coming of Europeans. In a series of different forms of **religious combination**, elements from European Christianity blended with Native American beliefs and practices. Sometimes, "new" religions sprang up, while in still different instances Native Americans became converts to various Christian denominations and put their native mark on Christian expression. Meanwhile, in a series of court cases, despite their losses Native Americans continued to challenge Euro-American views of religion and to insist on the seriousness of Indian sacred ways.

The story of American Indian religions is a microcosm of the religious encounters that would confront each of the immigrant groups that came to the United States. All would come with the ways of their ancestors; all would intend to preserve them. Yet each people was one among many "nations" present in the new country, and the presence of other ways led to changes in traditional religions. Religious combinations characterized American Indians and non-Indians alike. The people of Israel—the Jews—are a special case in point. Like Native Americans, for centuries they were sojourners more than settlers, and also like Native Americans, they sought to preserve their traditions even as they took religious ideas and expressions from their Protestant neighbors.

Chapter 2

Israel in a Promised Land: Jewish Religion and Peoplehood

When Christopher Columbus touched land in what came to be called the West Indies in 1492, among his crew were "New Christians." These were Spanish Jews who, in fear of the Inquisition, had converted to Christianity but many of whom secretly continued to practice Judaism. Their presence was one of those accidents of history that, in retrospect, seem fitting. Ancient Israel had, in its time, begun a religious revolution that became the source not only of later Judaism but of Christianity as well. So it was appropriate that the descendants of ancient Israel should be among the first Europeans to see the Americas.

In the late fifteenth century, some European Jews had pressing reasons to venture across the Atlantic. In 1492, the year that Columbus sailed, the Jews were expelled from Spain, and in 1497 the same fate befell them in Portugal. Thus, Jews sought refuge in whatever lands seemed likely to welcome or at least tolerate them. While many fled to Palestine and, notably, to Italy and Turkey, others turned to liberal Holland, where they flourished as the largest Spanish-Portuguese Jewish community in exile. After the Dutch won their political independence in the 1590s, they began to establish a far-flung colonial empire. Jews participated in the new Dutch success, and when in 1630 the Dutch moved into eastern Brazil, the Jews, with some New Christians already there, were partly responsible. So began a prospering Jewish settlement—only to be cut short suddenly in 1654 when the Portuguese reconquered their territory in Brazil. Once again, the Jews fled, some to Dutch colonies in the Caribbean, some back to Amsterdam in Holland, and some to New Amsterdam, a young Dutch colony in North America.

Peter Stuyvesant, the Dutch governor of this colony on the Hudson River, was not pleased. He was overruled, however, by the Dutch of old Amsterdam. As proprietors of the Dutch West India Company, which had Jewish shareholders, they urged that the Jews be permitted to stay. Within ten years, Jewish people were not only engaging in trade and commerce but also buying property, bearing arms, and joining the colonial militia. Then, in 1664, the colony fell to the British and became New York, only to become, little more than a century later, part of the new United States.

From the beginning of their history in the Americas, the Jews repeated an age-old pattern of wandering. Moving from place to place through European history, they had no land that, without reservation, they could call home. Indeed, their history of wandering was more ancient still. One of the oldest verses in the Bible reads, in the Revised Standard Version, "A wandering Aramean was my father" (Deut. 26:5); and although the origins of the Hebrew people are shrouded, their earliest representatives were nomads. As we will see, this nomadic sense was not only an external condition but also became an internal force that shaped Jewish religious experience and expression. Like Native Americans, the Jews were often compelled to wander. Like Native Americans, too, they dwelled in small, homogeneous communities in which religion and peoplehood were blended. In fact, some Americans told tales of kinship between Jews and Indians. As early as the seventeenth century, stories circulated in the United States describing Native Americans as remnants of the lost tribes of Israel. Yet there were many ways in which the Jews were unlike Indians and more like other Europeans who immigrated. The story of their arrival in America bears striking resemblances to the history of other ethnic groups.

The Jewish Immigrations

The oldest Jewish immigrants—in the colony and then state of New York—were **Sephardim**, with a religious culture and ritual practice that followed the Babylonian tradition of Jewish law and observance. Evolved in the sixth century of the common era (**CE**), this Babylonian tradition recalled the legacy of the Jews from the time of their Babylonian exile from their homeland and was also influenced by the Muslim domination of Spain. Distinctive, too, in language, the Sephardim spoke a Jewish dialect called Ladino, a blend of medieval Spanish with Hebrew, Arabic, and other elements. Their religious music was known for its rich, melodious chants.

The Sephardic Jews of New York were at first a very small community of mainly tradespeople. They lacked a rabbi and synagogue, and they frequently intermarried with the local population. By 1692, however, they had established the first synagogue in North America; and although they were never expressly granted the right to worship publicly, they literally took it, and no one in British New York objected. Meanwhile, other Sephardic Jews had settled in Newport, Rhode Island, where they acquired a burial ground and later built Touro synagogue. Gradually, the Sephardim, along with a number of Northern European Jews who had arrived by this time, established small congregations in eastern seacoast cities from Boston to Charleston, South Carolina.

After 1820 a new and much larger wave of Jewish immigrants swept into the United States. The newcomers were **Ashkenazim**, Jews of German origin who

Touro Synagogue of Congregation Jeshuat Israel, Newport. Exterior and interior views of Touro synagogue, dedicated in Rhode Island in 1763 and the nation's oldest synagogue. Note, in the interior lower left, the *bimah*, or sanctuary reading desk, for the Torah.

followed a combined Babylonian (from the exile) and Palestinian (from their homeland) tradition in law and ritual practice. When these German Jews came, there were only about 5,000 Jews in the United States out of a total population of some 13 million. Within the next half century, though, between 200,000 and 400,000 Jews from Central Europe entered the country, and the sheer size of their presence transformed Jewish life even though the Sephardim continued as a kind of Jewish aristocracy. Meanwhile, the Germans brought with them not only Ashkenazic customs and practices but also a movement toward the reform of Judaism.

As a result of the eighteenth-century intellectual movement known as the **Enlightenment**, new values emerged regarding human reason and the law of nature, and a new spirit of liberty and equality surfaced in revolutions in the United States and France. Jews found that various European countries began to invite them out of their ghettos—the segregated communities in which they had been forced to live. Now, they were told, they could experience the full enjoyment of civil rights. This **Emancipation**, as it was called, slowly eroded the close-knit Jewish communities of the past, as increasing numbers of Jews became middle-class citizens of their respective countries.

Now many Jews became concerned about "passing" in Gentile society. An emphasis on being like others began to affect the way some Jews conducted their synagogue services. The long, drawn-out chanting, the absence of a sermon, the Hebrew language, the prayer shawls that covered members of the congregation—all these seemed outmoded to a number of Jews. Their emphasis on practice, on what a Jew should *do* to be religious, was in keeping with the oldest traditions of Judaism. Proper practice, however, was linked to proper thought. The **Jewish Reform movement** of Germany began to question the authority of the rabbinic tradition as established in the **Talmud**, the huge compilation of commentary that elaborates on Jewish law. Reform Jews also rejected the expectation of a personal Messiah who would lead the Jews back to Palestine. They hoped instead for a messianic age, an era of justice, compassion, and peace for the world. Jewish people had no country, they declared, except the land in which they were born, bred, and exercised rights as citizens.

In the United States, the Reform movement grew among German immigrants. With their civic and social status more secure than it had ever been in Germany, Jews strived to mingle unobtrusively with their Protestant neighbors. In the twin lights of modernity and the American flag, much that had seemed acceptable in the old country came under new scrutiny—and was changed. When Isaac M. Wise (1819–1900) arrived in 1846, he quickly became the leader of the Reform party, and by midcentury, Reform had become prominent.

Whether or not they identified with the self-conscious Reform movement, most Jews wanted reform and were eager to embrace American culture. The majority of these new immigrants were modest peddlers and shopkeepers ambitious to succeed. Instead of restricting themselves to the eastern seacoast, they spread out across the country, so that soon cities like Cincinnati and San Francisco could boast flourishing Jewish populations. But Americanizing influences were countered by more community-binding ones. The immigrants spoke their own dialect, called Judeo-German; and in spite of the presence among them of some rabbis attracted to the United States from Europe, they produced no learned class. Even most of the Reform rabbis—as well as more traditional ones—strongly disapproved when immigrants intermarried with other Americans and lost their ties to the Jewish community.

The reform-minded German immigrants were outnumbered, soon, by a third wave of Jewish newcomers, more than 1.7 million strong. They arrived from about 1880 to 1914, when the outbreak of World War I and, a decade later, the immigration quotas of the National Origins Act effectively ended massive Jewish immigration. These Jews were noticeably different from earlier immigrants. They were Eastern Europeans, from countries like Russia, Romania, Poland, and Austria. They had endured hardship and persecution, living in **shtetls**, towns and communities within a designated area where Jews were permitted to dwell. No tempting bait of suffrage and civil rights had been held out to them, and they expressed no desire to mingle with Protestants and other mainstream Americans. They came to the United States in order to be free, and in the beginning they did not think that having freedom meant becoming otherwise like mainstream Americans. They were poor and mostly illiterate in English, and they settled in huge numbers in major cities such as New York and Chicago, becoming part of an army of factory workers or struggling along as artisans and small shopkeepers. Many of these people became the backbone of a self-conscious **Orthodox Judaism**, the strictest form of American Judaism.

For Jews already prospering in the country, the new immigrants at times seemed an embarrassment. Besides, the transition from traditional practice to the new Judaism promoted by Reform-oriented rabbis seemed impossible to imagine, let alone perform. Yet despite the poverty and seeming social awkwardness of the immigrants, the bond of Jewishness meant that the older American Jewish community could not look away. There was a warmth and inner meaning to the old ways that the immigrants brought, and the attraction of tradition, the responsibility of relationship, and, among some, a growing disenchantment with Reform encouraged the growth of a third form of Jewish practice and belief—**Conservative Judaism**.

The story after the Eastern European influx is one of growth and material prosperity, of education and involvement in the social and political life of the United States. It is also a story of a continuing search for the meaning of Jewishness in America.

Jewishness and Peoplehood

Being Jewish has always meant being a people. The ideas of peoplehood and worship of God were one in the minds of the Jews of history, expressed from biblical times in the belief that Israel's God had bound himself to the nation in a **covenant**. In this irrevocable agreement, the Jewish people believed, he had promised to be the God of Israel, even as Israel pledged to be his people. Thus, religious blessings and benefits were understood to come to the community as a particular historical group. And thus, the origins of Jewry were tied to an ethnic and a religious identity that were fused. To state the matter in the terms of the text, ordinary and extraordinary coalesced in traditional Jewish experience. It was only post-Enlightenment modernity that tried to bring about a separation, dividing **Jewishness**, an ethnic and cultural identity, from **Judaism**, a religion.

First, Jews were a people (Jewishness) because they viewed themselves as the inheritors of a common history. Their oldest remembrances, as recorded and interpreted in the Hebrew Bible, told of their descent from Abraham, their sojourn in Egypt and exodus from it under the divinely directed leadership of Moses, their acceptance of the gift of the Law from their God at Sinai, and their eventual entry into Canaan, the land their God had promised them. Other recollections dwelled on their exile in Babylon and their return to Jerusalem, where they raised up the Temple that had been destroyed by foreign troops. Still later, the rabbinic tradition would record the destruction of the Temple for a second time in the year 70 CE. With the devastation of the homeland, popular memory would continue to recall the stories of the faithful who remained in Palestine and of the remnants who scattered throughout the Roman Empire, making their way to parts of Europe, the Middle East, and Northern Africa.

Second, Jews were a people because their common history had been one of suffering. From earliest times, the ancestors of the Jews had borne years of war and insecurity. Later, when they no longer had a land to call their own, they still perpetuated the memory of Israel. Their strict monotheism and refusal to give up their distinctive customs and practices in the host countries where they settled led to persecution. As Christianity broke away from Judaism, its early scriptures reflected its struggle to be free of the synagogue, and anti-Semitism was spread by accusations that the Jews had killed Jesus. In this climate, the history of medieval Jewry was one of segregation, exclusion, and sporadic attempts at extinction. Organized massacres called **pogroms** were used at intervals in attempts to wipe out Jewish communities. Then, as in Spain and Portugal, a number of governments ordered mass expulsions of the Jews. Nor was the Enlightenment an out-and-out blessing when it came. Jews found their old and segregated communities no longer legally and socially recognized. Instead, they possessed a set of civil rights that in most cases did not confer social equality or even, practically speaking, legal equity. The ultimate horror occurred in "enlightened" Germany under Adolf Hitler (1889–1945). The **Holocaust** meant the destruction of 6 million Jewish people for no other reason than that they were Jewish.

Third, Jews were a people because their history and their suffering were bound to their sense of having been chosen by their God for special tasks. Their covenant with him, they believed, marked them off from other nations. It drew boundaries that identified them as a people united in their commitment to the Law of God. At the same time, they regarded the covenant as separating them from the rest of the world. In Jewish teaching, Israel's God demanded an exclusive allegiance, and by the time of the classical prophets in the eighth century before the common era (**BCE**), he was proclaimed the only God for all the nations. When

Christianity and, later, Islam drew their monotheism from Jewish roots, the Jewish sense of chosenness was reinforced. Hence, the bond of Jewishness was born in the dynamic tension among a common history, mutual suffering, and a sense of being chosen. Did the sense of being chosen lead necessarily to the history of suffering? Did the suffering bring about the idea of being chosen as a way to give meaning to pain? Or did the idea of chosenness itself invite antagonism from others so that persecution grew? We will never know the answers, but these questions point clearly to the relationship between Jewishness and boundaries.

As "others" throughout their history, Jews have been people on the boundary, living their lives in two worlds with a foot in each. As a marginal people, the Jews have experienced the strain of separateness, but they have also experienced its stimulation. Through the centuries, they have been remarkable for their creativity, in our own times advancing knowledge in the sciences and sensitivity in the arts. Likewise, through the centuries, they have been in a nearly ideal position to offer insightful criticism to a host culture. In every land where they settled, Jews knew enough to understand, but they also could penetrate cultural assumptions to find new models for thinking and acting. They have proved themselves intellectual and practical leaders. Meanwhile, their Jewishness was expressed in the religion that came to be called Judaism.

Judaism as Biblical Religion

In the discussion of Native American traditions, we saw that Indians in their emphasis on harmony with the natural world lived according to a religious belief in **correspondence**. For Indian societies, the human community was a microcosm, literally, a "small world" that reflected the macrocosm, or "large world," all around them. Religion meant adjusting any disruptions of correspondence in the human sphere, restoring wholeness through the power of sacred story and ritual. The earliest recollections of the Jewish people, present in the Hebrew Bible, suggest that they viewed the world in similar terms, seeing, for example, a close relationship between the fertility of land and crops and the reproductive fruitfulness of women and men. But gradually, Israel shifted its ideas by thinking more about time than about space. Instead of continuing to talk about the space of nature, people began to dwell on the time of **history**.

This shift was reflected in the transformation of religious festivals. Although in their earliest forms the festivals were probably seasonal rites following the agricultural cycle of planting and harvest, they came to have historical meaning. For example, Passover originally seemed to be a ritual event to mark the release of the earth from the grip of winter, the sowing of seed, and the renewal of clan and kinship ties. But as time passed, new interpretations were added, and the Jews came to see Passover as a historical feast to relive the exodus from Egypt and the birth of the Jewish nation. The Jews, they said, had passed over from slavery to freedom, even as the Angel of Death had slain the Egyptians but passed over the firstborn among the infant sons of Israel. The macrocosm—the larger world that explained Jewish identity—lay no longer in space but was instead in time.

Along with this shift came a sense of greater separation between divine and human than the idea of correspondence expressed. Briefly, in the newer idea of **causality**, Israel held that God had *caused* the world—but not out of his own "body." A gap existed between the sacred and the profane worlds, reflected in the account in Genesis of the fall of Adam and Eve. Because of the gap, it became necessary that things be done by God or by the Jews to ensure that, although separate from God, the world would still experience his power. Nature had been demoted, while the Jews even after the fall saw themselves as creatures made in the image of God and given by God the right and duty of controlling the natural world. In its full expression, this conception parted radically from beliefs about correspondence. When Christianity, the child of later Judaism, broke away from its parent, it took with it the heritage of causality. In the differences between correspondence and causality we have in rough outline the patterns for cultural collision between Indians and Europeans. If Jews were in some ways like Indians, they were also in significant ways different from them.

For their part, Jews saw their God taking the lead in turning the gap between divine and human into a bridge between them. God's covenant, they believed, had been both his revelation and his bond with them. And they felt that they could respond to God and tighten the bond by their faithful observance of the Law. In these ideas and the practices that came out of them, Judaism, the biblical religion, was born.

The covenant sense of a relationship with God also started Israel on a path that led to the pure **monotheism** of the eighth-century prophets. When these prophets began to interpret the history of Israel in light of the covenant they came to see the God of Israel as the universal God of *all* nations—an idea that contained the essence of monotheism. The prophets reasoned that the armies of foreign nations then marching against Israel were divinely controlled. God permitted their actions as punishment for the unfaithfulness of Israel to the covenant. Thus, foreign nations belonged to the same God as the God of Israel, and it was only a short leap to the belief that no other God existed—that the God of Israel was the God of all. Similarly, the covenant sense of relationship with God led to the discovery of history that lay behind the idea of causality. By pledging his commitment to the Jewish people in the Hebrew Bible, God, for the Jews, had entered history, establishing a pattern in which he could intervene in human affairs. And if the Almighty was seen to act in human events, then acting and doing became especially important. The God who acted led to a people who acted. As the idea of the covenant already implied, *how* people acted became a significant question.

With action so important in life, the Jewish people developed their traditions gathered in the **Law** in order to guide their activity. Implicit in the idea of God's covenant with Abraham, the Law became explicit in the first five books of the Hebrew Bible, called the **Torah**. Here, rules for living, prescriptions for both ceremonial and moral righteousness, were recorded for future generations. To be a Jew, then as now, meant to accept the burden of the Law. It was more what people *did* in their observation of the Law that made them Jewish than what they *believed*.

To sum up, Judaism as a religion grew out of a strong Jewish belief in the covenant between God and Israel. For Jews, the covenant healed a rift between the divine and the human that was expressed in the idea of causality. Time became an important dimension in which God acted. Because Jews saw God as acting, they came to see action and human history as also important. Hence, belief in a covenant with their God led the Jews to affirm their further belief in the importance of religious practice, of observance of the Jewish Law.

Jewish Tradition and the Consecration of Time

With this background of emphasizing practice, what of the Jewish immigrants in America? With less emphasis on belief than European Christians and their traditions, what Jews *did* became especially significant. So American Judaism meant a series of concrete acts that led to the consecration—the making sacred—of time. For the early immigrants who followed the uncontested orthodoxy of the past—and later for observant Reform and Conservative Jews—the consecration of time meant two kinds of doing. First, it meant ritual action in a regular communal cycle of feasts and in an individual life cycle made up of times of passage from one stage to the next. Second, the consecration of time meant commitment to moral action. For later immigrants, the rise of the different forms of Judaism was linked to arguments in the American Jewish community about *how* time should be consecrated and, as we have seen, about what role traditional ritual should play.

The Ceremonial Cycle

Perhaps the most compelling symbol of the Jewish consecration of time among the early immigrants was the Sabbath. The creation narrative of the biblical book of Genesis had led, step by step, to the climactic account of how on the seventh day God rested (Gen. 2:2), thus establishing the seventh-day Sabbath as a holy day. Yet the Sabbath holiness did not require for the Jews a temple or church. Since the sixth century BCE, when they were exiled in Babylon, they had learned to live without the animal sacrifices of the Temple in Jerusalem. Sometime in that era the beginnings of the later synagogue had developed. A special place in which the Torah could be read and studied, the synagogue required a religious teacher and leader called a **rabbi**. But even though the scrolls of the Torah were kept in the synagogue, the heart of Judaism lay in the home. Perhaps it took the earliest Jews nearly forty years to establish their first synagogue in North America because, so long as they had their homes and families, they felt that they had the essentials of Judaism.

A high point of the traditional Sabbath was—and is—a ritual meal eaten after sundown on Friday evening to begin the feast. With a clean house, a white cloth on the table, the best dishes and utensils, and the choicest foods and wine, the twisted loaves of Sabbath bread (called *hallah*) were placed under an embroidered napkin. The mistress of the house lit Sabbath candles (at least two) and spoke a blessing. At the beginning of the meal, the head of the household (the father) read or chanted a scriptural text, pronounced the *kiddush*, or sanctification, and blessing the bread, began to break it and distribute it to members of his family, all of whom had ritually washed their hands. The dinner that followed was far from solemn, for the Sabbath was a time of festival. Then, at sundown on Saturday evening, the Sabbath closed with another home-centered ritual to mark the end of its light. The head of the household took a special candle made of two or more plaited pieces of wax and, reciting a prayer to thank God for the separation of the sacred from the profane, which the Sabbath symbolized, extinguished it in a full glass of wine. In between, the Sabbath was traditionally observed with a strict separation from work and everyday activity. No travel was allowed, no business transacted, no money exchanged, no writing accomplished, and no other chores performed. The Sabbath called for leisure and recreation through visiting family and friends, going on strolls, and the like. But above all, it called for mental and spiritual re-creation through the reading and study of the Torah. This is why on Saturday morning it became customary to hold a synagogue service.

With its symbolism of separation to mark it off from the rest of time, the Sabbath continues to be for observant Jews the time of extraordinary religion. It memorializes the God of Israel, who created human beings out of nothing. And as a memorial to the God who acted—and acts—in history, the Sabbath aims to establish a religious monument that is to time what a cathedral is to space. At the same time, because in the Jewish scheme of things religion and peoplehood are one, the Sabbath becomes ordinary time. In the Sabbath meal, with its blend of ritual formality and spontaneous family conversation, we can see, encapsulated, the Jewish fusion of ordinary and extraordinary religion.

In making time holy, the Sabbath was—and continues to be—joined by an annual cycle of seasonal feasts. Judaism has observed these feasts according to a lunar calendar of 353 or 354 days, with an extra month added at set intervals to bring the reckoning into line with the solar calendar. Three major observances, originally attached to the agricultural cycle, provide the foundation for the yearly cycle. These are **Passover** (*Pesach*), at the beginning of the planting season, which was historicized to recall the exodus from Egypt; **Weeks** (also called *Shavuot* or Pentecost), at the end of the barley harvest, which commemorates the giving of the Law (Torah) to Moses on Mount Sinai; and **Booths** (also called *Sukkot* or Tabernacles), at the end of agricultural work for the year before the winter rains, which commemorates the wandering of the Jews in the desert before they entered Canaan.

In a chronology supported both by agriculture and history, Passover comes first, followed by Weeks, and then Booths. From the religious point of view, however, Booths marks the beginning of the Jewish year. In the Torah the wilderness wandering of the Jews directly preceded their entry into the promised land, and so the feast looks forward to new things. It seems fitting, therefore, that **Rosh Hashanah**, the Jewish New Year, comes just before the feast of Booths. So named because the Jews constructed and lived temporarily in huts, or booths, to remind them of their desert sojourn, Booths is the third stage in a long and solemn festival season. The New Year, Rosh Hashanah, comes first. Ten days later is the Day of Atonement, **Yom Kippur**, in which Jews fast, do penance, and confess what they feel to be their sinfulness before God. Finally, four days later comes the week-long Booths with its theme of new hope and confidence for the future.

Perhaps the most solemn moments of the Jewish ceremonial year occur on the **Days of Awe**, Rosh Hashanah and Yom Kippur, when the *shofar,* a special trumpet made of a ram's horn, is blown. Both the New Year and the Day of Atonement are days of religious remembrance. For Jews, God is recalling the deeds of his people, while the people remember their creation and covenant with God, their chosenness as his Israel, and their successes and failures in faithfulness. The shofar blows to remind Israel of its calling, piercing time to bring year after year into the covenant. Like all the solemnities of the Jewish year, the New Year and the Day of Atonement are not simply remembrances in the ordinary way in which we use that term. They are recollections that aspire to bring times of origin back again. That is, they aim to destroy the work of time to bring pious Jews in touch with the religious acts of tradition so that their imputed power can be tapped.

At the other "beginning" of Jewish festivals, the springtime Passover, the solemn ritual meal carries the same message. The meal, called a **seder**, recalls the biblical account of the meal eaten on the night the Hebrews fled from Egypt led by Moses. The Jews use unleavened bread (*matzah*) because in the biblical exodus story they had no time to wait for bread to rise. They eat bitter herbs to remind them of the story's bitter journey and a mix of chopped nuts, apples, raisins, and cinnamon, like the mortar they placed between bricks in the account of slavery in Egypt. Parsley dipped in salted water, a roasted egg, the shank bone of a lamb, and four ceremonial cups of wine—all have symbolic meaning, and all are meant to re-create, as vividly as possible, the story of the exodus. At the heart of the ritual is a recitation of the story of the flight from Egypt. To introduce it, traditionally the youngest boy in the family asks, "Why *is* this night different from all other nights?" The boy's father answers in kind: "This *is* the night we fled the Egyptians"—and goes on to tell the story. If the ritual succeeds, the family and its guests feel a sense of renewal from connecting with the moment of the exodus; they can continue their ordinary lives with the same fresh energy as at a major moment in Israel's beginning.

Beyond these celebrations, there are a number of other feasts and fasts linking the parts of the year to one another, making the entire year holy, and rendering the extraordinary an ordinary event. The most well-known of these in America became **Hanukkah**. Called the Feast of Lights or Dedication, Hanukkah recalls the rekindling of the candelabrum in the Temple of Jerusalem by Judas Maccabeus and his followers (165 BCE). The Syrian-Greek monarch, Antiochus IV, who held

Jerusalem under his power, had tried to make the Temple into a shrine to the Greek deity Zeus. Judas with his brothers and other followers stormed the hill of the Temple, drove out the Greek troops, ritually purified the sanctuary, and restored the traditional services. The eight-day festival that, according to tradition, the Maccabees then began is perpetuated in Jewish homes by the lighting each evening for eight days of the **menorah**, or candelabrum. On the first evening, only one candle is lit; on the second, two; on the third, three; and so on, until the eighth night, when all of the candles are kindled. Hanukkah is a festival of remembrance, and it points to the Jewish right to be different. The deed of the Maccabees proclaims that because the Jews lived in the middle of a Greek culture, they did not also have to be Greek. In America, somewhat ironically, Hanukkah became a way to be different but also the same, becoming for some the Jewish version of Christmas complete with a "Hanukkah bush." Not all Jews approve this development, and it has been the subject of some thoughtful reflection on the part of contemporary Jews.

Leaving aside questions about Hanukkah and other Jewish feasts, individual lives in Judaism are also surrounded by ritual. A Jew should be a son or daughter of the Law, and in one traditional custom the scroll of the Torah is carried to the door of the lying-in chamber where a newborn infant and its mother are resting. If the child is a boy, he is circumcised on the eighth day, so that, now formally admitted to the community of kinship, he can bear in his flesh a sign of the covenant. At thirteen, the boy becomes **Bar Mitzvah**, a "son of the commandment." He demonstrates his maturity by reading from the scroll of the Torah in the synagogue. In the United States, in Conservative and Reform congregations his sister becomes **Bat Mitzvah**, a "daughter of the commandment," as well. The large celebrations that typically accompany American Bar and Bat Mitzvah ceremonies point, once again, to how extraordinary and ordinary religion are blended within Judaism.

In a traditional Jewish wedding, too, ritual expresses to bride and groom the importance of the human duty they are to undertake. They stand together under a bridal canopy of white silk or satin; the marriage contract is read to them; and the Seven Blessings are pronounced. Then the pair drink from the cup of betrothal, and the glass is smashed to recall the destruction of the ancient Temple. At death, austere and simple rituals mark the event, with burial in the earth. After the prescribed mourning period, yearly commemorations of the dead continue, and surviving kin recite the *kaddish*, or prayer of praise. In the United States, an annual collective remembrance, the *Yizkor* service—and "Yizkor days"—became especially popular among Eastern European Jews, bringing them back in touch with their traditional ways.

Ritual also tells the devout the meaning of their Jewishness in everyday life. The dietary laws prescribe just what foods should be eaten and how. Animals are divided into clean and unclean, with "clean" ones characterized by a cloven hoof and chewing the cud. "Unclean" foods are forbidden foods, and in America this has especially meant pork. Aquatic creatures without fins and scales are also considered unclean, eliminating shellfish. Finally, meat and milk dishes cannot be eaten together, and at least several hours must pass before an observant Jew can drink milk after eating meat. The origins of these practices are lost in history, and speculation on their development has produced a host of explanations. In America, however, they quickly became a marker of Jewish identity. Inherited from a biblical past in which, Jews believed, God acted in history in an extraordinary manner, the dietary, or **kosher**, laws recall in ordinary time belief in the extraordinary mission of Israel. Only a minority of American Jews have kept to full kosher observance, in so doing adding to American religious manyness. Other Jews, especially in the Reform tradition, have for the most part rejected the dietary laws, expressing the pull of American religious oneness. Both acceptance and rejection have shaped Jewish identity in America.

The Moral Law

Beyond the ceremonial requirements of the Torah, the consecration of time meant for Jews a life of moral righteousness. According to the biblical account, there were two tablets to the Law that God had given to Moses on Mount Sinai. The second, and longer, has told Jews how they should live in their *human* relationships. The many ceremonial requirements of the Law point to the centrality of the **Shema** (Deut. 6:4). This solemn summary of the covenant, recited morning and evening by a pious Jew, proclaims that God is one. It leads as well to the code by which Jews are to live. They are to love God, and they must love and care for one another. But external behavior was not enough. Biblical teaching held that a person could sin, even without acting, if he or she looked with envy on the life of another. The covenant began and ended *within*, and right behavior without a right heart was not sufficient. Reversing the equation, for Jews a right heart *always* led to the world. Preaching social justice and compassion toward all, the prophets announced a universal ethical message—one that could apply to every people.

The Moral Law in the United States

As Jews responded to their new situation in the United States, these ethical prescriptions of the Law assumed added importance. The mid-nineteenth-century Reformers found the ethical teachings of the prophets central, and they held that "outmoded" ritual practices should fall away. For example, Isaac M. Wise taught that Jewish chosenness meant a divine mission to spread the prophetic call for justice and mercy. For him, a special fit existed between Judaism and the American nation, for with its democratic ideals the United States offered a perfect setting for the ethical action that the ancient Jewish prophets demanded.

Later, Kaufmann Kohler (1843–1926), Wise's successor as president of Cincinnati's Hebrew Union College, took these ideas to still more radical conclusions. Divine revelation, Kohler argued, occurred in the natural historical process. Hence, the revelation of Judaism was natural and historical. Its essence lay in ethics, and its true aim was to bring in the messianic age by the salvation of human beings in history. In 1885 a conference of Reform rabbis called by Kohler met in Pittsburgh to adopt the widely influential Pittsburgh Platform. This statement of Reform principles, while rejecting the vast body of Mosaic and rabbinic law, such as the kosher laws, held to the moral law taught in the Torah and expressed a commitment on that basis to the struggle of the poor. The mission of Israel, as Kohler and other Reformers saw it, was the moral redemption of society.

In their transformation of Judaism in the United States, the Reformers received unintentional help from one segment of the Eastern European immigrants after the 1880s. While many Eastern European Jews retained as nearly as they could their Orthodox customs and practices, others substituted social radicalism. This had happened for some before they immigrated, when they responded to anti-Semitic harassment by abandoning their religion. In the United States, however, the new motive for rejecting Orthodoxy became its foreignness. Numbers joined the Socialist party, formed socialist labor unions, and produced socialist newspapers. Meanwhile, as Jews became more prosperous themselves, they became leaders in social welfare programs. Doing the Law had been transformed into a modern zeal for justice in society.

Acculturation has been a fact in all of Jewish history, and seemingly it became even more the case in the United States. Yet the story is one in which Jews responded differently to their new circumstances. The story of the American Israel reveals increasing separation between Jewishness the culture and Judaism the organized religion. It also tells of the rise of three major forms of Judaism—Reform, Conservatism, and Orthodoxy—and a number of related religious movements.

American Forms of Judaism

The Reform movement championed the effort to shape Judaism as an organized religion. The Pittsburgh Platform had declared that its subscribers were no longer a nation but instead a religious community. Now the Reformers proceeded to implement their religious community with zeal. By 1889 they organized the Central Conference of American Rabbis, and by 1894 they published the *Union Prayer Book* as a new order of synagogue service. Under the new rubric, the synagogue came more and more to resemble a Protestant church of the period. The service, almost entirely in English, was conducted mostly by the rabbi, in contrast to the older Jewish pattern of full congregational participation. Prayer shawls disappeared, as did segregated seating for women, while organs and mixed choirs of men and women now could be seen. So far did Reform Jews go in some congregations that they adopted a Sunday Sabbath, more in keeping with the practices of their Christian neighbors. They kept to the annual cycle of Jewish feasts less strictly and laid other traditional rituals, such as the kosher laws, aside.

Still, even the Reform movement preserved the age-old custom of circumcision and a ban on intermarriage with non-Jews, indicating the hidden presence among these "liberated" Jews of allegiance to Israel's identity as a people. It was the emergent Conservative movement, however, that self-consciously began to preserve a Jewish sense of peoplehood. From the first, significant numbers of Jews were dismayed at the path Reform—a vocal minority—was charting. Moderates recognized a need to adapt some American elements but still saw tradition as a source of nourishment. Increasing discontent with Reform leadership came to a head in 1883, when the first graduating class from Hebrew Union College received rabbinical ordination. The festive dinner to honor the occasion horrified a number of the guests, and tradition has it that two rabbis rose from their places and left. The caterer had served four forbidden foods (clams, crabs, shrimps, and frogs' legs)—foods considered **trefa**, or unkosher, according to Jewish law.

The "trefa banquet" became a dramatic catalyst for a counter movement that began to grow rapidly. When the Pittsburgh Platform was adopted two years later by Reform rabbis, it provided an added spur. Meanwhile, Eastern European immigrant needs were also supplying fuel for the Conservative movement. Sabato Morais (1823–1897), the rabbi of a Sephardic synagogue in Philadelphia, emerged as leader, and his efforts, with others, led to the establishment of the Jewish Theological Seminary in New York. It promoted fidelity to Mosaic Law and ancestral traditions as well as love for the Hebrew language—all to become, increasingly, badges of ethnic identity. Then, after some hard times, Solomon Schechter (1847–1915) came from England to become the seminary's president. A Romanian by birth and a distinguished scholar, he attracted an illustrious faculty and spoke far more clearly than earlier leaders in terms of the ethnic emphasis that Conservatism was fostering. In his idea of the "catholic Israel," Schechter expressed his faith that by a deeply spiritual inner unity—a unity as a *people*—Jews would find a middle way between the full demands of the Law and the requirements of modernity.

Emphasis on the Jewish people persisted and flourished in new ways. In 1918 Mordecai Kaplan (1881–1983) of the Jewish Theological Seminary began a synagogue center movement. Throughout the twenties and thereafter, Jewish centers became popular institutions, adding to the traditional synagogue and its services a host of nonreligious activities. For Kaplan and his supporters, the center should be a place where all Jews, whether observant or not, could feel at home. Meanwhile, Kaplan in 1934 published *Judaism as a Civilization*, arguing his case that Judaism was a religious civilization rather than a religion. The following year Kaplan founded **Reconstructionism**, a movement that, as an offshoot of Conservatism, spread his ideas about the importance of traditional ceremonies and rituals not as expressions of supernatural religion but as distinctive signs of Jewishness. Reconstructionism remained small, but its influence was important. For example, the **havurah** movement that spread among Jews in the 1970s began within Reconstructionist ranks. Named for a pietistic, mystical, and scholarly movement within Judaism in ancient times, the new American movement promoted a renewed Jewish devotionalism, with small circles gathered for prayer and song. It sought to support a deepening Jewish commitment outside of established institutions but later came to work within them, encouraging community closeness.

The havurah movement was certainly not the first to draw Jews together from different branches of Judaism. One important movement that galvanized the American Jewish community was **Zionism**. Aiming for the reestablishment of a Jewish nation-state, the Zionist movement in its modern form began in the late nineteenth century with Theodor Herzl (1860–1904). The idea of a return to Israel was attractive to American Conservatives and also, to some extent, Orthodox Jews. However, Reform Jews at first strongly opposed Zionism because of their insistence that Judaism meant an organized religion and not a national group. It was not until 1935 that they moved to a position of official neutrality. Meanwhile, small groups of **Hasidim**, the descendants of an eighteenth-century Eastern European mystical movement, also strongly opposed Zionism. For them, the worldly ideal of establishing a Jewish nation-state violated religious hope for the Messiah who, according to tradition, would lead the Jews back to the land of Israel.

The Holocaust, however, changed Reform and Hasidic thinking radically. As the news of German atrocities and the full horror of what had happened reached the United States, the very foundations of Jewish belief in a covenant with God seemed called into question. Whatever religious answers they groped toward, Jewish people became convinced that they themselves must take an active role in shaping their future. They could no longer trust the nations of the world and the Western heritage of the Enlightenment. Nor could they any longer wait for their God. When the modern state of Israel came into existence in 1948, it received enthusiastic endorsement and support from American Jewry and has mostly continued to do so. In Israel, American Jews see their spiritual home.

If Reform stressed Judaism, the religion, while Conservatism promoted Jewishness, the ethnic and cultural identity, Orthodoxy became the Jewish attempt to keep faith with the past. A traditionalist orthodox (small "o") outlook already shaped normal Jewish practice in the nineteenth-century United States. With Isaac Leeser (1806–1872) as its clear pre–Civil War leader, traditional Judaism flourished. Leeser felt comfortable enough with change to promote Sunday schools, a Jewish catechism, English-language usage, and even a union of synagogues. Still, he insisted on full observance of the requirements of the Torah. In the late-nineteenth-century environment, however, Orthodoxy became a more self-conscious movement. With its Eastern European faithful, it tried to retain the religious observances of the past and to hold on to all 613 commands of the Law—or as much of that as it could. Reform Judaism, by its emphasis on organized religion as a separate function, tried to make of Judaism an extraordinary (if Americanized) religion. Conservatism fostered ordinary religion as it encouraged Jewishness among observant and nonobservant alike. And Orthodoxy sought to continue the Jewish combination of the two. Still, the lines were not nearly so clear. Conservatism often seemed to share the Orthodox assumption that peoplehood and religion were one. In our own times, Reform—perhaps influenced by ethnic politics and multiculturalism—has embraced the Jewish past. Increasingly, cantors in Reform synagogues have chanted portions of the service in Hebrew, and the Reform prayerbook contains noticeably more Hebrew than earlier versions. The havurah movement, too, has fed into a new devotionalism.

The growth of formal divisions within the Jewish community is a good example of how the American experience has changed a religion. The divisions looked a lot like the denominations present within Protestantism. As time passed, Jews became like Protestants in other ways, too.

American Judaism and Contemporary Life

First, Jews were already like Protestants in some ways from the first. They shared with Calvinist-leaning Protestants a religion that stressed law and deed. So the "Protestant ethic" did not seem foreign to the newcomers, and they immediately exhibited industry, perseverance, thrift, and prudence. With their heritage of adaptability to many different host cultures, they were able as a group to rise quickly to middle-class status. Their tradition of study of the Torah led them as easily to education and the university, and they speedily became professionals. Their closely knit families and mutual-assistance patterns provided security and encouragement in the new environment and echoed the family values of the Protestant mainstream.

Second, Jews changed to become more like other Americans. Nurtured by religious liberty, Judaism should in theory have grown stronger. Yet religious liberty in America meant freedom *from* religion as well as freedom *of* religion. In the former world of the Jewish shtetl, such choice had not been possible. Now Jews could defect from their Judaism, and many of them did. Those who remained Jewish in religion expressed American pluralism in their formal divisions, their "denominations," as we have seen. Unlike in the small and self-contained Jewish communities of Europe, no single authority spoke for the Jewish people. It is significant that various efforts at Jewish ecclesiastical unity met with only moderate success. Both Isaac Leeser and Isaac M. Wise experienced failure on that score in the mid-nineteenth century.

Departures from Judaism and divisions in Judaism have continued to be related phenomena. In the early twenty-first century, the Jewish community is close to 6 million. This number represents perhaps 2 percent of the general American population—a percentage that has gone down for decades. But—more troubling still for Jews—surveys from 2002 suggest that the actual *number* of Jews in the country has declined for the first time since the colonial era. Fertility rates are low; immigration has lessened dramatically; conversions are few; and intermarriage is a significant source of leakage. Jews themselves are often disunited, and there are boundary issues aplenty about who counts as a Jew. Are those born of a Jewish father but not a Jewish mother really Jewish (tradition holds that a Jewish mother is the defining sign)? What do converts to Judaism have to do to make them Jewish? Are Jews for Jesus Jewish? And what about Jews who practice Buddhist or Wiccan rites? For strict Orthodox Jews, do Reform Jews count as Jews (they do not for the Orthodox rabbinate of the state of Israel)? Meanwhile, large numbers can be located among those whom Jewish sociologist Samuel C. Heilman has called "heritage Jews"—content with symbolic expressions of their Jewishness. A smaller number can be claimed as active.

Still, Jews, whether or not they regularly attend synagogue, have displayed strong identification with a specific form of Judaism, and observers have noted a **revitalization movement**—a return to tradition—among numbers of them. For those who are affiliated with a synagogue (less than half of all American Jews), it is estimated that 45 percent are Reform and 42 percent Conservative. By contrast, Orthodox affiliation is probably about 9 percent and Reconstructionism 4 percent. At the same time, Orthodox Jews are often given an equal voice with Reform and Conservative representatives in Jewish community affairs.

Whatever their formal allegiance, Jewish people continue to read the Bible. Fewer, however, can say that their beliefs in God or revelation in the Bible are firm. Belief in life after death, underplayed in much of Jewish history, has declined. Yet as some strive to blend more completely with the general American population, others find new spiritual energy in the Jewish mystical tradition centered on the **Kabbalah**. In fact, a Kabbalistic revival spearheaded by the ultra-Orthodox Lubavitcher branch of Hasidic Judaism has spread outside it—even into today's New Age movement and new spirituality, with celebrities like Madonna embracing it. With its emphasis on the divine spark in every person, its cultivation of prayerfulness, and its devotion to the Torah and its inner message, Hasidism has nurtured mysticism and a related spirituality just at the time when the havurah movement has become more routine. Meanwhile, some scholars of Jewish mysticism have moved toward helping Jewish congregations look to the Kabbalah as a living spiritual tradition. Popular books on Jewish mysticism have multiplied, and students at Reform, Reconstructionist, and Conservative seminaries have increasing exposure to the mystical tradition. While rabbis have frowned at the Kabbalah of Madonna and other New Age enthusiasts as inauthentic, they have generally responded positively to the interest in Jewish mysticism that the Kabbalah movement has promoted.

Among the Orthodox in general, a right-wing movement toward strict fundamentalism in interpreting the commands of the Torah has been thriving. By contrast, in Conservative and Reform congregations and in the small Reconstructionist movement, women are serving as rabbis, and they increasingly participate in ritual and administration. Reform and Reconstructionist rabbis have also voted to accept gays within their ranks. In Conservative quarters, while there is conflict over gay and lesbian ordination, rabbinic authorities have welcomed gay and lesbian Jews into general congregational life. In response to the times, too, both Reform and Reconstructionism have addressed the issue of attrition through intermarriage by expanding the age-old rule that being born of a Jewish mother is what makes a child Jewish. Now the Jewishness of the father also counts, with the proviso, for Reform, that the child affirms Judaism—an acknowledgment of what has already been common social practice in many Jewish communities.

In the early twenty-first century, the fortunes and actions of the state of Israel continue to preoccupy American Jews. For example, virtually all responses to the September 11, 2001, attack on the World Trade Center have included concern over the effects American actions will have on Israel. September 11 has also added a new urgency to the broader issue of Jewish-Muslim relations. As the issue of Palestinian rights has emerged more sharply and as terrorism and fear of it have increasingly become important factors in Israeli life, the American Jewish community's response toward Israeli policy has had its ups and downs. If this is a sign of division among Jews, it also signals—although it is not the same as—the two directions in which American Judaism today looks. On one side, signs of Jewish renewal are seemingly everywhere. On the other, Jews are becoming less visible as Jews. Becoming many in the land of manyness, they have become more like other Americans.

In Overview

The story of American Jewry is the story of both a **people** and a **religion**. In three waves of immigration, the Jewish people brought to this country a religious identity forged by common history, mutual suffering, and a sense of chosenness. The biblical religion that was fundamental to this religious identity stressed **historical tradition** more than nature and organized its cultus around belief in a God who revealed himself and acted in relationship to the community of Israel. Bound to its God by a **covenant**, Israel consecrated time through regular remembrance and through ethical action, both of them the ways in which observant Jews fulfilled the requirements of the Law, or **Torah**.

In America differences over how the Law's commandments should be observed resulted in the growth of three major forms of Judaism. **Reform Jews**, who tend to separate Judaism as an organized religion from Jewishness as an ethnic identity, have been liberals. They have loosened social boundaries as they encountered the pluralism of the United States. **Orthodox Jews**, by contrast, drew the boundaries tightly and tried to preserve as much of European Jewish culture as possible. **Conservative Jews**, who occupy the middle position, also blend organized religion and culture (peoplehood) but strive to find a more practical path to fulfillment of the Torah in light of modernity. In recent times, Jewishness as the bond of peoplehood has become more important, but Jews also experience the results of assimilation and intermarriage in narrowing the division between them and other Americans.

Jews have lived in the tension between self-conscious religion and peoplehood, between extraordinary and ordinary, and between manyness and oneness. If they have found a promised land in the United States while they look to Zion in a different land, another group of Americans has also been living between two Zions. Roman Catholics came over the sea to reap American promises. At the same time, they, too, have kept one eye elsewhere—on the domes of St. Peter's in Rome.

Chapter 3

Bread and Mortar: The Presence of Roman Catholicism

When the ships of Christopher Columbus brought the first Jewish "New Christians" to the islands of the Caribbean, they sailed under the flag of Catholic Spain. Roman Catholics were thus among the first Europeans to set foot in the Americas. Supported by the wealth and power of the Spanish throne, Catholic missionaries determined to convert the natives, even as they ministered to soldiers and other colonials.

Spanish Missions

As early as 1513, Juan Ponce de Leon made his way into the Florida peninsula. Eight years later he brought priests to establish missions among the Indians, but the Indians drove them off. Other attempted settlements failed until St. Augustine was founded, and, by 1595, missionary work began in earnest. North of the Gulf of Mexico, in what is now New Mexico, Francisco Vasquez de Coronado arrived in 1540 with three friars among his party. By the end of the century, the Franciscans began a ministry there. These missions had their ups and downs, with a rebellion by Native Americans near the end of the seventeenth century, but by 1750 the Spanish counted twenty-two missions. Similarly, in what became southern Arizona the Jesuit Eusebio Francisco Kino founded San Xavier del Bac in 1700 and, with his fabled journeys that led to the establishment of other missions, claimed to have baptized 30,000 Indians. To the west, the Franciscan Junipero Serra planted a line of mission establishments on the main road up and down the California coast. At least 600 miles in length, the California mission system at its peak included twenty-one stations where over 21,000 Indians farmed, raised livestock, wove, and displayed other skills. But by 1821 Mexico declared its independence from Spain.

Thereafter the Mexican government dissolved the missions, and Indian converts melted away.

Outnumbered by the Indians, the Spanish Catholic missionaries brought their Native American converts a shotgun Christianity, assisted by soldiers in garrisons never far away. But they were also convinced that they had a divine command to bring the Christian message to the Indians. Without the perspective of a later age that would introduce a new regard for the religions of Native Americans, they thought that they were snatching Indians from Satan—and bringing them civilization as well.

French Missions

Catholic efforts in New France were similar, although the French perhaps encountered even more open hostility. The French made regular visits to the Newfoundland coast in the sixteenth century, and by the next century a French Protestant community, the Huguenots, made plans to establish an outpost in Nova Scotia. These Protestant settlers would have their own ministers, but the French government decided that Catholic priests should go along, too, to convert the Indians. So French Franciscans came, later to be joined by Jesuit priests in Quebec. Striving to master Indian languages, the Jesuits set up mission stations for the Huron Indians. These missions failed in the midst of Iroquois attacks, only token conversions, and some Jesuit martyrdoms. Then, for political reasons, the Iroquois made peace with the French. By 1668 the Jesuits had taken advantage of the situation and opened missions in upper New York.

Work among the Iroquois lasted only about two decades until the English swept in, but as early as the 1630s the Jesuits had also been preaching to the Ottawa in the Illinois country, where they established missions. One of these, La Pointe in Wisconsin, later acquired fame as the place from which the Jesuit Jacques Marquette set out to explore the Mississippi River with Louis Joliet. In the interim, French colonies began to encircle the missions, and French settlers intermarried with Indians, assuring Catholic influence. In Maine, Jesuits worked in missions to the Abenaki Indians, and by the end of the century, priests were working with the Natchez people in the South. They later formed a parish in what is now Mobile, Alabama, and began a mission near New Orleans. The city itself became a settled French colony with its Catholicism obvious. Further north, a group of transplanted Acadians settled. French people from Nova Scotia who had refused to accept British rule there after 1755, they brought with them their Catholic religion and customs, part of a growing Creole culture.

English Colonies

In contrast to both the Spanish and French, Roman Catholics entered the English territories not to convert Native Americans but to settle. When King Charles I decided to grant a charter to found a colony north of Virginia to George Calvert, the first Lord Baltimore and former privy councillor to King James I, his decision was a concession to an acknowledged Catholic. Although George Calvert did not live to carry out his plans, his son Leonard arrived in 1634 as the first governor of the colony. Maryland law guaranteed religious liberty to all, but Catholics were a minority in the population and when Puritans were able to take over, they outlawed Catholicism. Although Lord Baltimore later regained power, by 1688 and the Glorious Revolution in England, the Catholic defeat was complete. Catholics began to pay taxes in support of the Church of England, and from 1718 until the outbreak of the American Revolution they were refused voting rights.

In New England, after a brief period of toleration in Rhode Island, Catholics were not able to worship freely until after the American Revolution. Similarly, beginning in 1691, New York applied religious tests to exclude them from public office, even though earlier there had been a Catholic governor. Pennsylvania, instead, provided the best conditions after Maryland for Catholic settlement. Germans and some Irish came, the Jesuits worked among them, and by 1770 there were probably 3,000 adult Catholics in Pennsylvania, with some 10,000 in Maryland. Yet small as the English Catholic presence was compared to the missionary efforts of Spain and France, the English colonies created the constitutional structure within which Catholicism would later flourish. Moreover, land claimed by New Spain and New France would become part of the United States in the nineteenth century, and with this territory would come an assortment of Catholic communities. Still more, from overseas hundreds of thousands of Catholic immigrants would pour into the country.

Roman Catholic Religion

If the religion of Native Americans emphasized the sacredness of space and the religion of the Jews emphasized the sacredness of time, for the Catholic immigrants, space and time were equally consecrated. From the perspective of space, Catholics have **sacraments**, and from the perspective of time, they honor an annual cycle of feast and fast days. Meanwhile, space and time are combined in a series of popular devotions that have flourished alongside official rituals that Catholics call the **liturgy**.

The Consecration of Space: Sacramentalism

A **sacrament** in any religion is a sacred sign—a person, place, object, or action that is regarded as holy. More than that, a sacrament is a place where a divine world is experienced as breaking into the human one. It is, in other words, a boundary phenomenon; and as a bridge between two worlds, a sacrament is understood to contain, in some mysterious way, the sacred power that it stands for. In a sacrament, therefore, ordinary and extraordinary reality are considered present, the one revealing the other even as it disguises it in ordinariness. Coming out of an understanding of the world related to the idea of correspondence, Catholic **sacramentalism** has taught that the material world reflects the spiritual one so closely that it can both enclose and disclose the sacred reality that transcends the world. Matter for Catholics is sacred; the natural world, good and holy.

Catholicism developed its sacramental sense through the early and middle centuries of Christian history, combining a Jewish legacy with Greek philosophy and the remnants of Greco-Roman popular religion in the Mediterranean lands where Christianity spread. By medieval times, popular Christian belief held to seven sacraments—baptism, confirmation, penance, eucharist, holy order(s), matrimony, and extreme unction. Five of them formed a series of sacred actions that, ideally, assisted Catholics as they passed again across a boundary—from one stage in life to the next. The remaining two—penance and eucharist—were meant to aid them in the regular course of their lives.

Baptism in the name of the Father, the Son, and the Holy Spirit was intended to make an infant or adult convert a member of what Catholics called the **communion of saints**, the Christian community of all those now on the earth and those who had passed faithfully to the next world. It was said to obliterate the original sin that these Christians believed was passed down from Adam and Eve. **Confirmation** used chrism, or blessed oils, to anoint a Catholic Christian as a sign of his or her spiritual maturation. Similarly, **holy order(s)** used chrism to anoint men in a series of steps to the full Catholic priesthood. **Matrimony** used the spoken words of a man and a woman in a pledge of mutual faith and love to make them husband and wife. **Extreme unction**—in recent times called the **anointing of the sick**—once again used blessed oils to anoint a person in serious illness. The sacrament was meant to give support either to regain physical health or to move successfully through the time of death.

Before the end, however, Catholics turned to penance and to the eucharist for assistance along the way. **Penance** demanded the confession of sins and a sincere act of sorrow spoken by the penitent to a priest, who forgave the sinner in the name of the Christian Trinity. Finally, in the **eucharist** (the **Mass**), Catholics held that Jesus Christ, the Son of God, was made physically and spiritually present to become the food of Christian believers—in a ritual action that recalled both the biblical Last Supper of Jesus and his death on the cross as a sacrifice for sin. At its heart were the elements of bread and wine that, through a series of sacred words and actions on the part of a priest, were changed, Catholics believed, into the body and blood of Jesus Christ. Of all the sacraments the eucharist functioned at the center of Roman Catholic life and most clearly expressed its sacramental understanding of the world. Meanwhile, Catholics taught that the priest who offered the Mass was acting not in his own name but in the name of Jesus. Thus in the Mass, for Catholics, it was Jesus who was offering himself to his Father, and the priest became a sacramental sign—a vehicle through which Jesus could act. As in Jewish ritual, the sacred action was meant to cut through time to make people present not at a mere commemoration but at an actual event.

While the Mass was for Catholics a sacrifice, it was also for them a sacred meal, a memorial to the last meal Jesus had eaten with his followers and a foretaste of a heavenly banquet. So it was that the bread and wine, now sacramentally regarded as the body and blood of Jesus, were consumed at the Mass by the priest, who offered the bread to other devout communicants. Here, for the action to come full circle, the sacramental bread and wine must be used as they were in ordinary life. They must nourish human beings by giving spiritual grace. Again, the sacrament was meant to cut through time, so that the memorial to the Last Supper and the foretaste of paradise could become real in the lives of participants.

Sacramentalism did not end with the seven sacraments in Catholic history. Rather, it became a favorite way of conceiving of the church, human life, and even the natural world. In the Catholic scheme of things, the church ideally should be as broad as the human race. In practice, it should include all those born in a territory and a culture. Unlike a sect or denomination, which draws lines between its membership and the world at large, a church seeks to include all. For Catholics, the church became the sign of God's presence in the world through Jesus; and from the sacramental perspective the sign of God really *was* God present among humans. Similarly, the **pope** of Rome, as head of the church, became its sign, representing it to God and, at the same time, acting as the conduit through whom God, through Jesus, communicated with human beings. Hence, the pope's solemn and official teachings were popularly regarded as infallible for many centuries. (They were officially so declared by a church council in 1870.) In Catholic understanding, the Roman papacy, with its traditions and trappings, stood equal to the Bible as a source of spiritual authority, with Rome the specific human location where God had chosen to communicate. This was why the church was *Roman* Catholic, and this was why it was also authoritarian.

With the pope the representative of Jesus Christ, Catholics saw Jesus as the sign and sacrament of God revealed both in the scripture and in the continuing tradition of the church. In the Catholic view, by taking human flesh Jesus had spoken the clearest word about the goodness of the natural world and the sacredness of matter. If God had, for Catholics, become human in Jesus, then humanness—existence in *this* world—had its value. The church taught that value, and so Roman Catholicism had a thisworldly as well as otherworldly orientation. Indeed, Catholic tradition put spirit and matter together by understanding the church as the **Mystical Body of Christ**. Meanwhile, any natural object could become a "**sacramental**," an article in and through which, Catholics believed, humans could encounter the grace of God. A priest could bless water to make it holy, and he could confer a blessing, too, on a religious painting or statue. People could wear commemorative medals dedicated to Jesus; his mother, known as the Virgin Mary; or one of the saints. They could light candles as signs of their prayerful remembrance of a loved one, receive ashes on the day known as Ash Wednesday to remind them that they would one day return to the dust, use prayer beads called rosary beads to gain Mary's protection, and acquire and venerate relics of the saints.

The Consecration of Time: The Liturgical Cycle

Just as sacramentalism has expressed the Catholic consecration of space, the **liturgical cycle** has expressed its consecration of time. Structured very much like the Jewish annual cycle of feasts and fasts, the Catholic year begins with the December **Advent** season when believers await the coming of Jesus. Then on **Christmas** day Catholics commemorate his historical birth into the world as well as his spiritual birth in human hearts. The season that follows is punctuated with feasts that recall events recorded in the gospels—the remembrance of the "holy innocents," infants slain by the king, Herod, in his angry search for Jesus; the Epiphany, in which the Magi, or wise men, paid homage at the crib of Jesus; and the baptism of Jesus by John the Baptist. Then, beginning with **Ash Wednesday**, Catholics keep a forty-day period of prayer and fasting called Lent. It recalls the forty days that, in gospel accounts, Jesus spent in the desert before inaugurating his public ministry, and it culminates in the observances of **Holy Week** to commemorate the passion, death, and resurrection of Jesus.

As Holy Week opens, on the Sunday before Easter, known as **Palm Sunday**, Catholics receive blessed palms and process around their churches to relive the biblical account of the triumphal entry of Jesus into Jerusalem before his passion and death. On **Holy Thursday** (believed to be originally the same day as the Jewish Passover), Catholics commemorate in a special way the Last Supper and the institution of the eucharist. This is the day on which the oils to be used ritually during the coming year are blessed, and also the day on which the priest washes the feet of laypeople to imitate the Last Supper account of how Jesus washed his disciples' feet (John 13:4–5). As Catholics link themselves to their Jewish heritage, Jesus becomes the paschal lamb to be sacrificed so that his people can "pass over" from slavery in sin to freedom in grace.

Good Friday is the only day of the year on which Roman Catholics, properly speaking, cannot be present at Mass. The service resembles the eucharistic action of the Mass, but unlike on other days the priest does not consecrate bread and wine. Instead, the communion service uses the reserved sacrament, kept on a side altar after the Holy Thursday Mass. A sense of sorrow and loss pervades the scriptural texts, everything meant to underline the significance of the commemoration. But the most sacred day of the church year for Catholics is **Easter**, which proclaims the resurrection of Jesus. A long vigil service held the previous evening ends with a Mass at midnight filled with the symbolism of new birth and life—lighting a new fire from flint; blessing a huge new Easter candle to represent Jesus; blessing baptismal water for the coming year; solemnly repeating baptismal vows as a congregation. In the Mass that follows, the scriptural texts are sprinkled with alleluias, expressing joy in the belief that Christ has risen and remains with his people.

Forty days after Easter, Catholics celebrate the **Ascension** of Jesus into heaven, where, they believe, he reigns with his Father. Then, ten days later, they keep the feast of **Pentecost**—their own transformation of the Jewish feast that honors the divine gift of the Torah. Catholics, however, commemorate the coming of the Holy Spirit. In the biblical account, tongues of fire descended on the assembled apostles, the fire imparting courage and zeal to spread the gospel and the tongues enabling others to understand them although the apostles did not ordinarily speak their languages. The remainder of the liturgical year is a long series of Sundays after Pentecost, spread through the summer and autumn months, with successive aspects of the life and teachings of Jesus considered. Interspersed throughout this period, as through other parts of the year, come major feasts commemorating Jesus, Mary, or the saints. Almost no day in the Catholic year is without its special liturgy, with scriptural texts read at the Mass to bring its lesson home.

As in the Jewish calendar, the feasts of the Catholic year are historicized rituals, remembering traditional events that form the story of Christian beginnings or the men and women who are its heroes. Still, as in the Jewish ritual calendar, underneath the symbolism of history lies the symbolism of nature and the material world. Catholics await the birth of Christ— for them the light of the world—as the year lies "dying" on the last days before winter solstice. At Christmas, Jesus is presented as if born during the week of solstice, like the first ray of the sun that, ancient religions taught, conquered the winter darkness. Lent brings fasting during the last days of winter, while Easter—the Catholic feast of new life—comes on the Sunday following the first full moon after the spring equinox. Appropriately, Catholic customs in many lands include use of Easter eggs, natural symbols of fertility and birth.

Paraliturgical Devotions

In addition to the official liturgy, Catholics could participate in **paraliturgical devotions** (literally, devotions alongside the liturgy). Each Catholic country had its own favorite among them; and in the United States, therefore, popular devotionalism has flourished with imported practices. These devotions are special, personal ways for Catholics to worship Jesus, venerate Mary, or honor the saints.

Among special devotions to Jesus, the traditional cultus of the **Sacred Heart** was perhaps the most widespread among American Catholics. Originating in France, the devotion featured iconography portraying the pierced and bleeding heart of Jesus surrounded by a crown of thorns, often fashioned as a badge that a person could pin to clothing. By the middle of the nineteenth century, an official feast honored the Sacred Heart, and meanwhile devout Catholics tried to attend Mass and receive communion on the first Friday of each of nine successive months. They believed that Jesus had made a promise to the French nun Margaret Mary Alacoque, who began the devotion: if they kept the nine first Fridays, they would not die in a state of serious personal sin, and their salvation would be assured.

Other devotions to Jesus—popular before Vatican Council II ended in 1965—included special worship of the reserved eucharistic sacrament, exposed to public view in a special sacred vessel at a time called **Forty Hours**—to commemorate the time that, according to tradition, Jesus spent in the tomb before his resurrection. In **Benediction of the Blessed Sacrament**, the priest raised the sacrament in the same vessel to bless the assembled congregation. Additionally,

Catholics could "make" the fourteen **Stations of the Cross**, representations that recall, usually in raised relief along the walls of a church building, the last journey and death events in the gospel account of Jesus. Still other Catholics expressed devotion to the **Infant of Prague** (Czechoslovakia), a doll-like statue dressed in bejeweled satin with a crown on its head, representing the kingship of Jesus even in the child.

Devotion to Mary is even more widespread than paraliturgical devotion to Jesus. In the **rosary**, Catholics use a chain of beads on which, while repeating prayers to God as Father and to Mary, they recall traditional beliefs about her life as an inspiration for their own. In one popular tradition, Catholics manifested their devotion to Mary by wearing a **scapular**, two small pieces of brown wool cloth worn over the shoulders as a symbolic undergarment. No one, they believed, could die unrepentant or unprepared while wearing the scapular. Beyond these devotions, Catholics have venerated Mary under various titles, many of them deriving from the place names of locations in which she is said to have appeared in visions. Our Lady of Lourdes, Our Lady of Fatima, and—especially among Mexican Americans—Our Lady of Guadalupe are examples.

Nor were the Catholic saints neglected. St. Jude became known as the patron of hopeless cases, and St. Rita acquired a reputation as the saint of the impossible. St. Blaise was thought to help in the case of sore throats, with a special throat blessing on his feast day, and in the nineteenth century St. Thomas Aquinas became patron of Catholic schools. Each nationality among Catholics has had its favored saints. Indeed, one combinative result of the American experience is that St. Stanislas (the Pole) and St. Rocco (the Italian) have both received their due among American Catholics.

Especially before Vatican Council II, local church groups conducted still more paraliturgical activities. Often men could belong to the Holy Name Society, committed to avoiding profanity and blasphemy. Women could join the Sodality of the Blessed Virgin Mary, promoting chastity in and out of marriage and encouraging the other virtues Mary was said to embody. One organization dedicated itself to teaching Christian doctrine, while other groups sewed altar vestments for the liturgy or expressed their devotion to a particular saint through a formal organization. To be a Catholic, thus, was ideally to be surrounded with sacrament and liturgy from cradle to grave.

Ethics and Morality

Official Catholic attitudes toward ethics and morality have included the same regard for the natural world as in sacramentalism and the liturgical cycle. Stated clearly by Thomas Aquinas in the thirteenth century, the Catholic ethic is grounded in large part on ideas of **natural law**. This is the law thought to be present within any creature—plant, animal, or human. Here moral action for Catholics means action that follows this law of nature; immoral action means unnatural behavior. There is a natural instinct against killing one's own kind, they have said—a natural law written in human hearts that murder is wrong. Similarly, they have explained, right-thinking people respect the property of others, and stealing also violates the law of nature. It was in matters of sexuality, though, that the implications of natural-law teaching led Catholics—or at least their official church—down a path different from that to be taken by many of their Protestant neighbors. The sexual act, Catholic thinkers have argued, is naturally open to the production of children; whatever interferes with that openness violates the divine and natural purpose of sexuality. From this perspective, artificial birth control became wrong and sinful. And in the late twentieth century and after, when abortion became increasingly an issue, Catholics used natural-law teaching to condemn abortion as murder.

Natural law, however, was clarified and strengthened for Catholics by revealed law. Like their Jewish and Protestant neighbors, Catholics look to the Ten Commandments as the source of norms for behavior. With Protestants, they look also to the Christian gospels. But more clearly than Protestants, they have elaborated a scale of offenses against the law. After original sin is forgiven in the sacrament of baptism, Catholics have taught, humans are still capable of committing actual sins. They call a serious offense a **mortal sin** and have taught that, if unforgiven, it can condemn a person to hell for all eternity. A less serious sin they named **venial** and warned that it would weaken a person's resistance to more serious forms of evil and dull spiritual sensitivities. Catholics believe that both kinds of sin can be forgiven, if a person is truly sorry, through the sacrament of penance. Catholics have argued, though, that once having fallen it is always easy to fall again. Beyond that, they have taught that the **remains of sin** are still there, so that after death a person has to undergo a period of suffering and purification in **purgatory** before entering heaven. To lessen the time in purgatory, a Catholic might obtain an indulgence through pious acts or prayers specifically recommended by the church for that purpose. There was no tension for a devoted Catholic here: the pope, as the sign of Christ, who was the sign of God, could set an indulgence on an act or prayer, and heaven would obey. In the sixteenth century, the issue of indulgences became the catalyst for the Protestant Reformation, but in the Catholic scheme of things they have played an uncontroversial, if small, part.

The legalism in its own way reflects the fact that Catholics, like Jews, consider community to be primary. The ethic of Catholicism is ultimately social. It deals with the waging of war and the keeping of peace, with the problem of poverty and the distribution of goods, with the relationship between the claims of the church and the demands of the state. In medieval times, Catholicism existed as Christendom, a public and cultural reality that included both church and state. In the modern era, it still sought to weigh in on the proper roles of church and state and became especially sensitive to church–state separation in the United States. Modern popes, too, were particularly strong in highlighting problems of capital and labor in an industrialized society, and by the twenty-first century American bishops were speaking out against the war in Iraq as unjustified. Their message of social concern is part of the traditional Catholic heritage.

The American Saga of Catholicism

In America, this traditional Catholicism faced changes from both inside and outside the church. These changes stemmed from both the ethnicity of the American Catholic church and the pluralism of its setting. **Ethnicity** refers to the *internal* condition of being many national churches in one American Catholic church. **Pluralism**, in turn, means the *external* condition of being one church among many denominations. Together, the two conditions became part of one issue—how Catholics should respond to their new American situation. And together, the two conditions generated a tension that reflected the larger tension between oneness and manyness in religion characteristic of American society.

Ethnicity

As waves of Catholic immigrants poured into the nation, each ethnic group brought its own mix of ordinary and extraordinary religion, combining local custom with general Catholic teaching. There were bound to be organizational problems as worshipers from different nations shared communion plate and pew. Still more, there would be conflict about whose way of being Catholic was right. Both Catholics themselves and other Americans generally wanted to see a single church that could be easily understood. This is one among several reasons why the Irish came to dominate American Catholicism.

The earliest Catholics in America, as we saw, were Spanish, French, Native American, and English. Moreover, in colonial times Pennsylvania's Catholics were mostly German, whereas New England was the home of a small number of Irish Catholics. From the beginning, national frictions led to open conflicts. For example, in the late eighteenth century Germans expressed their hostility toward Anglo-Catholic leadership by forming a separate Holy Trinity Church in Philadelphia. However, the most serious ethnic struggles occurred in the second half of the nineteenth century when Irish immigrants became the backbone of American Catholicism and other groups fought to maintain their identity. The **Irish**, most of them refugees from the potato famine of Ireland, arrived in huge numbers in the 1840s and after. Without many resources, they were forced to settle in eastern city slums. Their knowledge of the English language helped them adjust, but their lack of literacy and working skills combined with their poverty to hamper them. Because their clergy had helped them in Ireland during the potato famine and also because their clergy had enough education to become culture brokers in the new and alien setting, the American Irish remained loyal to their religious leaders. As in Ireland, many were attached to the church by little more than baptism. Still, the many who were practicing Catholics tended toward legalism and literal observance of church law, at the same time emphasizing personal morality and piety but not intellectual values. Significantly, the Irish encouraged their sons and daughters to serve the church as priests and nuns.

St. Patrick's Cathedral, New York City. Constructed beginning in 1858, Gothic-style St. Patrick's Cathedral became a proud announcement of Roman Catholic—and Irish—presence in the United States.

So Irish Catholics, by the sheer power of their numbers—almost 1 million by 1850—and by their willingness to enter ecclesiastical service, dominated the hierarchy of the American church. Moreover, when a separate parochial school system began, Irish nuns for the most part staffed it—and passed to generations of Catholic schoolchildren their interpretation of Catholicism. Irish brick and mortar built the church—hence the "mortar" of the "bread and mortar" in this chapter's title. In the twentieth century and after, the Irish were still giving American Catholicism its public face.

Among the ethnic groups with whom the Irish dealt, the **Germans** were especially important historically. Present from colonial times, they increased their numbers until by 1850 there were over 500,000 in the United States. Generally more affluent and better educated than the Irish and other Catholic groups, they often headed for the Midwest and flourished in cities like Cincinnati, St. Louis, and Milwaukee as well as the farmlands of the area. The Germans were deeply attached to their language and traditions, and so they wanted parishes organized on the basis of nationality rather than territory. With their love of their native music, relaxed observance of the Sabbath, and opposition to the temperance movement, they were often at odds with the Irish.

Matters came to a head in what came to be known as **Cahenslyism**. In 1871, a businessman in Nassau, Germany, named Peter Paul Cahensly organized an international society to aid German emigrants before and after they left their native land. By 1891 the society presented a petition to the pope, claiming that immigrants to the United States were being lost to Catholicism in huge numbers because they lacked priests and institutions of their own nationality. The American church should be multilingual and multinational, they said. The movement brought support from European Germans to the German American struggle against the Irish. Although it failed in its most ambitious goals, it was a strong indicator of continuing conflict within American Catholicism.

In the last third of the nineteenth century, however, these immigrant tensions that had begun in an earlier age were complicated by frictions associated with the arrival of new groups. The "new immigration" from 1880 until World War I brought a steady flow of Southern and Eastern European Catholics. Well over 3 million Italians arrived by 1920 and nearly as many Poles. Yet for various reasons neither ethnic group seriously altered the public face of American Catholicism.

The **Italians** came largely from southern Italy and Sicily, poor and illiterate for the most part, and, like the Irish before them, they settled in eastern seacoast cities. In their large extended families, religion and culture mingled. Their preference for family over church had only grown stronger because of church–state relations in Italy. There the pope ruled the northern Italian Papal States until 1870, and because of that many Italian Catholics distrusted the official church in the same way that they distrusted the government. As they immigrated to the United States, these Italian Catholics were unwilling to give the church either their children, as priests and nuns, or their money, to build new shrines and schools. With their own spirit of relaxed adherence to official rules and regulations, they did not accept the legalism of the Irish.

By contrast, the **Poles** were intensely devoted to the institutional church. Coming from peasant backgrounds, many eventually became farmers, but numbers settled in cities like Chicago, Milwaukee, Detroit, and Cleveland. For centuries, the Polish people had joined their nationalism to their religion, and so in the United States, like the Germans, they sought to maintain a distinct national ethos, preserving their language in churches and schools. The pattern of conflict that developed was familiar—struggles between clergy and laity over financial matters. By the early twentieth century, many were calling for equal representation with other national groups in the American hierarchy. Indeed, tensions with a non-Polish hierarchy grew so strong that in 1904 they resulted in the formation in Scranton, Pennsylvania, of the separate Polish National Catholic Church. Still, most Polish Catholics chose to remain within the Roman Catholic church. They brought into the American church a series of new devotions, such as that to the Black Madonna of Czestochowa (Mary), and they gave their sons and daughters to Polish Catholic religious communities.

In the late twentieth and early twenty-first century, the story of European Catholic immigration had for some time been superseded by another. The 22.4 million **Latinos** of the 1990 national census became 37 million by 2003. A swelling Mexican presence had begun in the early twentieth century, spilling over the borders into Texas, California, and the Southwest. Later, by midcentury, Puerto Ricans were entering New York City in heavy concentrations, while the Cuban revolution of 1959 brought Cubans in large numbers to the Miami area, and a record number of Haitians arrived in the country, too. With Mexicans by far the largest national group, followed by Puerto Ricans and then Cubans, Latinos now exceed African Americans as the largest minority group in the nation. Moreover, official figures do not include the many who have entered the country without immigration papers. Changes in the United States immigration law in 1965 made entry from Central and South America easier, and political and economic conditions in various lands of origin have also often encouraged people to leave. Among the Latino population, even in a period of Catholic decline, Catholicism was the overwhelming religious choice of 70.2 percent of the population (ca. 25 million) in 2002.

Despite a Catholic heritage, however, this great influx has been the least church-oriented of any immigrant group. Latino Catholics tend to be anticlerical, and, in the United States as in their homelands, many have turned from their nominal Catholicism to evangelicalism and, especially, to an intense and active pentecostalism. Beyond that, large numbers practice combinative religious forms, joining Catholicism to active attempts to contact spirits in European-influenced spiritism and various Afro-Caribbean religions. Or, in the Mexican-American population, they combine Catholicism, spiritism, and herbalism in the healing work called **curanderismo** that blends European and Native American beliefs and practices.

When Latinos are Catholic, their religious expression is distinctive, and like the Italians, they overlap ordinary and extraordinary in noticeable ways. Among Mexican Americans, for example, devotion to the **Virgin of Guadalupe** dominates religious practice, and traditional women keep home altars to honor Guadalupe and bring her their family concerns. On the **Day of the Dead** (*El Día de los Muertos;* November 2, or All Souls' Day in the traditional Catholic calendar), public ritual activities and private cemetery visits signal a family network that extends beyond the grave. In another example, after the administration of the sacrament of baptism, the godparents, who have made the baptismal vows for the infant, cultivate a special relation with child and family throughout their lives.

By the late twentieth century, the composition of public Catholicism began to change because of the Latino presence. Latinos were now close to 30 and perhaps as much as 35 percent of the United States Catholic population, and whereas in 1972 there had been but one Latino bishop in the nation, in the early 1990s there were twenty. There was also a national Secretariat for Hispanic Affairs with regional offices scattered throughout the country, while Latino leaders themselves had begun the National Catholic Council for Hispanic Ministry.

These changes in the American Catholic church were fed, from the 1960s, by altered cultural currents and moods. In the late 1960s in Los Angeles, for example, the militant *Catolicos por la Raza* (Catholics for the People) protested the opulence of the church and its seeming indifference toward the political and social struggles of Latino peoples. Other groups of priests and nuns organized around themes of social justice and empowerment for Latino Catholics. Then in the 1970s the **encuentro** movement began. Encuentros, or national pastoral congresses, aimed to address the needs and concerns of Latino Catholics. Large numbers of laypeople attended, many of them delegates from an already existing grassroots movement. American Catholic bishops by the early 1980s acknowledged the changes and their own changed attitudes.

Meanwhile, new Catholic immigrants from Vietnam and elsewhere in Asia added to the changing population. And we already saw, in Chapter 1, the prominence of Kateri circles and the Kateri Tekakwitha Conferences for Native Americans, with their practices of inculturation. Among African Americans, groups like the National Office of Black Catholics and the Institute for Black Catholic Studies at Xavier University in New Orleans had been working since the 1970s and 1980s. And by 1984 the ten African American bishops could write a pastoral letter pointing to the richness of black culture and proclaiming the need to share their experience with others. In this mood, the bishops asked increased leadership authority for black Roman Catholics and called for an end to the racism that had long existed in the Catholic church. The small number of African American Catholics had by then shown a sizable increase. As the last decade of the twentieth century began, perhaps 2 million, or over 9 percent, of the American black community identified as Catholic. The American Catholic church, in fact, was the only major denomination with a white majority to experience increased black membership. Notably, large numbers of the new members were coming from among West Indian immigrants, especially from Haiti.

Among Afro-Caribbean immigrants in general, Catholicism has often functioned as part of new, and older, combinative religions, many of them from outside the United States—a theme the text will take up later. In a more self-conscious example, the former black Catholic priest George Stallings created the African American Catholic Congregation, growing to roughly 4,200 members in 1994. The **Imani Temple movement**, as it was popularly called, blended Catholic liturgical elements with African dancing and chanting. The Imani combination is in some ways a useful sign pointing the way toward the twenty-first century. For American Catholics, in general, the century means existing, as throughout American religious history, in a multiethnic church. Latinos, African Americans, Native Americans, and some Asian Americans, too, have joined the so-called "old ethnics" from Europe. Although the Irish continue to predominate, new forces are actively at work within the church as new people bring their styles to the religious combination that is American Catholicism.

Pluralism and Americanization in Historical Perspective

Alongside ethnicity, the second major factor that affected Catholicism in the United States is its pluralistic setting. This *external* condition means that whatever its theoretical claims to universality, the Catholic church in America is a minority. For outsiders, the Catholic presence has sometimes seemed threatening, and historically, Protestant fears generated a series of nativist and protectionist movements. For insiders, the influence of the American and Protestant mainstream led to a series of attempts by some to "de-Romanize" the church, while others more conservatively sought retreat to preserve their ethnic heritage. Pluralism and ethnicity were related issues.

Nativism was a continuing fact of Catholic life throughout much of the nineteenth century and after. In 1834, in an often-cited incident, a mob set fire to the Ursuline convent in Charlestown, Massachusetts, while in Philadelphia a decade later at least two churches were burned. Meanwhile, associations like the American Protestant Association and the Know-Nothing party were formed to combat Catholic power. Later, in 1887, the American Protective Association opposed Catholicism, and then in the 1920s the revived Ku Klux Klan fought against the Catholic church. These organizations expressed sentiments that were shared by many who did not belong to them. They were monuments to the strains that the Protestant United States was experiencing as it worked to come to terms with large-scale immigration.

Hostile toward Anglo-America in their turn, many Catholic working-class immigrants of German and Polish origins joined the majority of the Irish and their clergy in a strong conservative stance. Led among the hierarchy by Michael A. Corrigan (1839–1902), the archbishop of New York, and by Bernard McQuaid (1823–1909), the bishop of Rochester, they labored to isolate the church from the dominance of a Protestant culture. They especially feared the public schools, where, they thought, teachers were spreading a common-denominator Protestantism. It was in this atmosphere of caution and reserve that the Catholic school system was born when the Third Plenary Council of Baltimore in 1884 declared that every parish must establish its own parochial school.

For other Catholic insiders, however, mainstream American culture possessed an inviting face. Even at the beginning of the early national period, some lay Catholics had taken a strong hand in parish affairs. Influenced by congregational Protestants, they were often close to replacing their own pastors, sometimes separating themselves from their bishops to do so. **Trusteeism**, as it was called, took advantage of the fact that the civil law had been written to accommodate both church–state separation and Protestant church governance, giving corporate ownership of church property to the lay trustees of a congregation. Urged on sometimes by struggles between various national groups within the church, trustees invoked their democratic rights and thus challenged the old hierarchical and sacramental model. Eventually, property rights were vested in the bishop of each diocese, but not before some sixty years of disruption of traditional patterns.

The democratic trustees were succeeded in the latter part of the nineteenth century by democratic bishops, who formed a liberal camp in opposition to the conservatives. Led by James Cardinal Gibbons (1834–1921) of Baltimore and even more aggressively by Archbishop John Ireland (1838–1918) of St. Paul, Minnesota, a number of these bishops sought to open Catholic culture outward, countering the ethnic and separationist trend of others. They wanted to end every kind of Catholic isolation and to "Americanize" the church. Catholics, they thought, should wholeheartedly embrace the American style and the American way of doing things.

Thus, Cardinal Gibbons actively intervened in 1887 to prevent Rome from condemning the Knights of Labor, an early labor organization supported by Irish Catholics. With the strong endorsement of Cardinal Gibbons and Archbishop Ireland, Bishop John Lancaster Spalding of Peoria, Illinois, crusaded for the foundation of a Catholic university where graduate theological study could go on. His success was apparent in 1889 when the Catholic University of America opened its doors in the nation's capital. Meanwhile, Archbishop Ireland remained doubtful about the value of a separate parochial school system and repeatedly urged the American church to live in its own age and its own setting. For Ireland, the Roman Catholic church in America should become an *American* Catholic church. As he and other liberals saw it, the official separation between church and state in the United States was not just a practical arrangement. It was an ideal situation that American Catholics should enthusiastically support.

But the liberals did not continue their efforts toward the Americanization of the church undisturbed. Ethnicity became entangled with other issues, and matters came to a head in 1899 when Pope Leo XIII published an encyclical letter, *Testem Benevolentiae*, which condemned a number of opinions collectively labeled "**Americanism**." The pope found Americanism in a willingness to regard natural virtues more highly than supernatural ones. Here, natural virtues meant active and "thisworldly" gifts congenial to the Protestant American style. Supernatural virtues meant those more "passive" and otherworldly, like the traditional humility and obedience associated with Catholic saints. Second, the pope saw Americanism in a readiness to adapt to the theories and methods of modern culture, which could relax the strict spiritual discipline of the church. Third, the pope warned against an Americanist tendency toward individualism in religion, countering the traditional Catholic emphasis on the role of the church in salvation. As soon as the encyclical letter was published, American bishops unanimously asserted their freedom from the errors named therein, so much so that many called Americanism a "phantom heresy." Whether the bishops had been Americanists or not, Pope Leo XIII had effectively put an end to the Americanization of the Catholic church—at least for the time being.

On the popular level, however, Americanization occurred indirectly in the **Catholic mission movement**, which looked in some ways like Protestant revivalism. In the second half of the nineteenth century, the mission movement helped to stop defections from the church and stirred the piety of ordinary working-class people. Held in a parish, usually for one to two weeks every four or five years, a mission featured traveling preachers whose sermons warned of the dangers of eternal punishment and the need to repent from sin and recommit to Catholicism. Like Protestant revival preachers, mission priests used large-scale evangelistic techniques to reach their audiences, planting a cross, displaying an empty casket to dramatize a point, or tolling a sinner's bell at evening. The presence of the Catholic sacramental system, however, separated the Catholic mission from Protestant revivalism. For the Catholic who came to listen, the sermon was meant to lead to the confessional, where, in Catholic belief, sins could be forgiven.

Pluralism and Americanization: The Later Twentieth Century and On

In the twentieth century, it remained for Rome itself to help stimulate a new era of Americanization for the church. **Vatican Council II** (1962–1965)—a meeting in Rome of all the bishops of the church with the pope at their head—did not so much *cause* the changes as catalyze them by discarding older forms and admitting new ones. Already, in the 1950s, American Catholics had begun to come of age. They were reaching social and economic equality with their Protestant neighbors, and so they were both thinking and acting more like members of the mainstream. When Vatican Council II used the work of the American Jesuit priest John Courtney Murray in its official Declaration on Religious Freedom, it was offering an endorsement of the American way. The American Catholic experience with religious pluralism, with the manyness of free and individual choices, had helped to shape the teaching of the world church.

Just as significantly, in the wake of Vatican II American Catholics registered changes in the areas of worship and morality. In worship, the council paved the way for Mass texts to be read in the language of each nation instead of the traditional Latin. Many additions to the Mass that had grown up over the years were dropped, while scriptural sermons and congregational singing were stressed. The council explained the changes as ways to bring the liturgy closer to the pattern of the early church. However, the changes underlined the verbal content of the service at the expense of the symbolic. In so doing, they did not destroy sacramentalism, but they did modify it, bringing it closer to the model of Protestant services. At the same time, sociological study suggested that Sunday Mass attendance—always high because failure to attend was considered a serious sin—declined. Meanwhile, the devotionalism of the past seemed permanently eroded by the reforms. Once more, Catholics were coming closer in their religious practices and attitudes to their mainstream Protestant neighbors.

Beginning in the later 1960s, a **charismatic movement** swept the church. A successor in some ways to the old mission revivalism, it also went further. The movement stressed the pentecostal baptism of the Holy Spirit and featured tongues speaking, ecstatic behavior, exorcism, prophecy, and faith healing. It has continued to attract a well-educated middle class that includes many clergy, meanwhile downplaying theology, and actively cultivating relationships with American pentecostals. Charismatic Catholics have often borrowed religious language from pentecostals as well as characteristic gestures such as the raising of hands at prayer and the laying on of hands for healing. At first Catholics drawn to the charismatic movement often met in private homes to conduct their prayer sessions, but they did begin to institutionalize, with a central organization and annual conventions, continuing prayer groups, and covenant communities. Their movement grew quickly for some two decades, although growth slowed by the beginning of the 1990s. Still, in the early twenty-first century, the charismatic movement seems to be in the church to stay.

By borrowing from pentecostals, charismatic Catholics were taking cues from conservatives in the Protestant world. However, in morality and ethics, Catholics became more like Protestants by moving in a double direction—more liberal *and* more conservative. Overall, individualism in morality has grown at the expense of giving priority to community. From the liberal side, a more permissive sexual ethic began to spread, especially among younger Catholics. They have expressed more willingness to allow sexual activity outside of marriage and more support for artificial birth control and even abortion. At the same time, gay or lesbian Catholics could join an organization called Dignity, with chapters in major American cities and numbers of priests in its ranks. Although the hierarchy of the church has strongly condemned the organization and all same-sex relationships, for the Catholics who joined Dignity, individual conscience trumped church authority. At the heart of the change was a move away from a sense of absolutes based on belief in natural and revealed law for a community and a move toward a sense of the situational and the relative. Catholics were turning to an ethic based on history, and the change was leading them closer to a mainstream Protestant United States.

As increasing polarization beset the American Catholic church, still other Catholics more strongly embraced an ethic they shared with Protestant conservatives and evangelicals, as well as Orthodox Jews and Mormons. Here they taught and lived out old positions—especially against abortion and same-sex relationships—but they did it in new ways and with new political muscle. As events unfolded in the courts and legislatures and on the streets, the anti-abortion campaign escalated from impassioned speeches and the display of enlarged fetal pictures to marches, protests, and sometimes even physical harassment of the clinics where abortions were performed and of the women who chose to undergo them. The anti-abortionists resembled the Prohibitionists of an earlier era in the fierceness of their stand and the aggressiveness with which they worked to change laws to reflect their views. Moreover, Catholics used older forms of devotion to support their new activism. Forms of piety directed toward Mary—for Catholics, the Mother of God—have pervaded the anti-abortion, anti- (artificial) birth-control, and anti-gay movements. For example, some Catholics—like Nancy Fowler of Conyers, Georgia—have claimed to see apparitions of Mary. With doomsday warnings directed against the permissive fabric of American society, the Marian message has affirmed family values and condemned nontraditional life practices, especially regarding abortion.

For all the traditional Marian piety, Catholic anti-abortion advocates and those who support related causes have had a Protestant edge. How is this so? These protesters have acted much like prophets. A **prophet**, in religious terms, is a figure who criticizes the existing state of things in order to restore what the prophet sees as fundamental truth. Such a figure self-consciously stands outside, impelled by a different vision of what ought to be. With this message of criticism, a prophet diverges from a priest, whose role is to uphold the standing order by repeating its rituals. Every religion has had something of the prophet and something of the priest, but in the modern West it is certain forms of Protestantism that have most strongly cherished the figure of the prophet and Catholicism, by contrast, that most clearly chooses the conserving role of the priest. In America, Protestantism—with its Puritan roots—has often preached a prophetic morality. By contrast, Catholicism in its traditional form has usually preferred priestly action.

If Catholic pro-lifers and related sexual traditionalists in our time have behaved much like conservative Protestants in the politics of prophecy, other Catholics have embraced more politically radical prophetic stances. With a rising feminist consciousness, many came to question the hierarchical stance of their church, seeing it as patriarchal and oppressive to women. Feminist theologians led the new morality of resistance and reform from one direction, as did other, more loosely affiliated laywomen from another. By the early 1980s, the Women-Church Convergence joined some forty groups with predominately Catholic roots in what became a continuing, ever more ecumenical, and ever more liturgically experimental movement. Well before the century's end, Women-Church brought together women from different classes, races, and nationalities who also diverged in religious background and sexual orientation. As they worshiped together, they borrowed from traditions as varied as the Buddhist, Native American, and pagan as well as Protestant and Catholic.

Meanwhile, a broad Catholic feminism also reached out to others who were not Catholic in a movement called ecofeminism. Here environmental activism joined forces with feminism in concern for the earth as Gaia, a living (female) being undergoing a time of purification because of human environmental abuse. These forms of earth-based spirituality are related to the "creation spirituality" of the former Dominican priest Matthew Fox with his California-based University of Creation Spirituality and to the work of other contemporary creationist Catholic thinkers, like the priest Thomas Berry.

Other American Catholic prophets have been connected with the peace movement. For example, in the Vietnam War era the Berrigan brothers, Daniel (b. 1921) and Philip (b. 1923), both Catholic priests, spoke and marched against the war, raided draft headquarters, poured animal blood on records, and inspired dozens of others to behave in kind. By the mid-1990s, Daniel Berrigan had been arrested over 100 times. Catholic life values informed the left-leaning words and acts of the Berrigans and the others. Catholic life values, too, figured in the complex motives prompting anti-abortion activists and other Catholic prophets of the right. Still, the influence of Protestant America and its prophetic model has been pervasive. Catholics have become active players on both sides of the "culture wars."

In the midst of the culture wars, an older American individualism has assumed new forms. After Vatican Council II, Catholics acted out the individualism as never before. In a church that valued hierarchy, obedience, life commitments, and silence, increasing numbers of priests and nuns sought dispensations from their vows. Other priests and nuns demanded greater responsibility in governing their institutions, while some priests also demanded the right to marry. Similarly, the laity voiced concerns about the management of parishes and formed councils to assist their priests. They stopped short of nineteenth-century trusteeism but became more and more willing to challenge embedded practices.

The democratic values of American Catholics came home to many of the hierarchy, and to critics, in the pedophilia scandal that rocked the American church in the early twenty-first century. Overnight seemingly, the image of the altar boy changed from one of innocence to one of ruptured childhood. Newspapers blazed headlines about molesting clergy, cases went to court, and dioceses tottered on the edge of bankruptcy. Numberless lay Catholics felt abused and betrayed by the revelations. Yet members of the hierarchy who had hidden the criminal behavior of a small minority of priests and transferred them from parish to parish were operating on an older model that for years had prevailed in the church. Above all, instructed this model, it was wrong to scandalize the faithful—to expose the sins of the few and thus challenge the faith and trust of the many. This model preferred the collective good of the community to the individual good of abused children, whose lives one by one had been violated. The model was admittedly self-serving, but it was also community-oriented. When the laity rose up in protest, they were acting as Americans steeped in the democratic values that an Anglo-Protestant culture had taught them to value and respect—a culture in which individualism was prized and the individual was cherished.

The early twenty-first century revealed a Catholicism remarkably changed from its small beginnings in the United States. With a membership of between

65 and 70 million, the Catholic church continued easily to be the largest single American denomination—as it had been since the middle of the nineteenth century. Yet devotional practice had declined for many, and fewer thought that the pope was the vicar of Christ or considered him infallible. The church's traditional stand against artificial birth control had long since alienated many, and the refusal of the church to give official sanction to remarriage after divorce had disaffected many Catholics, too. (The use of annulment by Catholic church courts was, in effect, an endorsement of remarriage, and overall statistics showed an increase in the number of annulments granted.) The pedophilia scandal had pushed still others into an angry skepticism about their church. In general, the millions of Catholics who hung in picked and chose, deciding how and in what respects they would be Catholic—this despite the dismay of resurgent traditionalists who condemned "cafeteria Catholicism." The larger number of Catholics, however, did not embrace, as much as before, the church's teachings that suffering was a path to God and that the cross was a necessary part of a devoted Christian life. In end-of-life issues, they were more willing to withhold food and water from the dying to assist their passing—a practice supported by the American hospice movement but controversial especially among traditionalist theologians. Their commitment to democracy trumped their loyalty to the authority of the hierarchy on a variety of fronts. With a new voluntary style, Catholics selected what they wanted from their church's legacy, and they did not all select the same things. Clearly, the habit of pluralism had taken hold, and a combinative postpluralism could also be seen.

In one sense, the bread-and-mortar church was still there: the Irish were still noticeable in pulpit and pew, and the diverse ethnic character of the church was still a prominent feature. A huge network of Catholic schools and colleges had scarcely folded up and disappeared—although they did struggle with what it meant to be a Catholic college or university. The radical moralists of left and right had gained Catholics nationwide notice in the media, while the sacraments, still seven in number, gave solace to millions. Yet the sacramentalism that had shaped the Catholic understanding of religion and human life had begun to crumble. The refusal to accept the authority of the pope and bishops meant that they were no longer regarded, in the same traditional sense, as sacramental signs of Christ. The old order of things, in which ordinary and extraordinary mingled, was yielding to a new pattern. In some sense, this new pattern brought ordinary and extraordinary together in a different way in the prophetic politics of the culture wars. But overall, ordinary and extraordinary now were more separated and compartmentalized. By discarding some of their sacramentalism, Catholics were making clearer distinctions—like Reform Jews, and like mainstream Protestants, as we will see. American Roman Catholics were moving away from a medieval angle of vision and toward a modern one, and this move was shared by many in world Catholicism. But the move was complicated by its context "in America." American Catholicism combined with aspects of its cultural environment and gave broad hints that it was gradually becoming more Protestant.

In Overview

From the time of Christopher Columbus, Catholics have been present in North America. Early Spanish and then French missionaries brought their first taste of Christianity to American Indians, while with the arrival of English Catholic colonists in the seventeenth century, Catholicism entered the English seaboard colonies. The religion that these Catholics shared found holiness in nature as well as in biblical and historical tradition. With its **sacramentalism**, Catholics saw the material world as the symbol and the reality of divine things. This understanding crystallized in **seven sacraments**, but it was visible throughout the Catholic system. At the head of the system, for Catholics, was Jesus Christ, whose presence they acknowledged in an annual **liturgical cycle** commemorating events in the gospel accounts of his life, death, and resurrection. Meanwhile, in a moral system developed over the years, Catholics lived their commitment to **natural law**, to **scripture**, and to **tradition** as expressed in church teaching. Like Native Americans and Jews, in both cultus and code they blended extraordinary with ordinary religion.

With this heritage, the Catholic church in the United States faced changes brought by its internal **ethnicity** and the external **pluralism** of American culture. Spanish, French, Native American, and English Catholics were joined, as time passed, by German and Irish Catholics and later by Southern and Eastern Europeans and by Latinos and some African American and Asian peoples. These groups often worked to maintain the separate boundaries of their respective ethnic identities, and they sometimes collided. In the growing internal manyness with its tensions, the **Irish** by the mid-nineteenth century dominated. In turn, the pluralism of American culture—and its postplural habit of religious combining—led to profound changes that swung the Catholic church more and more away from its "Roman" axis. Extraordinary and ordinary religion generally grew more separate, as Catholic boundaries opened out toward American culture. In the early twenty-first century, catalyzed through the actions of **Vatican Council II** and later developments, the Roman Catholic church in America had become an American Catholic church. It looked increasingly like the churches of mainstream Protestantism in both liberal and conservative versions.

Who were the people who had so influenced the religions of Catholic and Jewish immigrants? What kind of religion had drawn them more and more toward itself? American mainstream Protestantism came in many shapes and sizes. Its liberal form—long a major cultural player—in the early twenty-first century was still a force in the nation, even if it was showing signs of decline. Like Catholics, liberal Protestants faced religious anxieties and, as we will see, worried about their spiritual condition.

Chapter 4

Word from the Beginning: American Protestant Origins and the Liberal Tradition

Probably every schoolchild in the United States has heard the tale of how the Pilgrims with their Indian friends celebrated the first Thanksgiving, a harvest festival to thank God that they had survived in North America for the year. Similarly, almost every child has heard the Virginia narrative of how Pocahontas, the daughter of the chief Powhatan, saved Captain John Smith from certain death at the hands of the Indians and of how some years later she became a Christian and married John Rolfe. In light of later American history, these are curious stories. Both tell of intimacy between English Protestants and Native Americans, but subsequent relations between these peoples contrasted sharply.

Yet if intimacy is based on common elements between people, the two groups did have something in common. For both, **manyness** was a way of life. Each Native American nation was surrounded by others that were separate and different. Many English Protestants were religious nonconformists and so had religious differences with others in Britain. Further, just as the many Indian nations had a basic **oneness**—similar mindsets and ceremonies—so the many American Protestant groups showed a tendency toward religious oneness. Although Protestants demonstrated the most religious diversity in America (in terms of numbers of members and numbers of denominations), their common ideal was so persuasive that it became the religious vision of all Americans. Protestants brought with them an inherited religious vision, and in time they transformed it into an *American* religious vision. Among the changes came the growth of **liberalism**.

The Religion of the Reformation

Protestantism arose in sixteenth-century Europe with the idea of reform at its center. The leading Reformers, **Martin Luther** (1483–1546) and **John Calvin** (1509–1564), acted the part of prophets in lodging their protest against the priestly religion of medieval sacramentalism. The Reformers saw its many layers of ritual expression not as links in a chain to heaven but as obstacles to true communion with God. They wanted to call the church back to what they considered its original purity. They wanted it to discard religious practices that for the Reformers got in the way, substituting the material for the spiritual, the human for the divine.

In the terms of this text, the Reformers wanted to do two things. First, they wanted to bring about a clear division between **extraordinary religion** (attempts to reach their God) and **ordinary religion** (aspects of human culture). Second, they wanted to purge Christianity of elements of the idea of correspondence that had crept in, returning to a purer version of the idea of causality. In other words, they wanted to emphasize a gap between the divine order of things and the natural human world. For the Reformers, without God's help through the grace of Jesus Christ, humans could not be saved. For the Reformers, too, they must live out their loyalty to the God who saved by decisive action in the world. Paradoxically, although Protestantism separated human constructions from the biblical God, it also led out of the churches and into the world.

Thus, the **prophet**, believed to be the inspired messenger of God, was key for Protestants. The prophet called people to a mission that linked traditional accounts from the past to the present—and to an intended future. Spoken out of a strong sense of conviction, the words of the prophet made Protestantism the religion of the "Word." Moreover, since words are formed seemingly without matter—of breath or wind—they could readily be thought of as "Spirit." It followed that the idea of the Spirit, or the spiritual, could become the means by which Protestants conducted criticism. Prophetic protest was the basic spiritual principle on which the other, more concrete principles of the sixteenth-century Reformation were built.

First among these principles was **scripture alone**. The Word was a specific Word present in the Bible: for the Reformers, it was Jesus and the law that the religion of Jesus enjoined. In the beginning, the gospel of John had announced, was the Word (John 1:1). Protestants never forgot the scripture as they rebuked the medieval church for its adherence to tradition and the Roman papacy. In Reformation thinking, sacramentalism led away from the truth of the original Word and corrupted the scriptural message of salvation.

A second principle that the Protestant Reformers preached was **justification through faith** and by grace. As they saw it, this principle was closely tied to the idea of scripture alone, with justification by faith the core meaning taught in scripture. Here, justification was a legal term for salvation, and faith meant trusting God in the person of Jesus—unlike the medieval church, in which it meant a set of doctrines to be accepted. By contrast, the Protestant idea of faith put the emotional experience of an individual at the center of religion, an emphasis that American

Protestants would later take further. As a complete statement, justification by faith announced that humans could do nothing on their own to gain salvation. It implied the doctrine of total depravity, or corruption, and the huge chasm that in causality thinking separates humans from the divine.

A third principle for the Reformers was the **priesthood of all believers**. Here, too, the Reformation departed from the medieval church. The older church, with its sacramental understanding of the role of the priest, saw him as the representative of the community before God, offering the community's common worship. Now, with the priesthood of all, Protestants brought individualism into church consciousness. If each person was a priest, then each as an individual was offering worship to God. Worship in a group brought the fellowship of common *worshipers* but not, as in the older Catholic sense, of one common act of worship.

A fourth principle of the Reformation was the **church** as the **communion of saints**. In the Reformers' understanding, the church was the gathering place for those who had received saving faith, the place where the Word was rightly preached and the sacraments (baptism and the eucharist) rightly administered. *Preaching* the Word assumed new centrality in this definition, and—strikingly different from medieval Catholicism—administering the sacraments came second to the sermon. Unlike the medieval church, too, Protestant fellowship was a gathering of the many. The idea of the communion of saints, although long a part of Christian teaching, still stopped short of the more cohesive metaphor of the Body of Christ.

Thus, the basic principles of the Reformation brought a subtle **individualism** to Christianity. In the context of sixteenth-century Europe, this individualism reflected trends that had already been present in the spiritual lives of monks and nuns. It also agreed with other trends present in the philosophy being taught in the universities. Most important, it spoke to the individualism that was growing with a new middle class. Their place in the middle of society, neither rich nor poor, encouraged personal striving and, therefore, individualism. Beyond this, the basic principles of the Reformation emphasized the *content* of preaching and therefore a new theological consciousness. In contrast to Catholicism, which mostly remained attached to the theology of the sixteenth century until Vatican Council II, Protestantism spawned vigorous theological debate. Finally, the basic principles of the Reformation led to a new call for moral action in the world. This meant that while the Word of the Reformation separated extraordinary from ordinary religion, it also aimed to cut away distraction, so that there could be a reunification. Protestants, as well as others, experienced an overlapping of boundaries between extraordinary and ordinary. But the overlapping of boundaries did not come, as in medieval Catholicism, through the natural world, which supplied the material for ritual action in the sacraments. It came, instead, through the medium of history, that is, through the men and women who, inspired by the preaching of the Word, worked in the world.

In the Lutheran Reformation of Germany, which spread to the Scandinavian countries, the Protestant movement proceeded cautiously, holding to the sacramental past even as it preached the reforming Word. There were clear signs of the new order, though. Congregational singing indicated the importance of the laity and their response to the action in the sanctuary. New church architecture often placed the pulpit in such a position that it competed with the altar for dominance. Ministers read the Bible in the language of the people instead of in Latin, and gradually the eucharist became an occasional, rather than weekly, celebration.

Different from Luther, Calvin arrived at other Protestant views. With his insistence more on the majesty and awesomeness of God than on the humanity of Jesus, Calvin devised a plan for worship that matched his vision. A Calvinist church in its bareness proclaimed the otherness and difference of God. With the table of the Ten Commandments the only ornament on the wall, the building directed people to the law. As new buildings came into existence, the pulpit was placed in the center of the sanctuary and proclaimed the centrality of preaching. Hymns, prayers, scriptural lessons, and the sermon all strived to cultivate the clarity of vision that Calvin sought. Communion, in which the presence of Jesus was acknowledged, was at first prescribed monthly and then four times yearly. Above all, for Calvin the presence of Jesus was revealed in the Bible, which was God's law book. Understanding it, he believed, would lead Christians elected for salvation into the world, where they could witness to Jesus by their lives.

In the Reformed free city of Geneva (now in Switzerland), Calvin—with the (sometimes reluctant) consent of the city fathers—transformed the government into a **theocracy**, a state ruled by the church. Far more than Luther, Calvin joined the religious and the political, making it possible to view religion as moral action in the public sphere. Moreover, the Calvinist Reformation encouraged a sense of the chosenness of those whom, according to Calvinist doctrine, God had elected for salvation. The sense of chosenness, with a conviction of righteousness not far behind, was hardly complete, at least in Calvin's time. The elect were thought hidden in church and city, and there were no signs to determine clearly who they were. The theocratic constitution of the city of Geneva was designed to create a social climate in which the saints could flourish, but Calvin never thought of Geneva as a city in which *only* the saved resided.

With his religion of law and his doctrine of the **predestination** of saints and sinners, Calvin had begun a spiritual system that led increasingly to what the sociologist of religion Max Weber called **innerworldly asceticism**. Calvin had initiated the earliest stage of the **Protestant ethic**, a moral system that seemed to thrive on the evidence of its own success. As believers became anxious about their salvation, they looked to their behavior for assurance. One of the signs of saving faith was, they thought, a righteous and reformed pattern of living. Gradually, though, believers began in practice to attach more weight to this pattern than to their faith, to put the cart of good deeds before the horse of grace, so to speak. It was not too much of a shift for them to begin to see external righteousness—good works—as a guarantee of salvation that itself could be strengthened by more and more good action. Thus, ironically, an ethic of works and work came to flourish at the center of the religion that had taught justification by faith. In the United States the Protestant ethic would help to mold a continent to Euro-American ways and to imprint its character on the public face of the nation. Moreover, it would assist in the assimilation of religious and ethnic groups, such as the Jews, who shared a commitment to the value of law and the ethic of thrift, industry, and hard work—the Protestant ethic.

The Reformation in England

Before Calvinism migrated to North America, however, it traveled across the English Channel. Here at first the Reformation was an act of state accomplished by King Henry VIII (r. 1509–1547) after the pope refused him a divorce sought on the ground that his wife had not given him a male heir. Under Queen Elizabeth I (r. 1558–1603), the **Church of England**, or **Anglicanism**, absorbed various tendencies in belief and kept them together in one church with uniformity of ritual. So long as men and women gathered around the same altar table, in effect, they might hold Lutheran, Calvinist, or even Anglo-Catholic opinions as they chose.

Hence, the Anglican church under Elizabeth and afterward sought to find a middle way between Catholicism and Protestantism. Renouncing the papacy and many medieval devotions, open to various Protestant interpretations and practices, it still retained much of the flavor of an older sacramentalism. Yet a growing body of English opinion held that Elizabeth's reforms had not gone far enough. Those who shared this view came to be called **Puritans**, because they sought to purify the church. Among them were **Separatists**, who thought that the only route to purity was complete separation from the Church of England, and **Non-Separatists**, who thought that the church could be cleansed from within. Among the Non-Separatists, by the 1640s some thought that each congregation should govern itself in complete independence from every other (the **Congregationalists** or **Independents**), and others believed that individual congregations should be related to larger bodies called **presbyteries** and **synods** (the **Presbyterians**). Finally, left-wing Separatist groups, important among them **Baptists** and **Quakers**, also arose.

For all, purifying the church meant purging it of the Roman holdovers from the past and adhering more strongly to Calvinism. They sought a new order in worship and identified it with the austere and simple patterns introduced by John Calvin. Moreover, they developed the theological rationale that accompanied their ritual reforms. As the movement grew, it also came to incorporate elements from the left wing of the continental Reformation, more radical than Calvin had been. Puritans began to think of their churches as **gathered**, or **free**—voluntary associations of individuals who professed their faith with understanding, subscribed to a church covenant or compact, and demonstrated their intent by the upright moral character of their lives. In contrast, both Calvin and Luther had seen churches as **territorial**, including all the inhabitants of a place.

New "meetinghouses" began to displace older churches, and architecture told its story with bare walls and dominant pulpit. As in continental Calvinism, Puritan worship was meant for the ear and the mind, not for the eye. Communion occurred only infrequently, and when held, it was understood as a sign of faith and love for one another. Sometimes, in order to stress that communion was a meal and to imitate the simple setting of the gospel Last Supper, Puritans sat around a table. Their leaders broke bread from common loaves and then passed the loaves to the rest of the people, who broke off their share as well. Still more, the services fostered a new experiential dimension that went beyond the churches of continental Calvinism. Worship, the Puritans thought, should be spontaneous, the expression of a personal relationship with their God. Thus, early Congregationalists encouraged extempore preaching, often accompanied by heartfelt groans from members of the congregation. Early Baptists (Puritans opposed to infant baptism) thought hymns artificial and would not allow them in their churches. In emphasizing adult baptism, they stressed that the ceremony was an act of decisive choice and not, as in the medieval understanding, a sacramental mystery. While this early spontaneity of Puritan worship would later decline, its experiential quality would leave an important legacy when the Puritans immigrated to the American colonies.

In the spirit of Calvinism, the English Puritans encouraged a new consecration of time. They preached against the holy days, some 165 of them, that interrupted the daily work schedule for religious festivals. For the Puritans, these observances sanctioned "idleness," which invited onslaughts from the devil. In Puritan belief, salvation came to those who expressed loyalty to God in the work ethic. Thrift, sobriety, industry, and prudence—all were to be cultivated instead of the looseness that for them the holy days invited. So in place of this old liturgical calendar—even in place of its central feasts such as Christmas and Easter—the Puritans stressed the **Sabbath**. Kept on Sunday in honor of the resurrection of Jesus, the Puritan Sabbath was a time when all work ceased so that people would pay attention to divine things. They should likewise avoid the recreation—the sporting, gaming, and playgoing—that Anglicanism permitted. In the Puritan view, such recreation served only to distract men and women from service to God.

In effect, the Puritans in their Sabbath campaign had separated extraordinary from ordinary religion. The festival cycle, which had knit natural and supernatural concerns together, was gone, while the abolition of all forms of worldly recreation on the Sabbath stressed the separation between human and divine things. Meanwhile, the time taken from the frequent holy days of the older order was freed for the pursuit of work, a pursuit that supported the demands that industrialization and the factory system would later make on people.

The Reformation in the English Colonies

In the English Atlantic colonies, this separation of religion from everyday concerns intensified. The story of European Protestantism in the English colonies is a story of its Americanization. The heritage of the Reformation was never lost for the early Protestant settlers, but the experience of a new (for them) land changed the older Protestantism in profound ways. The earliest Protestant immigrants to the English colonies were Anglicans and Puritans, both with pronounced

Calvinist leanings. Moreover, the Puritan movement gradually took shape as Congregationalist, Presbyterian, and Baptist churches. So considerable religious unity existed in Protestant America from the first and would continue. It was, however, a unity in diversity. **Denominationalism** became the framework for American Protestantism.

Unlike a church (in the strict sense), which included all of the people in a given territory, a denomination was voluntary and thus not universal. As denominations evolved in North America, they were seen as called, or "denominated," out of the larger religious whole—branches of the church and not its entirety. Here the free-church model became more important. Religious liberty gradually spread until, with the United States Constitution, it became the law of the land. Every church, no matter what its theological claims, became a **denomination**, a voluntary society of gathered members, separate yet not separated from every other Christian church. Moreover, while denominations were not the same as all-inclusive churches, they were also very different from sects and smaller groups. They affirmed the world and, even in their more critical moods, never withdrew totally, seeing their task as experience and action. They accepted the Christian tradition as transmitted by the Reformation and did not claim a new revelation.

From the first, boundary problems plagued denominations. Being separate, yet not separated, from the larger church meant living with ambiguity. Boundaries between a denomination and a church easily blurred. Protestantism with its denominational openness always faced the danger of merging into a kind of religion-in-general. At the same time, because the borders dividing groups remained relatively weak, mutual cooperation between denominations could be strong as they sought to make the later United States a Christian nation.

Anglican Virginia

In 1607, the first permanent English settlement in North America was launched at Jamestown. Here Anglicanism and the *Book of Common Prayer* prevailed. Like the New England colonies that followed, **Virginia** was founded, in part, to counter the Catholic presence of Spain and France in North America. For all the Anglicanism of the colony, however, Puritanism—although unofficial—was part of the religious mood. For example, honoring the Sabbath demanded more in Virginia, for a time, than it would in self-consciously Puritan New England. From 1610 and for almost a decade, the law required attendance at divine service and threatened death for a third offense of nonattendance.

With the introduction of tobacco cultivation in 1612, however, another religious style began to spread. Increasing numbers of African slaves worked the plantations, maintaining what remnants they could of the traditions of their ancestors. Meanwhile, the Anglican population was scattered, and religious devotion was not strong. Virginia lawmakers stepped in to provide government support for Anglican clergy, and when the colony became a royal province, its new governor legally controlled many aspects of organized religious life. Still, the parish system of

England did not work in the vast expanses of Virginia, where a parish could be sixty miles long. So a system of **vestries**—groups of lay trustees elected from among the men of a parish to run the local congregation's affairs—became the state of affairs. How long a minister lasted and what pay he received typically depended on the vestrymen, and a lukewarm congregation could perpetuate itself by avoiding ministers who would challenge its people. Ministers themselves tended to be few and often lacking in zeal. So the failure of Anglicanism to build a strong establishment created a vacuum into which other Protestant denominations, like Presbyterians and Quakers, could move. The weakness of the Church of England in Virginia—and in the other southern colonies as well—helped to determine the future of Protestantism.

Puritan New England

To the north, in what became **New England**, the **Pilgrims**, a group of **Separatist** Puritans (no longer part of the Church of England), began their own settlement. They had fled first to Leyden, Holland, when their church came under continuing harassment by the English government. Now, however, they were dissatisfied by the easy and indulgent life that surrounded them in the Netherlands. With the English permissions they needed, the small group of Separatists set sail to establish themselves within Virginia territory. But the *Mayflower* sailed off course, and the ship landed on the Atlantic coast well north of Virginia. Still on board ship in 1620, the Pilgrims agreed in the Mayflower Compact to form a "body politick" and so to govern themselves.

Yet it was the **Massachusetts Bay** colony, founded in 1630 by **Non-Separatists**—Puritans still part of the Church of England—that set the pace for religious life in New England. Like the Pilgrims, the new settlers managed to evade strong English control for their overseas venture. Both groups now could give substance to their visions of a model religious society that in some ways recalled Calvin's Geneva. They could work at their "errand into the wilderness," at first, by perfecting their own ordered communities with proper civil and churchly governance and, as time passed, by thinking more of making an impact on the world.

Before then, though, other colonies also flourished in New England, among them **Rhode Island**. A refuge for religious dissidents from the Bay colony who objected to the Puritan establishment in Massachusetts, the colony stood out for its tolerance of nonconformists. Roger Williams (1603?–1683) founded the colony in 1636 after he was exiled from Massachusetts for religious views that did not conform to official Puritan doctrine. Here, too, Anne Hutchinson, exiled for challenging Massachusetts church leaders with ideas of direct guidance by the Holy Spirit, made her way in 1638. And here Quakers and others of independent religious views also found refuge. But the nonconformity of all of these was *Puritan* nonconformity. They sought a purity even greater than that championed by the leaders at Massachusetts Bay.

Old Ship Meetinghouse, Hingham. Nineteen miles southeast of Boston, Old Ship Meetinghouse from 1681 reflected the seafaring culture of Hingham with a framed roof that looked like an inverted ship's hull. The spare and simple style likewise reflected Puritan culture.

New England's leaders innovated even on the Puritanism of the English church. They sought to unite gathered communities of committed believers—a sectarian model influenced by European radical reformers—under a state church. Here, without the bishops and organizational structure of Anglicanism, a congregational system of independent churches flourished under strong clerical leadership. At the same time, a sense of isolation from the corruptions of old England and of immersion in an untainted American "wilderness" encouraged belief in New England's chosenness and righteousness.

The Puritans expressed their sense of chosenness by increased attention to the doctrine of the **covenant**, which had been part of their English heritage. According to the doctrine, God had formed a pact with the Puritan settlers modeled on his biblical covenant with Israel, and they were the New Israel. If the Puritans, as God's elect people, fulfilled their part in the covenant through faithful and virtuous lives, God also would be faithful. In contrast, if plague or witchcraft, Indian wars or conservative Anglicans troubled their settlements, these were signs for the Puritans that something was wrong from their side of the covenant. Still further, covenants formed the basis of the civil government as well as the congregational churches, each of which had covenants of association for members.

By about 1636 in Massachusetts Bay, Puritans began to require a new experiential test for becoming part of these church covenants. Now intellectual assent to the Christian faith was not enough. An emotional conviction of one's sinfulness and a felt sense of saving faith were required. Thus, no matter how upright the character, no matter how loyal the adherence to duty, unless a person experienced **conversion**, there could be no church membership. After the first generation, though, the Puritans saw the membership rolls of their churches shrink alarmingly when their adult children were unable to testify to experiences of conversion. Many of this new generation believed firmly in Puritan Christian teaching and led lives of upright Puritan morality. But they could claim no emotional encounter with saving faith. So in 1662 a Puritan church synod accepted compromise. The **Halfway Covenant** provided that the children and grandchildren of the saints, even without an experience of saving faith, be baptized and made "halfway" members of the church if they met all other requirements. Because voting rights in the colony depended on membership in the church, this action had civic consequences. More important here, it hinted at religious changes that would come to New England as its Calvinism gradually declined and a new movement called **Arminianism** grew.

But there was more. By the third and fourth generations, many Puritans, instead of looking to a simple restoration of a covenant past, were anticipating times future. They awaited the **millennium**, the thousand-year reign of Christ as prophesied in the biblical Book of Revelation. In Christian belief an event associated with the second coming of Jesus (the first had been his recorded life in Palestine), the millennium was thought to launch a radically new era. For American Puritans, **millennialism**—the keen expectation of the impending arrival of the millennium—became a way to hope for the restoration of the past by re-imagining it in the time to come. Puritan millennialism would make a significant mark on the American future.

Pluralist New York and Pennsylvania

In the Middle Colonies, however, it was the Dutch who initially made their mark. As early as 1609 Henry Hudson had explored the river that would later be named after him. Dutch traders established posts there as well as on Long Island Sound and the Connecticut River, and then permanent residents settled Manhattan Island. The Dutch Reformed church, with its modified Calvinism, formed the religious backbone of the New Amsterdam colony. After it became **New York** in 1664, the Dutch Reformed church remained the largest religious body, but increasing diversity characterized the colony. Eventually, the Duke of York pursued a policy of toleration for all who professed to be Christian (the Jews were noticeably excluded); and when, in 1693, New York's governor made the Anglican church in effect the official establishment, the change was not significant. Overwhelmingly, the colonists were Dutch Reformed, or they counted themselves English dissenters.

By the eighteenth century, the former Dutch possession had become home to groups as various as French Calvinists, German Lutherans, New England Congregationalists, Puritan dissenters of Quaker and Baptist temper, Mennonites, Catholics, and Jews. By that time, New York had had a Catholic governor, and many New Yorkers had come to see religious toleration not simply as practical necessity but also as positive good. Protestant **pluralism**—the existence of many separate but publicly equal religious faiths with none of them having the upper hand—became the New York experience, and New Yorkers began to see religious and political benefits in their arrangement. Churches found that they could engage in cooperative efforts for what seemed the good of all.

Pennsylvania, the Quaker colony of William Penn (1644–1718), followed its founder's convictions by providing sanctuary for Europeans who had experienced religious persecution. Although Anglicans theoretically received preferred treatment, Penn's colony guaranteed freedom of worship and made a point of its respect for the rights of conscience. Indeed, Penn extended his respect to Native Americans. Aware of the "unkindness and injustice" they had experienced at white hands, he insisted on dealing with them equitably and negotiated a treaty in 1701 with this in mind. Penn's regard for Indians was a sign of the range of Quaker commitments. Persecuted themselves, the Quakers (the **Society of Friends**) came to Pennsylvania as a haven where they could follow their conviction that there was something of the divine in every human being. They taught a mysticism of inner light, which for them meant that there was no need for church, creed, or priesthood. In worship they sat quietly together and waited for what they believed to be the promptings of the Spirit before they spoke. Plain and simple in religious practice, Quakers also kept religious spaces plain. The bare walls of Quaker meetinghouses stood as a protest against Anglican ornateness. It was belief in the divine light in all human beings thus that supplied the ground for conviction of the respect owed Indians, blacks, the suffering, and the downtrodden.

Even so, the realities of life in Pennsylvania began to militate against the radical stance of the Friends. Contradicting their prophetic religion and their history of social criticism, the Quakers had become a religious and political establishment. At the same time, Quaker successes in commerce were making the countinghouse more significant for many than the meetinghouse. So by the eighteenth century many of the Quaker Philadelphia elite were turning to Anglicanism and, eventually, Episcopalianism. Meanwhile, Pennsylvania's open-door policy of toleration brought an increasing immigration. Pluralism—in fact as well as in theory—ruled the day, with Scotch and Scotch-Irish Presbyterians and German Lutherans. By the 1750s the Quakers had given up their place of leadership in the colony. But despite the tensions within the Quaker experiment, Pennsylvania—like New York and Rhode Island—pointed toward the religious future. In the democracy that would flourish in the new United States, there would be no official religious establishment. Pluralism—and then the **postpluralism** of religious combination—would mark the American religious landscape.

Colonial Foreshadowings of Liberalism

Pluralism and postpluralism provided the framework for a new **liberal** form of Protestant religion, which in turn expressed in religious form American political and social realities. The word **liberalism** comes from a Latin word meaning "free." In fact, the words liberalism and liberty are related in their common Latin root—a fact that recalls what the liberal tradition counts as important. By the time the liberal tradition fully flowered, it would be emphasizing beliefs like the presence of God in the world (divine **immanence**), the goodness and even divinity of human nature, the humanity of Jesus, and the millennial fullness of his kingdom about to come on earth. Liberalism would teach optimism about human society and preach a message of social reform that could be achieved through concerted effort. In certain forms it would emphasize personal experience and thus individualism in religion. All of this added up, in different ways, to religious freedom.

Liberal Protestantism grew slowly in the United States, and—although colonial religion was hardly liberal—the beginnings of liberalism could already be found there. Ironically, one important source of the liberal tradition lay in a radical Puritan movement that valued sectarian purity and isolation even more than the leaders of Massachusetts Bay had valued them. That movement was Baptist Christianity. **Baptists** rejected infant baptism, with its emphasis on the community's role in nurturing Christian belief, and insisted instead that a mature and committed believer was the only appropriate recipient of baptism. In Baptist understanding, therefore, the church was not an umbrella organization for as many as possible. Rather, Baptists sought the purity of the gathered few. The corollary for Baptists was that social arrangements must be created that left individuals free to consent to Christian baptism. An established church worked against Christian salvation as they understood it, and religious freedom was necessary to ensure that only the pure and committed would enter the church. By the time of the American Revolution and its aftermath of constitution-making, the Baptists were the most vocal among Christian believers in demanding an end to religious establishment. The First Amendment owes a good deal, then, to Baptist believers who sought sectarian purity.

Most Baptists continued to be strong Calvinists. They emphasized, like Calvin, the "**total depravity**" of human beings, that is, the inability of humans on their own to say or do anything that could merit them salvation. Baptists stressed the unlimited transcendence and sovereignty of a God whom they understood more as distant and authoritative than as near and compassionate. Like other conservative Calvinists, they thought in terms of an atonement, through the death of Jesus, that was limited to those whom God in his inscrutable wisdom had chosen. And Baptists counted grace as a force that could not be resisted and believers as people who, fortified with this grace, were bound to persevere in their faith. The relationship between these beliefs and the political and social matrix of freedom that Baptists demanded seems, in our times, a curious one. Nonetheless, it was real. A religious logic linked church freedoms to the old Calvinist theology.

Still, during the colonial period a significantly modified form of Calvinism—called **Arminianism**—foreshadowed Protestant liberalism. Named after the sixteenth-century Dutch Reformed pastor Jacobus Arminius (1560–1609), who initially gave it direction, this movement emphasized human freedom. It taught that people could resist grace and that salvation (or condemnation) was not foreordained. Developed by others after the death of Arminius, Arminianism became a religious system that softened the austerity of Calvinism as it was then interpreted—and, as important, stressed human responsibility. In Holland, a church synod held at Dort in 1618 had condemned the new teaching. And in an echo, New England Puritans thought that to call people "Arminians" was to question their orthodoxy and insult their religious integrity. Despite this beginning, the history of colonial Puritanism involved, on the whole, a movement from relative Calvinism to relative Arminianism, with Puritanism losing its identity in the process. "Creeping" Arminianism eroded the rigor of Calvinist belief and practice, entering New England's churches without great fanfare. It grew through a change in the character of the preaching, as increasing numbers of pastors stopped talking about hellfire for the unconverted and spoke instead of the need for virtue and benevolence. The shift, of course, meant an unspoken assumption that humans could *do* something that affected their own salvation. "Liberal Christians," as they came to be called, previewed a liberal Protestantism for the new republic.

In Anglican Virginia, rationalism and moralism also flourished in elite circles. Most preferred among writers was a group of English thinkers known to intellectual history as the **Cambridge Platonists**, among them Henry More (1614–1687), Edward Stillingfleet (1635–1699), and Archbishop John Tillotson (1630–1694).

From 1635, these and other Cambridge Platonists advocated toleration and breadth in understanding the nature of the church. They sought to settle disputes by referring to a presence of God in the human mind and by using principles established by reason. The successors to the Cambridge Platonists in the English church were called **Latitudinarians**, people giving wide latitude to matters of dogma, church organization, and rubrics of worship. Their Christian rationalism and interest in matters of morality were not lost on the Virginians.

Indeed, the eighteenth-century European **Enlightenment**, especially in its English version, made its mark on Virginia, Massachusetts, and other colonies. Enlightenment thinking exalted human reason, and it might seem that New England Puritans, with their emphasis on the authority of the Bible, would therefore reject it. Yet the Puritans, even at their most austere, never denied what reason or nature could teach them. They believed that the light of scripture would enable them to use the light of reason and the knowledge gained from nature. Here, interest in new scientific thought combined with attention to innovations in philosophy. For example, the well-known Puritan minister Cotton Mather (1663–1728) authored the *Christian Philosopher* in which—writing as an amateur scientist and religious poet—he placed the book of nature beside the book of biblical revelation as a source of knowledge of things divine. Similarly, Jonathan Edwards (1703–1758), although he is often remembered for his revivalism, read widely in science and philosophy. Edwards left a series of important writings in both areas, and he even justified revivals by a rationalist argument derived from the thought of British philosopher John Locke.

Liberalism in the American Revolution

During the era of the Revolution, liberal doctrines from abroad attracted some Protestant Christians in the teachings of "**natural religion**." Educated upper- and middle-class patriots had learned their natural religion from British thinkers whose books they acquired. Ideas like the reasonableness of Christianity and **deism** began to spread. In its root meaning, the term *deism* stands, literally, for "Goddism," since *deus* is the Latin word for "God." Thus, deism and its softer version in natural religion taught a simple creed of belief in a God. As important, deists taught belief in an afterlife of reward or punishment. The deist creed emphasized a good and moral life, and it looked to nature and its law as sources of revelation and guidance.

Deism found organizational expression in the fraternal societies of **Freemasonry**. The brotherhood supported an ethic of right relationship in one's doings and dealings with one's fellows. Freemasonic lodges carried deism into many quarters, and deists played a key role in the political process that brought the new nation into being. The revolutionary organization of the Sons of Liberty and the revolutionary committees of correspondence were tied closely to Freemasonry. Many of the signers of the Declaration of Independence were Masons, as were members of the Continental Congress. Moreover, nearly every American general in the Revolutionary War was a Mason. Enshrined in the Freemasonic lodges, deism—although in pure form not Christian at all—existed comfortably beside Protestant Christianity and by so doing moved Protestants who were Masonic brothers in a liberal direction. Blending with currents of Arminianism and rationalism, deism furthered the spirit of tolerance that, for practical reasons, flourished amid America's religious pluralism.

Early Liberal Heyday: From the Revolution to the Civil War

Although Protestant liberalism did not achieve its classic form in the United States until after the Civil War, significant developments were already afoot in the late eighteenth and early nineteenth centuries. These developments occurred in older denominations, and they brought the birth of new ones.

Despite the revivals of the First Great Awakening, which swept the colonies during the middle years of the eighteenth century, full church membership was probably not large during the latter part of the century. More important, whatever the statistics, late-eighteenth-century contemporaries thought that religion had declined. They blamed this perceived decline on a deism hostile to Christianity, which had reached ordinary people through English soldiers during the French and Indian Wars (1755–1763) and through French soldiers during the American Revolution (1775–1783). They also felt a disruption in the life of the churches occasioned by the war. With even pastors enlisting and with the countryside turned into a battlefield, church life could hardly have been unaffected. Still more, Anglicanism and an infant Methodist movement had close ties to England and after the war had to undergo reorganization. Probably most difficult of all to remedy, institutions and attitudes that were taken for granted in England had to fight to make their way in the new nation. On the Anglo-American frontier, a church was less necessary than a house, and a Bible less practical than a hunting rifle or an ax.

However, Protestant clerical anxieties in certain ways promoted liberal behavior and thought. Among older denominations, the felt need to bring more people to the churches generated cooperative efforts. In a key example, by the end of the war the Congregationalists and their denominational cousins, the Presbyterians, had joined forces, regarding themselves almost as a single church and dividing territory as practical need dictated. Under their **Plan of Union** in 1801, Presbyterians and Congregationalists cooperated in home missionary efforts on the Anglo-American frontier. Ministers in the two denominations shared each other's pulpits, clergy and laity worked together, and even membership became dual. Although conservatives in the Old School among the Presbyterians objected increasingly to the Congregational affiliation, liberals in the New School supported it, opening themselves to a toleration and cooperation that chipped away at the pure Calvinist model they had inherited.

From other quarters liberal practice was softening denominational separateness. By the early nineteenth century Protestant **voluntary societies**—formed without official denominational ties—were distributing Bibles and tracts and furthering moral reform. For them, as for most Protestants of the time, the leading problems for American Christianity were "infidelity" and "barbarism." Protestant Christians acting *together* could change things, they believed. Yet ironically, the new theology of liberalism was bringing a different kind of denominational separateness. Growing disagreements within Congregational ranks became apparent at Harvard College as liberals took over. Their movement spread, until in 1819 liberal leader William Ellery Channing delivered a landmark sermon on "Unitarian Christianity" at a Baltimore ordination. Different from a preexisting European version, the **Unitarianism** that Channing taught and that shaped a new American denomination saw Jesus as more than an ordinary human. At the same time, although he was seen as Savior, he was not considered God. The Bible was an inspired book but also one written in ordinary language that must be studied and interpreted like other books. Most of all, Channing and his followers taught a likeness between God and human beings. Humans had a "moral nature" that was the foundation of virtue. Jesus showed the way to the perfection—which was divine—that humans could achieve.

The mostly Boston-based Unitarians had their country cousins in the **Universalists**. Universalist views of salvation were expressed in their name, for they held that, through the sacrifice and grace of Jesus, God intended salvation for all. Although there had been universalist preaching in Pennsylvania as early as 1741, in the denominational sense the movement began with the work of John Murray. An English Methodist of Calvinist persuasion, Murray arrived in North America in 1770 and began preaching on the Atlantic coast, establishing groups of people with universalist convictions. The person who had the most to do with the direction Universalism would take, however, was another convert, Hosea Ballou. With Baptist roots and also with exposure to the thought of Boston liberals who emphasized human goodness and divine benevolence, Ballou published his influential *Treatise on Atonement* in 1805. In it he rejected Calvinist teachings of total depravity and eternal condemnation of the damned. Even more, he rejected the Christian doctrine of the Trinity and the traditional belief in miracles, stressing instead human goodness and capacity for perfection. Jesus, in Ballou's reading, was not himself God, but he was God's son. In short, the Universalism that Ballou preached moved close to what would emerge as Unitarian belief. (The two denominations would join at last in 1961 as the Unitarian Universalist Association.)

Both Unitarians and Universalists threw themselves into social reform, convinced that their work was God's work. Other liberals expressed their commitments in literary and philosophical terms in New England **Transcendentalism**. Begun among a group of Boston Unitarians educated at Harvard, many of them ministers, Transcendentalism flourished in a loosely knit club for conversation about literary, philosophical, and religious issues. The acknowledged leader of the movement was Ralph Waldo Emerson (1803–1882), whose small book *Nature* provided its gospel in 1836. Key to this work was a new form of the ancient theory of correspondence, in which Emerson and his friends looked to nature to teach them spiritual truths. They saw in the New England landscape symbolic statements of deeper realities, and by studying nature, they believed, they could uncover the secrets of their inner selves and a corresponding knowledge of the divine. Both suggested for them the presence of a God who was immanent—within oneself and the world. For Emerson and other Transcendentalists, humans were using only part of the full power they possessed. The Transcendentalists expressed great optimism about human goodness and capacity for reforming society.

A number of Transcendentalist ministers, either in or out of Unitarianism, began reforming society by their attempted reforms of the church. For example, the famed antislavery preacher Theodore Parker, while fellow Unitarian ministers ostracized him, formed the Twenty-Eighth Congregational Society. In his new congregation, which eventually became the largest in Boston, Parker abolished the custom of paying to own one's pew and also banished a regular collection. Other Transcendentalist ministers experimented with communal ideas. For instance, William Henry Channing, the nephew of William Ellery Channing, based his Boston congregation on the thought of the French socialist and communitarian Charles Fourier. And in West Roxbury, Massachusetts, in 1840, the former Unitarian minister George Ripley formed the Brook Farm community, a joint-stock company that aimed to express, in a communal-living experiment, Transcendental ideas of freedom and spontaneity. By 1844 Brook Farm became a Fourierist "phalanx," a self-sufficient cooperative community.

Other reformist concerns—especially antislavery—continued to occupy the Transcendentalists. Their movement, however, was only one expression of the European and American cultural movement known as **Romanticism**. The successor to the Enlightenment, this movement flourished after the French Revolution and became the dominant ideology of the nineteenth century. Like the Enlightenment, the Romantic movement exalted nature, but a nature viewed as organic, free, and spontaneous instead of, as in the Enlightenment, mechanical and ruled by law. More than the Enlightenment, therefore, Romanticism stressed human freedom and its expression through passion or emotion. It found little to fear in strong feeling, since humans, in the Romantic understanding, were basically good. As with the Transcendentalists, other Romantics likewise found significance in the inner life.

Romantic ideas found an important theological voice in Germany in the writings of the Reformed minister Friedrich Schleiermacher. His *Christian Faith* (1821–1822) announced that religion was the feeling of absolute dependence and that Christianity was the highest but not the only true religion. In the United States, Schleiermacher's work helped to shape the Transcendentalists. But it also helped to shape a broader movement of Christian Romanticism. Probably the chief exponent of this American movement was the theologian Horace Bushnell (1802–1876). A Yale Divinity School graduate and Congregational minister, Bushnell absorbed home-grown Unitarian ideas along with those of Schleiermacher and other European thinkers like English Romantic poet Samuel Taylor Coleridge.

His "progressive orthodoxy" did not win him much popularity in his own time, but it later received a full hearing in the seminaries that were training future generations of ministers. Bushnell advanced a theory of language that enabled Christians to bring past and present together. This "mediating" theology taught that words were symbolic devices that could only hint at the truth that lay behind and beyond language.

Bushnell thought of language as a social product, and therefore he underlined the importance of the processes by which children were brought, through language, into the cultural community. His *Christian Nurture* (1847) was widely influential in teaching the importance of religious education. Here Bushnell countered the revivalist language of the era, with its emphasis on sin and sudden salvation, with a gradualist view of continuing progress from good to better. Behind his thinking lay an organic and developmental view of Christian life: it was something that grew and matured with the years, he believed, through a process nourished by the institutions of family, church, and even nation. In fact, in his later *Nature and the Supernatural* (1858), Bushnell redefined the supernatural (literally, what is "above the natural") to include everything alive. His supernatural could not be separated from nature, and his God was immanent in the living world.

Bushnell's ideas pointed the way to what, well after the Civil War, would be called the Social Gospel, and he also laid the groundwork for later liberal Christian acceptance of the theory of evolution. In the meantime, increasing immigration—bringing new religious groups to the United States—also encouraged the growth of liberal Protestantism. German and Swedish Lutherans and the Dutch and German Reformed had long been present. These older national churches continued to receive new members from abroad, and now members of other national churches arrived, too. Still more, slavery became a source of friction for older, mainstream churches. Baptists, Methodists, Presbyterians, and (with qualification) Episcopalians divided into separate churches before or during the Civil War. From another quarter, although there had been independent African American congregations since the late eighteenth century, black denominational growth received a major boost after the war. In an atmosphere of often-passionate adherence to what believers regarded as gospel truth, no one group should be singled out for its "liberalism." Yet the presence of multiplying groups would have its results. The liberal endorsement of as much freedom as possible while maintaining some community identity would be strengthened by the presence of the many.

From Gilded Age into Twentieth Century

The post–Civil War era was known as the **Gilded Age**, because beneath the glittering surface of society there was said to be a sense of spiritual erosion and discomfort. Then the nation experienced a continued wave of prosperity until the outbreak of World War I in 1914 and, in 1929, the Great Depression. From the Gilded Age into the twentieth century Protestant liberalism reached its mature form, making its impact felt in the religious life of many believers. Liberals acted in a broad context in which Protestants either affirmed American culture, withdrew from it as much as possible, or tried to transform it. Liberalism helped to shape the first and third ways of responding to culture directly and the second indirectly by helping to provoke the second way's rejection of modernity.

With their varied responses to American culture and their liberal impulse, late-nineteenth-century Protestants formulated new theological statements with a characteristic American quality. Their new gospel Word was pragmatic, so that wealth and poverty, evolution and science, liberalism and the fear of it became the content of the theological message. Meanwhile, rank-and-file Protestants were already acting out theologies in the circumstances of their lives. First, Protestants affirmed culture through the content of popular preaching. Perhaps no better example can be found than in the life of Henry Ward Beecher (1813–1887). The clerical hero of the age, Henry Ward was the son of the memorable Lyman Beecher, bellwether for an earlier generation. From 1847 to 1887, the younger Beecher held the pulpit at the Plymouth Church in Brooklyn, New York, where his sermons drew crowds numbering in the thousands. He had moved decidedly to the left of even the modified Calvinism of his father. His **New Theology**, as it came to be called, was **evangelical liberalism**, centering emotionally on an individual relationship with Jesus and leading confidently toward an acceptance of the world. The humanity of Jesus inspired his emotional sermons, and Beecher saw the humanness of Jesus as a sign of natural human possibility. For Beecher, things as they were, were good. The goal of his preaching, with its sentimental warmth, was to lead each hearer to an experiential encounter with the gospel. The Reformation Protestantism of prophetic protest gave way to a new culture religion, and extraordinary religion was mostly forgotten. Still, there was a biting edge to Beecher's Word, for it led him to speak out on a range of issues, from slavery and women's rights to immigration and municipal corruption.

In the **Gospel of Wealth**, however, the biting edge seemed wholly lost. Liberalism became an affirmation of the freedom to prosper, a testimony to prosperity as divine blessing. God became immanent in the flow of material good fortune, and human nature became the ordained vehicle for the acquisition of wealth. A good example of the Gospel of Wealth was the preaching of Russell H. Conwell (1843–1925). Baptist Conwell—and others who agreed—transformed an older Calvinist belief in wealth as God's blessing into the declaration that poverty was sinful and that it was the duty of every Christian to become rich. Conwell's sermon "Acres of Diamonds" was initially delivered in 1861 and repeated some 6,000 times, proclaiming to hearers that there were acres of diamonds in their own backyards, if only they would take the trouble to dig them out. Conwell's preaching—and the Gospel of Wealth—acted as a Christian baptism for the burgeoning capitalism of the era. Still more, by the last decade of the nineteenth century, the good news of prosperity would be announced again in the kind of Christianity known as **New Thought** (to be discussed in Chapter 8).

Popular expressions of Protestant belief in a need to accept the world were joined by more intellectual ones. It was here that Protestant liberalism became its most reflective, responding to the science and scholarship of the era, including Charles Darwin's theory of evolution. In its most pronounced form, this liberalism of the intellectuals came to be known as **modernism**. The Christian task, for modernists, was to realize the gospel in the modern world. In the terms of the text, modernists sought to collapse ordinary and extraordinary into one continuous reality. By so doing, in some statements they seemed to make modernity the norm by which the Word was measured and to want to restructure the gospel along lines that science and general cultural development provided. For example, modernists reinterpreted traditional biblical accounts, such as the Genesis story, with the aid of critical scholarship coming from Germany. Known as the "**higher criticism**" to distinguish it from the textual ("lower") criticism inherited from the Reformation, the new scholarship emphasized the sources and literary methods that biblical authors employed. Unlike textual criticism, which sought to establish the correct text of manuscripts and to reconstruct textual history, higher criticism pointed to possible sources of a biblical author's text and so challenged older theories of revelation and inspiration. By suggesting the literary and theological creativity of biblical authors, higher critics likewise inserted biblical books into historical situations. They questioned old theories of authorship, dating, and meaning in biblical documents.

Still more, the modernists brought the liberal challenge to Calvinism to full maturity. Whereas the Calvinist perspective expressed awe at the transcendence of God—his distance from the human world—the modernists, in their teaching of immanence, saw God's presence in the world. Whereas Calvinism taught human depravity, modernism abolished original sin and taught human goodness. Indeed, modernists shared a basic optimism about creating heaven in the present world, and so they replaced the traditional heaven of the afterlife with an earthly version. Unlike Calvinists, modernists saw Jesus as an elder brother, someone who disclosed to humans all that they could know of God. Finally, modernists left Calvinist intellectualism behind and sought felt experience more. In late-nineteenth-century liberal teaching, evangelical pietism, with its emphasis on heartfelt feeling, continued in a new and more sophisticated form. The intellectual difficulties of new scientific theory and practice were short-circuited by a religion of the heart.

The challenge of the age was especially symbolized for later generations by Charles Darwin. Protestant response to **Darwin's theory of evolution**, particularly among people in the pew, was slow in coming. Not until the 1920s and the Tennessee trial of John T. Scopes (1925), a biology teacher accused of violating a Tennessee law by teaching the theory of evolution, did the matter evoke great interest. Many—indeed, most—Protestants who studied Darwin's theory before 1875 saw it as lacking in scientific credibility. After that, though, since many scientists had changed their minds, most Protestant intellectuals began to change theirs as well. Many began to see the idea of evolution as a blueprint for God's way of working in the creation of life forms.

Some Protestants, though, refused to accept the world that modernity presented, and they countered liberalism head on in a second response to change. They withdrew from the world as much as they could, rejecting the worldly forms that, for them, challenged the gospel. Protestant **fundamentalism** grew strong in the same climate that fostered a mature liberalism, and the fundamentalist–liberal controversy became the key to Protestantism in the late nineteenth and early twentieth centuries. But fundamentalism, like liberalism, grew out of earlier movements; and the same is true for other movements that at least partially rejected the world, such as the **holiness-pentecostal movement**. Important here, liberalism played a significant role in the birth of these movements of withdrawal, particularly the fundamentalist one. In liberalism, some Protestants saw the face of the enemy among fellow religionists. For these Protestants, liberalism became a more serious form of betrayal than the defection from the Christian gospel they saw in the world. So liberalism, indirectly, worked to promote countermovements.

The third response of liberal Protestantism after the Civil War aimed to transform American culture and society. Joined by some others who were more conservative, liberals threw themselves into the **Social Gospel**. The new gospel cause had precedents in earlier Protestant calls to reform society. Moreover, many of the roots of the Social Gospel lay in evangelical liberalism, although Social Gospelers were less content with social conditions in the post–Civil War United States than world-affirming liberals had been. Social Gospelers noticed that large numbers received little pay for their work and led lives of poverty in urban slums. Advocates of the Social Gospel saw the true tasks of Christians as rescuing the poor and renewing the political, economic, and social order. They thought that the Kingdom of God must come on earth—through human effort.

Under Washington Gladden (1836–1918), a Congregationalist minister from Columbus, Ohio, the movement began to receive notice in the 1880s. Gladden had first ministered to churches in Massachusetts, where he had become aware of exploitation and poverty that working people faced. He came to endorse the rights of workers and even favored ownership of public utilities by cities and municipalities. Gladden became increasingly outspoken in advancing his views, lecturing persistently and writing some thirty-six books. Later, Walter Rauschenbusch (1861–1918) provided a theological foundation for the Social Gospel in the early twentieth century. Rauschenbusch had labored as a young minister in the Hell's Kitchen district of New York City, and though he returned to his seminary in Rochester as a professor, he never forgot what he had seen. After a decade of seminary life, he published *Christianity and the Social Crisis* (1907), and later he produced *A Theology for the Social Gospel* (1917) and other works. Religion, for Rauschenbusch, was intended to change not only individuals but also the social structures that thwarted people. In the Social Gospel, salvation came in the reconstruction of society. A personal relationship with Jesus was not enough.

A number in the Social Gospel movement were directly inspired by the "Christian socialism" of the English Frederick Denison Maurice and Charles Kingsley as well as by German and Swiss Christian socialist thought. Americans were also becoming more acquainted with the ideas of Karl Marx and of British socialists in the Fabian Society as well as those of European political theorists who favored socialism. Thus, political science, economics, and especially sociology could be tapped in the interests of the Social Gospel. Some, for example, supported the development of new "settlement houses" to improve conditions in poor neighborhoods, such as Jane Addams at Hull House in Chicago.

With its practical directness, the Social Gospel, like modernism, stressed the ordinary dimension of religion. But it went beyond modernism in bringing belief in Christian revelation to its work. In other words, the Social Gospel insisted on the extraordinary, and this was perhaps why some Protestant conservatives could feel comfortable with it. But the old spirit of prophetic criticism, the Protestant principle, revived within the movement in a new way—directed at the world, not the church. The Social Gospel sought to transform society as a means of establishing contact with the divine. The God of the Social Gospelers, like the God of other liberals, was immanent.

Protestant Liberalism in Recent Times

The Social Gospel provided an enduring legacy to mainstream liberal Protestants in the twentieth century and after. The popularity of social Christianity waxed and waned, but the Social Gospel never completely disappeared. Meanwhile, a liberal–fundamentalist split seemed a permanent feature of Protestant life, with liberals and fundamentalists organized in separate denominations. But increasingly the divisions happened *within* denominations, so that some within the same church might be liberal and others conservative or fundamentalist.

By the late 1980s and 1990s the most liberal Protestants tended to be Episcopalians, members of the United Church of Christ (heirs to Congregationalism and other traditions), and Presbyterians. (Unitarian-Universalists had effectively moved beyond Protestant Christian boundaries.) Moderate Protestant churches, with memberships that had substantial liberal and conservative factions, included Methodist, Lutheran, and Northern Baptist groups. For the most part, in the 1980s these denominational families numbered among the largest Protestant bodies in the nation, but by the mid-1990s they had slipped considerably, ranking mostly among churches with the largest membership decreases. By contrast, the largest single Protestant denomination was the fundamentalist-oriented Southern Baptist Convention, and Protestant churches showing the greatest membership increases were overwhelmingly conservative.

In fact, liberal churches had declined for several decades at least, and signs of weakening appeared even earlier. With their continuing denominational manyness, they—like mainstream Protestant groups in general—faced a series of problems. First, the increasingly urban character of American culture caught many Protestants off guard and ill prepared. Protestantism had been a rural religion, and even the Protestantism of more city-oriented liberals had thrived in a simpler, less complex nation. Now, however, the future lay with city life with its greater diversity and complication. Second, the gradual separation of American public culture from deliberate attention to religion also worked against the churches. Radio, television, and film powerfully affected the social images projected into people's lives. Moreover, highly mobile life-styles, the quickening pace of life, an ascending divorce rate, and a declining birthrate played havoc with older religious values. Despite some prominent exceptions, ordinary religion was flattening the transcendent dimension of life. Meanwhile, the intensifying pluralism—the manyness—of American culture brought anxiety to numbers of liberals. Old-line denominations, particularly strongly liberal ones, looked increasingly alike, and outside the evangelical and fundamentalist camp, religion-in-general—with few clear boundaries—seemed to rule the day. Still further, as they grew to adulthood, the "baby boomers" of the post–World War II era proved less drawn to community-oriented churches. American individualism seemed stronger than ever.

In response, some churches tried to speak to urban dwellers by making worship only one facet of their mission. Elaborating on social patterns developed during earlier rural days, such churches held classes and picnics, conducted sporting events, and sponsored church suppers to reach out to a larger public. On a more reflective level, the movement called **theological realism**, or **neoorthodoxy**, challenged both liberal optimism and American cultural materialism. It tried, both in Europe and in the United States, to bring an end to what it saw as uncritical acceptance of the age of progress. Influenced by the thought of the American Niebuhr brothers, Reinhold (1892–1970) and H. Richard (1894–1962), some Protestants sought again the prophetic Word of their Reformation ancestors. With the Niebuhrs, they believed that evil in society could never be completely eradicated by human effort. The Word must stand in judgment over every political, economic, and social endeavor.

Both the absence of clear religious symbols in much of public life and increasing pluralism in the private sphere had something to do with the growth of the **ecumenical movement** for the reunification of separated churches. Both also probably contributed to the growth of various movements of cooperative Christianity, which worked not for denominational merger but for union in accomplishing common tasks. Here liberal Protestants took the initiative, and here to a partial degree they succeeded. An international movement of church cooperation and work toward Christian reunion had begun as early as 1910, when a world missionary conference was held in Edinburgh, Scotland. After other formative meetings, the World Council of Churches came into being in 1948.

But an American movement of interfaith cooperation had predated the world movement. Some Social Gospelers had believed that an official church federation could advance the work of social Christianity. Then, in 1905, the New York meeting of a group calling itself the Inter-Church Conference on Federation led to plans for the Federal Council of Churches of Christ in America. By 1908, the organization had come into existence, with thirty-three denominations its members. Here again, liberalism became less an intellectual movement than a willingness to work together at mutually conceived tasks. Nor did the liberal flavor of the organization go unnoticed among conservative Protestants. In 1942 they established the National Association of Evangelicals at least partially because of concern that the Federal Council was keeping fundamentalists out of religious broadcasting.

Despite the liberal–conservative rift that continued, Protestant cooperation in the United States achieved new form with the institution, in 1950, of the National Council of Churches. The old Federal Council of Churches and other coordinating organizations came together to bring the new structure into being. It became the largest cooperative body that Protestants had established, with roughly 33 million members organized in 143,000 congregations. Now, however, Protestants had shed their exclusivity, for a number of Eastern Orthodox bodies held institutional membership in the National Council.

Meanwhile, the mood of cooperation fostered the goal of church union, and the ecumenical movement, in the strict sense, began to have practical results. Lutheran national churches—some twenty-four of them in the early twentieth century—continued to merge until, in 1988, the Evangelical Lutheran Church in America came into being. Today there are two major denominations organizing Lutheran life in the United States: the more liberal Evangelical Lutheran Church in America, with over 5 million members in the early twenty-first century, and—roughly half its size—the conservative Lutheran Church–Missouri Synod. Other full denominational mergers occurred. One important union came in 1957, when the Congregational Christian Church joined with the Evangelical and Reformed Church to become the United Church of Christ, a body with over 1.3 million members in 2002. Yet another came in 1968, when the United Methodist Church was formed by the joining of the Evangelical United Brethren and the Methodists. In 2002, United Methodists could point to over 8.2 million members in their church—the second largest Protestant denomination in the nation. Presbyterians, too, succeeded by 1983 in uniting the northern and southern branches of their church, which had divided before the Civil War over slavery. The Presbyterian Church (U.S.A.) counted 3.4 million adherents in the early twenty-first century, although conservative holdouts maintained separate Presbyterian denominations.

Still, these numbers told a story of decline. The churches had seen larger numbers on their membership rolls. Some thought that the ecumenical movement, by blurring boundaries, encouraged decline; others, that the movement itself was a response to a decline already set in motion—an attempt to make the churches more appealing. Within this context of anxiety over denominational health, the largest effort at church union was the Consultation on Church Union (COCU), begun in 1962 to bring together denominations including the Methodist, Presbyterian, and Episcopalian churches, the United Church of Christ, and the Disciples of Christ. After over a quarter of a century without achieving its goals, however, COCU (which by then stood for the Church of Christ Uniting) began to work for "covenant communion." Member denominations would retain control of their internal affairs but cooperate in clerical ordinations and baptismal services as well as mission, education, and welfare work. With nine denominations participating—including three African American ones—by the mid-1990s, COCU moved slowly. Reconstituted in 2002 as Churches Uniting in Christ, today it still includes nine denominations, three of them black. Meanwhile, other attempts at union were being made between denominations, the most ambitious, by the early twenty-first century, between Episcopalians and Evangelical Lutherans with a goal of full communion between their churches.

Liberal churches continued to signal their commitment to change in other ways. New hymnals in some churches sought to banish sexism and militarism (leaving out hymns like "God of Our Fathers," for example, or "Onward Christian Soldiers"). Formal prayers addressed concerns like Alzheimer's disease patients, people in comas, and the removal of life-support systems. Websites devoted to prayer appeared on the Internet. More controversial than prayer, though, for liberal denominations were matters of race and sex.

Although the civil rights movement was in the most important sense a black revolution, white, as well as black, liberal Protestants did have a role to play. As early as 1952, two years before the United States Supreme Court ordered integration in the nation's public schools, the National Council of Churches declared officially that racial segregation opposed Christian faith. The council continued to support the civil rights struggle in official ways. At the same time, unofficial acts by white liberal Protestants were as important. Members of the clergy marched and allowed themselves to be arrested. They left their congregations to be present in picket lines at distant locations. They took part in sit-ins and in street demonstrations. Their new Social Gospel was politicized, aiming to address law and government. It saw material rescue as not enough and, in some cases, as a perpetuation of an oppressive political and economic system.

By the 1980s and 1990s, however, liberal attention shifted increasingly away from racial matters—in which there had been, at least publicly, consensus—and toward sexual ones, in which consensus proved to be far more difficult. Virtually every liberal denomination struggled over rubrics for sexual behavior in and out of the ministry. Virtually every liberal denomination, too, struggled to come to terms with the "woman" issue. In both cases, the denominations experienced the depths of their own divisions. They encountered strong groups of members who embodied new life-styles and worked with new aims and visions for the future and, opposing them, others who very much disagreed. Battles over sexuality continued into the twenty-first century, challenging mainline denominations as members drew lines in the culture wars. Numerous local congregations joined the Welcoming Church movement to signal their readiness to make gays and lesbians feel at home in their congregations. Meanwhile, the issue of openly gay and lesbian ministers refused to go away. By 2004, it was perhaps best symbolized in the battle that erupted in the Episcopal church over the appointment of a gay bishop. Conservatives in the American church found support from worldwide Anglicanism in their anti-gay stance. Some thought the denomination would break apart.

In the case of women, liberals differed strongly as well. They had long made feminism a major concern, and female members of their denominations had lobbied for change in a general climate that supported their goals. For example, in 1983 the National Council of Churches printed new translations of texts to be used in worship services designed to avoid language they considered sexist. But the ultimate restructuring proved to be that of church community. Doing away with male hegemony meant that women as well as men should rule, and so liberals worked to support the ordination of women in the denominations in which, historically, it had been denied them. For some liberal churches, of course, ordination was not an issue. Congregationalists, Northern Baptists, and Disciples of Christ had all ordained women since the late nineteenth century. Moreover, other denominations—Lutherans, Methodists, and Presbyterians—in the 1920s and 1930s created special lay ministerial structures to support a leadership role for women. By the 1970s, however, a new feminism demanded more. In a sign of the times, the Lutheran Church in America ordained its first female minister in 1970. And in the decision that became symbolic of the ministerial question, the Episcopal church approved the ordination of women as priests in 1976. By 1989 Episcopalians had their first woman bishop in Barbara C. Harris, and a traditionalist wing of the church, incensed at her Massachusetts episcopacy and the ordination of women in general, was moving to organize as a special church within the church. At the same time, in a decision just as significant, Joan Salmon Campbell, a black woman, was elected as moderator of the Presbyterian Church (U.S.A.). In the 1990s and after, continuing gains were registered for women in ministerial leadership. However, even with the number of female seminary students steadily increasing, when women left the seminaries and received ordination, they often served in lesser roles. Typically, they did not pastor churches but worked instead under male pastors or in bureaucratic and educational support services.

Controversy regarding women and sexual orientation fanned out, for the liberal Protestant mainstream, in a variety of directions. Abortion issues and biogenetic engineering, for example, occupied some, even as the general rights of gays and lesbians did still others. But there were numerous areas beyond these in which liberal Protestants continued to struggle to define a Christian stance in the face of rapid cultural change, and in the early twenty-first century liberals were clearly acting on a variety of fronts. Minority rights for Native Americans, for Asian Americans, for Latinos, and for others evoked continuing liberal concern. So, too, did causes and questions such as environmental advocacy, peace efforts, health reform, and relationships to the New Age movement and various other new religious movements, to name only some of the most visible. Moreover, beyond the noise of the war with conservatives—sometimes members of their own denominations—the liberals insisted that their response was not simply a march to the drumbeat of the times but that they looked to the guidance of the gospel to indicate appropriate action in the world. Even so, in liberal Protestant involvement in social and public concerns, the extraordinary had become ordinary. In general, a felt sense of the sacred was hard to find in the midst of the action in the world the liberals preached.

Clearly, the liberal solution to the relationship between Word and world, like the conservative one, was a Reformation legacy. Yet the liberal solution brought to the Reformation heritage a religious sense shaped by *American* history and culture. Here the oneness and manyness of society complicated the relationship between ordinary and extraordinary religion. If liberal Protestantism faced the danger of dissolving its boundaries and merging with American culture-in-general, it also had significantly shaped that culture. The public face of religion in America had long been Protestant, even if dramatic changes were shifting that picture by the early twenty-first century. Liberal Protestantism was still a significant part of the story.

In Overview

The Protestantism that began in the Reformation came a long way in England's Atlantic colonies and then the United States. The sixteenth-century Reformers preached a religion of prophetic protest based on the principles of **scripture alone, justification by grace through faith, the priesthood of all believers**, and **a fellowship of common worshipers**. These teachings of the Reformation brought into being a series of churches in which a subtle individualism combined with a new interest in the preaching of the Word and a call for moral action in the world. As Protestant church buildings became simpler and pulpits more prominent within them, they expressed a cultus and a code that led out of the churches and into public life. Paradoxically, the spirit of Protestantism separated extraordinary from ordinary religion in its emphasis on the gap between God and the material world. But it brought them together in another way in its insistence on a this-worldly ethic.

In England the spirit of Protestantism was reflected in the **Church of England** and, important here, in the **Puritan** movement. With its Calvinist leanings, Puritanism fostered a spirit of still greater reform. New England and (in the loose sense) Virginia were both settled by Puritans, and so was Quaker Pennsylvania. Gradually, other Protestant peoples, the Scotch-Irish, the Germans, and the Dutch among them, became part of colonial society.

With this background, the American **liberal tradition** grew slowly. The colonists accepted pluralism for practical reasons, but tolerance gradually came to be seen as advantageous. Moreover, religious freedom—important for dissenters who sought purity of faith—promoted the growth of still more groups. For many, **Arminian** ideas gradually modified **Calvinism**, while rationalism, moralism, and—by the time of the Revolution—even deism were noticeable. After the Revolutionary War and a time of concern about church membership, Protestant churches thrived, restructuring themselves in light of new needs. For many, an early liberalism meant accepting the value of cooperation. For others, a more intellectual agenda governed liberal choices. In urban eastern Massachusetts, late-eighteenth-century liberal Christians became nineteenth-century **Unitarians**, while their rural relatives turned to **Universalism**. By the late 1830s a new generation of Unitarians had begun to teach the liberal doctrines of **Transcendentalism** and, in many cases, to work for reform of church and world. And by midcentury other Protestant Christians were inspired by the **Christian Romanticism** of figures like Horace Bushnell.

In the Civil War era, increasing pluralism meant more emphasis on earlier liberal themes of tolerance. However, the post–Civil War period and the early twentieth century brought greater challenges to Protestantism from a rapidly changing American society. In general, Protestants either affirmed culture, as in popular **evangelical liberalism**, the **Gospel of Wealth**, and a more intellectual **modernism**; or they partially withdrew from the culture and rejected liberal doctrine, as in **fundamentalism** and the **holiness-pentecostal movement**; or, finally, they sought to transform culture, as in **Social Gospel** activism. By the early twenty-first century, liberalism and conservatism seemed permanent within Protestant life. On their side, liberal Protestants renewed their efforts at interdenominational cooperation and committed themselves to **ecumenism**. Meanwhile, they transformed the Social Gospel to address issues such as the civil rights of African Americans. But the inherited Social Gospel liberal consensus fell away in mainstream denominations when questions regarding sexual orientation, especially for ministers, and appropriate gendered theologies and roles for women came to the fore. The question remained for Protestants whether the success of their version of liberalism had changed it too much into the ordinary religion of present-day American culture.

Boundary questions plagued liberal Protestantism. Conservatives flourished partly because the liberal gospel became less and less clear about what separated Christians from other people of goodwill. More numerous than liberals—and in the early twenty-first century more vigorous than they—evangelical Protestants throughout American history responded to the times out of their own reading of the gospel Word. It turned out that, read by a less liberal set of Protestants, the gospel Word said different things, or at least said them in different ways and underlined a different list of priorities. What the gospel Word said to evangelicals most of all was mission.

Chapter 5

Restoring an Ancient Future: The Protestant Churches and the Mission Mind

Patty Lumsden had grown up Episcopalian. She led a privileged life as the daughter of Captain Lumsden, the largest landowner in a corner of southern Ohio in the early nineteenth century. She seemed aloof, regularly turned down suitors, and wore fine clothes and jewelry. Then one day, even though she had been warned regularly against lower-class Methodist circuit riders, she attended a forest meeting to hear one preach. According to the story, she felt "curiosity" but also "proud hatred" and "quiet defiance." Yet during the preacher's sermon, she took off her earrings and plucked the flowers from her bonnet. With this visible evidence of a radical change of heart, she renounced her former life to embrace the message the minister brought.

Patty Lumsden's conversion to Methodist Christianity occurred only in fiction, in a scene from an 1874 novel by Edward Eggleston. *The Circuit Rider: A Tale of the Heroic Age* chronicled the life of the familiar nineteenth-century itinerant minister known to Methodists and others as the circuit rider. In its own time Eggleston's book was a resounding evangelical success. Its circuit rider was fictional in name but faithfully represented real-life circuit riders of the time. Both Russell Bigelow, who converted Patty Lumsden in fiction, and real-life circuit riders of the era understood the Christian message as mission. That understanding had flourished for centuries before Protestant Christianity was born. As a monotheistic religion—a faith founded on belief in one God—Christianity proclaimed that universal power, meaning, and significance operated out of one sacred center. In more personal terms, the God of Christians created *all* peoples, including non-Christians, and to this God all should therefore turn. So the Christian God was "jealous" in the biblical Old Testament and wanted no other Gods to compete with his claims. In the New Testament, Jesus underlined this divine command in the Great Commission:

"Go ye therefore, and teach all nations, baptizing them in the name of the Father, and of the Son, and of the Holy Ghost" (Matt. 28:19). Those who made their commitment to the creator God through the Word of Jesus would seek to disempower other Gods by bringing all people to the Christian gospel and God.

Protestant Christianity inherited the monotheism and the Great Commission. Still more, to bring its message to people already considered Christian, the Reformers and their followers had to convince them of the deficiencies in the conventional Christianity of the time. True enough, the strictest Calvinist teaching dampened enthusiasm for mission: if God had predestined some to be saved and others to be damned, mission effort seemed almost pointless. Yet however convincing that view might appear in Europe, in America the realities and demands of a new situation altered the equation. Furthermore, the specifically Puritan background of much of American public culture carried the message that Americans, like the Hebrews of old, were a "peculiar" people. Americans, according to this way of thinking, were divinely blessed as God's new chosen people. And for the descendants of the Puritans and those who shared their mental world, divine choice brought duties and obligations. Living in a nation they saw as favored by God, they felt that they had been commanded to occupy the land and to transform its non-Christian inhabitants. As Protestant Christianity adjusted to the American experience, the **mission mind** became a guiding force.

That American experience, as lived by the English and other Europeans, translated an ideology of newness. When Europeans "discovered" their "New World," they felt as if they were walking in the Garden of Eden again. Although, for Indians, the Europeans had invaded an old world and, for Africans, they had created a totalitarian one, Anglo-Protestants and other free people reflected a very different perception. With a sense of new place and time, ideas about reforming the church seemed, to many, to have stopped short. Instead, they embraced newly urgent ideas about the church's **restoration**, aiming to wipe away the effects of time to recover an original and "first-time" vitality. Gone in this vision was change and history, and gone were adjustment, accommodation, development, and acculturation. In the "New World" wilderness, Europeans felt that they could revisit a time when the church was young and strong. Later, the Enlightenment and then the Romantic movement would add to the biblical imagery. Increasingly, stories would feature the origins of humanity and the innocence of the "noble savage," who represented "primitive" or "new" peoples.

But the "paradise" of the mission mind lay not only in the past. It came also in the New Jerusalem prophesied in the New Testament Book of Revelation. According to the predictions of the book as read by Anglo-Protestants and those who agreed, the second coming of Jesus was linked to a new and radically different age. Theological reflection in the United States seemingly never wearied of speculating on the exact sequence of events that would surround the coming of the millennium. So **millennialism** beckoned Americans toward the time to come even as restorationism drew them backward into a past that had been perfect. Pushed and pulled between past and future, Americans found it easy to live in a mental world colored by narratives and ideologies that reinvented former times and reshaped dreams of what lay ahead. Church life reflected these polarities, and the mission mind pointed in both directions and found in them little contradiction.

Mission on the Home Front

Even among people who had grown up in a Protestant culture, missionaries found work to do. Thus, **revivalism** became a practical technique—a tool—for evangelizing large groups. To "evangelize" meant, literally, to "gospel" the masses, to bring them the New Testament Word. Derived from the Greek *euangelion*, an evangel was "good news" and "gospel." The people who brought the gospel became, by the nineteenth century, **evangelicals** in an **evangelical culture**. As heirs to the Puritans, they continued to exalt the Bible and to promote a culture based on it. By teaching the doctrine of the "**new birth**," they also continued to underline the importance of the personal experience of conversion. And conversion led inevitably, for evangelicals, to the task of mission. The mission mind was, in fact, the hallmark of mainstream Protestant evangelicalism, and revivalism became a recurrent feature in American life.

Christianizing Relative, Friend, and Neighbor

For the Puritans, not only people from another town or social group but even friends and neighbors, close relatives and children, became targets for mission enterprise. Preaching became an avenue of outreach to the unconverted. Thus, it was only a matter of time before New England was swept by religious **awakenings**, or revivals. So were the other Atlantic colonies, beginning in some cases even earlier than New England. Economic factors and unsettled conditions influenced Americans, and so did a deep Calvinist sense of sin and the separation anxieties that distance from England created. In this atmosphere, the **First Great Awakening** spread from place to place.

Historian of American revivalism William McLoughlin assigned the years from 1730 to 1760 to the awakening, but its exact time span as a cultural event is difficult to pinpoint. In the Middle Colonies, first stirrings were happening as early as 1726. Then, at Northampton, Massachusetts, in 1734, the preaching of Jonathan Edwards sparked a strong response. People groaned, sobbed, and sometimes fell down physically before what they felt as the power of God. By 1740 the English Methodist evangelist George Whitefield was traveling through the colonies and fanning the sparks of revival into fire. Whitefield and Edwards were this awakening's "stars," memorable preachers who stood out for the character of their work. Thousands claimed conversion, and revival leaders thought their mission a success.

Whitefield brought a communications revolution. With Methodist founder John Wesley (1703–1791), his attempts to reach English factory workers relied on open-air preaching. Freed from the constraints of a church building, people could more spontaneously express their feelings about sin and divine mercy. The fact that the preacher was an **itinerant**, a traveler who moved from place to place, seemed to excite the crowds, too. Besides, the vividness of Whitefield's language as he worked the crowds was cause enough for fame.

Edwards, however, most clearly provided the theological grounding for the new preaching. Bringing basic Calvinism together with the thought of John Locke, Edwards believed that humans learned through their senses. According to this theory, called **sensationalism**, the more strongly a person's senses were affected, the more clearly he or she would understand. Edwards added to the five traditional senses (sight, sound, touch, taste, smell) what he called the "sense of the heart." In his sermons, therefore, he painted striking pictures of, for example, a sinner hanging like a spider by a thread over the abyss of hell. In this way, Edwards thought that he could be a tool to excite in the hearts of his listeners an awareness of their true spiritual condition. Then, he reasoned, if God had so chosen, the sinner would be converted.

Others agreed. Throughout the colonies, from all reports, revival preaching drew a strong emotional response. Probably 30,000 to 40,000 out of a population of about 1 million "fell" and then rose to claim a new birth. The trend continued when, from roughly 1800 to 1830, the **Second Great Awakening** brought new revival techniques and theory. In the East, Yale College became a site for revival under the preaching of Timothy Dwight, the grandson of Edwards. As president of Yale, Dwight conducted services in the college chapel that resulted in the conversion of over a third of the students. Ministers from Yale and other schools to which the revival spread carried its enthusiasm to their congregations in town or countryside.

In the West, the **Great Revival**—as it came to be called—provoked excitement. Often coming from fifty miles or farther, people assembled in huge **camp meetings**. Many times preachers from different denominations—Methodist, Baptist, and Presbyterian the most frequent—spoke at the same meeting. At evening the campground became a sacred space with a raised platform for the preacher in the front, a sinners' "pen" where those overcome with a sense of sinfulness could pray, and behind them space for the rest of the crowd. People publicly acknowledged their failings by their presence in the pen and by other physical signs.

Reports of meetings such as one at Cane Ridge, Kentucky, in 1801 told of people shrieking, crying, and falling into trance. Some could not control their motor functions, and they jerked, danced, or even "barked." Sin, for these believers, meant estrangement from God. But if all the revivals fed on a sense of estrangement, here the reasons for estrangement were multiplied. Away from eastern cities and the comforts of more settled territory, people saw themselves as surrounded by Indians and "wilderness" country and isolated from those they had left behind. It was this sense of separation that mission work was designed to overcome. **Evangelism** became a way to create community, which, preachers hoped, might control what some saw as a dangerous tendency toward religious diversity. Here, too, an important geographical element crept in. Protestant leaders saw controlling the West as part of God's command to his new chosen people. By the mid-nineteenth century Americans were talking about their "manifest destiny" to spread across the continent. The Great Revival in the West signaled, even earlier, the way in which themes of mission, radically new beginning, and expansionism could come together in powerful religious form. Within the mission mind, ordinary and extraordinary religion joined, and—in Christian terms—natural and supernatural goals united.

In both the eastern and western phases of the Second Great Awakening, the stern Calvinism of Edwards's day was giving way to Arminian views. The old doctrine of predestination was all but forgotten, and optimistic understandings of the role that people could play in their own redemption came to the fore. The message was that Jesus had died for all, not merely for the chosen few. And the corollary was that if humans truly desired salvation, the grace of God would find a way to do its work. This meant that missionaries could labor even more actively to convert. The process was demonstrated best in the revival theory and practice of Charles Grandison Finney. Beginning in the mid-1820s, he electrified his congregations in the **Burnt Over District** of upstate New York, so-called because of near-legendary revival fires. Finney later widened his field to preach in eastern cities like Philadelphia and New York, and he eventually moved west to become president and professor of theology at Oberlin College in Ohio.

Finney introduced a series of "**new measures**" that were widely imitated. His speaking style was more direct than that of previous revivalists: he used the second-person-singular "you," stared boldly, and pointed his index finger at individuals. He spoke spontaneously, and he was often theatrical. Finney instituted inquiry meetings and prolonged services late into the night. At these "protracted meetings" he set up an "anxious bench" in the front where, as in the sinners' pens of the camp meetings, people could receive special attention. Sometimes when he preached and prayed out loud, Finney called individuals by name, and he also encouraged spontaneous public prayer. Reports of women praying out loud in public at Finney meetings, as well as other Finney innovations, shocked the eastern establishment. But his new measures were destined to become standard techniques for professional revivalists thereafter. Moreover, theologically Finney's work helped to erode Calvinism further. He taught a doctrine of perfectionism in which, by trusting and dedicating themselves through the Holy Spirit, Christians would be empowered to work for social reform. His ideas became linked to antislavery sentiment, and Oberlin became known for its stand on abolition and for its openness toward other kinds of reform.

Meanwhile, as revivalism moved to the cities, it became more carefully staged and controlled. The old emotional and physical abandon would continue in the holiness and pentecostal movements, but mainstream revivalism itself became more sentimental. This milder form of revivalism became a challenge for mission work. In the new revivalism, revival hymns stressed the joys of heaven and saw it as "home." But how could fervor be maintained without the forbidding image of hell? How could beliefs about the anguish of the sinner and the joy of the convert be maintained if a Calvinist sense of opposites was undercut? The answer came through the greatest technician of a new form of preaching, Dwight L. Moody.

In Moody, urban revivalism had its most successful innovator, and the late nineteenth century its most important revivalist. Unlike earlier revival leaders, Moody was not an ordained minister. In the 1870s and after, he promoted his revivals with shrewd business judgment and dramatic skill. An advance team would precede his arrival in a city, publicizing the revival and generating interest and excitement. At the event itself, the famed gospel singer Ira D. Sankey accompanied Moody, and the two worked closely to ensure the outcome. Moody filled his sermons with Bible stories, anecdotes of home and family, and continuing themes of salvation. Simple, sentimental, and nostalgic, his message urged hearers to a conversion as easy as accepting Christ, and he welcomed his converts into any evangelical church they chose. The Christian life for him was not an initiation into theological abstraction. Instead, bankrolled by wealthy business leaders, Moody created a world of down-home religious comfort that helped to keep urban dwellers content and attached them more firmly to middle-class values. In the crowd of strangers at a revival, hymns and sermons brought decision for Christ, feelings of moral purification, and—in the revival moment—an immediate community based on shared emotion.

Twentieth-century revivalism generally followed the path that Moody charted. Early in the century, William A. (Billy) Sunday—a former baseball player—captivated audiences by mimicking the sport and peppering his sermons liberally with slang. In place after place he preached sermons weaving together themes of fundamentalism and Prohibition (of alcohol) with hostility toward modernists and toward America's German enemies in World War I. Hailing God, home, and motherhood, Sunday declared his patriotism by waving an American flag from his pulpit.

By the time William F. (Billy) Graham began preaching his "crusades" in the second half of the century, with the first large success in Los Angeles in 1947, revivals were becoming more restrained and media-oriented. On into the twenty-first century, Graham used radio, film, and then television to bring people to their "hour of decision." He became the friend of presidents, but was deeply embarrassed when Richard M. Nixon's guilt in the Watergate scandal of the early 1970s became clear. By the 1980s he was speaking out against nuclear war and, until the Persian Gulf War, advocating a peace stand. Graham had begun by preaching that the end of the world was coming soon, entwining mission with millennialism in a familiar American theme. Then in his political middle years his message shifted, as he supported a government establishment based on the belief in the continuance of a strong and thisworldly nation. Finally, Graham's antinuclear advocacy mostly returned him to a transformed version of the initial millennialism. For Graham, the world would end soon unless Americans claimed responsibility.

Evangelical women, like the popular nineteenth-century lay revivalist and holiness teacher Phoebe Palmer made their impact, too, differing in style but similar to evangelical men in aims, methods, and effects. Meanwhile, **pentecostalism** fanned revival fires, and its **Azusa Street revival**, as we will see, outlasted anything that had come before. In the last decade of the twentieth century the "**Toronto Blessing**" brought "holy laughter" to scores of congregations in the United States and to still others internationally. Pentecostal Christians and their charismatic sympathizers claimed the presence of the Holy Spirit in the "blessing." It spread from church to church as visitors returned from the original Canadian congregation where the phenomenon began (a member of the Association of Vineyard Churches, and then, asked to leave, an independent church). A related revival at the Brownsville Assembly of God Church in Pensacola, Florida, helped to spread the revival still more throughout the United States.

Revivals heightened millennial fervor, and they also encouraged the efforts of those who sought to restore the church. But for restorationists and others, revivals were only instruments. Religion for them required more permanent form if it was to maintain its role in American culture. In the end, they felt, the mission mind needed the solidity that organizations give.

Institutionalizing the Mission Mind

By 1790 the new United States had entered a time of rapid development. The population in that year was some 4 million, with one out of every twenty people living west of the Appalachian Mountains. By the time of the Civil War (1861–1865), there were over 30 million people in the country, and about half of them had left the eastern seaboard for new settlements to the west. Church membership, meanwhile, increased ten times from 1800 to 1850, and whereas in 1800 probably only one out of every fifteen persons was a Protestant church member, by 1850 one out of seven belonged to a Protestant church.

A series of **voluntary societies** sprang up during the period—the American Home Missionary Society, the American Bible Society, the American Sunday School Union, the American Tract Society, and other groups that tangibly expressed a commitment to mission. Overwhelmingly, however, the era was a time of **Methodist** expansion. Well over 1 million by 1850, Methodists formed the largest American Protestant congregation, with the Baptists trailing them by some 500,000. They achieved their success for at least two reasons. First, their religious message fit the mood of Americans in the nineteenth century, entwining concern for mission with perfectionism, millennial optimism, and restorationist themes. Second, Methodist organization was well adapted to new conditions on the Anglo-American frontier and also to more settled areas in the East.

Methodist spirituality and worship were attractive. John Wesley, Methodism's founder, used hymns in his services that affirmed the presence of Christ in the eucharist, and he urged Methodists to take communion frequently. Yet Wesley told his American followers that they were at liberty "simply to follow the Scriptures and the Primitive Church." Thus, the formal and elaborate ritual of communion became infrequent, and more intimate and communal love feasts became the rule. The spontaneity of the love feast seemed, to Methodists, to capture more clearly

The Circuit Preacher. This lithograph by A. U. Waud appeared in *Harper's Weekly* in 1867. By that time, the circuit rider had become a national symbol of religion on the Anglo-American frontier, as Edward Eggleston's novel *The Circuit Rider* (1873) also suggests.

the gospel spirit. Moreover, it was a *Protestant* gospel spirit, for the love feast was a banquet of the Word in which first-person testimonies created what Methodists called a "melting time." By sharing their personal spiritual experiences, Methodists encouraged one another.

The very name *Methodist*, however, suggests the importance of organization. Methodists lived by a rule, or method. By 1784, when the Methodist Episcopal Church in America became an independent entity, it acknowledged two superintendents, or—as they later were called—"bishops." Under them and later bishops, the American church was divided into districts. Each district had its presiding elder and, in turn, was carved into circuits, huge areas over which traveling preachers, such as the one who in fiction converted Patty Lumsden, would ride. Preachers aimed to visit Methodists regularly in their far-flung territory. In the interim, each circuit contained local units called classes, visited on occasion by circuit riders but conducting worship largely on their own. They met weekly, prayed, studied scripture, and offered testimony. When they could find one, they turned to a lay exhorter, who would preach and hearten them. In short, the class enabled Methodists to improvise on a biblical base, looking to the church of apostolic times.

Methodist ministers improvised on a biblical base, too, in their conferences. To be "fully connected" meant membership in a general conference, in which early Methodism conducted its ecclesiastical business and also experienced times of revival. General conferences were joined by district and annual ones, so that conferences became, for preachers, as all-encompassing as classes for the laity. Methodists had successfully institutionalized the mission mind, and Methodism became the predominant form of American Protestantism.

The "**Methodist era**" also marked much of Protestantism with its religious style. Here the mission mind took precedence over the legal mind of Calvin and the intellectual discourse of the Puritans. Although the Methodists, Baptists, and other major denominations displayed zeal in founding schools, Protestant Christians moved increasingly away from an intellectual gospel. Mission work instead fostered sentimental piety and religious individualism. Meanwhile, as the "Methodist" style of religion spread among other Protestant groups, the mission mind became allied with millennialism and restorationism.

Such alliances produced a number of new religious groups in Protestant America. Largest among them was the **Disciples of Christ**, even though its founders—calling themselves "Christians"—did not originally intend to start a denomination. These leaders, in fact, drew on previous religious ideas and organizations promoting a return to New Testament Christianity. The ideas were congenial to a new and democratic society that, by cutting its ties with Europe, seemed to be cutting its ties with history. Moreover, restoration ideas seemed to point to a way to begin the millennium, for the early church stood symbolically for the perfection that existed before the passage of time had tarnished it. In this conception, last days and first days were the same: the circle would be complete if Americans could restore the wholeness of the beginning. For then, according to belief, the end could come.

The largest impetus to an organized restorationism came from the two movements that joined to produce the Disciples. Barton W. Stone, who led the first of these movements, became part of a group of revival ministers formally suspended by the Presbyterian Synod of Kentucky in 1803. The group banded together in what they called the Springfield Presbytery, but before ten months had passed they produced "The Last Will and Testament of the Springfield Presbytery." In this document, a landmark of restoration thinking, they officially dissolved their organization to take the Bible as "the only sure guide to heaven." They called themselves "Christians," and they read the Bible as endorsing an Arminian theology and an independent congregational style of church government.

Alexander Campbell, who led the second movement that joined in the Disciples of Christ, had grown up in northern Ireland but in 1809 joined his father, Thomas Campbell, in the United States. In the "Christian Association" that he formed, the elder Campbell announced what became a byword for the later restoration movement: where the scriptures spoke, he and other Christians should speak; where the scriptures were silent, they should be silent, too. Once again, biblical beginnings were being underlined, and the new order was understood as a restoration of the old. Alexander Campbell eagerly embraced his father's views as he became aware of them. A Baptist for a time, he later began to publish a magazine in 1830 called *The Millennial Harbinger*. The title of the new journal is significant, for it showed the link between the recovery of "primitive" Christianity and the coming of the millennium.

Unlike Stone, Campbell was a rationalist, and he had already acquired a reputation for religious debate. Yet he and his movement shared much with the revival-oriented Stonites. Campbell first met Stone during a visit to Kentucky in 1824, and the two leaders noticed their similarities. Despite some differences, the emphasis on restoring the New Testament church, the rejection of creeds as nonscriptural and as obstacles to union, the endorsement of congregational organization—all of these brought them and their followers together in a new church. From 1830 to 1860 Disciple farmer-preachers spread their message, fanning westward from Ohio, Virginia, and Kentucky. At the time of the Civil War, so persuasive had the Disciples become that they numbered 200,000 members.

Meanwhile, **Baptist** farmer-preachers also preached in revivals in the South and West, bringing attachment to the older Calvinistic theology but disdain for seminary education. Not so itinerant as the Methodists, Baptists were also not so organized. Each local Baptist congregation was independent, but groups of congregations came together in regional associations. Missionary work likewise brought Baptists together as they formed societies to advance publishing, educational, reform, and philanthropic goals. Important among them, the American Baptist Home Mission Society came into being in 1832 to help create churches and schools and to evangelize Indians and other unchurched people. Still more, Baptists, like Methodists and other Protestant Christians, founded schools. The roster of Baptist colleges and seminaries with at least partial ties to the pre–Civil War period is long and distinguished, including such present-day universities as Brown, Baylor, Colgate, and the University of Chicago.

Among the Baptists, a "**Landmark**" movement aimed to follow the scriptural admonition to "remove not the ancient landmark, which thy fathers have set" (Prov. 22:28). For these Baptists, the "landmark" meant historic Baptist rejection of other churches and their ministers because they were not considered true representatives of New Testament Christianity. But the new situation that provoked concern for old "landmarks" included the growing religious pluralism of the times, the revival-driven evangelical cooperation of Baptists with other groups, and the formation—dominated by eastern interests—of interdenominational benevolent and missionary societies. By contrast, Landmarkists taught that true churches were structurally identical to the original church of Christ. They were not universal entities spread over the globe. Rather, said the Landmarkists, they were particular manifestations of the church of Christ in a given place and time. On these premises, the Landmark movement grew and flourished throughout the South, becoming during the second half of the nineteenth century the most powerful voice in the Southern Baptist Convention (organized in 1845 in the context of tensions that led to the Civil War).

In a related **antimission movement**, a feature from the 1820s and 1830s of the Calvinist wing of their denomination, Baptists taught strict predestinarian ideas that precluded missionary work because God had already determined who would be saved and who condemned. But, as in Landmarkism, antimission talk provided symbolic expression for fears of loss of local control. Mission opponents worried that new overarching societies, often dominated by easterners, would erode their ability to stand autonomously. Thus, restoration "**primitivism**," especially in the Baptist case, became entangled with the language of antimissionism. Still, antimission rhetoric often cloaked mission concerns. As the nineteenth century progressed, even the most adamant Calvinist faced a religious culture that had softened under the Arminian message. Revivals, after all, were Arminian means, and a revival climate, such as existed on the southern and western frontier, promoted the mission mentality. In these terms, what opposition to missions really meant was conviction that missions should be local efforts directed to one's friends and neighbors.

Moreover, Baptist primitivism was only exaggerating what all Baptists believed. Baptist churches, they thought, were New Testament churches, founded by Christ and removed from the corruptions that had entered Christianity during the fourth century or at other points in Christian history. Equally important, first times were also end times. What happened in New Testament times, they anticipated, would unfold again, and—in a heightened atmosphere of millennial expectation—restoring the true church would inaugurate the new age.

Presbyterians, too, claimed that their denomination had restored the ancient pattern of church government. For them, the combination of individual autonomy and the larger authority of **presbyteries** (district bodies with legal authority) and **synods** (assemblies made up of members of several presbyteries) faithfully followed the New Testament charter. Presbyterians believed as well that they maintained true doctrine, reiterating what the Bible taught for their times. In the years after the Civil War and later, however, other groups became especially strong examples of the mission mind. These groups shared beliefs in **premillennial dispensationalism**.

Premillennial thinking held to the belief that Jesus would come *before* the millennium to begin it. By 1875 premillennialists were preaching their message especially in the form called dispensationalism. Promoted in North America by visiting Briton John Nelson Darby (1800–1882) of the Plymouth Brethren, dispensationalism viewed time in terms of distinct ages, or **dispensations**. During each dispensation, according to Darby and his followers, God changed his ways of dealing with humans. At that very time, they taught, people were living in the era before the second coming of Jesus that would begin the millennial dispensation. The world was growing steadily more evil, the Antichrist would soon control it, and after this period of tribulation, Jesus would return, conquer the Antichrist, and establish his kingdom for 1,000 years. Meanwhile, the members of the true church would, according to scripture, finally meet Jesus in the air (I Thess. 4:15–17), a **Rapture** that dispensationalists said would occur before the Antichrist came. Still more, even though Darbyites also believed that the final events were divinely arranged, they found new work for missionaries.

Perhaps more significant than the exact sequence of predicted events was the emphasis on the literal nature of these beliefs. Paradoxically, people who were antihistory—who preached first times and last times as, essentially, the only meaningful "moments" in time—were insisting on the historicity of what would happen. People who rejected high-church sacraments—in which the material sign was thought to become the literal divine presence it symbolized—were introducing by the back door their own sacramental consciousness in their teaching about a literal Rapture. And people who rejected the magical world of what they saw as non-Christian "superstition" among Indians, blacks, and pagans were reinstating a magical mindset in which natural laws, as currently understood, would be overruled.

Dispensationalist views spread in a series of summer Bible conferences held at Niagara, Ontario, beginning in 1868. Moreover, those who attended also embraced rationalistic study and interpretation of the Bible. They took their ideas from the so-called **Princeton Theology**, the form of biblical interpretation taught by Charles Hodge (1797–1878) and others at Princeton Theological Seminary for the major part of the nineteenth century. Influenced by the new prestige of science during the era, the Princetonians and their dispensationalist admirers saw the Bible as a book of facts. Its "scientific" concreteness, therefore, promoted both literalism and regard for its inerrancy.

Premillennial dispensationalism and Princeton rationalism became two of the major roots of what people, by the 1920s, were calling **fundamentalism**. But beyond these characteristics, an identifiable social style marked fundamentalists. They were militants, and they fought against the modern world—especially the modern world as embraced by other, more liberal Protestants. Shaped also by the revivals and the holiness movement (to be examined later), fundamentalists acted out their flight from modernity in their own sense of the mission to restore.

That mission to restore was evident in the very name *fundamentalist*, used self-consciously by Curtis Lee Laws in a 1920 editorial in a Baptist publication. Laws rejected designations like "Landmarker" or "premillennialist" for those who, he said, still clung to "the great fundamentals." His choice of words was likely enhanced by the continuing success of the twelve small volumes called *The Fundamentals*, published between 1910 and 1915 with the leadership and financial support of the California oil magnate Lyman Stewart and his brother Milton. Since the late nineteenth century, conservative Protestant evangelicals had been expressing their need to restore the "fundamentals" of their faith, to promote in doctrinal terms the quest for purity expressed in restoration views. The short list of fundamentals varied but usually included affirmations of the inerrancy of the scriptures, the divinity of Jesus, his birth from a virgin, his death on the cross in substitution for the sins of all human beings, and his bodily resurrection and imminent second coming.

In this and all the forms the fundamentals took, they brought a new insistence on supernaturalism and on absolute surety. This emphasis was especially clear in the concern that conservative evangelicals expressed for scriptural **inerrancy**. Not only was the Bible verbally inspired, fundamentalists said, in its original "autographs," or manuscripts; the Bible also avoided error in every historical allusion or opinion. Moreover, fundamentalists linked their doctrine of inerrancy to the interpretation of biblical prophecy regarding endtime events. They taught that the world was swiftly worsening and that only the power of Jesus in his second coming could save the elect. So they understood the Bible in terms that for them dissolved difficulties that science and the modern world—and other Protestants who were liberals—presented.

Both the climax and the close of the early period of fundamentalist success came in 1925 with the **Scopes trial**. John T. Scopes had been accused of violating, while teaching biology, a Tennessee law that forbade the teaching of—to quote the statute—"the theory that denies the story of the divine creation of man as taught in the Bible." His trial became famously a forum for expounding fundamentalist and opposing liberal views of the Bible, especially as related to modernity and science. Scopes had certainly violated the law, and on narrow legal grounds the issue was clear. But the American Civil Liberties Union provided his defense, with Clarence Darrow squaring off against fundamentalist champion William Jennings Bryan. Common report had it that the fundamentalists won the battle but lost the war. At any rate, the years following the Scopes trial were times of regrouping and quieter growth for fundamentalists. In yet another quarter, however, the mission mind expressed restorationism. Holiness and pentecostal people, like those in the fundamentalist movement, at least partially rejected the world and disdained the meaningfulness of historical time.

The **holiness-pentecostal** movement had major roots in the Methodist doctrine of Christian perfection taught by John Wesley. It had other roots in the Calvinist theology of sanctification taught at **Keswick**, an English town in which annual religious conferences were held beginning in 1875. Wesley posited two distinct operations of grace: **justification** (at conversion) and **sanctification** (a later experience associated with perfection and freedom from sin). Wesley himself seems to have understood sanctification in progressive terms. Americans, however, increasingly saw sanctification as a distinct state brought by a clearly defined **second-blessing** experience of the Holy Spirit. The quest for such perfection, or **holiness**—both the experience and the state—had attracted many to Methodism earlier in the nineteenth century.

In his revivals, Charles G. Finney also spread a form of perfectionism. Instead of sinlessness, however, Finney taught empowerment in work for Christian social causes. This Finneyite—and Reformed—version of Christian perfection through the Holy Spirit helped to create a climate in which the theology coming from

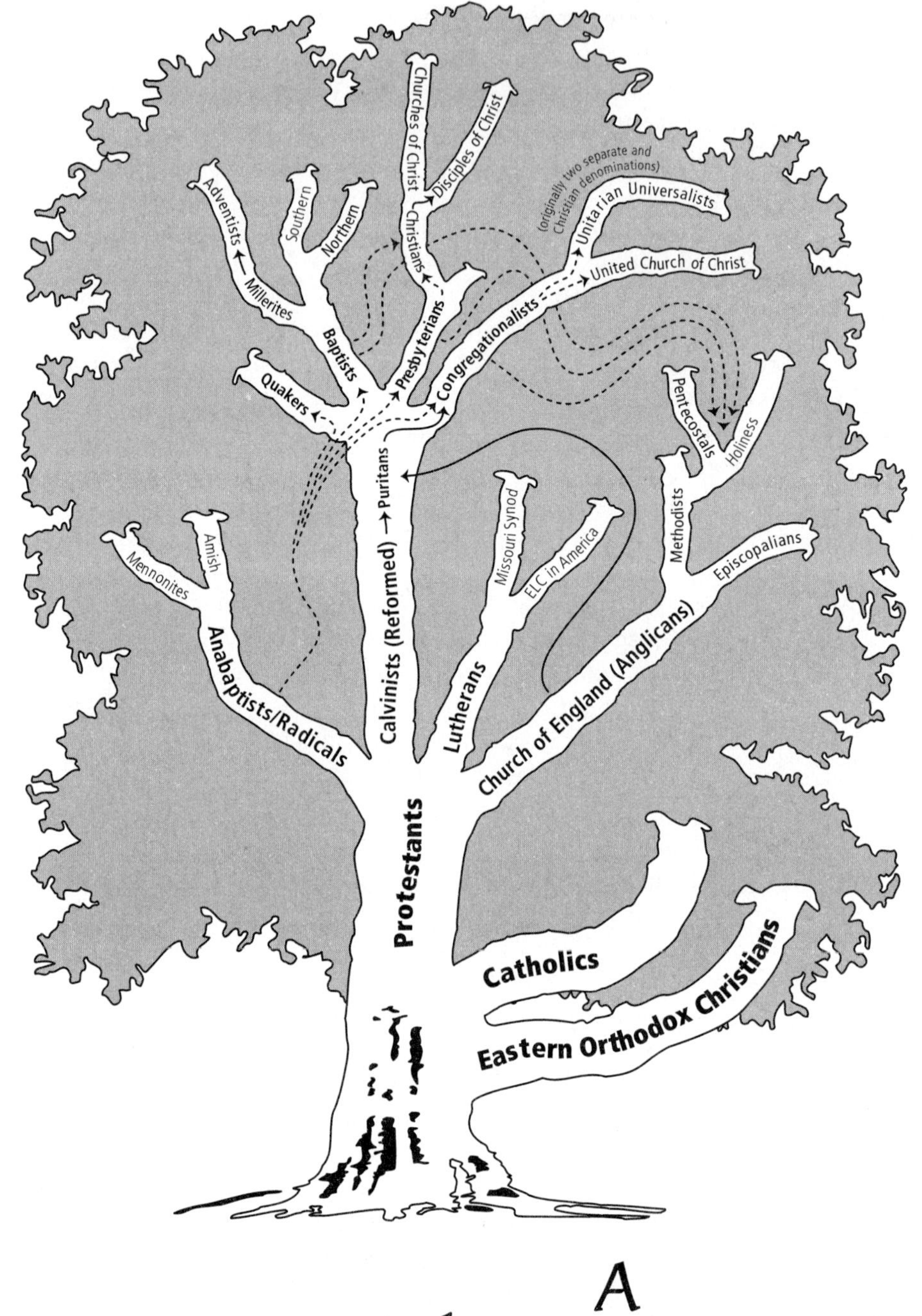

A Christian Tree in America

- Branches are not drawn to scale.
- Broken lines indicate weaker influences.
- Relationships shown are general and do not detail many of the historical changes that lead to present-day denominations and groups.
- Lower branches on the tree separated before the American period; see the text for more details.

Keswick was readily accepted. As the **higher life movement**, or **victorious life movement**, it found a home in Baptist, Congregationalist, and Presbyterian churches. For advocates of these views, sanctification occurred gradually throughout the course of a person's life, and, in a distinct work of grace, the Holy Spirit empowered an individual for Christian service and mission. Premillennial dispensationalism supported these ideas, as some Christians saw in the rise of holiness an event that they associated with the second coming of Jesus. Added to these for pentecostalists was a new theology of **faith healing**. Spread by rising "faith homes" for the sick, this restoration theology agreed with the New Testament that Jesus had made physical as well as spiritual healing possible.

By the last third of the nineteenth century, as many Methodist churches grew more formal and restrained in worship, a holiness revival began. After a holiness camp meeting at Vineland, New Jersey, in 1867, the National Camp Meeting Association for the Promotion of Holiness came into existence. Other holiness organizations followed, and for a while holiness remained within the Methodist church. After increasing tensions, by the 1890s various holiness associations either seceded or were expelled from the Methodist church, and holiness began an independent history. The largest and most well-known denomination that emerged was the Church of the Nazarene.

Pentecostalism was not long in following as an independent movement, too, spurred on by a rediscovered form of New Testament religious experience. Pentecostals took their cue from the New Testament writings of Paul and from the account of the descent of the Holy Spirit as tongues of fire at Pentecost (Acts 2:1–20). They sought to receive the **baptism of the Spirit** with **speaking in tongues** (a form of ecstatic speech) and additional scriptural gifts of prayer, prophecy, and healing. Supported by these signs of God's presence, they felt, they would be ready for the imminent return of Jesus. In the late nineteenth century, there had already been reports of tongues speaking at some holiness meetings. But one definitive moment for the pentecostal revival came in Topeka, Kansas, at the turn of the century. Charles F. Parham (1873–1937), with a background of faith-healing and Holy Spirit beliefs, founded Bethel Bible College. He had already decided that the baptism of the Holy Spirit had as its sign the ability to speak in tongues. Indeed, he thought of the "tongues" as foreign languages, miraculously given to believers so that they could, as missionaries, spread biblical teaching in foreign parts. Students sought the Spirit under Parham's direction until, he claimed, beginning with the century on 1 January 1901, "fire fell," and one of the Bethel students reported speaking in tongues.

However, William J. Seymour (1870–1922), Parham's later student, played a larger role for the spread of pentecostalism in its second definitive moment, the **Azusa Street revival** (1906–1909). An African American preacher, Seymour affirmed total sanctification, miraculous healing through faith, and the restoration of the New Testament gifts of the Holy Spirit as joined to the imminent second coming of Jesus. In the longest continual revival until then in American history, Seymour used a rented hall in Los Angeles that had once been an African

Methodist Episcopal church and later a stable and warehouse. Aided by the anxiety generated by the San Francisco earthquake of 1906 and by newspaper reports, the crowds at the revival grew. Ethiopians and Chinese, Indians and Mexicans, members of various European nationalities, Jews, and African Americans prayed and were mutually convinced of the presence of the Spirit among them. They believed they were living in the power of the first, New Testament, times, and they expected that the second coming of Jesus would be soon.

Pentecostalism grew in denominations like the Church of God in Christ (founded in 1897 and turned pentecostal in 1907); the Church of God in Cleveland, Tennessee (founded perhaps as early as 1902 and formally pentecostal by 1910); the Pentecostal Holiness Church (formed by the merger of holiness sects and Presbyterian bodies until it reached its enduring form in 1915); and the Assemblies of God (an amalgam of various groups that came together as the General Council of the Assemblies of God in 1914). Pentecostalism flourished, too, in the International Church of the Foursquare Gospel (formally incorporated in 1927 in Los Angeles under the leadership of the charismatic Aimee Semple McPherson); in the United Pentecostal Church (officially formed as late as 1945 by so-called "oneness pentecostals" as a non-Trinitarian—"Jesus only"—movement); and in numerous other groups.

Pentecostalism would spread worldwide with more practitioners outside the United States than inside and numbers of adherents that collectively exceeded the membership of the largest single Protestant denomination (the Southern Baptist Convention) by far. In our own times, pentecostals have made vast numbers of converts in the United States and Latin America among formerly Catholic Latinos.

By turning inward for an experience of holiness and for the ecstasy of the Spirit, the holiness-pentecostal movement paralleled fundamentalism in its rejection of Protestant liberalism. Moreover, holiness-pentecostal people took the scripture as literally as the fundamentalists did. Both groups likewise sharply divided extraordinary from ordinary in doctrine (stressed by fundamentalists) or experience (emphasized by holiness-pentecostal people). For both movements as they became institutionalized, the Word continued to speak out against the world. Yet, different from traditional Protestantism, the message led mostly, until recent times, not to public concerns but to private quests for God. Both movements sought to restore scriptural purity to the Christian church, and both saw in restoring the beginning the promise of the end, of the swift return of Jesus. Preferring to live in extraordinary space and time, members of both movements found the need for mission a compelling part of their witness.

Christianizing Nearby Strangers

In these movements and others, the mission mind inspired attempts to convert relatives, friends, and neighbors. But what of the stranger close to home? Was it appropriate for missionaries to work to convert the native people they encountered in North America? Should missionaries turn their resources toward converting African Americans to Christianity?

For Native Americans, attempts at conversion became one expression of the imperialism of various European nation-states. These efforts at conversion took place amidst an extended argument about the human status of Indians. In one expression, as early as 1550 in Valladolid, Spain, Juan Ginés de Sepúlveda and the Dominican Bartolomé de Las Casas sparred verbally over whether the native peoples of North America were by nature slaves or whether they were human beings who were fit subjects for Christianization. Sepúlveda, championing the ancient Greek philosopher Aristotle with his theory of natural slavery, won the debate. In their turn, both French Catholics and English Protestants understood the Indians as savages and therefore as wild and lawless. Indeed, sometimes both understood Indians as even without the capacity for religion. The cultural inferiority of Indians was assumed by English Protestant missionaries as by the missionaries of other European nations. At best, missionaries believed they would "raise" and "elevate" Native Americans with Western civilization and the Christian message. In another version, they would reclaim the Indians as lost American descendants of the ancient tribes of Israel. Or, more cynically, they would stem the tide of barbarity to make North America safe for white representatives of Western culture. Yet the missionaries were also responding to another impulse. The mission mind commanded the conversion of Indians.

English Protestants made it clear that evangelizing the Indians was one of their intentions in colonizing North America. However, the English were slower and less enthusiastic than the Spanish and French in making good on their plans. Even so, at Martha's Vineyard and Nantucket, the Mayhews, beginning with Thomas, Jr., worked among the Algonkian-speaking Indians for well over a century. Thomas Mayhew learned the local Indian dialect, and the work that he began among individual Indians in 1644 led to a regular mission three years later. In seventeenth-century New England, too, John Eliot learned the Massachuset language and began to preach in it, also translating the Bible and other works for Indian converts. Eliot settled fourteen villages of "praying Indians" where the Massachuset underwent a profound cultural transformation, learning to live permanently in towns, to sustain themselves almost completely by agriculture, and to read a Christian catechism.

The First Great Awakening gave new impetus to missionary work. In Lebanon, Connecticut, Eleazar Wheelock established a boarding school for Indians (unpopular among them). Farther south, the Presbyterian David Brainerd and his brother, John, spread Christian teaching among the Delaware. Meanwhile, the Moravian David Zeisberger studied the Iroquois language and later lived and worked among the Delaware for sixty-four years, with numerous literary productions for his Native American converts. As these instances suggest, Protestant missions in British North America were tied to a sense of the importance of the Word. Moreover, Christianizing the Indians fit the postmillennial mood that dominated much of eighteenth- and nineteenth-century Protestant culture. For those who were **postmillennialists**, the concerted efforts of Protestant Christians were needed to bring on the millennium and, at the end of it, the return of Jesus. Working to bring Indians to Christianity would, they believed, help prepare the world for endtime events.

Mission societies—either general ones or others specifically founded to spread Christianity among Native Americans—also supported the work. Meanwhile, the Civilization Fund, established by the United States Congress in 1819 for Indian education projects, distributed federal funds through mission schools. So it was not surprising that **Indian Removal**—the government policy to move Indians west of the Mississippi to make way for white settlement in the Southeast—created controversy among missionaries, who stood on both sides of the question. Entanglement with government continued even after the Civil War, when churches were invited to name individuals who could serve as Indian agents. At that time various denominations actively supervised some seventy-three Indian agencies until, in the 1880s, belated questions were raised about church–state intimacy. By the twentieth century, outright evangelism declined in favor of being available and assisting in need. Missionaries grew more conscious of cultural imperialism and more interested in Indian contributions to Christian renewal. Increasingly, evangelical and pentecostal groups worked as missionaries, even as older denominations seemed less committed.

The mission mind operated in similar ways for African Americans. Biblical restoration and postmillennial anticipation fueled mission efforts. As for the Indians, Anglo-Protestants hesitated before they began serious mission work. Slaveholders provided the first line of resistance. If slaves were converted to Christianity, they asked, would baptism make them equal to their masters? Was it right for children of God to hold other children of God as slaves? Conversely, were blacks less than human, as many thought, and thus without souls that could be saved? Would introducing them to Christianity turn them into worse slaves because they would hear the New Testament message of equality? Or again, would the process of teaching Christianity take too much time away from the slaves' work?

Beginning in 1664 in Maryland, colonial legislatures served notice that conversion to Christianity would not alter a slave's material condition. Meanwhile, missionaries began to urge religious instruction for slaves, pointing to the Christian duty of masters and the advantages of Christianity in producing more well-behaved servants. When the Anglican bishop of London in 1727 wrote a formal letter to urge the conversion of American slaves, he cited "the great value of those servants who are truly religious." Still, missionaries had other motives for converting slaves. New England had seen its first slave baptism in 1641, and before the end of the seventeenth century, American Puritan leader Cotton Mather had found enough support to organize weekly meetings for a Society of Negroes. The same John Eliot who preached to the Indians announced his willingness to preach to blacks if their masters would agree. And more formally, the Church of England's Society for the Propagation of the Gospel in Foreign Parts, founded in 1701, understood its mission to include the evangelization of American slaves.

In the South, however, the Anglican clergy—especially in Maryland and Virginia—had more than slaveholder resistance to hinder them. The vast size of their parishes proved a major deterrent. They also complained of their small numbers, a lack of legal support, and the cultural differences between themselves and the slaves. Indeed, in the end it was African Americans themselves who held the key to their religious future, a story entwined with the rise of evangelical religion.

Baptists and Methodists, and to some extent Presbyterians, brought a revival version of Christianity to African Americans. As among Native Americans, the First Great Awakening helped catalyze a new Protestant mission-mindedness and resulting overtures toward slaves. For a time in the 1780s, white Protestants in the North and upper South created almost a popular Christian trend in freeing their slaves. Perhaps their gesture aided the conversion enterprise. At any rate, by 1793 perhaps one-fourth of all Baptists were black, and by 1797 nearly one-fourth of all Methodists were black as well. Nineteenth-century missionaries proceeded under the evangelical banner as poorer, less educated white preachers communicated their New Testament enthusiasm to black listeners. Some black preachers preached to racially mixed and, on occasion, all-white audiences. Still, by 1820 most African Americans had not been deeply influenced by the Christian message.

Then, as the Methodist and Baptist churches divided into their northern and southern branches in the mid-1840s, concern for converting the slaves grew. The new southern denominations underlined the beneficial effects that Christianization would have on slaves' behavior. Likewise, missions spread westward aided by the growing conviction of slave masters that the missionaries were right. Methodists and Baptists got involved, and Presbyterians, too, expended efforts toward slave conversion. By the eve of the Civil War, missionaries could look to a slave population in which large numbers were at least nominally Christian, although the great majority of the slaves did not belong to churches. Moreover, even before the war, missionary work was proceeding among freed African Americans. After the war, mission concern influenced the national congress to create the Freedmen's Bureau in 1865, with the bureau using the educational services of northern churches and their missionary agencies.

The mission mind had made its compromises in order to encourage work among African Americans. Entanglement with the national government in the Freedmen's Bureau was only one instance. In its southern form, the mission mind had agreed to a consciously one-sided version of the Christian message that stressed obedience to masters, humility before owners, and the like. Still, the missionaries must have said enough about ancient Israel and the bondage of the Jews, on the one hand, and about the return of Jesus and the coming of the millennium, on the other, to inspire the slaves and those newly free. As the next chapter shows, African American Protestants embraced restorationist (here Old Testament restoration) and millennial themes with enthusiasm. Moreover, when, both before and after the Civil War, blacks formed independent churches, restoring first times and preparing for end times continued to be important to them. In the twentieth century, evangelical Christianity became the preferred religion of the majority of African Americans, repeating the concerns of the mission mind.

Missionaries also found strangers close to home among immigrants. Evangelical Protestants saw new people to convert—and to acculturate—among European Catholics and Jews and, by century's end, among religiously diverse East Asians.

Protestant efforts for these immigrants, like those for Native Americans and African Americans, had mixed motives. Even so, evangelicals aimed to restore the gospel in the shadow of the millennium, skipping over history to do so.

Mission to the World

Home missions provided a cultural staging ground for world mission projects. Interdenominational societies widened the influence of evangelical Protestantism beyond the boundaries that individual denominations could reach. Yet even before the appearance of these groups, the demands of Christian empire prompted some evangelical Protestants to look to the world beyond the United States. Many Protestants hotly debated the issue of whether mission on the home front should come before or after mission to the world.

Evangelical tradition finds a beginning for world mission effort in the "haystack prayer meeting" of 1806. In that year, it is said, a chance thunderstorm surprised a group of students at Williams College in Massachusetts during their regular meeting for prayer. The students moved under a haystack for shelter and there pledged their lives to missionary work abroad. Later they formed a society to advance their goals and took as their motto "We can do it if we will," eventually seeking a formal organization to support their work and that of other missionaries.

So, in 1810, began the **American Board of Commissioners for Foreign Missions (ABCFM)**. The board's Congregational base quickly expanded to include Presbyterian and Reformed membership, and, also, American Baptists. By 1814 Baptists formed their own mission board, and it became a strong force within the denomination until Baptists divided over slavery. In this mood of evangelical commitment, Burma as well as India and Ceylon (present-day Sri Lanka) became the main theaters of missionary action during the first half of the nineteenth century. Work extended, too, to Southeast Asia, West Africa, Turkey, Hawaii, and even to a few nations in Latin America. Denominational organizations arose to support these efforts. Among the Methodists a missionary society was established in 1819, while the Episcopalians followed suit two years later. Presbyterian Old Schoolers, in turn, left the ABCFM in 1837 to begin their own organization. More interdenominational cooperation also occurred in this period than in the later years of the century.

The millennial doctrine within the call to mission had already been expressed in the eighteenth-century theology of Jonathan Edwards, who linked Christian cooperation in the work of redemption with the coming of the millennium. By the second half of the nineteenth century, the political doctrine of American "manifest destiny" to rule the continent gave added support to this message. As many understood the doctrine, the United States, through the enlightened government of its democracy, would provide the place for the millennium to begin. As soon as continental expansion was completed, the nation would experience the millennial time. Thus, Edwardsean Calvinism was mostly replaced by the emphasis on human agency that came with the revivals and with the political mood. So it was not surprising that, after the revival of 1857–1858, new organizations for mission work appeared, a number of them begun by women.

In the 1850s and in the shadow of manifest destiny, too, the central terms of a debate between two opposing conceptions of mission emerged clearly. Echoing ideas that had surfaced in missionary work among Indians earlier, the debate would continue into the twentieth century. According to the prevailing position, missionaries needed to westernize, or "civilize," non-Christian populations before they could receive Christian teaching. Now, however, Rufus Anderson, foreign secretary of the ABCFM from 1826 to 1866, challenged that view. He opposed the use of English in mission schools, not to mention the commitment to education itself. Anderson thought it misguided to send specialists in agriculture or medicine or various technologies into the field. Missionaries were there, he believed, to proclaim the biblical message. They would better spend their time preaching and translating the scripture—and letting indigenous peoples control their own churches. As he argued his case, Anderson looked to first-century Christianity as his model. The gospel alone, he said, would perform the work of civilizing. Anderson, in short, was taking a primitivist stand in a foreign-mission context.

The Civil War and its aftermath brought a decline in foreign-mission interest and support. Home-mission work occupied Protestants now, as freed slaves, immigrants, the poor, and alcoholics alternately attracted the attention of the missionaries. After 1880, however, foreign-mission interest showed a decided upswing. Indicative of the mood of many was Josiah Strong's book *Our Country* (1885). The work expressed a doctrine of Protestant responsibility based on theories of "scientific" racism fashionable at the time. In Strong's reading, the Anglo-Saxon "race" (meaning "ethnicity") was inherently superior and so had certain gospel duties. Anglo-Saxons, argued Strong, possessed both the purest form of government (democracy) and the purest form of religion (Christianity). Therefore, they should spread their culture even as they spread their religion.

For foreign missions, the message was that human effort would hasten the millennium and that Jesus would return only *after* Americans had established the gospel. Thus, Strong and many of his contemporaries linked the restoration of gospel purity with self-promoting theories about American cultural superiority. Another kind of missionary restoration was replacing Rufus Anderson's foreign-mission primitivism. In the shadow of Strong and those who agreed, the "civilizers" were often winning the day. Until at least the 1920s, an elite Protestant establishment of postmillennialists led the way in missions.

In their turn, premillennialists—growing with the birth of early fundamentalism—looked to dispensationalist theory to spur foreign-mission work. If the return of Jesus was near, premillennialists believed, they should do all they could, in the short time that remained, to preach to those who had not heard Christian teaching. Some, influenced by Reformed and Keswick ideas, joined postmillennial "civilizers" in their acceptance of social aid as a function of foreign missions. Others, with more individualist views of sanctification and the Christian life in general, moved toward so-called interdenominational "faith missions." Best exemplified by the China Inland Mission, begun in 1865, the **faith mission** employed laymen and single women as missionaries. Without a denominational sponsoring body or the financial support of an interdenominational one, a faith mission relied on prayer rather than formal fund-raising activity. Faith missions, moreover, encouraged missionaries to blend with native cultures, adopting their dress and language although preaching strictly on biblical themes.

The urban revivalist Dwight Moody inspired another major effort. With its beginnings in a summer conference Moody sponsored, by 1888 the **Student Volunteer Movement for Foreign Missions (SVM)** was formally organized. Led by John R. Mott and Robert E. Speer, it aimed at "the evangelization of the world in this generation." The lay-controlled SVM became the dominant mission organization until 1920, sponsoring huge "Quadrennial" conventions that acted as catalysts for mission recruitment and producing materials for mission study endeavors. Mott had ecumenical ideas and chaired the 1910 world missionary conference at Edinburgh (noted in the last chapter). But the division that came between liberal ecumenists and conservative evangelicals after World War I generally did not trouble the SVM earlier. As new mission stations opened, members of the movement considered evangelical success to be evidence that the millennium was coming soon. They generally recognized the evils of uncontrolled imperialism; but they thought, optimistically, that these could be replaced by a more benevolent cultural and spiritual expansionism. Meanwhile, with East Asia replacing South Asia as the most prominent field for mission labor, Japan, Korea, and, particularly, China became familiar mission terrain.

The **Laymen's Missionary Movement (LMM)**, which the SVM indirectly helped to spark, also worked to spread the gospel abroad from the early twentieth century. In so doing, its cultivation of the business community in support of mission efforts was decidedly new. It stressed advertising and public relations, so that capitalism became party to Christian enterprise. Bringing a gospel foundation to foreign lands was good business and worth capital investment, it maintained. Meanwhile, growing numbers of pentecostals sent missionaries abroad, as did other, increasingly self-conscious, conservative evangelicals. Eventually, the Southern Baptist Convention became the largest national supplier of foreign missionaries. At the same time, the proportion of missionaries abroad, outside of North America and Europe, shifted toward greater American dominance. Whereas in 1900 just over one-quarter of world missionaries came from the United States, by 1925 Americans represented nearly half of all foreign missionaries. Yet for all the numerical increase, the theological conviction that had spurred missions in the nineteenth century was, for many, eroding.

Symptomatic of new times and new questions was the report of the Laymen's Foreign Missions Inquiry in 1932, or, as informally known, the **Hocking Report**. The work of William E. Hocking, a Harvard philosopher and a liberal, the report was based on a field survey of missions in South and East Asia. It moved past the civilizing-Christianizing debate to suggest, more controversially, that conversion should not be the goal of foreign missionaries at all. Instead, missionaries should look for those aspects of their own faith that were echoed in the religions of others. Such similarities, argued the report, should be used as means for interfaith cooperation and collaboration.

The Hocking Report did not sit well with most Protestants. Still, mainstream denominations increasingly worked to turn mission stations over to indigenous peoples. For conservative evangelicals, of course, the clear goal of mission effort was conversion, and they often resisted such indigenous control. In the long term, moreover, conservative clarity about intentions, along with liberal ambivalence, was reflected in the changing Protestant foreign-mission establishment. In the mid-1930s, conservatives showed small support for foreign missions considering the commitment they had made. But by 1980 conservative evangelicals had taken over the mission establishment, and missionaries had increasingly gone to new places. In the 1980s the largest mission field had become Latin America, and ironically, Europe had become an important mission field. By this time, what American religious historian William R. Hutchison has called a "three-way division" in missionary thought and operation had happened. A small body of ecumenically minded liberals was far outflanked by members of two other groups, who, in turn, expressed the evangelical mission mind in quite different ways. On one side were those evangelicals, usually affiliated with large agencies, who were open to indigenous control of mission churches and to some social-service work. On the other side was the larger body of conservative missionaries who opposed any but traditional missionary patterns. For the majority of Protestant mission workers who were part of the unaffiliated movement, missionary work should not be compromised by anything that hinted of liberal adaptation.

The presence of liberals and the threat of their policies played a significant role in shaping and catalyzing major aspects of the mission enterprise into the twenty-first century. Liberals, in fact, were "complementary" antagonists, necessary enemies for conservative evangelicals. Without liberals, the historic commitment to mission would most likely have grown weaker. Liberals reminded conservative evangelicals of who they were and of what they stood for. And what conservatives stood for was the mission mind. Led by it, conservative Protestants sought to transform ordinary life into the extraordinary. With mission as the call to stand out and be different, conservatives sought to stop time. They disdained ordinary history in favor of a privileged role at the (for them) extraordinary moment of New Testament beginnings, and they as fervently awaited the millennium. Conservative Protestants argued that they were the true heirs of Puritan forebears, Revolutionary War patriots, and nineteenth-century evangelicals.

In Overview

The churches of mainstream Protestantism had begun in North America with a commitment to evangelical themes and ends. To "**evangelize**" meant to spread the New Testament Word, and the drive to spread knowledge of the Bible was for evangelicals the fruit of a deep personal experience of "**new birth**." Conversion, in short, bred a need to keep converting.

With this commitment providing the basic structure of religious experience, mainstream Protestants built an evangelical culture that by the mid-eighteenth century found primary subjects for conversion close to home. Christianizing relative, friend, and neighbor became the goal of a series of **revivals** that were recurring features of the American religious landscape. Beginning with the preaching of **George Whitefield** and **Jonathan Edwards** in the **First Great Awakening**, revivals brought community and intense individualism, sincere conversion and thoroughgoing hostility. Whitefield's **itinerancy** and **open-air preaching** proved important innovations for later revival technique. Others in the nineteenth century continued to perfect the technique, with **Charles Grandison Finney** pointing to the human role in revivals and employing "protracted meetings" and the "anxious bench." After the Civil War, **Dwight L. Moody** promoted revivals in the cities and adapted big-business practices to ensure success. Meanwhile, revivals were transformed from the earlier intensely emotional and physical experiences of western camp meetings to the relatively restrained gatherings of Moody's urban tabernacles.

Twentieth-century revivalism brought, in some cases—like that of Billy Sunday—histrionic preachers and, in others, an evangelical religion-as-usual. In their turn, **pentecostalists** conducted the most memorable revival until then at **Azusa Street** in Los Angeles. But the revivals were strongly assisted in the work of Christianization by the denominations and the vast network of institutions they built: schools and colleges, publishing houses and periodicals, and voluntary societies for accomplishing evangelical goals.

Among the denominations, the **Methodists** built an organization that gave its name to an era. Methodist circuit riders and conferences, class meetings and love feasts became staples of evangelical culture during the first half of the nineteenth century. Methodist **perfectionism** encouraged human agency in winning others to Christianity and also urged a **restoration** of the New Testament gospel. A series of new denominations, however, took up the restoration theme more explicitly and self-consciously, most prominent among them the **Disciples of Christ**. These New Testament "Christians" looked also to the **millennium**, when they believed Jesus would return, and so they sought to restore the past to prepare the way to the future.

Other older denominations shared the restorationist desire, among them the **Baptists**. In their **Landmark movement**, restorationists became a major force in the Southern Baptist Convention during the second half of the nineteenth century. After the Civil War, **premillennial dispensationalism** bolstered restorationist themes. Dispensationalists awaited the imminent arrival of Jesus and then the final dispensation, or age, of the millennium. But they turned as much to biblical beginnings, with their doctrine of the **inerrancy** of scripture. Moreover, dispensationalism became a leading formative factor in the growth of **fundamentalism** and the **holiness-pentecostal movement**.

Fundamentalism itself formed gradually from sources that included, in addition to dispensationalism, a rationalist Princeton Theology and revival-born ideas and attitudes, including holiness views. By the 1920s fundamentalism had come into its own as a militantly antimodernist movement of Protestant evangelicals. By this time, too, a separate holiness movement had long crystallized from Methodist and Reformed elements, and a series of pentecostal churches had formed, adding to holiness doctrine an experiential emphasis on tongues speaking, faith healing, and other prophetic gifts.

The mainstream mission mind also urged the conversion of "strangers" at home—Native Americans, African Americans, and, by the mid-nineteenth century, immigrants. After initial hesitation about the goal, numbers of missions to convert Indians and blacks were launched with varying degrees of success. Native Americans were slow to convert, and Puritan—and later—missionary efforts were, in general, less than enthusiastic. Among African Americans, initial resistance gave way, but by the eve of the Civil War the great majority of blacks were also not church members. Still, for the numbers of African Americans who belonged to churches, Methodist and Baptist churches were the preferred denominations.

Conversion of the stranger at home led to attempts to convert the stranger abroad. Fed by **cultural expansionism**, mainstream Protestant missionaries began to evangelize other nations. They worried, as they did so, about whether they needed to westernize and, as they understood the matter, "civilize" before they could introduce the Bible. American foreign-mission history stands as a record of that debate. Moreover, as separation between liberals and conservatives grew, evangelical mission work passed largely from liberal hands to conservatives.

However, some Protestants had been happy neither with the ordinary character of American liberal Protestantism nor with the extraordinary manifestations of the evangelical mission mind. Nor, finally, had they been happy with the character of American culture. A nation within the Protestant nation, these people also spilled over its borders, remembering their separate past and wondering if they would also have a separate future. These Americans had African roots, and, like the Indians before them and the Jews, their religion and nationhood closely blended. **African Americans**, like others among the many, had their own religious center.

Chapter 6

Black Center: African American Religion and Nationhood

Toward the end of August 1619, a Dutch ship slipped into harbor at Jamestown, Virginia. On board were at least twenty "Negars," who were sold as indentured servants. Over the next several decades, a slow trickle of human cargo came to Virginia to labor on the tobacco plantations. After 1660 statutes began to acknowledge slavery and set forth conditions of enslavement, and by the end of the seventeenth century, other Africans were pouring into Virginia and the neighboring Maryland colony. To the north, seventeenth-century Puritans also began to engage freely in the slave trade and reap their profits. Almost without thought, the colonies started down the road to the bondage of Africans, a road that would bring 427,000 or more blacks to their land. They continued to import African slaves legally until 1808, when the practice was outlawed and, although some smuggling went on, declined. By around this time, some 1 million blacks lived in the nation, representing some 20 percent of the population. In short, one person in five was black, and African Americans had become a significant group. Whether Euro-Americans liked it or not, blacks would have much to do with the future shape of American religion and culture.

West African Religions

By and large, enslaved Africans came from West Africa and the Congo-Angola region. They included Mandinke, Yoruba, Ibo, Bakongo, Ewe, Fon, and other nations, some of them followers of Islam and many of them practitioners of traditional African religions. Here, in a situation roughly analogous to that of Native American cultures, religious diversity prevailed, with each people possessing its sacred accounts of origins, its Gods, and its ritual and magical practices. Yet underneath the diversity, a common fund of meaning and value existed.

West Africans based their sacred world on a strong sense of **community**, so that no person could live in isolation, either materially or spiritually. Without a sense of sin in the Christian sense, West Africans considered wrongdoing an offense against someone in the community, and upon this ground of relationship, their cultures flourished. Similarly, West Africans felt themselves tied to people from the past. Like a continuous thread, memory linked the living to their dead, and ritual reinforced the memory. Elaborate burial ceremonies included numerous customs, from the preparation of the body to continued periods of mourning at set intervals after death. West Africans believed that the **ancestors** still lived and that they took an interest in their descendants. They might grant fertility and health, or they might punish neglectful kin. As guardians of law and custom, they mediated between the Gods and ordinary people, sometimes becoming Gods themselves as ancestors of entire clan or kinship groups and sometimes, conversely, living on in their descendants.

These beliefs suggest the continuity that West Africans saw with the spirit world. No sharp break separated heaven and earth, and so West Africans found spirit power in the world, which they thought could be tapped for good or ill. At the same time, they acknowledged the existence of the Gods, who were distinguished for West Africans by their extraordinary power. Among them, a **high God** who had created all things was the ultimate force upon which they depended. In West African thinking, however, once this high God had started up the world, generally he did not intervene. Thus, West Africans did not often pay homage in a regular way. They called on God from time to time but did not make him the object of a cultus. God for West Africans was just *there*, a simple and unavoidable fact of life. He did not change history, and no West African would have expected him to prevent slavery.

Other deities, however, got more involved. According to West African belief, while they might once have been among the ancestors, they might also have arisen independently. Associated with natural phenomena like thunder, rain, or animals, these Gods directed the world in its course and brought good and evil to human beings. Meanwhile, various **Tricksters**—hares, spiders, or other small and insignificant creatures (as among Native Americans)—also blurred the West African boundary between sacred and ordinary. West African stories told how they worked chaos, confounded the proud and wise, and introduced the possibility of a new order.

Traditional accounts more generally explained the origins and interrelationships between the Gods and the world. Sometimes, too, these accounts mingled with recollections of the past. Present and past—more than future—were the important moments, and rituals performed to contact the Gods supported memory. **Animal sacrifice** brought gifts of life to honor the Gods. **Divination** employed various techniques to discern their will and intentions. Especially, **music and dance** became vehicles for experiencing communion with them. With the rhythm of drums to set the pace, people danced out their spiritual desire until, in West Africans belief, a God would "mount" the dancer and begin to dance him or her. Possession by a God in West Africa meant the integration of self with the divine, as a boundary between this world and another seemed to dissolve.

Magic of various kinds thrived, as devotees worked to bring extraordinary power to the ordinary world. They used magic to try to heal illness or to inflict harm on an enemy, to bring fertility to nature and to women, or to assure the success of a venture in love or war. So religious expression became part of the ordinary business of living. People usually turned in worship to a God who had been honored by their parents, and they saw intermediary Gods not simply as otherworldly beings but as practical go-betweens who could lend assistance in ordinary concerns.

New Land, New Religion

With their capture and enslavement, many West Africans found themselves uprooted and systematically deprived of their kin, their culture, and their Gods. As a business, the slave trade transformed human beings into marketable commodities, and so during the middle passage between African ports and American destinations, blacks were deliberately isolated from those who came from their community or spoke their language. Without support, slavers reasoned, an African would be unlikely to plot a revolt. He or she would be forced to become docile, depending for survival on what little the captors provided. Under this brutal system, many Africans died in the holds of ships, and those who managed to survive became slaves under a law code that deprived them of basic human rights. Unlike slavery in West Africa, where captives from enemy societies could inherit property and contract marriage, blacks who came to the English colonies in North America could do neither.

Yet legal fiction could never hide the fact that the slaves were people. More than that, they were *a* people who, although they had often been warring enemies in Africa, had also been very much alike. They shared a basic view of life and the relationship of the Gods to the human condition. They spoke for the most part dialects—although not easily translatable into one another—of perhaps two major languages. So there was much that enslaved American blacks could mutually affirm. Their fundamental ways of looking at religion and at life had been and would remain similar. Their common experience of servitude would give them another and different set of bonds to share.

African American religion was built on pieces of a common African past, reconstructed in a new situation. It was built, too, on the experiences that the slaves endured in America, mixing their sense of involuntary presence into their religion. And finally, it was built with materials that came to the slaves from the Christian tradition, the religion of their new masters. Together, these three sources—the **West African background**, the **condition of slavery** in the present, and the **language of European Christianity**—provided the elements for a religion to fit the conditions of a distinct people in a new land.

From West Africa, blacks kept customs and practices that had become habitual. But West Africans also kept their internal way of looking at the world. Most fundamentally, they continued to see life in terms of a blend of extraordinary and ordinary worlds. The old African Tricksters continued to be present in a new set of tales the slaves told about figures like **Brer Rabbit**. Small and insignificant, like the hare of Africa, he outsmarted the great and powerful, showing that his cunning matched any animal's strength. Brer Rabbit and his animal friends gave blacks a way to express their hostilities and to celebrate the triumph of the weak (like slaves) over the strong (like masters). At the same time, the new animal tales contained the same religious philosophy as the West African tales—that chaos was the source of creativity and that, by upsetting the standing order with his antics, Brer Rabbit was restoring the situation, making the world vigorous again.

Similarly, the practice of **conjure**, which flourished among the slaves, revealed West African ideas. Here, under the guidance of a **root doctor**—in many ways like a West African priest-healer—spells were cast and healing practice went on. Conjure aimed to bring extraordinary power to the ordinary details of life. Its magic was believed to kill or cure, work love or create havoc. Using herbs and other natural substances (and sometimes manufactured goods), **root work** typically employed a **conjure bag** intended for some one person, who would knowingly or unknowingly touch it and so be affected in dramatic ways. In their attachment to conjure, African Americans were expressing their belief—like that of the New England Puritans—that nothing just "happened"; everything had its spiritual cause and cure. Disease, for example, was often considered the work of an indwelling evil spirit or of the spell cast by an enemy's malice. Attributed to extraordinary causes, thus, illness had to be healed by specialists in the extraordinary—in America most often women, who combined their work as midwives and herbalists with their knowledge of spells and magical practice.

Frequently called **hoodoo**, conjure by this name revealed its connections with the religion of **voodoo**, which grew especially among blacks in New Orleans. By 1850 voodoo was at its height in the city, and its influence was spreading in Louisiana and other parts of the South. Based on *vodun* or *vodou*, a Dahomean (West African) religion that flourished in new form in Saint-Domingue (Haiti) and other parts of the French West Indies, voodoo had been present in French Louisiana since its early days, when blacks had come from the Indies. But after the Haitian Revolution of 1804, numbers of new blacks from the West Indies entered New Orleans, many of them with French masters fleeing from the victorious black regime. The influx of these **Afro-Caribbeans** succeeded in making New Orleans the center of voodoo in the United States.

As a system of worship, voodoo made use of drums and dance, song and possession. With priests and, more often, priestesses presiding over its ceremonies, it provided a ritual context in which the West African theology of personal transformation under the felt power of a God could be lived out. In the cultural mix reflected in the ceremonies were elements derived from Roman

Catholic worship, such as altars, candles, and prayers to the Virgin Mary. But as in the West Indies, Catholic elements expressed West African or African American religious meanings.

In places where voodoo never completely reached and in times after voodoo had declined, root work, or hoodoo—the magical and healing practices associated with it—continued in the South and even the North. As in voodoo, hoodoo contained distinctly Christian elements. Sometimes a Christian minister also functioned as a conjure man. Other times the Bible became a "conjure book" for divination. Conjurers and their clients could work to cast spells by praying, or they could speak in tongues while conjuring. As among Native Americans and many others, religious combinations flourished. By the twentieth century, significant religious combining of African and Christian elements marked a series of thriving movements among both American-born blacks and Afro-Caribbean immigrants. And even when African Americans turned more or less exclusively to Christianity, they brought to it, often without taking notice, their prior heritage.

Black Christianity

In Louisiana and in Maryland some blacks became Catholics. Significantly, French Catholics had settled Louisiana, and English ones Maryland. Moreover, although Catholic ritual formality deterred the trance behavior of West African religions, the sacramental character of Catholicism, with its use of material elements, proved attractive. So, too, did the saints, who functioned as intermediaries with God in much the same way as the many specific Gods of West Africa interacted with the high God. So Catholicism enjoyed a modest and continuing presence among blacks, even if African American Catholics were a small fraction of the total black population.

By contrast, the majority of African Americans embraced American Protestantism and then changed it to express their own past history and present situation. In the process of doing so, African Americans grew in a sense of inner autonomy and developed a conviction of separate peoplehood. Both carried them through slavery and continued to support them through emancipation. As in West Africa, blacks who were now African American Protestants looked to a religion of affirmation in the present, even when the present involved suffering.

The most important factor in the Christianization of the slaves was their own decision—not the racism and fear of slaveholders or the practical difficulties of missionaries. Initially, blacks clearly expressed indifference to the Anglican missionaries' literary model of religion. They disdained the emphasis on catechetical schools, the reading of the Bible and the *Book of Common Prayer,* and the mastery of Christian doctrine. As Anglicans gave way before an army of Methodist and Baptist preachers, however, blacks found the new form of Christianity more attractive. By 1760 the conversion of blacks to the new religion had become noticeable, and throughout the pre–Civil War years, the spread of Christianity among the slaves increased. However, two different forms of Christianity characterized the world of the slaves.

First and most visibly, white masters promoted an official Christianity for slave consumption, stressing humility, obedience, and "good" behavior. They encouraged special plantation missions to bring slaves into the church, even though these missions were never large-scale and they hardly reached all the slaves. Second and more powerful for blacks, however, was the Christianity that they directed for themselves.

The Invisible Institution

This second form of Christianity among the slaves has often been called the "**invisible institution**"—a church or churches without membership rolls, ordained pastors, official meeting places, or approved ceremonies. The invisible institution had begun under the eyes of the masters when they sometimes permitted their slaves to hold separate services in a local church or chapel. But after about 1830 to 1835, slave revolts based on prophetic and apocalyptic ideas among the slaves—like the one in Virginia led by **Nat Turner** in 1831—frightened the owner class. New laws prohibited religious services held by slaves without white supervision. So the invisible institution became the religion of a double blackness, carried on in the shadows and under cover of the night, always in danger of punishment so severe that it might mean the death of a slave. Yet the invisible institution made the slaves more intensely a community: it brought blacks together as a people, a nation within the nation.

Centering on prayer and worship, the invisible institution created sacred space and time in which members of the slave community could express their religious ideas and sentiments. On some plantations, blacks could go to a **praise house**, a special chapel constructed for their needs, where regular services, prayer sessions, witnessings, and the like occurred. But most of the time and especially after 1831, blacks held meetings in the woods at evening, secret sessions in the cabin of one of the slaves, or even spontaneous hymn sings. Wherever they made their places for prayer, or "**hush harbors**," black people raised their prayer in whispers and song in the quietest tones. They stationed lookouts, and they often overturned a huge pot or kettle because the slaves believed it helped to contain sound. If someone began to shout in religious excitement, the others quickly silenced the devotee.

Just as blacks found sacred space in the hush harbors, they found sacred time in the rituals that marked significant moments during each one's lifetime and in the distinctive happenings called conversions. They found it, too, through the words of their preachers and the melodies of the **spirituals**. Both words and melodies became art forms. A sermon was said to be "spiritual" to distinguish it from a more learned style of preaching delivered from a prepared manuscript. If the preacher was "in the spirit," he would begin by quoting a text from scripture. But as the text worked itself out, he would begin to chant at a swifter and swifter pace, using repetition and association to construct the lines. His chant became an unrhymed poem, with a rough and breathy sound at the end of each line to mark the rhythm. Meanwhile, the congregation became active, humming rhythmically and interrupting the preacher with shouts. Finally, together preacher and people broke into song.

The rhythm of the spirituals kept time beside the chanted sermons. With words and thematic content based on the Bible, their melodies had developed over the years, probably through a blending of West African and Protestant musical forms. The spirituals could be sung anywhere, but they were above all *communal* songs, meant to create intense experiences of sacred presence and unity with one another. At intentional prayer meetings, they were songs in motion, accompanied by hand clapping and head tossing, by cries and moans, and by a form of sacred dancing called the **ring shout**. In the largely West African ritual, a leader lined out verses while a group of others, called shouters, moved around in a circle. Singers who stood outside the circle gave out the chorus, at the same time tapping their feet and clapping their hands in support. With a shuffling step, the inner circle moved quickly to the beat set by the singers and shouted the sounds, sometimes all night long, that gave the ring shout its name.

Always, the spirituals showed spontaneity and flexibility, so that they could express the moods of various members of the group. Often someone particularly depressed could be heartened by these songs, in which words could be invented to suit the situation. Often, too, words and choruses could carry double meanings, so that even as the slaves sang of spiritual freedom in the other world, they also expressed their yearning for physical freedom in this one. "Go down Moses . . . Tell old Pharaoh / To let my people go," sang one spiritual—so clear in its allusions to the slave situation that it was reportedly censored. Sometimes the spirituals could even provide a code language for plots to escape on the "underground railroad" to the North or to Canada. "I am bound for the land of Canaan" might be a revealing signal.

Chanted sermons and spirituals based black people in a community of prayer from which they drew support. That same community was also sensitive to the cycle of each member's lifetime. For example, at baptism both preacher and people participated, the preacher to do the immersing in a stream or pond and the people to give support with their spirituals and shouts. At marriage—a doubtful proposition, often broken by the sale of one of the partners—the ceremony in the presence of the community affirmed the integrity of the partners despite the situation. Most often, the couple jumped over a broomstick either together or in sequence, and sometimes a preacher presided. At death, in a solemn ceremony, often held at night, people typically carried pine knots as torches and moved together to the burial site, singing spirituals along the way. At the grave, the preacher offered prayers, a post marked the location, and—in a custom brought from Africa—people deposited old belongings and broken earthen pots, suggestive of the spirit that had broken away. A sermon usually came sometime later, sometimes a collective one for all who had died in a given period. As in Africa, death meant the cultivation of remembrance.

Appliqué quilt, Athens, Georgia. Constructed by former slave Harriet Powers, this quilt (1895–1898) was pieced together from dyed and printed swatches of cotton, with gilt embroidery added. Thematically, biblical stories were joined to astronomy and local lore, suggesting the combinativeness of African American religion.

Behind these events lay the prior experience of individual conversion. Here, African Americans thought of God as a "time-God," who acted when he would. So the idea of waiting on God was built into religious culture. Many accounts of conversion stressed the action of an arbitrary God who worked according to whim rather than logic. Often highly visionary, these accounts began with a person's experience of "getting awfully heavy" with the felt burden of sin. Conviction of sin was reinforced, for example, by visions in which a little man conducted a tour of hell. Crying for mercy and feeling hopeless in the situation, the soon-convert claimed rescue by the mercy of God. A vision of the Almighty on his throne or of the heavenly regions filled with angelic choruses might accompany this experience. Frequently, colors of white and gold predominated in these visionary landscapes, along with the green of country. Jesus might be white with golden hair, his outstretched hand gleaming. His message, though, transcended the visual language in which it was cast: it was a message of relief and salvation. The convert felt surrounded by the grace of God and able to overcome all obstacles. Shouting with joy, according to accounts, the new convert rushed to tell others.

In the experience, God had acted as the Master; he controlled the slave-convert by his will and acted in his own time; he was white or dressed in white; and he presided over a heaven that resembled a giant plantation. Yet, precisely by imaging God in these terms, a slave-convert relativized the human condition of bondage, and the earthly fiction of slavery was decisively modified in the face of the belief in divine ownership. Conversion narratives also expressed West African religious ideas. In them, as in Africa, God transformed a person, even physically, without changing the social or historical situation. As in Africa, too, freedom seemed to many a kind of magical flight through visionary experience. Finally, African Americans wove in Protestantism by their choice of language about Israel and the exodus from Egypt. Just as the biblical nation of the Hebrews had been slaves in ancient Egypt, so the slaves saw themselves leading lives of bondage in the American Egypt. But just as, in the Bible, Israel had reached freedom by the power of God and the staff of Moses, so, too, they believed they would one day be free by the power of Jesus and, at the time of the Civil War, the hand of Abraham Lincoln. In a world in which ordinary and extraordinary were felt as one continuous reality, these beliefs did not seem incongruous.

The Black Church in Freedom

Formal denominations had begun among free blacks in the North by the end of the eighteenth century, although it would be nearly a century later before the church would be autonomous in both the North and South. While not all African American religion took place in the black church, from the first, church organizations provided a vehicle for religious and even political expression. It was no surprise, therefore, that later the leadership for the black civil rights movement would come largely from the church.

As early as 1787 **Richard Allen** (1760–1831) and **Absalom Jones** (1746–1818) founded the Free African Society in Philadelphia, a nondenominational religious society and mutual aid organization. Then, in a story that has become near legendary, in the early 1790s Jones was pulled from his knees while praying in a gallery section closed to blacks in a Philadelphia Methodist church. The insistence on segregated seating showed the limits of Methodist toleration, and the incident catalyzed the Free African Society to raise the funds for an African American church. This was Jones's new Church of St. Thomas (Episcopal). Allen, however, chose to remain Methodist, and his Bethel African Church was dedicated by Methodist Bishop Francis Asbury. Then, by 1816, Allen's movement took on a more formal character when a number of churches came together as the **African Methodist (Episcopal) Church**. Meanwhile, in New York **Peter Williams, Sr.** (1760?–1834?), left a white Methodist church at the head of a group of blacks and founded the Zion Church. By 1821 it, too, was organizing as a national church, and in 1848 its official name became the **African Methodist Episcopal Zion Church**.

In the South, before the changes of the 1830s, Baptist congregations expressed particular openness to the independence of African American churches. Because of the nature of Baptist governance, separate black churches had enjoyed some freedom, and black committees within white churches had worked with church members who were black. Even after the enforcement of restrictions in the era of slave revolts, some African American churches managed to survive. For example, in 1845 the Baptist Sunbury Association of Georgia had seven black churches with, among them, four ordained preachers. Earlier, in 1821, the black Gillfield Baptist Church in Petersburg, Virginia, could boast of 441 members. Separate black Baptist churches existed throughout the Southeast and as far west as Kentucky and Louisiana. Sometimes they succeeded in wielding considerable authority despite the efforts of white associations to limit or even disband them.

After the Civil War, the African American church came into its own, with blacks overwhelmingly **Methodists** and **Baptists**. Both the African Methodist Episcopal Church and the African Methodist Episcopal Zion Church sent missionaries to the South, where they gained many converts among the newly freed blacks. At the same time, a series of independent black church organizations incorporated themselves, separating legally from mainstream Protestant churches. Meanwhile, thousands of other blacks continued to worship in congregations organized under the white Methodist and Baptist denominations. It was through these churches that African Americans had fashioned their own religious expression, and their loyalty to these churches continued in the decades following emancipation and after.

Problems and tensions accompanied the new church organizations. Some in the more traditional black churches made an issue of decorum. With middle-class aspirations and values, they were often former house slaves (or their descendants), who had worked close to their masters in a two-class system of plantation slavery. In the new situation the spirituals, for example, offended them. They were upset, too, by a permissive sexual ethic that prevailed among numbers of free blacks and wanted instead a firm commitment to Victorian morality. The majority, however—mostly former field slaves or their children—had lived on the plantations without close contact with whites. Now they felt alienated by the "airs" of the would-be middle class. More than that, they sought a church where they could feel at home in a confusing and often hostile world. Like many white Protestants from a similar socioeconomic background, they wanted a religion of the Word—but a Word that could be felt and expressed intensely.

Despite the difficulties, the black churches succeeded. They became schools in responsibility and community leadership, and their membership swelled. As the nineteenth century drew to a close, at least one-third of all American blacks were church members, with numbers reaching to some 3 million—a striking contrast to a century before, when only 4 or 5 percent had been within the church. Black churches got involved, too, in education, supporting universities and seminaries. They helped to organize benevolent societies for mutual aid, and in addition to these "sickness and burial" societies, they cooperated in forming fraternal organizations such as the Knights of Liberty and the Grand United Order of True Reformers. In short, they surrounded the members of their congregations with spiritual and material assistance in a world in which they were learning the ambiguities of legal freedom.

Black Religion in the Twentieth Century and After

The new century dawned with a huge migration from southern farms to cities in both the North and the South. Whereas 75 percent of African Americans lived in the rural South before 1900, by the last third of the twentieth century three-quarters of them were city dwellers, and half of all blacks lived in northern cities. Meanwhile, African American nationalistic hopes were expressed in a series of movements, from the back-to-Africa strategy of Marcus Garvey to an intellectual trend called black theology.

In the northern industrial cities where blacks arrived, feelings of rootlessness and alienation troubled many. Sociological divisions became more pronounced, and upper, middle, and lower classes more clearly defined. Types of church organization and worship style increased, too. Like Jews and Catholics, the upwardly mobile among African Americans felt the pull of mainstream Protestantism. Meanwhile, separate African Baptist and Methodist churches flourished among the middle class, independent yet conforming to the style of mainline Protestant churches. Among poorer people, the new holiness and pentecostal movements attracted some, a series of smaller movements in northern cities drew others, and, by the late twentieth century, **Afro-Caribbean immigrants** brought distinctive religious forms to urban centers north and south. Yet nearly two-thirds of African American church members counted themselves Baptists, and almost a quarter identified as Methodist.

The Holiness-Pentecostal Movement

African Americans were prominent in the formation and growth of holiness churches and, as we saw, they played a crucial role in the beginnings of pentecostalism. With their stress on the felt presence of the Spirit, **holiness-pentecostal churches** appealed to African Americans who wanted an experience of ecstasy within a small, supportive community. They cultivated a familiar style of preaching. They transformed the spirituals in a new development called **gospel music**, which combined the spirituals with blues and jazz and also incorporated drums and tambourines. And they encouraged the work of healing—something familiar to blacks from the long tradition of root work and conjure. At the same time, these churches taught perfection—holiness—and demanded from their followers a disciplined and sanctified life. In this way, they provided a structure to guide people in the midst of unfamiliar urban settings. Still more, many of the holiness-pentecostal churches thought of Jesus as a black man, and as they did so, they expressed a regard for blackness in itself. From its beginnings in these churches, this new esteem for blackness began the process of transforming African American religion.

Denominations proliferated among the holiness-pentecostal churches. Notable among them, the **Church of God in Christ** originated in a cotton-gin house in Lexington, Mississippi, and later incorporated in Memphis, Tennessee. Its founder, **Charles H. Mason** (1866–1961), had gone from holiness to pentecostalism and in the process become a legend in his time, with many white pentecostalists seeking ordination at his hands. His reorganized (pentecostal) church spread not only in the United States but also throughout the world. It claimed close to 5.5 million American members alone by 1991—the last date that it reported—making it the single largest pentecostal church in the nation.

Combination and Creation in New Religious Movements

Meanwhile, thousands of new and indigenous urban religious groups sprang up in storefronts and local residences. Many were influenced by voodoo and spiritualism (discussed in Chapter 8), and, in general, their "spirit-filled" leaders were come-outers from more established churches. They often proclaimed a revelation that departed in major ways from tradition. With a charismatic leader and a new revelation, the religious group that grew up, though relatively small, was clearly distinguishable. Moreover, it often fostered intense religious experience through distinctive spiritual practices. Different from a denomination, the new **spiritual practice group** did not see itself as part of a larger religious body. Different, too, from a sect (as we will see in the next chapter), the spiritual practice group was smaller and religiously more radical. But like a sect, the group did enforce its boundaries, providing an antidote for the facelessness of city life. In its supportive cultural system members could fuse extraordinary and ordinary religion, seemingly for every need.

A good example of a charismatic leader and his successful group is **Father Divine** (1879–1965) and his **Peace Mission Movement**. Born as George Baker, Jr., and silent later about his past, M. J. Divine found nurture in storefront churches in Baltimore, became acquainted with Methodism and Catholicism there, drew close to the mind-cure and prosperity thinking of New Thought in the Unity School of Christianity, and experienced pentecost at Azusa Street. For a time he functioned as part of a religious triumvirate in which he called himself the "Messenger," God in the degree of Sonship. Then, striking out on his own, Father Divine traveled in the South, teaching a blend of mysticism and practicality in which, if a person were truly identified with God, health and plenty would result.

Grounded in this spirituality, he made his way north, started a religious community, and moved to an eight-room house in Sayville, Long Island, in 1919. So began a long era during which Father Divine presided over a community of devoted followers whose lives, they claimed, were transformed. In keeping with both holiness and New Thought, Father Divine banned drugs, tobacco, and alcohol, and he demanded a disciplined life-style among members. His hospitality and generosity became legendary, as members of the Peace Mission sat around a laden banquet table. In its unspoken theology, if the Father who was also Messiah were present, there ought to be a messianic banquet; and Father Divine did not deny the conclusion that he was God. The belief flowed naturally from holiness religion, in which, in the enthusiasm of worship, a person could feel seized and taken over by God and, so, literally, one with God. According to some, Father Divine even claimed that he would not die and also held that if a follower were genuinely devout, he or she, too, would neither grow sick nor die.

Preaching the doctrine of peace on earth, offering food and shelter at a nominal price, and helping blacks to find employment, often by encouraging the creation of cooperative businesses, Father Divine opened his doors to white followers, too. When, after his first wife died, he married Edna Rose Ritchings, a white Canadian woman, he became an example of black-white unity. Indeed, after his death, it was Mother Divine who continued the movement from its headquarters in Philadelphia, where it had been relocated in 1941.

For Father Divine's followers and many other groups, the satisfaction of material needs flowed from union with God. The link between ordinary and extraordinary religion seemed omnipresent for all of them. So, too, did religious combination. For example, the **Spiritual churches of New Orleans** from the 1920s have held services with a holiness-pentecostal style in order to communicate with spirits—in sanctuaries adorned with statues of Catholic saints and the Native American Black Hawk. Prophecy and healing have flourished, women have dominated the leadership, and there are elements, as well, derived from voodoo. By the late twentieth century, noticeable examples of religious combination were coming from Afro-Caribbean groups in cities like New York, Atlanta, and Miami.

In one major instance, Haitian immigrants have practiced forms of **vodou** distinct from the New Orleans variety called voodoo in the United States. Based on extended family networks, already in Haiti vodou moved from rural to urban space. In New York and other American cities, increasingly women have headed vodou house-temples. Here, in supportive environments, devotees honor ancient African Gods as spirit powers called *lwa,* whom they identify with Catholic saints. They develop a sense of close relationship with one or more of the lwa, and, as initiates, they seek experiences of trance possession in which, within the ritual, the lwa will take over their bodies. The "family" that an initiate joins is now no longer made up totally of blood kin, but—with the word *vodou* roughly meaning "spirit"—the family has become, appropriately enough, spiritual. Spiritual families, though, provide nurturing communities for the resolution of material concerns. Healing work—for bodies and for relationships—goes on in the temples, and so do quests for money, jobs, the untangling of legal difficulties, and the like. Combining matter and spirit, African religion and Christian forms, rural memories and urban life, vodou practitioners frequently also combine their initiatory practice with membership, especially, in the Catholic church.

A similar combinativeness has characterized Afro-Cuban **santería**, or the "way of the saints." A nineteenth-century religion that developed among Yoruba people enslaved in Cuba, santería came to the United States with Cuban exiles after the revolution of 1959. Ritual practice centers on devotion to Yoruba *orishas*, whom believers connect to Catholic saints—with both seen as manifestations of the same underlying spirit entities. Initiated priests or priestesses (*santeros*) preside in a religion that is African in its regard for ancestors, its cultivation of personal relationship with the orishas, and its sense of the ritual community as a spiritual family. Practicing divination with shells and palm nuts (to seek guidance), animal sacrifice, and spirit communication, those who follow santería believe they attain the highest engagement with the orishas through their own initiation, in a near-mystical bond between devotee and orisha. Especially in Miami and New York, small retail stores called **botánicas** sell ritual materials and herbs for the ceremonies, with new devotees coming from among Puerto Ricans and American-born blacks. As in vodou, song, dance, and spirit possession have marked santería, along with a sense of the closeness of divine forces, and a sense, too, of empowerment with spiritual insight and material success.

The Religion of Blackness

Both home-made groups (like Father Divine's Peace Mission Movement) and immigrant ones (like those engaged in Haitian vodou and Cuban santería) echoed holiness religion in their encouragement of intense experience, altered states of mind, and spiritual healing. Echoing holiness-pentecostal religion again, African Americans by the twentieth century began to forget the plantation past with its white God and to look to a God who preferred **blackness**. In so doing, they combined their sense of the sacred with a new sense of personal esteem and collective nationalism. Because he was black and considered divine, Father Divine pointed to the personal aspect of this change. Some, however, in a new blending of ordinary and extraordinary, spoke of a free black nation.

Consciousness of peoplehood among blacks existed even during slave times, as the slave rebellions witnessed. After emancipation and the turn of the twentieth century, these stirrings took more concrete form. In a key example, Jamaican immigrant **Marcus M. Garvey** in 1914 established the Universal Negro Improvement Association. In the early 1920s, Garvey's star rose, as he preached a gospel of the African heritage based on the affirmation of a black God. To underline the religious character of his message, he was instrumental in founding the African Orthodox Church in New York City. Anglican in background, the church fostered racial pride and fought white domination in black religion. At the same time, Garvey urged blacks to create an independent state in Africa to which—like Zionist Jews—they would return. Garvey's dream for the black Israel was interrupted by his deportation in 1927 after accusations of financial fraud, but his legacy of a religion of blackness lived on.

In Jamaica, Garvey's movement combined with a cultural fascination for Ethiopia. **Ethiopianism** linked biblical symbolism to nationalistic yearning, as **Rastafarian** groups sprang up, honoring Ras ("prince") Tafari, who became the emperor Haile Selassie in Ethiopia in 1930. The Psalm verse "Ethiopia shall soon stretch out her hands unto God" (Ps. 68:31) became a millennialist message in which (black) Ethiopia was heaven, Haile Selassie was God, and those with African blood would return to the Ethiopian homeland through the power of the emperor-God. In the late twentieth century, Jamaican immigrants entering the

United States brought Rastafarianism with them. Their beliefs about Haile Selassie modified, their reggae music became well-known, and their uncombed dreadlocks and beards brought—important here—a prophetic style to black religious nationalism. African Americans of non-Jamaican background readily joined them.

Earlier, **Black Jews** had also self-consciously promoted the African American people as the true Israel, accepting the Jewish Talmud as their holy book and observing Jewish dietary laws. Others, in a similar rejection of Christianity, turned to Islam. The **Moorish Science Temple of America** offers an early example. Founded by Timothy Drew in 1913, it thrived in the same atmosphere that fueled the Garvey movement. After the prophet's sudden death in 1929, one of the factions of his movement in Detroit came under the spell of the mysterious **Wallace D. Fard** (Farrad Mohammad or Wali Farrad). A peddler thought to be of Arab extraction, he taught many to read, and he urged the black nation to awake to the deceits of "blue-eyed devils." He told them that Allah, the true God, was using whites as instruments through whom blacks might learn their own past history and prepare for their future destiny.

Within three years, Fard had established an impressive organization with a temple, a University of Islam (an elementary and secondary school), a Muslim Girls Training Class, and the Fruit of Islam, a military company for the defense of the faithful. Among those who rose to responsibility within the movement was a man from Georgia named **Elijah Poole** (1897–1975). Renamed **Elijah Muhammad** by Fard, he became his Minister of Islam, and when Fard disappeared mysteriously in 1934, Elijah Muhammad emerged as leader of the **Nation of Islam**. Fard, he preached to followers, had been God in their midst. As in holiness religion, Elijah Muhammad taught a life of family solidarity and self-discipline. But the Nation of Islam's story of origins reflected its militant difference from holiness. **Yakub's history** told of black superiority and a demonic plot that, over centuries, had produced a bleached-out white race. The Nation also preached the formation of a separate national territory for American blacks and warned its members not to vote, hold public office, or serve in the armed forces.

Even during the lifetime of Elijah Muhammad, variant interpretations of the Nation of Islam and the religion of blackness arose. **Malcolm X** (born Malcolm Little), one of Elijah Muhammad's most trusted lieutenants, came to see the message of Islam as universal human solidarity. After a pilgrimage to Mecca, he could no longer endorse the radical separatism of Muhammad's Nation, and he broke with the movement in 1964 to form the Muslim Mosque, Incorporated, and then the Organization of Afro-American Unity. In this second organization, especially, he began to explore the meaning of black nationhood without attaching it openly to Islamic ideology. So at the same time, Malcolm X was moving blacks closer to orthodox Islam and urging them toward a clearer sense of their own identity.

Malcolm X was shot to death in 1965 by members of the parent Nation of Islam, but a decade later, some of his ideas returned. After the death of Elijah Muhammad, his son **Wallace D. Muhammad** assumed control, taking the movement even further in the direction of Malcolm X. Educated in Egypt and an Arabic speaker, Wallace Muhammad ended official black separatism and moved the Nation toward orthodoxy. He banished Yakub's history and the prohibitions against voting, holding political office, and joining the armed forces. Malcolm X was honored in death with the title of Shabazz (the ancient tribe of Abraham), and a temple in Harlem was named after him. Muhammad's transformed organization welcomed whites, and it promulgated a new symbolism of the Qur'an (Koran) as the universal open book.

The old Nation changed its name twice—to the World Community of al-Islam in the West and then to the American Muslim Mission—but by 1987 Muhammad dropped all names and dissolved the organization. Henceforth, members of the former Nation were to join local Muslim mosques and consider themselves part of the international Muslim community. Meanwhile, Warith (as he had changed his name) Muhammad began to act as official distributor of Arab-donated missionary funds to Muslim organizations in the United States. In a still more honorific acknowledgment (for ritual reasons), world Islamic leaders designated him to certify American Muslims for participation in the Islamic annual pilgrimage to Mecca. Muslim prayer leaders now mingled in associations of black ministers. Muhammad intended to be fully Muslim, and he clearly also wanted more accommodation to American society. Still, persistence in being Muslim—not Christian—has continued to tell of the limits of acculturation and the enduring presence, in some form, of the religion of blackness.

In the old Nation of Islam, however, some saw the changes introduced by Warith Muhammad as betrayal, and among them Minister **Louis Farrakhan** led a countermovement. Attracting a membership outside the former Nation and especially among the young, Farrakhan reconstituted (or continued) the Nation of Islam, acknowledging Elijah Muhammad as the Messenger of God and once more telling Yakub's history of the origin of blue-eyed devils. Sharply condemned by the mainstream media for radicalism, racialism, and anti-Semitism, he yet became a national figure in 1995 when he successfully led the "Million Man March" in Washington, D.C. The event bonded huge numbers of black men (with estimates of 400,000 to 1 million) as they pledged responsibility for their families and communities, renounced spousal abuse and other forms of violence, and rejected drug use. It is significant that Farrakhan is the son of West Indian immigrants in New York and that his mother lingered on the fringe of Garvey's movement. Like the Rastafarians who have also drawn from Garvey, Farrakhan's Nation of Islam sees blacks as a divine community and the chief actors of biblical times, while whites appear as evil. In Farrakhan, the religion of blackness has expressed itself in strictly separatist form. Despite profound reasons for alienation, however, the majority report for African American Muslims is less radical and more aligned with traditional expressions of Islam, with perhaps a third of Muslims in America being blacks.

The religion of blackness also found expression in the Protestant churches, and in the civil rights movement of the 1960s, the more traditional black churches provided leadership. **Martin Luther King, Jr.** (1929–1968) gave the movement its clearest symbol and most effective organizer. With his father a prominent preacher, King grew up as a product of the black church. When he began to employ the tactic of nonviolent resistance, his first model inevitably came from ancestors who had endured their lot on southern plantations. During King's years at Boston University, theological reading helped to develop his views. Then, beginning with the Montgomery, Alabama, bus boycott of 1955, history provided the stage. As minister of a local Baptist church, King found himself the leader of the boycott movement. Later, in Birmingham, Alabama, and Albany, Georgia, in Selma, Alabama, and Washington, D.C., blacks marched with King at their head. Meanwhile, the United States Congress seemed to tread in their steps. The Congress passed Civil Rights acts in 1957, 1960, and 1964, and in 1965 the Voting Rights Act.

Fired by his dream that one day the children of former slaves and former slaveholders would sit together at the same table, King evoked for many the figure of Moses leading the Jews out of Egypt. His religion of blackness had been nourished in the rural churches that, in honoring a black Jesus, had encouraged self-esteem. But on a different front, as King marched, another group of blacks was beginning to spell out for intellectuals the meaning of the religion of blackness. Precedents for them existed in the writings of **W. E. Burghardt DuBois**, a Harvard-educated sociologist at Atlanta University at the turn of the twentieth century. DuBois had written long reflections on the meaning of the black Jesus and the nature of black spirituality. In the 1960s and 1970s, a new generation of preachers and scholars took up these themes, the most well-known among them **James H. Cone**.

For Cone and for others attracted by his **liberation theology**, the Christian gospels had revealed Jesus as a religious leader proclaiming freedom about to come to the oppressed. Since black people historically had been the most oppressed among the nations, Jesus must be on their side, Cone argued. To be a Christian, in this reading, all people must become spiritually black; that is, they must identify with oppressed people and their cause. In *Black Theology and Black Power* (1969) and *A Black Theology of Liberation* (1970), Cone developed these and similar themes. As he did so, he took much of his material from the European Christian tradition, and much of it had little impact on black laypeople. Yet in many ways Cone's work springs from the same roots as the black laity sprang. In his liberation theology's quest for black empowerment and in its mingling of religion and peoplehood, it echoes the African and African American past.

Today African American church membership is higher proportionately than that of any other religious family. Among worshipers, the largest black denomination besides the Church of God in Christ (with some white membership) is the **National Baptist Convention, USA,** with 5 million members in the early twenty-first century, making it the third or fourth largest Protestant body in the nation. Other major African American denominations include the National Baptist Convention of America, the African Methodist Episcopal Church, the Progressive National Baptist Church, the African Methodist Episcopal Zion Church, and the Christian Methodist Episcopal Church.

Against a background of racialism and pain, African Americans developed a clear sense of their identity among the many in the United States. With little opportunity for cultivating their past, they demonstrated what it meant to seek roots. Like American Indians, Jews, and Catholics, they felt the pull of the one center, the mainstream Protestant axis of American religion. Yet more than Jews and Catholics, blacks have explored paths of resistance. Like American Indians, they have sought ways to make their separate past a present source of strength. They have combined and recombined spiritual resources to create new religious forms. For blacks, the African past is over; the African American present continues to unfold.

In Overview

The African American experience began in the seventeenth-century slavery that brought West Africans involuntarily to the Americas. While they were diverse, their religious heritage included common elements: a strong sense of **community**, an equally strong regard for **ancestors**, belief in a noninterfering **high God** and, at the same time, a sense of the **nearness of intermediary Gods**, and **rituals** that expressed both extraordinary and ordinary religion.

In America, blacks preserved some religious customs and practices. More important in the long run, they continued to look at the world in African ways. They mixed ordinary and extraordinary religion in tales of **Tricksters** like **Brer Rabbit** and in **conjure**. As they encountered Christianity, a few blacks became Catholics, but—after a slow start—the largest number became Protestants. In the "**invisible institution**," these black Protestants created their own religion. They found sacred space in public **praise houses** or in secret **hush harbors**, and they created sacred time with **sermons**, **spirituals**, **ring shouts**, and other rituals. As converts who proclaimed they had been "struck dead" by the power of God, blacks both affirmed and overcame the **involuntary condition of slavery** to express spiritual freedom.

Meanwhile, in the early nineteenth century, free blacks organized in the **African Methodist Episcopal Church** and in what became known as the **African Methodist Episcopal Zion Church**. Under the **Baptist** form of governance, some enslaved blacks in the South also controlled their churches to a degree. After the Civil War, a series of independent black churches came into existence, and by the twentieth century and on, a **religion of blackness** thrived. A nation within the nation, blacks had already turned to a **black Jesus** in northern **holiness** and **pentecostal** churches. In smaller movements, they honored blackness in their devotion to African American **charismatic leaders** and to **ideologies of chosenness** such as those provided by the **Nation of Islam**. In the **civil rights movement** of the 1960s and the creation of a **black liberation theology**, newer versions of the religion of blackness arose. Meanwhile, in both American-born and immigrant-derived forms of spiritual practice, blacks have engaged in numerous expressions of religious

combination. Even as blacks have combined in some ways with other Americans, though, they have carefully drawn the boundaries between themselves and the white world. African Americans continue to mingle ordinary and extraordinary religion in a separate black center.

Yet in the United States, other centers and hopes have flourished. As the slaves described their visions of paradise and their children looked for ways to begin to build more modest versions on earth, different Americans staked a claim to their piece of a heavenly landscape. Nineteenth-century new religions grew out of the visions of their founders. To imagine in the United States seemed to mean to create and to construct.

Part Two

MANYNESS: NEWMADE IN AMERICA

Two centuries after the original cast came together in America, they had experienced extensive change. Ties to tradition were real, but by the 1800s, a fascination with newness was offering radical competition to the past. New lands—new places to live and build—were by this time a fact of life for millions, even for many Native Americans displaced by European immigrants. New people—strangers from many places and traditions—were also entering the nation.

For some, the traditions of the past, even as revised for the United States, were no longer adequate. Instead, they began to reach toward religions newly made in America, religions that in marked ways cut traditional ties and struck out on their own. Mormonism, Christian Science, spiritualism, Theosophy, and New Thought were all examples. So were changed forms of premillennialism as among Seventh-day Adventists and Jehovah's Witnesses; and of perfectionism as among members of the Shaker and Oneida communities. In these experiments with newness, people began to take parts that no one had foreseen. They combined and recombined elements from the past to create innovating roles and perspectives. Religious change became ever more noticeable as the American religious scene grew more complex. From now on, **newmade** American religions and their followers would speak important lines in the play that was American religious history.

Chapter 7

Visions of Paradise Planted: Nineteenth-Century New Religions

On a spring day in 1820, a teenager named Joseph Smith from a poor family in upstate New York knelt to pray in the woods. Confused by the claims and counterclaims of mission-minded sectarians in his area, he did not know who was right. So he decided he would ask God. Smith was not doing anything exceptional in a district given over to religious excitement, but his story of what happened next was extraordinary. According to Smith's account, he watched as a pillar of light came gradually down upon him, and then he saw two "Personages." As they stood in the air above him, one pointed to the other, calling the second his beloved son and telling Smith to hear him. When Smith asked the two which of the sects was right, he was told that they were all wrong and that he should join none of them.

Sectarianism and Nineteenth-Century New Religions

The results of Joseph Smith's vision story live on the Church of Jesus Christ of Latter-day Saints and a few related groups. As the account indirectly hints, Smith—as founder—and his Mormon followers (their familiar name) would think of themselves as an all-inclusive church. But others for a long time considered Mormons to be members of a **sect**. Classic statements in the early twentieth-century sociological work of Max Weber and Ernst Troeltsch help in thinking about the meaning of this term. For Troeltsch, sects were voluntary societies of people bound together by religious experiences of new birth. They lived in small groups separated from the world, emphasizing a life of committed love and law rather than one of free grace, or unmerited divine aid. Above all, they lived in expectation of a coming kingdom of God that would end the present world. Thus, people moved into sects as the result of some decisive religious experience. And although their own religious change often turned them into missionaries, their groups mostly became refuges for the totally committed. Theirs was a chosen society of saints instead of a huge, extended church that included saints and sinners.

Christianity, which had once itself been a tiny Jewish sect, produced numerous sectarian groups, especially after it became established. For American sectarianism, however, perhaps the most useful model is the **Radical Reformation** of sixteenth-century Europe. Radicals departed in major ways from the mainstream Protestant Reformation led by Martin Luther, John Calvin, and others. Different from mainstream Protestants and Catholics alike, Radicals understood the church as a free society of people gathered out of the world. They believed that not all of those who lived in a place should be part of the church but instead only those who chose willingly. Once, they thought, the Christian church had lived up to that ideal; but long ago, in the fourth and early fifth centuries, it had fallen. What the church needed, therefore, was not reformation, as mainstream Protestants thought, but the **restoration** of primitive Christianity.

Moreover, whereas for Luther and Calvin **salvation**, or **justification**, came through faith in the gospel Word (Jesus) that had been preached, the Radicals saw the gospel as law. For them the process of **sanctification** took central place. In their view, the church meant an association in which people would support one another in right living. Salvation came by works, and Jesus became a model of how to live and die more than a sacrificial victim who had atoned for sin. For the Radicals, sacraments (called **ordinances**) were signs and memorials, teaching events that reminded believers powerfully of Christian truths, but they were not in their material substance guarantees of God's presence. Since all were called to be saints, Radicals thought, all were called to be priests both in theory and practice. Combining this quest for holiness with a mood of expectation of the return of Jesus, they disdained any involvement with the state, sometimes treating it with indifference as a relic of the past and sometimes acting with hostility toward it. Pacifism, the prohibition of oaths, and the avoidance of magistracies or other government service were all examples of Radical avoidance of the world.

Direct descendants of the European Radicals existed in groups like the Pennsylvania and Ohio Amish and the Hutterites of the upper Midwest. But other groups who could not trace their lineage directly to the Radicals nonetheless partly resembled them. In seventeenth-century North America, for example, the Puritans in some ways held sectarian views. They emphasized restoration and millennialism, made conversion the gateway to social and civil participation, and possessed missionary intentions. Some—like the Baptists of Rhode Island—sought even greater purity. Still, Puritans as a whole had absorbed enough of Calvinist thought to stand by the doctrine of predestination and to be wary of law as a saving force. They found the Christian state necessary. Making war, taking oaths, and serving as magistrates were matters of fact that were also, for them, matters of Christian duty. Similarly, by the nineteenth century, Radical Reform ideas of restoration and millennialism spread through evangelical culture. But, like the Puritans, evangelicals played out these themes in a softer, more inclusive style. And like them, too, they mostly found an ally in the Christian state.

Other groups, however, resembled the Radicals more fully even in colonial times. By the nineteenth century, sectarians and their movements caught the public eye significantly and grew more than at any time before. Of course, important differences existed between sixteenth-century Radical views and nineteenth-century American ideas. But the similarities are worth noticing, and they provide a picture of a series of new religious groups that may usefully be called sects. They broke sharply with conventional Protestantism of the time, both in its liberal and evangelical versions. So from a religious point of view it is not fair to call them "also-rans" among the Protestants. They were not simply smaller or less popular than Baptists and Methodists or even the Disciples of Christ. They pursued a more totalizing vision, one that departed more completely from mainstream American culture. They experimented with forms of ritual and behavior distinct from what others regarded as standard. While mainstream Protestants emphasized the Word and exalted the Bible that contained it, radical American sectarians put their premium on the deed—on the major changes in life-style that their religious convictions demanded. Thus, like American Indians and like Jews and sometimes Catholics, they often succeeded in bringing ordinary and extraordinary religion together. With the zeal of their newness, they made the ordinary—each detail of daily living—a way into another world.

Although the sectarians never attracted huge numbers of people relative to the Protestant mainstream, they were acting and living out themes central to the culture. In a time of marked political and cultural change, a mood of experiment flourished. People wanted to match the newness they felt about their place and their democratic political experiment. Many believed, as we saw, that either they would restore Christian origins or, turning the time of beginnings inside out, they would create brand-new societies to launch the millennium. In short, many believed that they could plant paradise on American soil. Such excitement, however, could not last indefinitely. Sectarians often could not maintain the intensity of their vision for more than a generation or two. So usually they gradually changed to become denominations. In the United States, this is part of the story of how manyness became oneness.

It is helpful here to imagine a broad continuum of nineteenth-century new religions. At one end are those that, while they maintained their exclusivity, still relatively allowed for individual initiative. At the other are religions that carried the sectarian principle as far as they could, demanding a total—even totalitarian—commitment in full community living. Thus, moving across the continuum we find groups such as Mormons, Christian Scientists, and Seventh-day Adventists, all of whom made—and often still make—considerable, but not totalizing, demands on their members. Jehovah's Witnesses have probably asked even more than these three but have stopped short of total community. Groups such as the Shakers and Oneida Perfectionists, however, made full community demands.

The Mormons

The Mormons—officially, the **Church of Jesus Christ of Latter-day Saints**—passed from a time of near-total community living to a later and more individual, but still strongly bonded, membership. So they are interesting in terms of the sectarian continuum. Central to the Saints themselves, however, were their beliefs about new revelation. **Joseph Smith** (1805–1844) claimed to receive such revelation first through a heavenly messenger named **Moroni**. In his reported conversations with the angel, Smith's religious anxiety and his paid occupation as a treasure (money) digger using a "seerstone" came together. Moroni, said Smith, directed him to a place where golden plates were buried, forming a written testimony to the spiritual history of early America. Smith also said that, buried in the same place, he found two stones in silver bows and attached to a breastplate, the **Urim** and **Thummim**. After a delay of five years, Moroni allowed him to take all. The plates contained what came to be known as the **Book of Mormon**, and Smith began to use the stones (seerstones of a higher order) to translate it. Furthermore, he said, Moroni supplemented what was written on the plates with other prophetic words and teachings—most significantly concerning the future destiny of American Indians and of America itself as the site of a New Jerusalem.

Standing beside the Bible as sacred scripture, the Book of Mormon told the story of Lehi and his family of the tribe of Joseph, who left Jerusalem in 600 BCE and were led by God to America. But two of Lehi's sons, Laman and Lemuel, along with their followers, rebelled and became wicked. Hence, God cursed them with dark skin, and from them the American Indians descended. These **Lamanites** turned on the white **Nephites**, the other branch of Lehi's family, and destroyed most of them. But Mormon, one of the Nephites who remained, buried in the Hill Cumorah of upper New York state the plates that contained the Book of Mormon. In addition, he gave a few of the plates to his son, Moroni, who, according to the book, was the last surviving Nephite.

The Book of Mormon, therefore, established the Hebraic origins of American Indians and supplied the nineteenth-century United States with a biblical past. The nature of its account shaped the growing movement. Since God *acted in history*, both in the Bible and in the Book of Mormon, action in time became the essence of religion, and Mormonism early expressed this religious idea in a number of ways. For Mormons, **revelation** lived on in the present because, they believed, God continued to speak to the prophet Joseph Smith and his successors. Moreover, they understood themselves to be repeating the years of wandering of Israel recorded in the Old Testament. In 1830, they moved to Kirtland, Ohio, and then, in 1837, to Independence and to Far West, Missouri. When the hostility of their neighbors drove them from Missouri, they migrated to Illinois, where they founded Nauvoo. But in 1844, hostility again brought an armed confrontation, and it led to the murder of Smith while he was jailed in Carthage, Illinois. In the midst of the turmoil and the moving, Mormons looked toward a future time of "gathering," when an American Zion would be established. Under **Brigham Young** (1801–1877), the

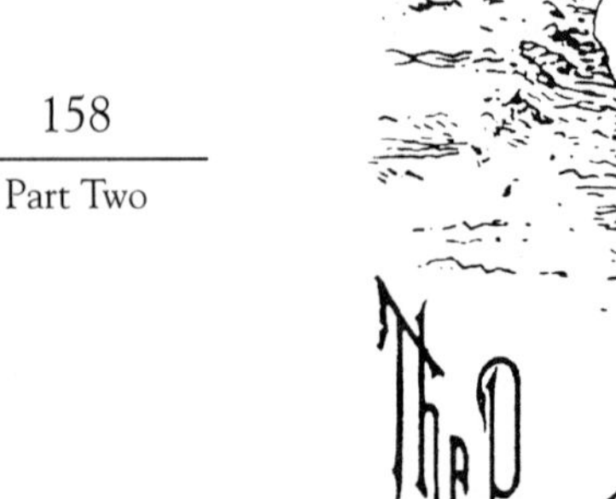

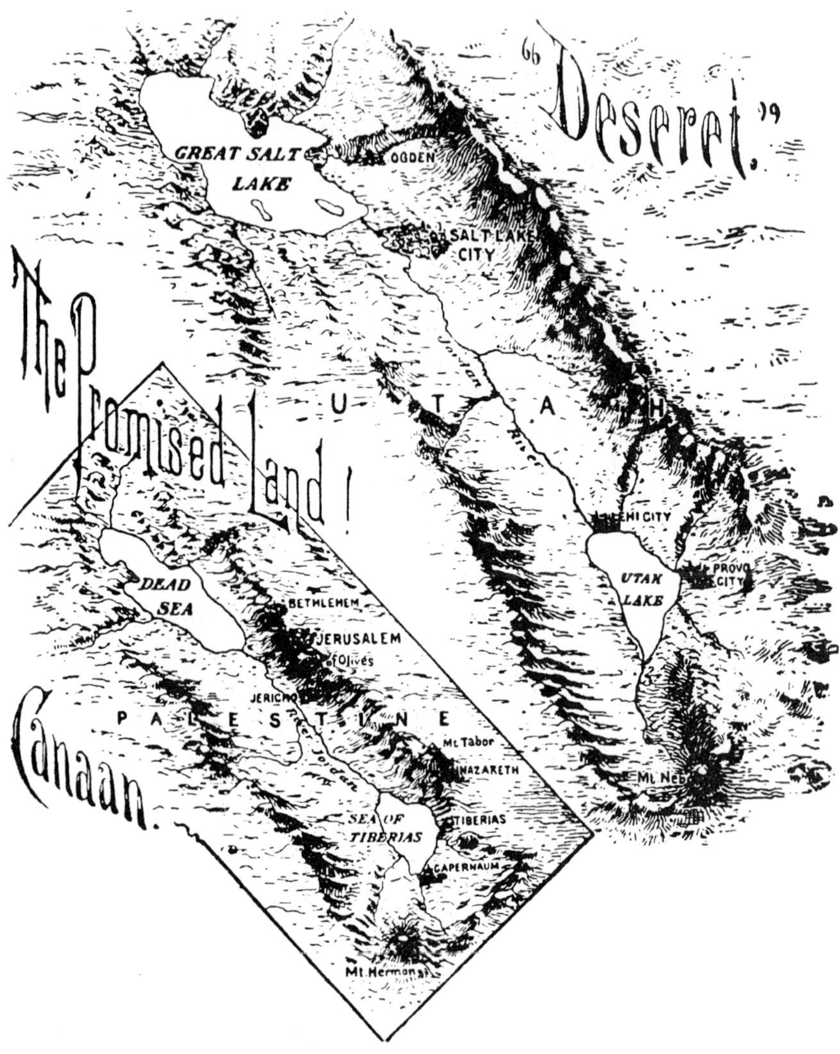

Salt Lake Valley, Utah. This Mormon-inspired drawing (source unknown) was published in William E. Smythe's *Conquest of Arid America* in 1900. Mormon (Old Testament) restorationism is strikingly imaged in the juxtaposition of biblical Canaan and latter-day Deseret.

main body set out on a journey that brought them at last to the Great Salt Lake in what is now Utah. Here they founded their own Zion in the mountains, the state of **Deseret**.

It is clear that doing the Word was central to these early Mormons, as it would be to later ones. At the same time, in their conception of the nature of the church they self-consciously separated themselves from their Protestant neighbors. Like the Radicals of the sixteenth century, the Mormons thought that reformation was not enough and sought restoration of the church instead. They agreed with the

Radical Reformers, too, in their beliefs concerning the abolition of infant baptism and the coming of the millennium.

However, the Mormons were also *American* in their religious vision. For example, unlike most of the Radicals, the Mormons believed that Zion would be gathered in the flesh. Like all sectarians, they demanded full commitment in a radical life-style that at some points involved the surrender of possessions to the church and the practice of **polygamy**, or plural marriage for the men, as in biblical times. Yet their exclusivity often led them to the center of the political process. In order to preserve their separateness, they had to obtain the worldly power that would enable them to form their own societies, independent of the general government around them. Thus, while in Illinois, Smith announced that he was a candidate for the presidency of the United States, and Brigham Young, at the head of Deseret, worked for years for the admission of the Utah Territory to statehood and for a time was its official governor.

The content of Mormon revelation is also more "American" than the religions of most Americans. Mormon interest in the history and destiny of American Indians and belief in America as the promised land for the New Jerusalem are examples. Still more, in their teachings about the nature of God and of human beings, Mormons have given major values of American culture a theological basis. They preached—and continue to preach—a doctrine in which the material world is sacred and ultimate. Their God is not an infinite and omnipotent creator. Rather, in a universe that has always existed, God is a finite being who does not have the world totally under control, does not interfere with human freedom, and cannot prevent evil. In fact, Mormons hope one day to enter the celestial kingdom where they, too, will be "as Gods." Here they are teaching a **polytheism** in which the divine principle has many expressions.

Mormons say that their souls preexisted in a spirit realm before entering their present bodies. And instead of affirming the dualism between spirit and matter that is basic to orthodox Christian theology, they have viewed spiritual things as the refined essence of the material world. For them, all spirit is matter. Because of this teaching, the human body has held a privileged status. Historic Mormon prohibitions of the use of alcohol, tobacco, and caffeine and their sparing use of meat are indications of their regard for matter. In a nineteenth-century culture that pursued material success and worldly progress, Mormons told other Americans that, if matter and progress were good, this was because revelation had shown ultimate reality to be both material and progressive. And yet, in a twist that hinted of the biblical literalism of twentieth-century American fundamentalism, Mormons held to a literal understanding of the teachings of Smith and their later prophets. For them, the revealed Word should be respected in its material integrity and not "spiritualized" away.

The Mormon cultus—its secret **temple work** not open to outsiders—has dramatized these beliefs. After a revelation in 1841, Smith told his people to build a temple in Nauvoo where the Saints could present to God the records of their dead. From this time, Mormons date their practice of **baptizing the living for the dead**.

That is, as in the past, present-day Mormons immerse themselves in the baptismal waters in the name, usually, of individual relatives who died without conversion. They hope, thus, to bring all the worthy dead to salvation. Meanwhile, in their **Endowment ceremony**—for themselves and later for ancestors—Mormons have participated in elaborate rites considered necessary to assure life after death. Given by Smith in his lifetime, the ritual forms have continued, with only slight modification, until today. In their marriage ceremonies Mormons are encouraged to seal themselves to one another "for time and eternity." Since God is both Father and Mother, humans worship by entering such a union, and full salvation cannot be reached without it. Indeed, temple work has included sealing ceremonies for those who died before the time of Mormon revelation. In all of this work, Mormons have continued to express their confidence in the power and sacredness of matter. For them, the dead must be subject to material rites, and the sexual as well as spiritual bond of marriage will endure in the world beyond. The millennium will not bring an end to the world but will perfect the American Zion to come—*in* time and not beyond it.

Finally, the Mormons have expressed their Americanness in their governance. Like New England Puritans, they tried to build a **theocracy** in which otherworldly and everyday concerns were regulated by one set of authorities. This blending of temporal and spiritual agreed with Mormon teaching about the importance of matter, and the early theocracies made near-total demands on the Saints. The law of consecration and stewardship at first required each Mormon to surrender all goods to a bishop, who would then give back for use what each Mormon family needed. Later, Mormons were still required to tithe. The church continued to showcase its organizational efficiency, divided into stakes and wards, with stake presidents and bishops, councils, elders, and priests, and at the head a president who inherited the role of Smith. After a presidential revelation in 1890 that officially ended polygamy, theocracy gave way to statehood for Utah. But the fusion of church, state, and culture informally lingered on, as in a revelation in 1978 that removed the racial barrier to the highest (male) priesthood. Occasioned by missionary concerns for people of color throughout the world, the American civil rights struggle of the 1960s also had something to do with the timing. Now African American men could be full Mormon priests.

From the twentieth century on, Mormons experienced increasing wealth and respectability, and in many ways they moved away from the sectarian ideal to become a broad and inclusive church. Liberalizing intellectuals and feminists (often the same people) among them have raised searching questions about some aspects of inherited teaching and practice. Still, change has come only gradually, and Mormons have retained so much of their past that the sociologist of religion Joachim Wach hesitated to call them a church and labeled them instead an "independent group." Whether as church or as independent group, though, the Church of Jesus Christ of Latter-day Saints today can boast of an inclusive membership of well over 5 million, making it the fifth largest religious body in the nation. Rate of growth is the highest among all churches, and commitment levels have remained strong. The nineteenth-century new religion has become, in our times, an established social entity.

The Christian Scientists

Another view of the relationship between sectarianism and new American religion comes from **Christian Science. Mary Baker Eddy** (1821–1910), who founded it, grew up in New England and spent years as a Congregationalist and so as part of the American mainstream. Yet Eddy's claims of extraordinary religious experience, like the claims of Joseph Smith, shaped Christian Science as a distinct sectarian movement. For years Eddy moved from place to place after the death of a first husband and the unfaithfulness of a second. She also suffered from physical complaints and a chronic spinal disability. Then in 1862 she sought out **Phineas P. Quimby** (1802–1866), a celebrated mental healer, who began to help her and to teach her that erroneous thinking was the cause of disease. Four years later, Quimby, in his sixties, died, and about a month after that, Eddy fell on ice and suffered what seemed a concussion and a possible dislocated spine. "On the third day," however, while reading the gospel story of Jesus healing a palsied man (Matt. 9:2), Eddy claimed a profoundly moving experience in which she glimpsed spiritual truth and was instantly healed. She dated the beginning of Christian Science from that moment.

The decade from 1866 to 1875 brought Eddy more years of wandering. But inwardly, these were years of quiet thinking and writing. They culminated in 1875 in the first edition of ***Science and Health***, the book that for later Christian Scientists ranked beside the Bible and explained it. In four years more, the **Church of Christ, Scientist**, was formally chartered, and the story after that became one of growing wealth, influence, and prestige. Still, during this time, the founder and her movement experienced a series of defections, when former students struck out on their own as part of a more general mind-cure movement. Perhaps alienated by Eddy's claim to spiritual authority, perhaps inspired by it to experience their own, these former Scientists in some ways served to enhance the sectarianism of those who remained with Eddy. The original group, now plagued by accusations and even lawsuits, turned within. So the bonds that separated Christian Scientists from the world grew stronger, and their sense of identity sharpened.

As for Smith and the Mormons, teaching and practice for Eddy and her followers expressed continuing divine revelation. At certain exceptional moments in human history, Eddy believed, individuals rediscovered this revelation, and when they did so, they experienced a breakthrough of light and power in their lives. In such a moment, she had "discovered" Christian Science, and in such moments later Christian Scientists would find the power to heal the sick. At the basis of all of this, Eddy said, was Jesus Christ, the only person in human history who fully demonstrated what it meant to be the Son of God. She urged that the revelation of Jesus was a practical ideal for others to imitate, since all people should strive, like Jesus, to realize completely their relationship to God. This meant bringing to light the perfection of their actual and God-given natures, instead of accepting the limitations of their apparent natures. For Eddy, Christian Science was the way to break out of a world of illusions.

Eddy's teaching extended, too, to include a **metaphysical** reading (see Chapter 8) of the nature of God, human beings, and their world. In her vision God was more than a person in the ordinary sense and existed more as the divine Principle or Life expressed in the universe. So, for Eddy, God became Soul, Truth, and Love. Using gender designations, God was **Father–Mother**, with love (motherhood) as the divine Principle that created spiritual beings and the universe as a reflection of infinite Mind. It followed for Eddy that, as **Mind**, God dwelled in all reality, and—most significant for Christian Science practice—that matter had no substantial reality. Spiritual rather than material laws bound God and nature together. Only one true Science, the law of this divine Mind, actually ruled. For the **material sense**—the limited sense of reality that people shared—Eddy said, matter was completely real. But she thought that from the perspective of God's Mind, the real nature of human beings, as reflecting the divine Principle, was immortal. Seemingly bound by the laws of matter, humans were actually entwined only in their own false conceptions of the nature of things. So for Eddy, **error** was at the bottom of sin and sickness, and **Truth** could dispel them both as the redemption of what she called "**mortal man.**" Such truth came for her through Jesus Christ. In her view, salvation meant following the example of Jesus, and **atonement** meant at-one-ment with Christ, which brought an end to separation from God and, consequently, sickness and sin.

This vision of the nature of things, with its lingering Calvinist concern regarding evil and its metaphysical idealism, took—and continues to take—concrete form in the work of Christian Science **practitioners**, who have devoted themselves professionally to healing the sick. They visit, counsel, and, above all, pray for their patients. Prayer here becomes not a plea for God's help but instead the practitioner's meditation on the sick person as thought to be seen by and related to God. So practitioners try to discern what they feel is the real (spiritual) truth of each person for whom they work—understood as seeing through an illusion of illness to a person as he or she exists in the sight of God. Practitioners hold such thoughts in mind until they feel that they have broken the falsity of their patient's illness in the truth of God. When they feel the treatment is completed, they firmly expect to receive word of the sick person's healing. At the same time, practitioners have also typically made demands on their patients. Aside from charging a fee for their work, they may ask a sick person to study certain passages from the writings of Eddy, to discipline their thoughts, or to try to realize certain truths about their lives. Meanwhile, Christian Scientists avoid alcohol, tobacco, and sometimes caffeine, wishing to eliminate the presence of drugs of any kind. Whether prescribed by a physician or used in the form of socially accepted stimulants or depressants, for them drugs operate in terms of human belief in their power.

To sum up, Christian Science taught a broad interpretation of Christian revelation, expounded a metaphysical system to help modern people understand it, and practiced healing as the logical outcome of its beliefs. As for the Radical Reformers, Jesus for Christian Scientists was the great example of human perfection. Salvation came through imitating the model that he provided. Moreover, like the Radical Reformers, Christian Scientists thought that they were *restoring* the teaching of an early church in which healing had been central. While Eddy would also claim that no one before her had discovered the truth of Christian Science and that all of previous Christian history had missed the revelation, her sometime emphasis on restoration was significant. So, too, was the theology of material error, which led Christian Science to adopt a position toward politics and the social order similar to that of the sixteenth-century Radical Reformers. For if the material world was illusory, participation in its business, attention to its problems, and adherence to its political or social systems could at best be only secondary. True, near the end of her life Eddy founded a newspaper, *The Christian Science Monitor,* to offer a healing approach to social issues. But since, in her view, human conflict and suffering resulted from false belief, Eddy believed that a Christian Scientist ought to minimize worldly involvement.

However, if—like Mormons—Christian Scientists had their sectarian side, they also showed themselves to be citizens of the nineteenth-century United States. First, there was their name. In a century that witnessed startling advances in science, the word carried considerable prestige. For Mary Baker Eddy and her followers, it meant the laws by which God governed the universe, but it also pointed to the methods, or rules, used for Christian Science "**demonstration**" and the certainty with which these rules could be applied. Christian Scientists asserted that their healings, like scientific experiments, were repeatable, so long as one had studied and practiced correctly. The prestige of science also helped shape Eddy's continual references to her followers as "students" and her steadfast conception of her role as that of teacher. In 1881, just two years after the official incorporation of her church, she received a charter for the Massachusetts Metaphysical College, in which she trained future Christian Science practitioners. And for years before a church organization of any kind came into being, she taught students her principles in rented rooms.

Second, the organizational structure that Eddy built looked as American as the businesses that in the late nineteenth century were becoming sizable corporations. Although in the beginning she had not wanted a formal institution at all, her later efforts reversed this direction. She grew dissatisfied with the rudimentary structure she had fashioned through the Church of Christ, Scientist, the Massachusetts Metaphysical College, and then the National Christian Science Association, ending both the college and the association. At the same time, she reorganized the Boston church, urging Christian Scientists throughout the country to apply for membership in this **Mother Church**. From then on, most Christian Scientists belonged to both a local organization and the Boston church. Here a self-perpetuating board of directors assumed enduring power, while in the branch churches pastors were replaced by term-appointed readers. Worship now meant recitation of assigned passages from the Bible and *Science and Health,* its sanctioned interpretation. Under these circumstances, the Christian Science organization became a model of efficiency.

Third, the character of Eddy's life and the lives of those who joined her suggests an American background. In many ways, their problems reflected what historians call the **Gilded Age**, a time when the surface brilliance of American culture seemed to hide spiritual sickness. Recovering from the Civil War and expanding at a great rate industrially, the United States was enlarging old cities and creating new ones, with people arriving from the American countryside and also, as immigrants, from abroad. The old symbols of a supernatural order no longer rang true for many. In this new world, Mary Baker Eddy's movement and message provided some form of resolution. Herself a product of social dislocation, Eddy offered followers security in the Mother Church. A strong leader at a time when a woman's place was largely domestic, she created in her church a place where she and others could act forcefully and effectively. Many of those who joined were middle-aged and middle-class women (although there were also many—and prominent—men), and she offered all a purposive life that could be lived *alone*. At a time when community values were breaking down, she taught self-reliance through metaphysics and spiritual practice. Meanwhile, the rejection of the primacy of the social world implicitly rebutted a male-oriented culture that denied a public place to women.

In short, Christian Science, like Mormonism, has made the ordinary extraordinary. But in the very act of doing so, Christian Science has also made the extraordinary ordinary. Its healings tell believers that the world as it appears, is malleable, and in that conviction Christian Science reveals its American spirit. Even so, the church is today small, without an ordained ministry, and without published membership statistics. It shows all the signs of decline. In the 1980s and 1990s, rifts developed within its leadership. A series of court cases challenged Christian Science spiritual healing practices with their rejection of conventional medical treatment, even for children. Financial troubles vexed the church, and to help resolve them leaders agreed to publish a controversial biography of Mary Baker Eddy that seemed to deify her. Bliss Knapp's *The Destiny of the Mother Church* (1991) before century's end brought over 50 million dollars to the church through the terms of a will that the printing of the book fulfilled, but many Scientists objected.

All of that acknowledged, Christian Science still reveals much about indigenous and lay-directed American theologizing. It is equally significant in what it reveals about religious organization and about selectivity in religious practice. Through the religious **combinativeness** of Christian Science, a new theological hybrid grew out of a transformed American Calvinism joined to metaphysical idealism. Just as important, in Christian Science, theology met American corporate talent and linked it to a religious quest for healing. Nineteenth-century Christian Science was in some ways a sign of the religious future.

The Seventh-day Adventists

Assenting neither to the Mormon theology of materialism nor to the Christian Science theology of its denial, Seventh-day Adventists from the first showed strong interest in a future world. The term **Seventh-day Adventist** came into official existence in 1860, when a general conference of Adventist Christians—bound together by religious, social, and economic ties—decided to adopt it. They were expressing their version of the millennialism that thrived within nineteenth-century Protestant Christianity on both sides of the Atlantic.

Decades before, however, their immediate ancestors, the **Millerites**, expected the second coming, or **advent**, of Jesus to be very soon. They followed a New England Baptist named **William Miller** (1782–1849), who drew large crowds as he moved from place to place, convincing many that the second coming would occur "about the year 1843." He had so concluded after study of the prophetic books of the Bible and, in particular, Daniel 8:14: "Unto two thousand and three hundred days; then shall the sanctuary be cleansed." For Miller and others, the time of the sanctuary's cleansing was the time, also, of the second coming. With interpreters generally agreed that a biblical day equaled a year of ordinary time, Miller taught that the 2,300 "days" (years) had begun 457 years before the time of Christ with the rebuilding of the city of Jerusalem. He predicted that the end of the present world would come between 21 March 1843 and 21 March 1844, a period he specified after others urged him to be more precise. Later, when Jesus did not come by March 1844, one member of the movement convinced Miller and others that, because of differences in the Jewish calendar, the return could be calculated for 22 October 1844. After the **Great Disappointment** of that day, many left the movement. Others, however, accepted the interpretation of Hiram Edson, who declared that, although Christ had not come on earth, in heaven he had entered the holiest part of the Jewish sanctuary as a preliminary to his earthly advent. Still others simply gave up time setting but retained their belief that the end was near.

The Seventh-day Adventists arose from the remnants of the Millerite movement. Prior to the Great Disappointment, a number of Adventists had followed the practice of keeping the ancient Jewish Sabbath (Saturday) instead of Sunday as their weekly day of worship. Influenced by the example of **Seventh Day Baptists**, some Adventists became convinced that the Bible should be taken literally and that they should honor the seventh rather than the first day of the week as the Sabbath. Among those who later accepted the Sabbath teaching were a former sea captain named **Joseph Bates** and a sickly woman, **Ellen G. White** (1827–1915), along with her husband, **James White**. Now these three provided new leadership for former Millerites who were still Adventists and had become **Sabbatarians**. They linked Adventism and seventh-day Sabbath keeping together, believing that the restoration of the genuine Sabbath prepared Adventists for the second coming. Conversely, they believed that worship on Sunday formed an idolatrous image to the Beast representing the powers of evil in the New Testament Book of Revelation. Such worship, they said, substituted a papal institution for the biblical command in the Ten Commandments.

Because of the unusual character of her religious experience, Ellen White quickly became prominent in the new movement. According to her report, in December 1844, when only seventeen, she had seen a vision of Adventists traveling along a path toward the New Jerusalem, lighted on their journey by the message of 22 October. For Adventists, White's account was divine confirmation, and when she claimed further visions they were ready. As the years passed, her reports of visions as well as inspired dreams enabled White to offer pronouncements on a variety of concerns, ranging from child nurture and education to missions and church organization. Especially, she addressed issues of dietary reform and health. In keeping with the thought of a number of nineteenth-century health reformers, White saw God calling the Adventist people away from not only alcohol and tobacco but also tea, coffee, and meat, with special prohibitions against pork. She also urged dress reform for women, condemning tightly fitted garments and trailing skirts in the interests of health; and she preached general rules of hygiene to maintain the vigor of the body.

Because of this history, the sectarian character of Seventh-day Adventism has been strong. Followers settled near one another in towns like Battle Creek, Michigan, and Loma Linda, California, while close-knit medical and educational organizations sprang up in the United States and throughout the world. Beliefs in the nearness of the millennium, in the prophetic guidance of Ellen G. White, and in Sabbatarian and dietary practices have set Adventists apart. Yet like many other sectarians, Adventists have counterbalanced their exclusivism with a missionary urge so strong that their story strongly features the spread of Adventist world missions. Like other sectarians, too, Adventists have been suspicious of government. The earliest Adventists avoided any relationship to government, and by the early 1850s they began to identify the government of the United States with the Beast in the Book of Revelation. Even in the 1880s and later, Adventists remained at the edge of the political process. Their logic sprang from their millennialism. If the end was soon, it was foolish to become involved with worldly government.

Similarly, Adventists declined to fight wars. They pointed to the biblical warning not to kill as well as to the practical difficulty of keeping the Sabbath in an army in which Sunday was the officially recognized day of worship. They entered military service with noncombatant status, serving generally as medics. Seeking the restoration of the primitive church rather than a reformation of the present one, thinking more of sanctification than of justification, Adventists, like Mormons, resembled the Radicals of the sixteenth century. They preached the gospel, as one Adventist scholar has put it, but they did not cease to preach the law. Like the Mormons, too, though not so markedly, Adventists questioned God's control over the part of the universe that involved humanity; they held that humans with their free will could change the course of events and so the plans of God.

Today Adventists look to a time when the world as we know it will cease to be. Yet with their **Sabbatarianism**, they just as strongly affirm the material world. Unlike the Sunday observance that expresses faith in the *resurrection* of Jesus, a symbol of spiritual triumph over the material world, the Saturday Sabbath points to belief in God's work in creation from which, on the seventh day, he rested. Thus, it honors the natural and material, and it looks to the beginning of things as much as to the end. Implicitly in Adventist theology, the first advent of the divine came with creation. The implications are that the natural, material world is a significant source of value, and so, for Adventists, the present becomes an important moment stretched between past and future. Ellen White, like Joseph Smith and Mary Baker Eddy, functioned for them as the mouthpiece for a *progressive* divine revelation in history, with ordinary matters achieving extraordinary status through divine interest. Adventists took the literal word, from White and the Bible, at face value. Just as the Sabbath meant Saturday, creation meant the direct and immediate work of God and not new nineteenth-century teachings such as the theory of evolution.

Although Seventh-day Adventists worked to remain distinct, like Mormons and Christian Scientists, they also reflect the **oneness** of American religion and culture. Both materialists and millennialists, with their far-flung educational and medical empire they still intensely await the second advent. There is an almost humorous commentary on just how much Adventists have assented to the general culture in the reference of one Adventist apologist to the "scientifically proven visions" of White. (He meant that the advice attributed to God through the visions was corroborated by scientific evidence.) Still, Adventist **missionary expansionism** gives even stronger evidence of Adventist Americanism. After a remarkable foreign-mission effort, world membership in the church stood at over 7 million by the last decade of the twentieth century. By contrast, in the early twenty-first century, fewer than 1 million of them were American Adventists. Matched against Adventism, the work of mainstream Protestant missionaries seemed less enthusiastic as an expression of the mission mind.

At the same time, Adventist services, with the exception of quarterly communion and footwashing rituals, have been largely indistinguishable from general Protestant worship. For the most part, ministers are teachers more than preachers and rational more than emotional, as in many mainstream Protestant services. Today, some affluent and highly educated American Adventists ask themselves the question, Do we belong to a sect, or are we members of a mainstream Protestant denomination?

The Jehovah's Witnesses

For the people who by 1931 called themselves **Jehovah's Witnesses**, little doubt existed about being sectarians. They separated themselves sharply from mainstream denominations, and their leadership insisted on the point. In fact, Jehovah's Witnesses typically have talked about their "congregations" in **Kingdom Halls** and not about their "churches," even as sociologists have labeled them an "established sect." Yet the Witnesses come from the same roots as Seventh-day Adventists.

Charles Taze Russell (1852–1916) founded the **Watch Tower Bible and Tract Society** in the 1880s. He had grown up Presbyterian and turned to Congregationalism, the same denomination that shaped Mary Baker Eddy. But he found, while still a teenager, that he could not accept church teachings about predestination and eternal punishment. So he renounced religion altogether for about a year. In 1869, however, he heard Adventist Christian church leader Jonas Wendell, in a lecture, reject the doctrine of hell. Wendell was affirming an Adventist belief in the annihilation of the individual at death, with the dead brought back through resurrection. Thinking about Wendell's ideas, Russell found himself again a Bible-believing Christian, formed a Bible study group, and gathered students around him in Allegheny (Pittsburgh), Pennsylvania. Unlike many other Adventists who no longer set a time for the second coming, though, Russell felt drawn to dates and times. He became convinced that Jesus had come again in 1874 as an invisible, spiritual presence and that he continued to be around. Collaborating with another Adventist, Nelson H. Barbour, Russell produced a book to spread this belief. The two, however, subsequently parted company—in part over Barbour's failed prediction that the church would be removed to heaven in 1878.

Russell's fascination with **time setting** would follow the Jehovah's Witnesses as they evolved. After 1874, the dates 1914, 1918, 1925, and, most recently, 1975 assumed endtime significance among them more or less strongly. Russell himself by 1879 was publishing a magazine called *Zion's Watch Tower and Herald of Christ's Presence*, its millennial interest already clear in its title. Moreover, he began to teach that the presence of Jesus would reach its climax in 1914, the year when God would judge all nations and establish his kingdom. When Russell died in 1916, he firmly believed that World War I was the Battle of **Armageddon** as prophesied in the Book of Revelation. But he left a society at loose ends, not only because the war did not turn out as prophetically as believers hoped, but also because different factions were struggling for control. **Joseph F. Rutherford** (1869–1942), the society's lawyer, won out and became its second president. It was he who called the Watch Tower group Jehovah's Witnesses, and he also began famously to summarize Witness belief with the slogan "Millions now living will never die." Forced to acknowledge that World War I had not been Armageddon, Witnesses under Rutherford now saw 1914, rather than 1874, as the year when the invisible, spiritual presence of Jesus began. Once again, though, they had to deal with failed prophecy. Rutherford claimed that in 1925 worldly powers would cease to exist and a series of Old Testament patriarchs would rise from the dead. His prediction did not materialize.

At Rutherford's death, **Nathan Knorr** (1905–1977) became president of the Watch Tower Society and undertook its transformation into a strongly authoritarian and hierarchically organized religion, with a presidency like the Catholic papacy (even though the Witnesses are militantly anti-Catholic). A board called the **Governing Body** took over, and books and periodicals came from Witness presses in vast numbers, all of them without naming authors. Witnesses created their own Bible translation in the *New World Translation*. They learned to speak to strangers about the Bible and developed strategies for success in converting them. By the 1960s, they turned to time setting once again, with publications theorizing that 1975 would bring the beginning of Armageddon. That year, said the unknown authors, marked the 6,000-year anniversary of the biblical creation of Adam and Eve. Once again, though, the Witnesses had to face a prophecy that failed. Some became disillusioned and left, but most Witnesses hung on.

What kept them was a strong sense of community and a purposive life with all questions answered and all obligations clear. Later, when new leaders and generations of Witnesses came on the scene, the failed prophecy of 1975 faded from mention or memory. Meanwhile, the two Witness magazines *The Watchtower* and *Awake!*, which are sold globally in millions of copies, detail the enormous power the society has had in members' lives. Giving them a religion that is rational (in the sense that it is based on knowledge of the Bible and the use of biblical texts as proofs) and not emotional, Witness publications are absolutist in their demands and do not allow for questions or controversy.

Nor do they give members a religion that is in any way devotional. Prayer and meditation are not favored occupations. Leaders prohibit celebrations for Christmas and Easter, along with observances for national holidays and even personal birthdays. The only Witness "holiday" commemorates the death of Jesus in a "Memorial Supper." The occasion is not festive but is instead a solemn and symbolic meal fully shared only by those who think themselves among the "remnant" who share the rule of the heavenly Christ (see the following paragraph). Instead of devotion and celebration, Witnesses study and learn in order to teach and convince others. With their nineteenth-century roots in Adventist ideas, they have taken on the militancy of twentieth- and twenty-first-century American fundamentalism. For Witnesses, though, the militancy expresses a set of beliefs that puts them at variance with most Protestant fundamentalists.

Proclaiming that theirs is the one true faith, they reject the doctrine of the Trinity and see Jesus as the earthly incarnation of the spirit that Jehovah (God's biblical name) originally created as the Archangel Michael. A being with vast power as Jehovah's only divine creation, Jesus, according to Witnesses, ransomed humankind from the devil by giving his life—not on the cross but on a simple stake—and took up his divine position again after his resurrection. Now, though, he has the added role of ruling over creation under Jehovah. Meanwhile, for humans, death ends existence, and no afterlife or hellfire awaits the spirit. Still, except for the "willfully wicked," all who die before Armageddon will be resurrected. Witnesses say that an "anointed" group of 144,000 (the number taken from the Book of Revelation) will reign with Christ in heaven as God's spirit sons. For the "great crowd" of others, however, earth will become a paradise, and they will dwell here forever. Most of those now living will be in this second group, along with pre-Christian believers.

These distinctive beliefs draw a line between Jehovah's Witnesses and other Christians and mark them off as sectarians. So do a number of their practices. Besides avoiding devotion and celebration, the Witnesses—in cases that have led them into law courts—renounce blood transfusions as violations of a scriptural command to abstain from blood. With the end coming soon, their leaders have warned them against participation in civil activities. Witnesses do not vote, lobby, hold political office, or salute or display the flag (once again a source of trouble with the law for them in the mid-twentieth century). Personal rules of purity, similar to nineteenth-century holiness teaching, have set other boundaries. With a strict sexual ethic and a plain, labor-intensive life-style, Witnesses reflect their belief that salvation comes not just from faith in Christ but also from their own hard work. Their missionary practices directed toward nonmembers become more important as ways for the hard work to go on, and these practices have created boundaries in yet another way.

With no ministerial class among them, ordinary Witnesses are ministers or **publishers**, and they publish by going from door to door to bring others to their truth by talk and the dissemination of Witness literature. Averaging perhaps ten to fifteen or more hours monthly doing publishing work and three or more hours any week, Witnesses receive careful training for their roles. They practice their entrance lines, learn how to deflect attempts to dismiss them, and study ways to capitalize on the fears of early twenty-first-century people about nuclear attack, terrorism, crime in the cities, and the like. Nearly all Witnesses take part, with some doing still more work as "auxiliary pioneers," "pioneers," and "special pioneers." Virtually all of the membership is low-income and blue-collar, a pattern that suggests almost total absorption in Witness work. Moreover, besides publishing, Witnesses attend five separate weekly meetings when possible, two of them following each other on Sunday mornings at local Kingdom Halls, a third at a member's home on a weekday evening, and another two, one after the other at Kingdom Halls on a weekday night. Bible study and training for ministry dominate these meetings, with their agendas clearly controlled by the society leadership based in Brooklyn, New York. Women, since the late 1950s, have participated in the meetings, and they have worked as publishers. However, their role is clearly subordinate in a patriarchal organization.

Rigorous discipline and rules for dealing with transgressions through **counseling** and—if that fails—**disfellowshipping** (total ostracism of the offender) characterize Witness culture. Many converts are related to each other by blood or marriage, so the ostracism can be especially difficult and is sometimes ignored. Even more, the demands of Witness life have generated a steady stream of **apostates**, individuals who have left and then paint life among the Witnesses in damaging terms. Yet, as in the African American Nation of Islam, strictness of life has not deterred minority membership. As far back as the 1960s, 20 to 30 percent of Witness membership came from among blacks, and today Witness membership among Latinos is growing noticeably. The Witnesses come third, behind only pentecostals and Baptists, in numbers of non-Catholic Christians among the Latino population. Meanwhile, in the early twenty-first century Witness membership in the United States and throughout the world is huge. With over 90,000 congregations worldwide, nearly 12,000, with over 1 million members, were flourishing in the nation by 2002. And with pulp publications—translated into over 100 languages—spelling out gospel "truth" for Witnesses, revelation among them is in practice as progressive as among the other nineteenth-century new religions. Joseph Smith, Mary Baker Eddy, and Ellen G. White spoke with no more authority than do Witness proclamations in *The Watchtower* and *Awake!*

Communalism

The four religious groups so far examined in this chapter—Mormons, Christian Scientists, Seventh-day Adventists, and Jehovah's Witnesses—all count as sectarian, with the Witnesses clearly the most restrictive and all-encompassing in their demands. Even more demanding, however, were nineteenth-century—and later—groups who lived together in communities. From the eighteenth century on, for some Americans religion meant working to create perfect societies in which all would live together in harmony. Often they saw their planned societies as blueprints for reforms that later would spread or, like other sectarians, as millennial beginnings. Still, with stronger boundaries than the established sects and with **charismatic leaders** to guide them, these groups cherished distinctive sacred stories, effectively dramatized them through rituals, and encoded them in rules for living—to a greater length than other sectarians did. Above all, they adopted a communal life-style in which they challenged two fundamental principles of social independence—**private property** and **sexual exclusivity** in the family.

The Shakers

A classic example is the **Shakers**. Very little can be documented about **Ann Lee** (1736–1784), their founder, before her appearance in New York in 1774. But by the nineteenth century, American Shakers evolved a traditional account that stressed the spiritual significance of events in Lee's life for believers. According to this account, she had experienced visions from her childhood in Manchester, England, and had come to identify the root of human sin in sexual intercourse. After her marriage to Abraham Standerin (Standley), her four children died in infancy (burial records can be found only for one), and she became even more convinced of this belief. Lee, already a member of an ecstatic group that had broken away from the Quakers, reportedly received a vision in 1770 in which she saw the original sin in Eden. After that she began to teach the importance of celibacy, and the Shaking Quakers, or Shakers, came to call her Mother Ann, or Ann the Word. Tradition taught that a later vision urged her to go to America, and a small group of eight believers took ship with her and finally arrived. The Shakers remained in New York state throughout the American Revolution, and although they endured their share of harassment, they continued to preach until Lee's death.

Only thereafter did the **United Society of Believers in Christ's Second Appearing** become communitarian. Living together in "families" of celibates who shared all property in common, the nineteenth-century Shakers taught, like Joseph Smith and Mary Baker Eddy, that God was Father–Mother. On earth, Shakers said, the fullest male manifestation of God had come in Jesus Christ, and the fullest female manifestation in Ann Lee. Moreover, with the sectarian conviction that they were restoring the New Testament church, the Shakers preached community of property and sexual abstinence. They also insisted on the necessity of a separate government, the Christian duty of pacifism, and the power of spirit over physical disease. The millennium was about to begin, they thought, because the second coming of Christ had already happened in Ann Lee.

Shaker **dance**, originating in the ecstatic movements of the Shaking Quakers, became the organized enactment of the sacred story of community based on the dual sexuality of God. Here male and female members of the community revealed that they were equal members of one body, reflecting the divine community. Similarly, the dance dramatized millennial belief because in it the barriers between this world and the next seemingly dissolved. When the Shaker dancers continued their stylized movements long into the night—until the movements gradually lost their stylization and the Shakers whirled themselves into ecstasy—they felt that they experienced a union with one another in God and "Mother" Ann and a foretaste of paradise. From 1837, a period of ritual intensity known as **Mother Ann's Work** set in. Mediums who claimed they could communicate with spirits became important officiants in the rituals. Shakers reported that they had entertained spirit visitors from American Indians to George Washington. They acted out visions as their mediums directed, convinced that in the process they were the privileged recipients of heavenly gifts.

Later, when the greatest involvement in spirit activity declined, **spirit drawings** took over. These drawings or paintings on spiritual and mystical themes, executed

From Holy Mother Wisdom to Grove Blanchard. This Shaker spirit drawing, executed in ink on blue-colored paper in May of 1847, announces in part: "Come lovely child, rejoice with me; And beat the drum of victory, For surely I your Mother true, have sent this plate to comfort you."

by women, were gifts, Shakers said, from heaven and often directly from Holy Mother Wisdom—recollections by the artists of visionary experiences they had known. At their height, these spirit drawings were executed in bright color and careful symmetry, often emphasizing floral, leaf, and arboreal patterns. Symbols of the Father–Mother God filled them, as did representations of a wealth of material goods (musical instruments, jewelry, exotic foods, and the like) that in their actual lives the Shakers denied themselves.

After the Civil War, the Shakers increasingly lost members, until by the early twenty-first century only four remained in one surviving Maine community, which continues to admit new members and has attracted a community of support around it. In their years of greatest vigor in the late 1820s, however, Shaker societies spread from New York and New England to Kentucky, Ohio, and Indiana, numbering nineteen separate establishments and perhaps 4,000 or more members. Despite the harmony expressed in Shaker creed and cultus, considerable evidence of tension between the eastern and western communities existed. Still, the Shakers were renowned for the order of their lives. Shaker furniture, with its simplicity, still suggests the functional efficiency that regulated community endeavors. Noticed for their practical inventions, for their agricultural seeds and pharmaceutical supplies, Shakers gave every evidence of being as pragmatic as they were mystical. They blended otherworldliness with thisworldly success. As they so clearly illustrate, religious groups that thrive seem to be able to balance a variety of concerns, to hold in tension values that are often opposed. Like other sectarians, Shakers knew how to make the ordinary extraordinary.

The Oneida Perfectionists

Not too different from the Shakers, **John Humphrey Noyes** (1811–1886), the founder of the Oneida community, believed that the millennium had already arrived—in the year 70 when the second coming had occurred. Jesus had expected the end within a generation of his personal ministry, and Jesus, argued Noyes, could not have been wrong; so those who followed Jesus in the nineteenth century need fear sin no longer. As perfected saints on earth, said Noyes, they should experience a foretaste of heavenly bliss. Further, because Christ had declared that there would be no marriage in heaven, Noyes thought there was something wrong with marriage as his age understood it. At the heavenly banquet, he said, every food should be available to every guest; on earth, restrictions of the marriage bond seemed to him part of a false, and even sinful, system.

These thoughts received concrete expression in the communities that Noyes established, first, at Putney, Vermont (1840–1847) and later at **Oneida**, New York (1848–1879). The Putney community began the practice of communism and then Noyes's practices of **male continence** and **complex marriage**. Male continence offered a reliable system of birth control through self-control, for in this practice men completed their sexual activity without ejaculation. Complex marriage, made possible by male continence, meant that every man was "husband" to every woman in the community and every woman was "wife" to every man. Only mutual agreement was needed to engage in sexual relations. At the same time, exclusive relationships between any two members of the community were not tolerated. In Noyes's teaching, sex should become the bond of community; it should not prevent the members of one body in Christ from loving each and all.

When difficulties with outraged neighbors brought trouble to the Putney community, Noyes and his group moved to northern New York at Oneida. Here began the most successful years of the **Perfectionists**, who readily engaged in business and manufacture. The community profited from their steel traps, and they also produced a variety of other goods. By 1878 membership had reached about 300, and meanwhile there were experiments in branch communities. Some new members freely joined the community. Others, however, were born into it through unions that were carefully reviewed and approved by Noyes for the production of offspring. Life in the community, from many reports, was pleasurable and satisfying, with various kinds of art, literature, and amusements. Still, by the time the second generation of Oneida Perfectionists had grown to maturity, internal dissension became a factor in community life. Some reacted against their elders in outright agnosticism or secret disapproval of what they saw as the immorality of complex marriage. The misgivings of these Perfectionists, combined with the hostility of outsiders shocked by the community's practices, eventually led Noyes to flee to Canada and to urge the end of the community. Finally, Oneida reconstituted itself as a joint-stock company and ironically is known today for its silverware.

At its height, however, Oneida combined religious theory with practical efficiency. A near-monastic discipline marked all aspects of daily existence. Both complex marriage and communism of property aimed to teach detachment—complex marriage by lessening sexual passion and communism by lessening intense ambition. Members engaged in monastic fashion in the regular practice of **mutual criticism**. They often requested a criticism themselves, or at times, when they seemed to be causing problems, they could be asked to undergo one. Sometimes before all members and sometimes before a selected committee, the person to be criticized listened to what was said about his or her actions and the spirit in which they had been performed. The public nature of the proceeding was meant to act as a check, and personal vindictiveness against any one person was discouraged lest it lead to criticism of the critic. At the end of the meeting, criticisms were summarized, advice offered, and encouragement given. Mutual criticism was found so successful that it became a form of treatment for illness, with Oneidans gathering at a sick member's bed to chasten the patient. Like Christian Scientists and many others of the era, the Perfectionists seemed convinced that spiritual means could—and did—cure.

Oneidans believed that apostasy, unbelief, obedience to "mammon," private property, and death were part of the "**sin-system**," links in a chain that had been destroyed at Oneida. In their place, they thought, the community was building a new chain of redemption. In the Oneida view, Christian love and responsibility would bring freedom, equality, and enduring life to all, since Christian communism had ended the "work-system" and the "marriage-system" in favor of a life fit for the time of the millennium. The Perfectionists, with their carefully drawn boundaries, saw themselves as the first wave of a future available to all who confessed Christ. Yet the material prosperity of Perfectionists, Shakers, and others like them seems a capsule summary of what many, perhaps most, Americans of their time desired. In a land of individualism and pragmatic opportunism, Oneida and other communities offered balance and sanctuary for those uprooted by new industries and cities. They seemed spin-offs of a modernization process that had reached its farthest frontier in the United States.

Paradise Found and Paradise Lost: An Afterword

Alongside Shakers and Oneida Perfectionists, numerous religious communes thrived throughout the nineteenth century and continue to be a noticeable feature of American religious life. Without the distance of a century and more, the not-so-classic communes of contemporary religious culture raise questions more clearly than their often romanticized predecessors. Effective community requires total commitment—expressed concretely in a totalitarian life-style. But what happens to individual followers in such an arrangement? How and when does the power of a charismatic leader infringe on private consciences and feelings? What does it mean to be exposed to such extraordinary personal magnetism when it is considered sacred and when the rules imposed by an established religious tradition are missing?

The **Branch Davidians** of Mount Carmel near Waco, Texas, provide a case that can help us to explore these questions. The group—with roots in Seventh-day Adventism—exploded into public awareness in 1993. Their small community, after a fifty-one day siege, was engulfed in flames as federal law enforcement officials invaded. The Davidians possessed a store of weapons and, it was alleged, had sexually abused their children. Some seventy-four Davidians died, including **David Koresh** (1959–1993), their leader. But the community had existed for many years as an adventist restorationist movement that sought to "correct" a too-easy relationship with American culture.

Victor Houteff (1886–1955) in 1929 began the Davidian adventist movement from which the Branch Davidians, as a splinter group, later came. As a Seventh-day Adventist, Houteff condemned what he saw as the group's compromise with the world and sought to convince a biblical 144,000 to create a church of purity. In 1935 he and his followers moved to Waco as a temporary home: they expected within less than a year to establish the Davidic kingdom (after the biblical King David) in Palestine, where the 144,000 cited in the Book of Revelation would dwell. But the community dug in at their Mount Carmel Center in Texas for longer than that, and they experienced the failure of prophecy when, after Houteff's death, his wife predicted the coming of the millennial kingdom in 1959. Like the Millerites of old and the Jehovah's Witnesses, the Davidians experienced severe disappointment.

Among the splinter groups that thereafter emerged was Ben Roden's Branch Davidian community. It was to this group that the future David Koresh was drawn in 1981. Two years previously, as Vernon Howell, he had joined the Seventh-day Adventist church in Tyler, Texas, where he had acquired a reputation for his ability to quote scripture. Like the earlier Davidians, he believed that the Adventist church had grown corrupt, and he spent long hours at prayer seeking divine confirmation as a prophet and leader. Adventist church leaders remained unimpressed, and he was officially dropped as a church member. Among the Branch Davidian community, though, Howell began to gain prophetic recognition. He changed his name, echoing the biblical King David's and also, in his new surname, Cyrus of Persia, a biblical hero who defeated the Chaldaean empire of the Babylonians. At the same time, with beliefs regarding a final apocalyptic battle between good and evil dominating his theology, Koresh pondered the Seven Seals of the Book of Revelation.

Koresh now directed his message no longer to the Adventist church but edged toward conflict with the symbolic center of worldly power, the United States government. Likewise, he renounced the pacifism of the Adventists and the Houteff community by moving—like Cyrus whom he so admired—into an armored world, in which military might could advance a righteous cause. He also began teaching as revelation that the men of the group should abstain from sexual activity even as he, Koresh, had sex with their wives—so that the new generation of the coming kingdom would all be children of the Prophet. He believed that he was the final manifestation of Christ's Spirit, the Davidic Christ on earth. Shaped by these beliefs, Koresh and his followers saw the flaming demise of the Mount Carmel community as an apocalyptic scenario that, as prophecy foretold, pitted the forces of good (the Branch Davidians) against the forces of evil (the government). The Branch Davidians had been devout, honoring Jesus and taking communion two times daily. They had studied scripture diligently, and they were convinced that Koresh had taught them the true meaning of the biblical Word. They died as martyrs to their belief and to the way of life that embodied it.

Both the federal government and the media at the time failed to come to terms with the religious content of Branch Davidian belief and practice, calling those in the group "cult" members and "fanatics." Yet the Branch Davidian episode raises questions about religion and, especially, its destructive potential. If religious commitment, by its nature, demands surrender and letting go into the unknown, how do people keep themselves within the boundaries of what most regard as "safe"? If transformative religion can be either life-affirming or life-negating, how do people know when the extraordinary world they seek to enter can damage them? These concerns point toward the role of the "border police" of the world's organized religious traditions. Established religions have not simply introduced people to a sacred world. They have also tried to *protect* people from such a world because, like electricity or other unbridled powers of nature, religion can be a destructive as well as healing force. Protection, of course, comes at a price—for many too high.

In Overview

Whatever their later history, the groups explored here, like **sects** in general, originally flourished as voluntary societies with strong boundaries. Claiming experiences of conversion to a life of love and law, members of the sects could be compared to the **Radical Reformers** of the sixteenth century in their zeal for the restoration of true Christianity, their stress on right living, their general indifference toward politics, and their millennialism. Not "also-rans" among the Protestants, they embodied a religious vision of their own, giving to each detail of ordinary life their sense of its extraordinary religious quality. At the same time, like their Protestant neighbors, sectarians reflected the American experience. Their religious experiments emphasized American themes of newness and human possibility with millennial themes. It was no accident that restorationism and millennialism were also important to many evangelical Protestants.

Some groups—like **Mormons, Christian Scientists, Seventh-day Adventists,** and perhaps **Jehovah's Witnesses**—did not demand all from their members. For the first three, their later histories led closer to mainstream denominationalism. By contrast, **Shakers, Oneida Perfectionists**, and, by the late twentieth century, **Branch Davidians** demanded a totalistic life-style. They believed that **private property** and **conventional marriage** divided communities and worked to replace both. All of the groups display a continuing concern for boundaries in the pluralist and postpluralist United States. Yet the groups responded to their situations in religious terms. Their blends of ordinary and extraordinary religion often worked effectively, even if a potential danger always lurked and sometimes emerged. In every case, sectarians exhibited the religious **combinativeness** that has continued to characterize American culture. Others, however, expressed even more combinativeness as they turned to metaphysical movements that encouraged them to take down religious boundaries and go freely where they most wanted to be.

Chapter 8

Homesteads of the Mind: Belief and Practice in Metaphysics

The year was 1848, and the place a ramshackle house in Hydesville, New York. Home to the Fox family—John, a blacksmith; Margaret, his wife; and their two daughters, Maggie, a teenager, and Kate, not yet twelve—it became the site of mysterious knocking sounds. After a week or so of the noises, the girls moved their trundle bed into their parents' bedroom. The new setting made them braver; snapping their fingers and clapping their hands, they asked the knocker to respond. A series of raps came in answer, and thus began what seemed a dialogue with an invisible presence. Soon the raps became the talk of the neighborhood, even leading some to claim discovery of the identity of the rapper—a murdered peddler buried in the cellar. Such reputed contact with the dead meant that, once again, religious excitement was spreading in the Burnt Over District of upstate New York, already the site of Mormon, Millerite, and Shaker preaching.

The incident marks the birth of modern mass **spiritualism**. For students of American religions, it points also to the **metaphysical movements** that proliferated in the United States in the nineteenth century and after. They added to the manyness of religions in the nation and also expressed a new oneness. Spread by word of mouth as well as the media and shared by members of the mainstream, the ideas and attitudes of those who joined these movements spilled beyond their boundaries.

The Religious Meaning of Metaphysics

From one perspective, **metaphysics** is simply an old-fashioned word for philosophy. In America, metaphysics refers to a type of religion present from colonial times to the early twenty-first century, with distinctive developments in the nineteenth. All the metaphysical forms of religion move away from dominant Western conceptions of the divine. Either believers change or mute a sense of the personal in notions of their God, or they avoid the issue of a God altogether by looking instead to extraordinary power or powers that can be used to aid their lives. Metaphysical religions focus, too, on **mind** as a saving force. When "mind" does its work mostly by employing thought or language as its tool, we have mind-oriented religions like **New Thought**. By contrast, when "mind" imagines itself into the material world with symbolic objects, gestures, and ceremonies, we have **occultism**, spiritualism, and sometimes **theosophy**.

Historically, elite forms of metaphysical religion crystallized in the West in a body of secret knowledge and practice passed on by small groups. Until the eighteenth-century Enlightenment, metaphysical religion remained in touch with major strands of the common European culture such as its science. While the Christian church warned against it, some of the clergy agreed with its basic ideas and engaged in its practices. At the same time, among less educated classes metaphysical ideas and practice had their counterpart, handed down from generation to generation, often in rural places. This vernacular metaphysics shared some ideas with the elite varieties, but it emphasized secrecy less than practicality and performance. After the Enlightenment, the new science brought a radical revision in the way educated people viewed the world. As the prestige of science grew, metaphysical religion increasingly became, thus, rejected knowledge. It had always mixed elements from various pagan traditions and combined them sometimes with Judaism and Christianity. Now the educated regarded the mix as thoroughly suspect—remnants of superstition from the early ages of humanity.

In America, at least four forms of metaphysical religion have flourished. First, early America was home to the same elite esoteric religion that characterized English and European culture generally in the seventeenth and early eighteenth centuries. Second, in the Atlantic colonies a traditional, popular occultism came with the herbal and magical practices of settlers and native peoples. Immigrants with rural European ancestry, Indians, blacks, and others all cultivated the beliefs and practices that their cultures had passed on to them. Third, in the nineteenth century and after, metaphysical religion dissolved elite secrecy and spread among self-conscious and educated middle-class people like many spiritualists. Fourth, in the late nineteenth century, a new type of nonsecret metaphysical belief and practice arose. This mind-oriented metaphysical religion—in New Thought and, to some extent, Christian Science—stressed the power of the mind to heal disease and channel spiritual energy to enhance life.

Underlying both more material (occult) and more spiritualizing (thought) forms of metaphysics is the idea of **correspondence**, in which many levels of the universe replicate one another. Metaphysicians believe that since our world exists within a larger one, action on one piece of the world can affect other parts. If everything is like everything else and really is part of everything else, then anything has potential to act on something else. The rationale for **magic** exists in this formula. Magic becomes for its practitioners a valid activity, grounded in an explicit theory about how the world is put together. Even mental healing becomes an ordinary fact of life from this perspective, a form, in fact, of **mental magic**.

Metaphysical believers live in a mental world with fluid boundaries. A universe in which microcosm and macrocosm share the same reality and in which any action has truly cosmic repercussions cannot be neatly divided into separate compartments. In social terms, at least by the nineteenth century the new self-conscious metaphysicians also had little common sense of peoplehood to locate them within well-defined boundaries. Nor did a sense of historical tradition offer boundaries for many of them either. Metaphysical believers floated, seemingly, in universal space. They were cosmic migrants for whom everything was religious and every place was home. Especially, they delighted in religious **combination**. So they mingled Western tradition with Eastern imports at times and also spread their message throughout American culture until often it became indistinguishable from that culture. Although they began from a position of seeming separation, many of their views and attitudes were, or became, thoroughly mainstream.

Metaphysical Sources in the Western Tradition

Metaphysical roots existed in the **Hellenistic world**—the world shaped by the Mediterranean Sea and the language of ancient Greece—during the first three centuries of the Christian era. Here a mixture of Greek, Roman, Christian, Jewish, and other elements fused to produce a cosmopolitan religious synthesis. After Christianity became the official religion of the Roman Empire, elements of that older Hellenistic synthesis provided the ingredients for a metaphysical combinativeness that persisted. Access to the Hellenistic world became newly available to clergy and intellectuals in Europe, especially in the fifteenth century. Fundamental in terms of future influence was a religious philosophy called **Hermeticism**. With the rediscovery in the Italian Renaissance of the bulk of the writings attributed to an ancient Egyptian priest called Hermes Trismegistus, a new interest in magic and mysticism grew in elite circles. Until critical scholarship proved otherwise, Hermes was revered as a great and mysterious seer, and his teachings possessed great authority. The Hermetic texts offered a comprehensive synthesis of mystical teaching from pagan sources, exalting Mind as intuition and giving magical lessons.

Hermeticism, in turn, became a cultural catch-all for similar Hellenistic mystical systems. Among them was **Neoplatonism**, descended from the teachings of the Greek philosopher Plato, who had taught that the real world was the world of Ideas on which the physical universe was modeled. Neoplatonism revised Platonism to see the highest Idea as the One, followed by Mind and then the World Soul, from which came individual souls and, even lower in the hierarchy, the manyness of the material world. The religious task, as Neoplatonists understood it, was to reclaim oneself for the One, retracing the path back by an upward ascent of the soul.

A second Hellenistic system that traveled alongside Hermeticism was **Gnosticism**. The term refers collectively to religious teachings and practices considered to be secret knowledge with power to save the knower from the present, evil world. Believers held that a saving spark of this knowledge had already been planted within a true Gnostic. In a well-known version, once realizing the treasure within, the Gnostic should begin a process of liberation—conceived as a long journey to reunion with a divine counterpart within the Godhead. **Astrology** offered still another system that thrived in a general Hermetic metaphysical synthesis. Present in ancient Mesopotamia, astrology did well in the Hellenistic era and continued to do so. While some used astrological materials in an uncombined form, Hermeticism gave practitioners a chance to mix their astrology with other religious disciplines.

Even before the rediscovery of the Hermetic texts, a number of elite Europeans engaged in **alchemy**, and it blended well with other ideas and practices in the Hermetic world. Alchemy, the ancestor of modern chemistry, meant attempts to change less valuable metals into more favored ones, especially gold. So, for religious alchemists, the process became an external symbol for an internal change the person sought—a mystical merger of self with God. Meanwhile, at least by the twelfth century, the **Kabbalah** became available as a mystical system. For Kabbalists, the Torah dressed truth in an earthly garment, and that garment had to be removed to behold spiritual beauty. Behind the God of Hebrew scripture lay En-sof, who had created the material world from ten emanating intelligences called Sefiroth. In a series of correspondences, Kabbalists explained connections between the Sefiroth and different parts of the human body, names for God, and classes of angels. From its beginnings, the Kabbalah blended elements from many different traditions but changed them to give the material a Jewish stamp. In the Hermetic synthesis, it often acquired Christian trappings and blended still again.

After the Renaissance spread to Northern Europe and time passed, other mystical systems took their place within Hermeticism. Among them were ideas, especially about healing, attributed to the sixteenth-century Swiss physician **Paracelsus**, whose applications of the theory of correspondence to the human body were at once mystical and practical. By the seventeenth century, others in Northern Europe and England turned to **Rosicrucianism** as their chief expression of Hermeticism. Based on publications, attributed to a nonexistent Christian Rosenkreuz, that claimed secret knowledge of ancient Egyptian mysteries, Rosicrucianism provoked great excitement in some circles of the time. Connections between Rosicrucianism and **Freemasonry** have been alleged but are difficult to pin down. In England, especially, **Freemasonry**, based on symbolic use of tools from the building trade, became a system for mystical access by privileged gentlemen.

Not only Freemasonry but all of these systems thrived in post-Renaissance Europe and made their way, as part of Hermetic culture, to Elizabethan England. So with the arrival of the sons and daughters of the Elizabethans in North America, elite metaphysics came to the English colonies. Here it joined the sometimes similar practices that came from the English country magic of nonelites, from the similar practices of Germans, and from Indians and blacks.

Traditional Practice in the Colonies

In early America, both learned and less educated people accepted metaphysical beliefs and practices as they had been handed down. By the end of the American Revolution, however, a clear division marked the two groups. The scholarly elite rejected the old beliefs and practices. The larger body of people, especially in rural America, held onto them as they were passed from one generation to the next. However, even among this wider populace a slow decline began and continued.

Astrology

A leading example is astrology, which came to North America from the England of Queen Elizabeth I. Learned Elizabethans had based their astrology on their understanding of the material composition of the universe. They held that it was made up of various combinations of four elements—earth, water, air, and fire—and four qualities—hot, cold, moist, and dry. For Elizabethans as for earlier peoples, each of these had a definite part to play in the functioning of a healthy body, and when one or the other of them predominated, it stamped its imprint on a person's character. Within this ordered universe, astrology charted the course of the heavens and related the lives of human beings to the stars. The elements and qualities were thought to be present in the stars and to correspond to the same elements and qualities within human beings, with different stars governing each. For astrologers, the stars became cosmic clues, and they used them to determine good and bad days for various activities. In other words, astrology taught that there were signs of the times, making it possible to understand the character of a person by the time in which he or she had been born and making it possible, too, to give advice or even foretell the future.

Like the Elizabethans, the colonists continued to distinguish two kinds of astrology. First and most common was **natural astrology**, which concerned the relationship between the stars and other material things such as the rhythms of nature, the weather, and the human body. Second was **judicial astrology**, which probed the relationship between the stars and human choice and action. This second form of astrology challenged the Christian doctrine of free will because it suggested that the stars controlled human destiny, and it was least accepted. The colonists, however, readily employed natural astrology. Textbooks at Harvard and Yale taught it, and natural astrology appeared, too, in the private libraries of prominent individuals in the late seventeenth and early eighteenth centuries.

Among less educated people, almanacs—found in virtually every colonial household—spread natural astrology. Probably more widely read than the Bible, the almanacs provided their readers with representations of the twelve signs of the zodiac as well as the names and symbols of the seven planets known to antiquity. In many of the almanacs, these signs were only the most basic in a series of symbols on the astrological charts and considered useful for farming, weather forecasting, and medicine. For this last, almanacs usually printed the "anatomy," the picture of a cosmic man surrounded by the signs of the zodiac said to govern parts of his body.

Each day or so the moon could be found in a different sign of the zodiac. Thus, by locating the moon in relation to the sign, a person could decide whether, according to the system, it was a good or bad day to treat some part of the body medically.

Witchcraft

Witchcraft also prospered among the colonists. Like astrology, witchcraft included a learned version, the object of scholarly inquiry, and a nonelite type, which attracted more people. The Pennsylvania German community nurtured a learned form of witchcraft, especially in the brotherhood established under Johannes Kelpius in Germantown, now part of Philadelphia. Here witchcraft was the religion of nature that had once dominated Europe and had only gradually yielded before Christianity. The group inaugurated their settlement with the rites of summer solstice according to early German tradition. They built bonfires out of trees and bushes, raised ritual chants, and invoked sacred powers to bless the place where they were making a home. The **Woman in the Wilderness**, as their community came to be called, offered its inhabitants a blend of pagan, Christian, and Jewish elements. The brothers wore astrological amulets, used incantations in their healing rituals, and studied long hours to learn to control nature by magical means. In their ceremonies, they expressed ideas found in the old pagan religions.

Among the general population, too, magic took hold in the colonies. Many settlers turned to "**cunning folk**," who reportedly could heal the sick, find lost items, locate precious metal with a divining rod, or send a fair wind to a sailing ship. Like the learned German magicians, these witches drew on special rituals to try to contact the powers of nature. In treasure hunting, for example, after the treasure was believed to be located (with a divining rod), the witch might draw circles around it to protect it, recite words held to have special power to overcome unwilling spirits, and use nails to "pin" the treasure down. None of the gestures was meaningless. Rather, the circles imitated the shapes of nature and centered the object as a source of concern. The ritual words sought to empower corresponding forces in nature for the protection of the treasure. Even the nails acted as symbolic statements meant to prevent the treasure from being moved.

The colonists believed, too, in other, evil witches, who used their powers to the disadvantage of some. Many times those who acquired a reputation as evil witches were poor, eccentric, and elderly women, unpopular in their communities because of their begging, their strange ways, or their biting tongues. They could allegedly harass their enemies and bring them illness and even, in some cases, death. Popular belief added to these feared individuals a fourth and still more disquieting type of witch. This was the Satanic witch, who was thought to have gained power by means of a pact with the devil. Those considered evil and Satanic witches at times ended up in trouble with the law in the colonies, and the Salem witchcraft episode of 1692 is one example. For others, the old fertility religion of witchcraft had been more benign, and its ordering of life through nature had been a meaningful way to think and act in an agricultural society. Like astrology, it brought ordinary religion to countless numbers of people and directed their lives in the ways they desired.

The Metaphysical Revival of the Nineteenth Century

Although these older forms of metaphysical religion went into decline, by the nineteenth century a new and deliberate form of metaphysics grew rapidly, a significant part of it once again among an educated elite. Its groundwork was laid in part by the American **Transcendentalists**. Based on their theory of correspondence, the Transcendentalists began to speak and write in a new way. With Ralph Waldo Emerson, their leader, they began to ponder the meaning of the Oversoul, the World Soul of the Neoplatonists to which individual souls were considered bound. They experimented, too, with new ways of living, sometimes in communities like Brook Farm formed to express the unity they saw among all. Always though, whether or not they chose community life, they followed Emerson (never a member of a commune) in a quest for self-culture. In this nineteenth-century version of the journey toward saving knowledge, each individual turned within to cultivate the qualities that would lead to harmony with self and universe.

Emerson and the other Transcendentalists, like many with metaphysical interests, were combinative. They mixed elements from Asian religious sources, from Neoplatonic philosophy, and from European Romantic writers. From India, they took the belief that the world, God, and human beings all participated in one substance and that beyond the illusion of matter lay the reality of spirit. From Neoplatonism came the complementary teaching about the One and the Many united in the Oversoul, in which every soul had its being. With admiration for the European Romantics, the Transcendentalists participated in the revolt against the Enlightenment, which had exalted reason and law. The church became one expression of such law-bound existence, and so a number of the Transcendentalists desired to escape from the formality of the Unitarian church.

Finally, they learned Hermeticism, especially from the metaphysical system of the eighteenth-century Swedish mystic **Emanuel Swedenborg** (1688–1772). The son of a Lutheran bishop and a member of the Swedish nobility, Swedenborg through his education developed a strong interest in the natural sciences and wrote extensively on scientific subjects. But his questions concerning life led him to turn to philosophy and to conclude that only through intuition could a person know God or the inner nature of reality. Still more, from midlife Swedenborg began to report visions and communications with angelic beings in a series of spiritual writings. Reviving Neoplatonic and Renaissance themes, his teachings now rested on beliefs about the correspondence between natural and spiritual worlds. The natural world, for Swedenborg, had been created in the image of a higher spiritual realm, and both worlds received an influx of the divine. In this explanation, Swedenborg presented an especially detailed description of spiritual spheres surrounding the earth. In Swedenborg's teaching, three were spheres of heaven and three of hell. Later American metaphysicians would build their own systems on a modified version of this idea.

Popular Metaphysics in a New Nation

The America in which Transcendentalism flourished was undergoing intense change. Emerson, in fact, capitalized on the change and traveled widely to publicize Transcendentalism. Even as he did so the Industrial Revolution was rapidly spreading. A new factory system was centralizing the production of manufactured goods, while a revolution in transportation was making it possible to travel by rail and steamboat many times faster than stagecoaches and sails had allowed. Meanwhile, a nation of migrants was moving westward to create new settlements or cityward to produce large metropolitan centers. The old homesteads were becoming a thing of the past, replaced by an emerging urban middle class with affluence, education, and leisure.

People praised the inventions of the age of progress and spoke of the manifest destiny of the United States to reach from one end of the continent to the other. But along with the optimism and excitement, migrants and immigrants were experiencing geographical, social, and intellectual dislocation. The ideas that traditional Christianity taught seemed less persuasive. At the same time, science was beginning to challenge religion from another quarter, and Romanticism encouraged people to step beyond accepted borders. In this world of newness and confusion, metaphysical religion provided spiritual havens. It offered homesteads on a mental landscape to replace the physical ones that, seemingly everywhere, were disappearing. Spiritualism, organized Theosophy, and New Thought are all examples.

Spiritualism

The Fox sisters were hardly the first spiritualists in the United States. The Shakers, for example, had frequently claimed spirit visitors. Meanwhile, in the larger culture, popular Swedenborgianism grew. In one well-known instance, when John Chapman, better known as Johnny Appleseed, moved through the Ohio country planting apple seeds and providing saplings to the settlers, he also distributed Swedenborgian literature. Similarly, **mesmerism** (later known as hypnotism) paved the way for spiritualist groups. Introduced from France in 1836 and also called **animal magnetism**, mesmerism brought induced mental—and physical—states similar to those in which contact with spirits was reported.

It was **Andrew Jackson Davis** (1826–1910), the "Seer of Poughkeepsie" (New York), who provided a theoretical grounding for spiritualism. Before he was twenty, he became convinced that in induced mesmeric trance states he could see through material objects as a clairvoyant, and later, on his own, he claimed that he made contact with the spirits of Galen, a famous doctor and writer of the ancient

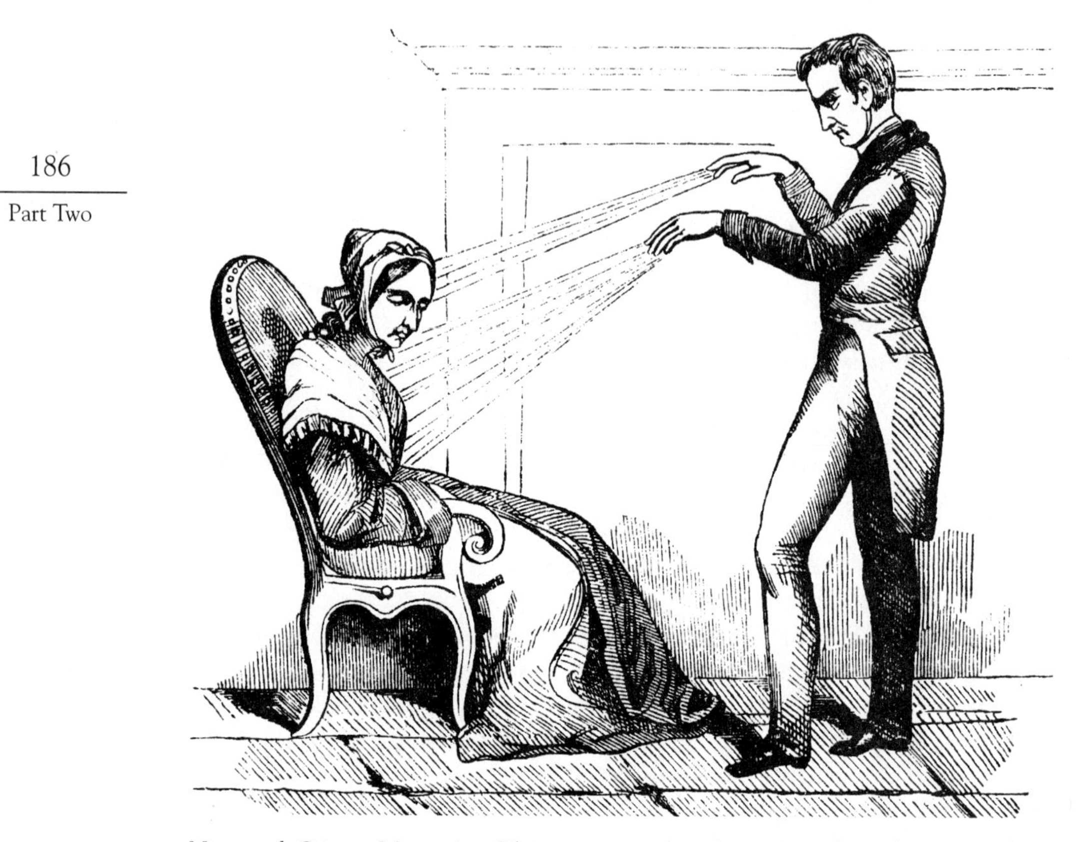

Nineteenth-Century Mesmerism. This anonymous wood engraving from about 1840 depicts a mesmerist directing magnetic "lines of force" toward an entranced female subject who is presumably his patient.

world, and Swedenborg. Davis began to make a name for himself as a healer and prolific writer. He took Swedenborg's theory of six spheres surrounding the earth and modified it so that each of them became a spiritual plane on the way toward a divine Sun. When all human beings had progressed to the sixth plane beyond the physical, he taught, a new set of spheres would appear. Davis thus saw a world of eternal progress, with spirits on various planes, closer or farther from their goal. Contact, especially with spirits closer to earth, seemed to his followers a realistic possibility.

While Davis explained his views, **mass spiritualism** spread. For the many who flocked to **séances**, spiritualism meant belief in and practice of communication with the spirits of the dead through the help of human **mediums**. Those who came were often elderly and often mourning the loss of a loved one. A number were prominent, and many of them—and of the mediums—were women. Mediumship thus gave women a way to assume a leadership role in religion normally reserved for men. Going into trance also enabled them to speak in public in an age when no respectable woman could easily do so. And trances gave them an authority that they could not normally acquire. That a number of female mediums later became active in the women's rights movement testifies to the climate of support for public activity they found in spiritualism. Meanwhile, spiritualism as a movement embraced the major social causes of the nineteenth century. Andrew Jackson Davis, for example, wrote, lectured, and campaigned actively for reform during his career and was especially concerned for women's rights and marriage reform.

To its practitioners, spiritualism seemed reasonable. At a time when religious beliefs were challenged, it promised proof that could be seen and heard that the dead lived on and a world beyond this one existed. Moreover, spiritualists often explained the unusual happenings, in which spirits seemed to materialize and strange objects appeared at séances, by a metaphysical form of scientific language. Many were eager to open their meetings to objective investigators who give their stamp of approval. At the same time, spiritualism brought a Romantic approach to religion. The Romantic spirit of impatience with formal religious institutions and stress on personal experience were part of it. In their felt communication with spirits, devotees believed that they were pioneers moving outside the boundaries that organizations had frequently set. They thought, like the Transcendentalists, that the world was one whole and that close ties joined the spiritual and material worlds. Spirit, for them, was higher and more perfect matter.

More important than theory for spiritualists was practice. Over time, two kinds of mediumship developed—mental and physical. In **mental mediumship**, spiritualists believed, a controlling spirit took over the medium's mind with psychic phenomena the result. By the twentieth century, the medium might engage in billet reading by responding to questions submitted on small pieces of paper and directed to a spirit. Or the medium could practice psychometry, aiming to get in touch with vibrations of a physical object to learn about people (now dead) who had once touched it. The medium might prophesy by reading auras, bands of colored light believed to come from every human being and thought to record the person's life history.

In **physical mediumship**, the spirits were said to acquire material form. Besides their rapping, it was claimed, the spirits tipped over tables and sent objects flying through the air. In automatic writing, mediums said that spirits used them to deliver messages, and in independent writing the spirits were said to write, without guidance, on paper. On some occasions, spirits reportedly made an object disappear in one place and reappear in another. At other times, they were said to use specially constructed trumpets to speak. Spiritualists eventually worked out an elaborate system that declared spirit Indian Chiefs and Spirit Doctors to be acting as assistants to the mediums. For them, Indian Chiefs often worked as Gate Keepers to send unwanted spirits away, and Spirit Doctors as lecturers or advisers on spiritual subjects. Moreover, mediums sometimes claimed healing gifts through a force flowing from their fingers.

Spiritualists, however, were not so successful with larger organization. In the nineteenth century they experienced a groundswell of public interest, especially in the decade after 1848 and after the Civil War. Yet they splintered into small groups around different mediums or groups of mediums. Finally, in 1893, the National Spiritualist Association of Churches came into existence with a congregational government in which independent churches joined in state organizations. This became the largest and the most conservative of the spiritualist organizations, but it was neither strong nor universal and today is very small, with probably between 1,000 and 2,000 churches. Most other metaphysicians have shared this looseness in organizational terms. Metaphysicians have tended to be people without boundaries. As they move beyond the most liberal forms of Protestantism, they reflect their mental universalism in the diffuseness of their organizations.

Theosophy

From the late nineteenth century to the present, spiritualists have often tended toward Theosophy, and this movement itself grew out of a desire to reform spiritualism. The two chief founders of the **Theosophical Society** met at a farmhouse in Chittenden, Vermont, where reports of the materialization of spirits drew spiritualists and other curious visitors. **Helena P. Blavatsky** (1831–1891), world traveler and recent Russian immigrant to the United States, was among them. So was **Colonel Henry S. Olcott** (1832–1907), corporation lawyer, agricultural expert, and sometime government official. The two struck up an immediate acquaintance and, drawn by their mutual interest in spiritualism—and condemnation of what they regarded as its moral indifference and philosophical simplism—became fast friends. In 1875, with **William Q. Judge** (1851–1896) and a group of others, they formed the Theosophical Society in New York, an organization to carry on occult research.

Theosophy, in the generic sense, means metaphysical speculation regarding the nature of the divine, and so knowledge was key to the new group. So Blavatsky, or "HPB" as her followers liked to call her, led the way in the pursuit of an occult form of knowledge, while Olcott provided organizational leadership. Between 1875 and 1877, Blavatsky wrote *Isis Unveiled,* a lengthy book glorifying reputed old spiritual masters and aiming to reveal their secrets for the nineteenth century. Blavatsky wanted to show the presence of a wide-ranging occultism behind the philosophies and religions of the world and especially to show that the Brahmanism of early India and, later, Buddhism were the sources for other religions. Exhibiting an interest in Asian thought similar to the Transcendentalists', like them she also taught the doctrine of correspondence. Matter, for HPB, was the crystallization of spirit, and magic was possible because of the harmony between earthly and heavenly spheres.

Blavatsky claimed that she wrote her vast work with the aid of **Mahatmas**, members of a select brotherhood who, while still human, had evolved to exalted degrees of perfection. The Mahatmas, she said, usually dwelled in the Himalaya Mountains in Tibet, but they possessed magical abilities to materialize at will or to communicate by letters that arrived at their destination as soon as sent. Blavatsky had met the Mahatmas earlier in her wanderings, she reported, and they had been directing her life purposively since, not simply for her own sake but in order to help human beings attain greater spiritual growth. Blavatsky claimed that it was for this reason, too, that with even more assistance they helped her to write *The Secret Doctrine* (1888). In this, her major work, she aimed to set forth the original knowledge from which all later religion, philosophy, and science grew. She gave an account of the beginnings of the world and of human life, explaining an Unmoved Mover and Rootless Root of all things as pure impersonal Be-ness. She told, too, of a law of becoming—the law of **karma**—in which each individual reaped what he or she had sowed and was periodically reincarnated to gain spiritual maturity. And she expressed her belief in the unity of all souls in the Oversoul, the belief that Emerson had affirmed.

Meanwhile, the Theosophical Society slowly assumed its mature form. Its purpose had become threefold. To the quest for occult knowledge, it added its intentions of forming a universal "brotherhood" of all people and of promoting the study of comparative religions. By now, ideally, Theosophists lived according to a disciplined program. As ordinary members of the society, they performed faithfully the duties of their place in life, lived according to the precept of brotherhood, meditated, regulated their diet (vegetarianism was preferred), and progressed spiritually through study and service. If they became part of an inner circle, called the "Esoteric Section," they received the special teaching attributed to the occult masters, or Mahatmas, and at the same time lived by the regular discipline already described. At the top of the hierarchy, the masters themselves were believed to form the third degree of membership.

After Helena Blavatsky died, **Annie Besant** (1847–1933)—an Englishwoman with a background in social reform—led the Theosophical Society. During her era, the group prospered, and by 1930, 50,000 Theosophists could be counted in forty countries, 10,000 of them in the United States. Typically, they were urban, middle-class people, many of them professional and prominent in their fields. Yet even before the death of Blavatsky and Olcott, factionalism beset the society. In 1895, William Judge led out a huge portion of the American membership to form the independent Theosophical Society in America. Other schisms followed. Once again, the boundary problem troubled those striving to live metaphysically, and the group itself was never very large and continued to dwindle into the present time.

Yet Theosophists have possessed an importance for American religious history beyond their numbers. The Theosophical Society provided the first organized channel for the introduction of Asian religious thought into the United States. Although it began as a spiritualist reform society, the formation of the society can be read as a spiritual pilgrimage of discovery to the East, a search by American "strangers" for their religious home abroad. The Theosophical Society also offered an institutional model for mixing East and West. As a combinative organization, the society enthusiastically took ideas from religious seekers in many traditions who seemed to share a similar mystical and metaphysical message. In the

United States, where popular Transcendentalism, Swedenborgianism, mesmerism, and spiritualism flourished, Theosophy absorbed elements from all of them and made the elements its own. Finally, Theosophists introduced a language of expectation for a "new age" and became a major source for the New Age movement of the late twentieth century and after. Theosophy took from traditions of the East and West an elaborate explanation of nature and humanity, rejected a traditional belief in the Western God, and offered instead the complicated details of its metaphysical account of Absolute Reality. The message would prove attractive to many who never joined the society or even knew of it.

New Thought

Even before Theosophy attracted the attention of some Americans, the foundations for **New Thought** were taking shape. Christian Science was its close relative, but while Mary Baker Eddy created a strongly authoritative sect, New Thought followed the pattern of spiritualism and Theosophy. It, too, was diffuse and lacked boundaries—so much that it became in its furthest outreach part of mainstream American culture.

The seed for New Thought lay in the teaching and healing practice of **Phineas P. Quimby**, the mental healer who had also played a significant role in Eddy's life. As a young man, Quimby encountered mesmerism and experimented with it when he could find a willing subject. He began to work with Lucius Burkmar, who in mesmeric trance aimed to diagnose and heal disease, and after the two had been together for a while, Quimby, himself in poor health, experienced a Burkmar cure. The healing depended on Burkmar's ability to change a person's belief, Quimby decided. This assessment became the start of a career dedicated to healing the sick, and when Quimby opened an office in Portland, Maine, he attracted his most famous patients and students, among them not only Mary Baker Eddy but also future leaders of New Thought.

Although neither well educated nor a system builder, Quimby pondered the basis of his healing ever more deeply. He came to reject the use of mesmerism, and his writings instead display a Swedenborgian influence. No doubt through Swedenborgian friends, Quimby had absorbed the idea of correspondence. He saw human beings as spiritual in nature, and he thought of the soul as in direct relationship with the divine mind. It followed for him that when a person was healed, it was because of the operation of the divine spirit on the human soul. For Quimby, this came about through an awakening by which a patient became aware of his or her inner spiritual nature. Sometimes Quimby identified the means to this awakening with a wisdom or science he called the Christ, and at least once he described his teaching as Christian science.

Far more the systematic thinker for the emerging New Thought movement was **Warren Felt Evans** (1814–1889). Formerly a Methodist minister, he became a member of the Swedenborgian Church of the New Jerusalem, based on the teachings of the Swedish seer. Around the same time, suffering from chronic illness, he sought the help of Quimby, was healed, and—encouraged by Quimby—opened his own healing practice. By 1869 he had produced his first book, *The Mental Cure*, in which he argued that disease was the result of a loss of mental balance that in turn affected the body. For Evans, disease was the translation into flesh of a wrong idea in the mind, and the way to get well was to think rightly.

The God whom Evans recognized in his numerous works recalled the Neoplatonic Idea of the One. Yet, in incorporating Christianity and reshaping Quimby's teaching, Evans thought that the One was present within every person as the Christ Principle. Union with this Christ Principle, the divine spark within, said Evans, brought wholeness and health. By contrast, when union with the divine was interrupted, sickness resulted, and another individual—a doctor—could be needed to help. If the patient really wanted to get better and trusted the healer, urged Evans, he or she could submit mentally to the doctor. This would bring a flow of thought from the healer to the patient and begin a restoration.

Above all, Evans seemed convinced of the power of suggestion. He built his view of the relationship between patient and doctor on this idea. Even further, he saw benefits in a state of light mesmeric trance in which the patient could be at once alert and submissive to healing influence. Likewise, Evans spoke of the power of conscious **affirmation**, and his thinking turned New Thought toward the practice of **affirmative prayer**. For later New Thought, the sick person needed to affirm health in deliberate internal statements of "Truth" and banishing disease as error.

Besides the practice of Quimby and the thought of Evans, the existence of Christian Science and its students contributed to the development of New Thought. Mary Baker Eddy's *Science and Health* from 1875 attracted readers who also read Evans. Those who were uncomfortable within the sharply drawn boundaries of Christian Science under Eddy's authority often found themselves leaving the organization. Indeed, some of the most widely influential early New Thought teachers had been Christian Scientists. For example, **Emma Curtis Hopkins** (1853–1925), a member of Eddy's 1883 class in Boston and later editor of *The Christian Science Journal*, left Eddy's movement after she was dismissed as editor and then founded her own seminary in Chicago. More combinative and mystical than Eddy, with her speaking and writing she taught a generation of future New Thought leaders, from Charles and Myrtle Fillmore, who started Unity, and Malinda E. Cramer and Mona L. Brooks, who began Divine Science, to Ernest Holmes, who founded Religious Science.

By 1882, former Quimby students Julius and Annetta Dresser began to practice mental healing in Boston. Many former Christian Scientists came to them, and the very strength of the Christian Science movement forced them to explain the meaning of their work more clearly. Around the same time, members of the movement were speaking of it as mental science. They had come to believe that thought was the greatest power in the world and that harmony with divine Thought, or Mind, was the way to health and happiness. Their interest in Emerson's ideas grew to the point that people in mental science came to regard him as the "father" of their movement. Emerson attracted because, unlike Christian Scientists,

The Long Roots of Metaphysics

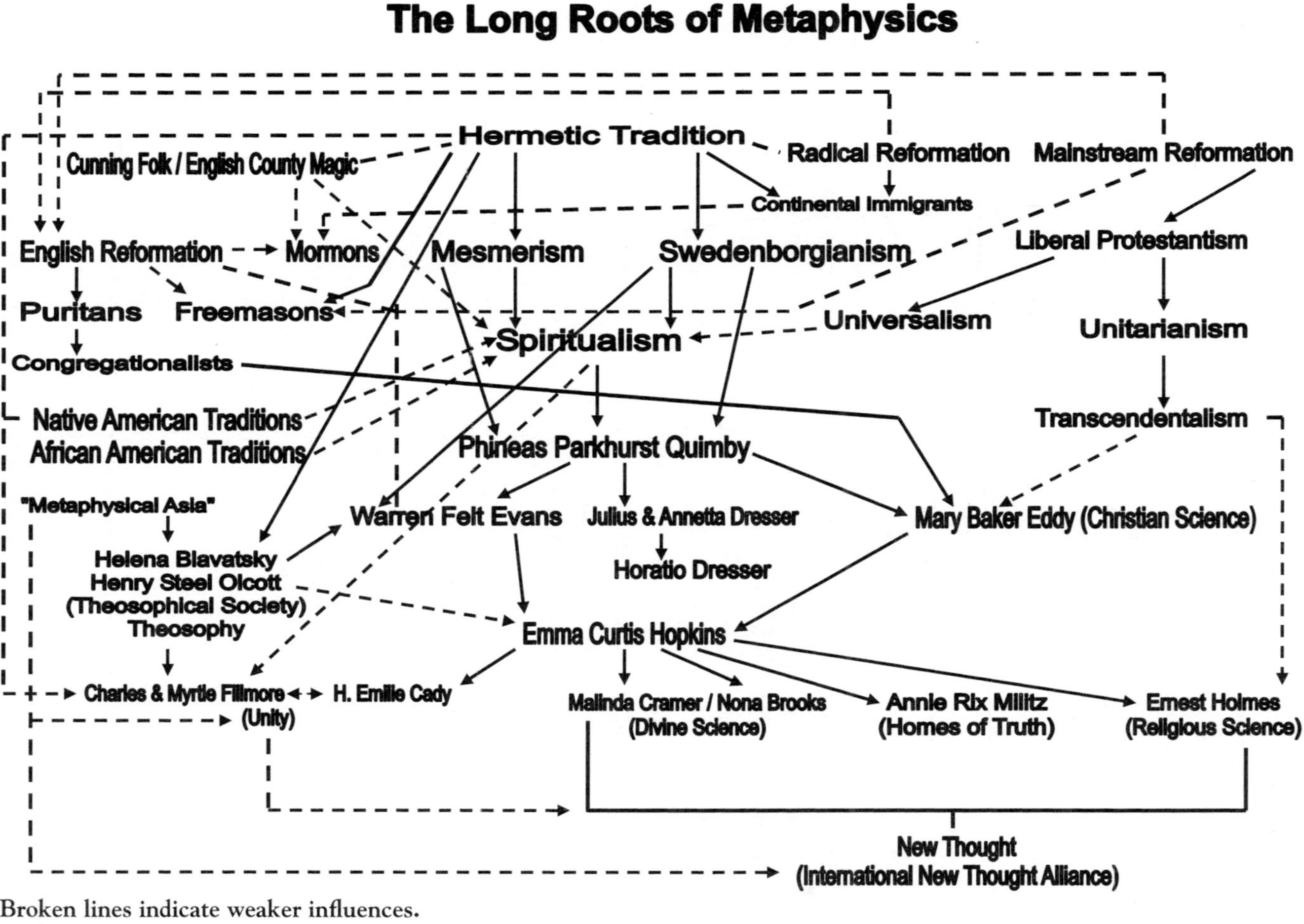

Broken lines indicate weaker influences.

who claimed a basis in divine revelation, mental science proponents sought a foundation in philosophy. Some formed an Emerson Study Club by the 1890s, and by this time too, mental scientists were calling their movement New Thought. They formed the Metaphysical Club in Boston in 1895, and it became the center for the movement's national and international development. Yet they resisted the idea of becoming a denomination or denominations.

Also by this time, a division could be noticed among teachers. Some—in the more rationalistic side of the movement that also affirmed worldly desire—stressed the powers of the human mind to heal disease, achieve prosperity, and bring personal success. This group, dominated by male teachers, most influenced the popular conceptions of New Thought that emerged. A second wing of the movement, though, was more emotion-oriented and self-denying, stressing the capacity and need for love in individual and society and even, in some cases, promoting socialism. Many, if not most, of the well-known female teachers followed Emma Curtis Hopkins in this version of the general New Thought message.

By the turn of the century, an International Metaphysical League announced its aim to teach the universal fatherhood and motherhood of God. Later, from 1915, International New Thought Congresses took place annually; an organization called the International New Thought Alliance continued to provide leadership; and the Unity School of Christianity, with its vast publishing enterprise and ministerial training program, became probably the best known of the New Thought institutions. Other New Thought groups such as Divine Science, based in Denver, and Religious Science, headquartered in Los Angeles, helped to spread belief. Leaders revised traditional religious services to express New Thought ideas, and new words were set to older melodies to create appropriate music.

Yet New Thought's ambivalence about existing in separate denominations proved a continuing theme. The movement made its biggest mark through its publishing, with many of its books becoming best sellers on the "self-help" market. For example, Ralph Waldo Trine's *In Tune with the Infinite*, written in 1897, has sold well over 2 million copies and continues to be reprinted regularly. Even more, New Thought influenced general Protestantism so that many who were part of the mainstream absorbed its ideas and values and began to spread them. In the best example, Norman Vincent Peale, with his *The Power of Positive Thinking* (1952), brought mental healing and the success ethic to millions of people outside the movement, while his other books and magazines continued the trend. But Peale was only the most successful of a series of writers who brought Americans a similar message. New Thought individualism, optimism, and affirmations of health and prosperity blended unobtrusively with mainstream American culture.

Mystical and Psychic Frontiers

New Thought and related movements had their theorist in **William James** (1842–1910), who synthesized the metaphysical conceptions of Emerson and general nineteenth-century American culture. As a Harvard professor with interests in philosophy and psychology, he was fascinated by claims of mental healing. Later, his curiosity about altered states in religious experience led him to experiment with nitrous oxide and even a peyote button. James's book *The Varieties of Religious Experience* (1902) stressed the inner, personal nature of religion, often giving examples from the private experiences of individuals; and James also played a leading role in the organization of the American Society for Psychical Research. James taught the philosophical position known as **pragmatism**, with its central conviction that truth could be known by its consequences and that what worked in the life of an individual or a society should be considered true. Using James's ideas, individuals might reconcile metaphysics with the world of modern science: if metaphysical religion worked to create a meaningful universe for a person, its truth could not be disputed.

Even as the legacy of William James lived on, others pursued their own mystical quests and mind-expanding experiments. Among them, **Aldous Huxley**, an English novelist who settled in California, followed James's example in the 1950s by experimenting with psychedelic drugs. In his book *The Doors of Perception* (1954) he broke ground in describing the experience. Underlying the experiments, for Huxley, was his interest in what he called the **perennial philosophy**. This term was his way of naming the major teachings of the metaphysical tradition, which he said lay at the basis of all religion. Huxley taught that the perennial philosophy saw divine reality within both things and minds and that, therefore, religious practice should mean seeking union with the divine spark within and finding there the ground of all being.

Later American Metaphysics

By the last third of the twentieth century a coherent tradition could guide seekers in the pursuit of mysticism and metaphysics. American culture had helped to prepare them. Protestantism, in general, supported the importance of knowledge in religion. Liberal Protestantism, in particular, in stressing the presence of God everywhere and the goodness of human nature, underlined American spiritual optimism. With liberal Protestantism's lack of strong boundaries, it accustomed people to live comfortably without tight organization. From its place in American culture, the holiness tradition, too, encouraged a perfectionism that, as in the case of Father Divine, could easily be linked to metaphysical views. Meanwhile, urban life and economy militated against strong communities and encouraged individuals to rely more on internal resources. So metaphysical practitioners have blended easily with the cultural mainstream. Because they seek universality and avoid strong institutionalization, they have been hard to count. Because their message has been so similar to what many have already been hearing, they have been as difficult to identify. Nearly everyone, it seems, has incorporated a metaphysical belief or two.

Yet by the 1960s some countered metaphysical diffuseness by finding ways to unite their spiritual quests with a new sense of boundary definition. A series of short-lived but intense religious movements resulted in which often a decided contrast emerged between what practitioners believed and how, in sociological terms, they lived. Linked to some extent conceptually to the New Age movement (see Chapter 10), these groups may be distinguished by their cohesiveness as well as their theological distinctives. They have shaped their spiritual practices in ways that—like their theologies of universalism—have departed significantly from Christianity, however reconstructed. Still, although these groups are often described as countercultural, it is more correct to say that they have exaggerated certain tendencies within American culture. Such groups, thus, have affirmed American culture even as they have rejected it. They have ranged along a continuum from those who carry on the tradition of self-conscious magical practice as communities and others who follow a more mind-oriented metaphysics, also as communities. Witchcraft **covens** (groups of witches) offer one example of the first, and **scientific-technological groups** of the second.

For witchcraft devotees, the law of correspondence has transformed the natural world into the macrocosm to which human beings should conform their lives. Contemporary witchcraft, or **neopaganism**, has taught reverence for nature as the source of fertility and life. Through the use of ritual, members of a coven seek to raise energy (their own) and to create harmony for themselves and others with the order of the natural world. Ritual, in this understanding, becomes a magical means to assure the operation of nature and—as important—to empower themselves. In their turn, scientific-technological groups have linked science with metaphysics in ways that echo spiritualism and New Thought. In a well-known instance, L. Ron Hubbard's **Scientology** has promoted an electrical device called an E-meter in order to help users become "Clear" (like the "clear" button on a calculator). Practitioners, say Scientologists, can liberate their consciousness so that it can control matter, energy, space, and time. The goal is total freedom, and the means—as in all the scientific-technological movements—is the pursuit of knowledge as a form of power.

So while witchcraft groups have turned people toward nature through magical rituals, scientific-technological groups have taught them that the real world lies beyond matter in saving knowledge. Yet for both, as for metaphysics in general, the mind is the place where sacred pathways begin and end. There, where extraordinary religious experience is seen as possible, believers seek strength for the ordinary religion of living. Since the law of correspondence tells believers that mind equals world, extraordinary and ordinary religion for them become one. Hence, as in sectarian groups, these communities have demanded seemingly everything, and converts have still been willing to sign on. And as in the Christian sectarian groups whose potential for commitment could become totalitarian, metaphysical groups have faced similar possibilities and have sometimes exhibited the destructive side of religion. Consider, for example, the metaphysical community called **Heaven's Gate**, whose thirty-nine members ended their own lives in a mansion near San Diego in 1997.

With a scientific-technological orientation, the Heaven's Gate group reflected themes present in **UFO groups**, who took their cue from unexplained flying objects in the space age. Members of these groups have claimed contact with visitors from outer space and say they have boarded their vehicles. They have seen these visitors as higher and more perfect beings who want to teach willing human beings a life-transforming knowledge. However, the Heaven's Gate people separated themselves from other UFO believers, whom they saw as deluded, through their adherence to their leader Marshall Applewhite's teachings about the "Next Level." With a combinativeness that brought together gnosticizing elements not only from the UFO groups but also from the *Star Trek* films and television series, computer technology, Theosophy, spiritualism, premillennialist Christianity, and monasticism, Heaven's Gate created a virtual reality that, for believers, could not be falsified.

The group announced that in the early 1970s, as—in effect—walk-ins, they had taken over the bodies of adult humans to do the work required to reach the Next Level. They had prepared by lives of monastic discipline, observing strict celibacy and, in some cases, even physically neutering themselves, since in the bodies of Next Level life, they believed, no reproductive organs would exist. They accepted, too, the claims of Applewhite to be a reincarnation of the same being who had once incarnated as Jesus of Nazareth. And they thought that his former companion and co-leader, Bonnie Nettles, who had died in 1985, was, in fact, his Older Member, or "Heavenly Father." The end of the present corrupt civilization was at hand, Heaven's Gate declared, when humanity would be "spaded under." For all the negative twists and turns of their theology, members yearned to be new creatures in the Next Level, clearly demonstrating the potentially radical nature of religious claims. They quoted Christian scripture about laying down their lives for the sake of following Christ and, in their combinativeness, translated gospel language into a command of literal death—this under the sign of the then-visible Hale-Bopp comet and, close behind it, a spaceship that was waiting to take them to Next Level life.

As the history of Heaven's Gate has shown, homesteads of the mind can be places of danger. In the main, though, as among the Christian sectarian groups of the previous chapter, metaphysical belief and practice have conducted people safely beyond ordinary boundaries and achieved better results. Both newer and older American metaphysical groups developed long and highly elaborate explanations of the nature of humanity and the universe. For them, the real world existed in the mind or in the universe. Moreover, ritual, found useful in mysticism and magic, was a way of making the metaphysical world concrete. It, too, led to a mental landscape, even if metaphysicians expressed clear social interests along the way—in spiritualism, in Theosophy, and in New Thought. Above all, homesteads of the mind were *American* homesteads. The picking and choosing that combinative religion brought was congenial in a land where every religion was equal in the eyes of the law and where many peoples and traditions encountered one another. The practicality of metaphysical religion agreed with general American practicality. Even spectacular journeys into the "other" world, for American metaphysicians, seemed to help them to gain power in this one.

Finally, homesteads of the mind have been places for people who need to create community in the midst of strangers. In the later twentieth century and the twenty-first, with a diminished sense of place and peoplehood, the children of the highway and the divorce court were looking for refuge. They found it in felt experiences of communion with the All, or divine Mind, through a divine spark within. Seeking union with universal being took the place of existing union with members of a community who shared a common history. In the end, metaphysical religion appealed because most Americans—with their histories of migration and mobility—have been either dislocated persons or descendants of the dislocated.

In Overview

Metaphysical religions have had a long history in the West. **Hermeticism**, along with **Neoplatonism**, **Gnosticism**, **astrology**, **alchemy**, and **Kabbalism**, numbered among its earlier forms, to be joined by later movements like **Paracelsianism**, **Rosicrucianism**, and **Freemasonry**. As religious systems, these movements and their successors offered secret and, by the nineteenth century, rejected knowledge to educated elites. During colonial times, among a broader segment in North America, popular metaphysical practice thrived in astrology and witchcraft. Then in the nineteenth century new and self-conscious forms of nonsecret metaphysics sprang up. The New England **Transcendentalists** provided a combinative theoretical expression for metaphysical believers, and later **spiritualism**, **Theosophy**, and **New Thought** gave vernacular expression to metaphysical religion. By the turn of the twentieth century, **William James**, as psychologist and philosopher, was exploring mystical and psychic frontiers. In the late twentieth century and after, a variety of small and intense movements perpetuated the metaphysical legacy, among them witchcraft covens and scientific-technological groups. The dangerous quality of borders and boundaries to an extraordinary world has been as apparent in metaphysical belief and practice as elsewhere. So have been its positive results—often, especially and sometimes paradoxically, in material terms. In general, metaphysical religion has been popular among all classes of people.

Metaphysicians base their theories on the idea of **correspondence**, and so they have mingled ordinary and extraordinary religion and used the extraordinary to achieve pragmatic and thisworldly results. Even further, without strong communities of support, metaphysical practitioners have tended to be people without fixed social boundaries. For them, universalism has been a condition of living as well as a condition of mind. Metaphysical believers have often reflected the upheavals of traditional community in modern urban and industrial society. Frequently, they have created mental homesteads to replace the human communities they cannot find.

But even as some dislocated Americans found homesteads of the mind, others still felt estranged. For no groups did this observation seem more true than for those who found themselves in the West either as inheritors of a non-Western religion or as converts to one. As the East became West in America, new religious forces offered still more chances for religious **combination** and demanded yet more decisions about moving toward what was new or retreating to preserve religious cultures as they were.

MANYNESS: PATTERNS OF EXPANSION AND CONTRACTION

The ancient Chinese classic *Daedejing* (*Tao Te Ching*) is built on a series of paradoxes surrounding the **Dao** as the source of all things and **yin** and **yang**, opposites that in Chinese philosophy come from it. Although yin and yang are hard to define, in Chinese belief they alternately complement and antagonize each other. Yang is considered an expansive force, and yin, a contractive one. Although it may seem odd to cite a Chinese religious text in a book about American religion, the reference makes sense for the post–Civil War period. In the decades following the war, some 300,000 Chinese came to this country, especially to California. Later the Japanese came to the West Coast—over 100,000 from 1901 to 1907. Meanwhile, Americans had mixed feelings, at best, regarding immigration. On the one hand, American culture, like the yang of the Dao, stretched itself to include peoples who seemed exotic and "other." On the other, Americans in a yin mood retracted their welcome.

These patterns of **expansion** and **contraction** also characterize American religion in general from the Civil War to the present. Americans have stretched to embrace religious beliefs and behaviors that seemed to them new, different, and often exotic. Simultaneously, they have contracted culturally to keep out the new and to consolidate. Thus, expansion and contraction formed a cultural system, an expression of the social body's engagement in a balancing act. In turning to Eastern religious forms, Americans have expressed religious expansion, while Easterners themselves have shown expansiveness by adopting aspects of an American religious style. Conversely, in cultural enclaves that have kept out religious difference, both Americans and Eastern immigrants have exhibited patterns of contraction. By the late twentieth and twenty-first centuries, new spiritualities were offering all Americans chances for religious expansion, while various forms of religious conservatism were enabling them to keep to patterns of religious contraction and consolidation.

Chapter 9

East Is West: Eastern Peoples and Eastern Religions

In 1893 the United States celebrated the 400th anniversary of Europeans' arrival in the Americas. The Columbian Exposition, named for Christopher Columbus, drew over 27 million people from at least seventy-two countries to its specially erected buildings in Chicago. As an open display of American attitudes, the exposition championed economic development and also exhibited the unexamined imperialism and racism of the age. In a more subtle display of the nation's values in conjunction with the exposition, representatives of major world religions assembled for the World's Parliament of Religions. With liberal Protestant leadership, parliament members took stock of the religious work of the century that was ending and planned for the future.

Members of the group that met clearly expressed religious difference. Annie Besant, the rising leader of Theosophy, impressed listeners with her addresses, and, rumor had it, a devoted Indian swami slept outside her room to protect her. The persuasive Hindu Swami Vivekananda, with his dramatic turban and orange and crimson garments, also addressed the congress. Buddhist Anagarika Dharmapala, later to establish Mahabodhi Societies in America, had come, and so had his fellow Buddhist, the Zen master Soyen Shaku, from whom a Zen lineage in the United States would derive. George A. Ford, a Presbyterian missionary, read the paper of a fellow missionary in Syria, closing with a quotation from Baha'u'llah, the founder of a religion called Baha'i.

In the speeches and social events that accompanied the parliament, East had come West, and visibly so. Although parliament organizers tried to control, especially, the Asian presence—so that the message of the parliament would finally be that all religions led to Christianity, the highest religion of all—the non-Western representatives had their own cases to make and, in many ways, did so. More important, the parliament proved to be the symbolic beginning of a new era for American religious history as, increasingly, Eastern religions would flourish in the nation. The World's Parliament of Religions signaled the growing American interest in Eastern religions, and at the same time it signaled a period of immigration that brought Asian peoples, as carriers of their native religions, to the country. In both a demographic and religious sense, the pattern was one of **expansion**.

Looking from Europe and the East Coast, from the Nearer East came **Orthodoxy**, the Eastern form of Christianity. From the Middle East came **Islam**—the religion of one-seventh of the world's people—and **Baha'i**, a nineteenth-century new religion related to it. From the Farther East, India sent its traditions called **Hinduism** by Westerners. China and Japan exported numerous forms of **Buddhism**, and Japan also contributed movements derived from **Shinto**. Tibet brought its mystical forms of Buddhism, and other Asian nations brought their own religious groups as well. As the religions of immigrants, these were **ethnic** religions that for centuries had been part of the heritage of the people who brought them. They were religions of particular places and peoples, and they blended extraordinary and ordinary religion. As the religions of American converts, however, the incoming religions were **export** religions. As people from Protestant, Catholic, and Jewish backgrounds embraced them, in the case of the Asian traditions they to some extent changed the religions. The new (to non-Asians) religions made it possible for converts to live an extraordinary religious life, offering a sense of liberation that traditional Western religions had not provided. To a lesser degree, the same generalizations could be made about Eastern Orthodoxy.

While Eastern religions were embraced by some Westerners because the religions were considered "other," Easterners themselves felt separate from American life and culture. Eastern Europeans, Middle Easterners, and Chinese and Japanese Americans had for decades experienced harassment and discrimination. The Chinese, many of them attracted to the United States as railroad construction workers, were early targets. So pronounced did West Coast hostility, and even physical violence, against the Chinese become that as early as 1882 Congress passed the Chinese Exclusion Act. The law was only the first in a series of legal measures designed to lessen the Chinese presence, and government policy led to a rapid reduction of the Chinese community, from 107,000 in 1890 to only 75,000 by 1930.

Japanese Americans also suffered hostility. In 1907, the so-called Gentlemen's Agreement between the United States and Japan restricted immigration to nonlaborers. Then in 1913 and 1920 the Anti-Alien Land Laws of California prevented the Japanese from controlling farmlands, making further immigration unappealing. A Supreme Court decision of 1922 prohibited Japanese immigrants from becoming naturalized American citizens, and in 1924 the Oriental Exclusion Act cut off the immigration of people who were ineligible for citizenship, effectively halting Japanese immigration. Later events in the twentieth century were even harsher. During World War II, Japanese Americans were forcibly evacuated from their West Coast homes and sent to internment camps.

Experiences such as these encouraged religious contraction among Asian religious groups. Ironically, they felt their foreignness even as numbers of mainstream Americans were becoming seekers of Eastern wisdom. Yet many Easterners became Christian converts and still others modified their birth religions in light of Western Christian ways, while many non-Asian Americans strongly rejected Asian religious ideas and practices. So for both groups—Eastern immigrants and mainstream Americans—patterns of expansion and contraction existed at the same time.

Nearer East: Eastern Orthodoxy

One major Eastern religious group, however, was non-Asian. **Eastern Orthodoxy** is the collective name for the Christian religious traditions of various national churches in Eastern Europe and the Eastern Mediterranean. Orthodox religious

Russian Orthodox Cathedral, Sitka, Alaska. Until 1872, Sitka was the cathedral city for the huge Russian Orthodox diocese that included all of the United States and Canada. This photograph of the cruciform-shaped wooden cathedral dates from about 1900.

contact with the North American continent began as early as 1743, when a Russian soldier baptized some Alaskans. Before the end of the century, eight monks made their way to Kodiak Island, off the Alaskan coast, to build a **Russian Orthodox** church there. The native peoples of Alaska welcomed them, and soon several thousand had become Christian. In the nineteenth century, Orthodox religion continued to grow in Alaska, until by the start of the twentieth century about one-sixth of the population, over 10,000 people, were church members. After Alaska became a possession of the United States, the church moved its headquarters to San Francisco, where Russians, Greeks, and Serbians from Eastern Europe turned to Russian Orthodoxy. By century's close, the Russian Orthodox had come officially to New York, while the number of Russian immigrants to the United States was increasing rapidly. Within a decade, from 1906 to 1916, Orthodox church membership grew fivefold, from 20,000 to 100,000 people.

With the twentieth century, the **Greek Orthodox** exceeded the Russian as a result of large-scale immigration. Greek churches appeared in New York and Chicago before 1900—even though the Russian Orthodox leadership pursued a "pan-Orthodox" policy, welcoming Greeks and others and giving them clerical authority. The Greeks, however—like other nationals—wanted to worship in their own language and to follow familiar religious patterns. Now, with a huge Greek immigration, that became possible. Membership swelled throughout the twentieth century, until the Greek Orthodox constituency (close to 2 million in the mid-1990s) grew to be noticeably larger than the Russian church. At the same time, another contingent, almost as large as the Russian, participated in various separate national churches, including the Albanian, Bulgarian, Romanian, Serbian, Syrian, and Ukrainian. With this huge numerical presence, many came to view Eastern Orthodoxy as a major faith in the United States and ranked it only behind Protestantism, Catholicism, Judaism, and Islam.

Eastern Orthodox Religion

Different from the Roman Catholic church, with its emphasis on being one religious body, the Eastern church cared more about expressing local community. And while the Roman church concerned itself with matters of law, Easterners stressed contemplation more. Later, when Protestantism appeared, Eastern Orthodoxy seemed to Westerners even more radically "other." If Protestants felt urged by the Word to action in the world, Orthodoxy has thought of the Word as a precious object surrounded by ritual and a model for prayer. And if Protestants tend to separate ordinary from extraordinary religion, Orthodoxy has created through its **Divine Liturgy** a unity expressed at many levels, both spiritual and material.

For Orthodoxy, the local community is the church. Organized in self-governing, or **autocephalous** (literally, "self-headed"), churches, the Orthodox give first rank of honor to four ancient churches called **patriarchates**: Constantinople, Alexandria, Antioch, and Jerusalem. After these four, they recognize eleven other autocephalous churches, among them the Russian and the Greek, which have both figured so prominently in North America. Below these come churches called **autonomous**—self-governing in most ways but not fully independent—and finally come provinces. What holds all of these local communities together is their adherence to "right," or "correct," religion. The word **orthodoxy** means just this, and Orthodox churches have understood **right religion** to have two sides.

First, they consider it to be **right belief**, a union of Christian people in faith and doctrine through acceptance of a common tradition. Inherited through scripture, through the writings of the fathers and other authorities, and through word-of-mouth teaching, tradition was initially passed on, say the Orthodox, through the authoritative teaching of the seven ecumenical ("worldwide") church councils, the last in the year 787. Second, the Orthodox see right religion as **right worship**. Acknowledging the same seven sacraments as the Roman church, the Orthodox emphasize their common worship of God through the sacraments and, especially, through the Divine Liturgy in which the eucharist is celebrated. Like the Catholic Mass in structure, the Divine Liturgy creates a community at worship in which outward organization matters less than collective presence around the altar.

Orthodox difference from the West grew up over centuries. During the eighth and ninth centuries, a controversy over the place of images in the churches helped to crystallize Orthodox thought and practice. One group, called **Iconoclasts**, considered religious art a form of idolatry and demanded that **icons**, or religious images, be destroyed. Another group, called **Iconodules**, venerated icons and wanted to preserve them. At issue was the question of what Orthodoxy thought of the material world and, ultimately, of the human nature of Jesus. If matter could be a way into the spiritual world, then for the Orthodox Christian the doctrine of the Incarnation, the taking of human flesh by the son of God, was possible. In the end, the Iconodules won out, and Orthodoxy became a religion of icons. Behind its iconic preference lay the same sacramental belief that ran through Catholicism. But the Orthodox developed this belief further, and, especially, they developed it to express qualities of vision and sight. An icon encouraged the gaze of the contemplative person and, for the Orthodox, became a meeting point where the sacred world could enter this one.

Iconic theology grew. The Orthodox saw the Bible as an icon of Jesus Christ and humans as icons of God—so that the Orthodox emphasize sin less than Catholics or Protestants do. Similarly, the Orthodox have viewed the church as the icon of the Trinity in which Father, Son, and Holy Spirit are one. Finally, the most important icon for Orthodoxy is Jesus Christ. Seen as the image of divine glory and light, Jesus is portrayed in Orthodox churches as divine king and victor over the forces of evil. Even in representations of the cross, the Orthodox express their belief in the Godhead of Jesus, and their images of the crucified Jesus show him crowned with gold and precious stones.

The mystical teaching of the East has shaped Orthodoxy as much as the iconic theology did. Through the centuries, the church fathers of the East contributed to a growing body of mystical literature. **Mysticism** here means belief in the possibility of an experience of total union between the divine and the human, and the religious experiences based on that belief. **Hesychasm** became the particularly Orthodox way of understanding mysticism. Coming from the Greek word for quiet, the term refers to a form of mysticism stressing the need for inner quiet and tranquility to wait for the transforming light of God. With the goal of seeing divine light, it developed techniques of physical and mental control. Seekers directed their breathing, posture, and eye movements according to specific exercises. Mentally and sometimes verbally, they repeated a short prayer to help produce a state of inner quiet.

Emphasis on mystical light linked hesychasm to the iconic thought and practice of Orthodox worship. Mysticism, like the veneration of icons, encouraged a form of seeing. The third element that shaped the history of Orthodoxy, however, was a matter of *not* seeing. While the West, by the sixth century, saw the pope of Rome as the sole head of the church on earth, the East looked at matters differently. Opposition to a Western insistence on the **primacy** (the firstness) of the pope grew. A phrase inserted through papal authority into a traditional Christian creed proved especially troubling. Whereas in its original form, the creed declared that the Holy Spirit proceeded (came forth) from the Father, the addition to the creed proclaimed that the Spirit proceeded from the Father *and from the Son* (in Latin, ***filioque***).

Since ecumenical councils had earlier forbidden changes in the creed, a clear choice existed here between the authority of the pope and that of the councils, between the one monarch and the community and its representatives. The Orthodox chose the councils and the community, regarding the papal claims as a departure from original Christianity. In the year 1054 the split between East and West was dramatized when a messenger from the pope left a decree of excommunication for the patriarch (bishop) of Constantinople on the high altar of his cathedral. The Orthodox, however, point to the year 1204 as the point of no return. In that year the European Christian soldiers who had joined the Fourth Crusade stormed the city of Constantinople (modern Istanbul, Turkey), sacking and pillaging it. The Orthodox saw the carnage as the final stroke in the conflict between the two churches. For them, the damage had become irreparable.

Orthodoxy in the United States

In the United States, Orthodoxy—as in all its history—continued as a religion of mystical contemplation and ethnic solidarity, especially among people from the immigrant generation. But overall, Orthodox practice has declined as second- and third-generation children of the immigrants grew away from their heritage. For a number of them, Americanization—and the pattern of expansion—has meant a weakening of ties with ancestral faith. Yet Orthodox leaders have worked to accommodate the needs of American adherents. Like Jews and Catholics, many of the Orthodox reformed their liturgies to bring them closer to Protestant America. English came into use in services, often alternating with the national languages spoken in the churches. The Orthodox also altered their calendar of feasts and holy days to bring it into conformity with the Western Christian calendar. Many churches introduced seating so that people would not have to stand—the custom of the past—during the Divine Liturgy. Often, too, churches brought in instruments and mixed choirs.

The **manyness** of the United States has strongly affected Orthodoxy. With so many national churches, jurisdictional claims became confused and frequently erupted into disputes; religious contraction and separation were not hard to find. By the 1970s, at least three separate branches of Russian Orthodoxy (the legacy of the Russian Revolution), three groups of Ukrainian Orthodox church members, and two groups of Syrian Orthodox adherents all flourished. Throughout the century, small splinter churches also formed. Other Eastern Christians, called **Uniates**, remained outside the Orthodox umbrella but—in different national churches and with distinctive rites—came under Roman papal jurisdiction. Still other Eastern Christians—those who had separated from the main body of Christendom even before the Orthodox-Roman break—found their place in the United States, members of the Armenian Apostolic Church and the Coptic Church among them. Then, in 1996, major administrative change came to the largest Orthodox contingent when Greek leaders separated the Greek Orthodox Archdiocese of North and South America into four jurisdictions, including the newly formed **Greek Orthodox Archdiocese of America** for the United States. At the same time, new calls for unity sounded throughout the American Orthodox community.

Meanwhile, Russian Orthodoxy has maintained its historic role of intellectual and social leadership. The largest of its three branches—the **Orthodox Church in America**—through its St. Vladimir's Theological Seminary has produced a continuing stream of publications on mystical theology and other themes. Both the Greek Orthodox Archdiocese and the (Russian) Orthodox Church in America belong to the Standing Conference of Canonical Orthodox Bishops in America, the one organization that can speak for all of American Orthodoxy and that seeks to foster cooperation in the face of Orthodoxy's many divisions. And both have participated in the National Council of Churches, although not without tensions. Even with its divisions and problems, Orthodoxy has clearly prospered in the United States. Its manyness does not seem unusual in a nation of religious manyness. Its preference for contemplation has become a growing choice among other (non-Eastern) Americans who find their lives too cluttered and too fast. In fact, a growing number have found their way into Orthodoxy, attracted by its Divine Liturgy and mystical worship style. So religious expansion has once more marked the Orthodox way.

Middle East: Islam

Close to Eastern Orthodox lands and in some cases overlapping them were the homelands of **Muslims**. **Islam**, their religion, was—and is—*Middle* Eastern both geographically and spiritually. Located between Asia and the West, it has shared much with Jews and Christians, but it has also been significantly different. In the

United States it became a religion of "otherness," and, aside from their recognition of blacks as Muslims, for many years most Americans hardly knew that Islam existed in their country. Yet the relationship of Islam to the Americas is a long one.

According to Arab geographers, Muslim ancestors from Spain and Portugal landed in South America as long ago as the tenth century. To the north, in the sixteenth century Marcos de Niza, a Franciscan friar sent to explore Arizona, used "Istfan the Arab" as his guide, and an Egyptian known to Americans as "Nosereddine" (Nasr-al-Din) lived in present-day New York state. In the Appalachian mountain regions, too, some claim that people of "Moorish descent" early amalgamated with other groups to form the multiracial Melungeon people. Scattered references to Muslims exist elsewhere. The largest group from the seventeenth through nineteenth centuries, though, were West Africans, who came as slaves.

Toward the end of the nineteenth century, other Muslims began to arrive. With small numbers at first, the largest group were Arabs from Syria and what is now Lebanon. They concentrated their settlements in industrial centers such as New York, Chicago, and Detroit, where they peddled dry goods, operated small businesses, or engaged in unskilled labor. Generally economically successful, most remained in America to the end of their lives even though that was not their original plan. But other non-Arab Muslims also immigrated to the United States. Some were Europeans from Poland, Albania, and Yugoslavia. Others came from South Asia, many of them to rural California as part of the mission-minded **Ahmadiyya Movement in Islam**, a nonorthodox group.

The major impetus for South Asian—and other—Muslim immigration came with the **Immigration Act of 1965**. In a major piece of legislation, Congress abolished the previous system of immigration quotas based on each national group's representation in the United States population in 1890. The new system no longer favored European immigrants over South and East Asians or other national groups. So by the 1980s, Muslim immigrants came from more than sixty countries. Arabs, Middle Easterners, Europeans, and South Asians joined Central and South Americans and even Indians from Fiji. Arabs and Iranians constituted the largest immigrant communities, followed, after 1965, by Pakistanis and Asian Indians.

With Islam a universal religion, American converts also came. In 1888, Mohammed Alexander Russell Webb, a former journalist and then-diplomat, became the first mainstream American to embrace Islam after his contact with Indian Muslims in the Philippines. Other converts from Protestant, Catholic, Jewish, and Mormon backgrounds followed, mostly through marriage. Meanwhile, the Muslim message of universal community and equality attracted African Americans, who heard the Muslim tradition that a daughter of Muhammad, the founder of Islam, had married a black man. By the late 1970s, the former Nation of Islam was moving clearly toward mainstream Islam and winning Arab approval. Other African Americans joined the Indian Ahmadiyya Movement and other Muslim organizations. Taken together, Muslims in the United States today either already outnumber Jews or are very close to doing so. They can be found in almost every American town of any size, with significant numbers engaged in all the professions. With a continuing flow of immigrants, a high birthrate, and attractiveness to converts—both African Americans and others—American Islam is thriving.

The Religious Meaning of Islam

According to traditional accounts, the founder of Islam, **Muhammad** (570?–632)—humble in background but a member of a powerful clan, entered the service of the wealthy Khadijah of Mecca as a merchant, married her, and prospered. Thereafter he reported a series of visions and voice revelations in which **Allah** (God) informed him, through the angel Gabriel, that he had been chosen as Messenger. Tradition taught, too, that gradually Muhammad became convinced of the authenticity of the message and began to speak it. There was no God but Allah, and Muhammad was his Prophet, proclaimed Muhammad. With this formula, Muslims announced themselves the spiritual relatives of Jews and Christians. Like them **monotheistic**, Muslims resembled Jews and Christians in other ways, too. They embraced a religion of history, concerned with public events and right action in the world. They adhered to a law by which to live and a sacred book, the **Qur'an**, to teach it. And they testified to a relationship between God (Allah) and their community in service to him.

Here Muhammad joined religion and nationhood under the banner of submission to Allah. The name of the new religion—Islam—meant submission to Allah and the peace that it brought. Before Muhammad's time, clan kinship provided the basis for Arabian social organization. Now the new force of faith united people in the community, the **umma**, theoretically open to the entire world. In this, Muslims brought ordinary and extraordinary religion together, just as ancient Israel had done, and they declared for universality, just as Christianity had. No surprise, therefore, that Muslims held Muhammad to be the last in a line of prophets that included Abraham, Moses, and Jesus. Their reputed **jihad**—a term often used today to signify violence and even terrorism—meant first the spiritual struggle within each person to submit to Allah, a struggle that should end in peace. In its outward form, jihad included armed defense and militant expansionism at different moments in Islamic history, but these as part of a righteous struggle to bring together the community of faith and so bring peace.

The **Five Pillars of Islam**, basic to the practice of any Muslim, have continued to reflect these beliefs. First, observant Muslims affirm the central confession of the faith: there is no God but Allah, and Muhammad is his Prophet. Second, they perform ritual prayers five times daily, facing the holy city of Mecca and using prescribed gestures and words. Third, Muslims give alms through a religious "tax" and other voluntary offerings. Fourth, during the month of Ramadan, they fast from food and drink from sunup to sunset, taking meals only after dark and before dawn. Fifth, at least once in a lifetime, if health and circumstances allow, observant Muslims make a pilgrimage to Mecca (in present-day Saudi Arabia), where the Kaaba—Islam's holiest shrine—stands and, in it, the black stone said to have been brought by the angel Gabriel.

Muslim dedication to keeping to the **sunna**, or customs, which supplement the teachings of the Qur'an, also reflects the fusion of ordinary and extraordinary. Handed on from generation to generation and acquiring written form, the sunna bind Muslims to practices believed to have guided the everyday behavior of the first generation. So important are they that the later history of Islam saw division into different religious communities over their interpretation. The **Sunni Muslims** formed the largest. They have aimed to follow the sunna of the original Muslim community and to honor the early history of Islam with its conquests by leaders called caliphs. The **Shiites** have countered Sunni claims. They follow the family of Ali, son-in-law and cousin of the Prophet, who reigned as caliph from 656 until 661, when he was murdered. For them, Ali is first in a line of sacred figures called **imams**, who replaced the caliphs of Sunni Islam and, in their persons, have embodied law and authority—so that the law of the Islamic community becomes less important than the living lawgiver. Moreover, the Shiites await the reappearance at the end of time of an imam, the **Mahdi**, from the house of Ali, to bring the final victory of justice and deliver the dead to resurrection. Intensely emotional in their religion, the Shiites became the dominant Muslims of Persia—modern-day Iran—and an important element in the populations of Iraq, Lebanon, and other Islamic states.

Different from both Sunnis or Shiites, the **Sufis**—Islamic mystics—gained reputations as wanderers, engaging sometimes in self-denial and at other times in the songs and dances that brought them renown. They gathered in religious communities, or orders, in which a group of disciples followed the mystical teachings of a spiritual master called a **sheikh**. The Sufis have noticeably influenced the growth of new religious movements in recent American life.

Transformations of Islam in the United States

The fear of losing Islam at first delayed the influx of Muslims to the United States. They recognized that adults could lose contact with their past and that children could grow up without a strong Islamic foundation. Middle Easterners came first, and like many other newcomers, they tended to live together in communities modeled on their former relationships. Often, in a city neighborhood members of almost an entire Syrian village would live within blocks of one another, renting apartments in huge buildings acquired by one wealthy villager among them.

In larger cities, tensions sometimes grew between Sunni and Shiite Muslims, with Sunnis building **mosques** (Islamic places of worship) and Shiites preferring "national clubs." However, the strangeness of their new location and the perceived threat to their heritage often led Muslims to ignore the differences of the past. Besides, with Islam a religion of community and of law, the mosque and its religious service had never been central. So in the United States Muslims built only slowly, the first mosque at Highland Park (Detroit), Michigan, in 1919. Even in the early 1970s, only about twenty mosques existed in the country, with perhaps six official imams (here, prayer leaders) for all of them. But by the 1990s, that pattern had clearly changed, and in the early twenty-first century numerous mosques stand in cities and towns all over the nation.

As important, the ways in which the mosques function suggest their Americanization. No longer simply houses of prayer, they have become Islamic centers with multiple purposes. Even more, the mosques have developed a "Sunday" tendency. Following the lead of their Christian neighbors, Muslims began Sunday morning schools for their children in order to hand on their religious heritage and then came to offer services for all at noon, thus replacing traditional Friday observances. Moreover, with the American Islamic emphasis on the education of children, women have gained a role of greater prominence. Although Islam is traditionally male-oriented, as Muslim educators women have participated increasingly in the public life of Islam, with all Muslims dependent on them in a new way.

Meanwhile, as Muslims coming from many backgrounds experienced American culture, they expressed diversity not only in their separate pasts but also in their relationship to Islam and its practice. At the same time, they began to search for public unity, and new organizations grew. Among them, the Islamic Center in Washington, D.C., became a symbol of the future from its beginning in 1949. Then, by 1952, the Federation of Islamic Associations, under the leadership of second-generation American Muslims of mostly Lebanese ancestry, provided an organizational umbrella for increasing cooperation among Muslims. From 1963, the Muslim Students Association aimed not only to preserve a sense of Muslim identity and religious activity among college students but also to work toward the establishment of pan-Islamic religious community. So, by 1981, it gave its formal blessing to the Islamic Society of North America, an organization designed to foster unity among Muslims from different ethnic groups and to carry forward a mission to non-Muslims. Already at this time, some Americans feared Muslims because of radical Islamic movements abroad. Building on a long history of Muslim conflict with the West that began in medieval times and continued through the modern period of colonialism, these radical **Islamists** sought a re-creation of Islam that threw off Western, and increasingly American, influence.

Still, by the early 1990s, a Muslim offered public prayer to open legislative sessions in both the United States Senate and House of Representatives. Not without friction, Muslims seemed to be making headway in their bid for acceptance by all Americans. Less than a decade later, however, Islamists—out of touch with mainstream and traditional Islam—flew planes into the World Trade Center in New York City and into the Pentagon, outside Washington, D.C., killing thousands and horrifying the nation. **September 11, 2001**, shocked and outraged Muslims as it did other Americans, but American Muslims bore the brunt in a special way. They joined most other Muslims throughout the world in categorically condemning the acts of terror and mourning the loss of so many lives. Like other Americans, too, they called for the capture and prosecution of those who had planned and supported the event—Saudi Arabian Osama bin Laden and others in the network known as Al-Qaeda. But—as they and others with Middle Eastern features faced increasing harassment and personal danger—American Muslims also expressed their concern that other Americans not discriminate against them. Groups like the Council on American-Islamic Relations and the Muslim Public Affairs Council worked to protect Muslim civil rights and to counter negative public images of Muslims.

Islam, like any major religion, has strong transformative power. If a few used that power toward destructive ends, the many understood that the jihad of their tradition was mostly an inner battle and that Islam was a religion of peace. In this context, September 11 made American Muslims more self-conscious about their religious identity and the degree of their religious practice. For most of the twentieth century, religious observance had declined among traditional American Muslims. Especially in the third generation and at midcentury, for many Arab Americans nationalism and politics seemed to take the place that religion once had occupied. Numbers of the young who had been educated in American public schools and now looked at their religious history from the vantage point of the American mainstream experienced Islam as foreign, and the majority of second- and third-generation Muslims have remained "unmosqued." Yet Muslims did not run headlong to embrace American culture, and the ordinary religion of Islam continued in Muslim communities. Family and an extended network of kin formed the basis of community, and the public male dominance of traditional Islam was apparent in Muslim neighborhoods. Although many Muslims had stopped praying five times daily, in other ways Islam kept on directing them in their ordinary lives and attitudes toward one another.

Then, with the influx of immigrants after 1965, came a sea change. The solidarity brought by numbers helped foster renewed devotion and conscious dedication to the faith, as the multiplication of new mosques suggests. The events of September 11, 2001, underlined the Muslim sense of difference. Some women, for example, began self-consciously to veil themselves, and others—men and women—have used religious practice to mark their identity in a time of trial. So even as Islam has expanded its presence in American society, it has looked within, consolidating its community in the presence of not-so-friendly American strangers. Islamic cultural accommodation increasingly has included reaching back to the Muslim heritage and reinserting it in a new context.

Islam and New Religions: The Example of Baha'i

Out of the mixture of the Muslim heritage with native cultures, new religious movements arose. Among them is a religion that originated in nineteenth-century Persia (present-day Iran), spread into numerous countries, and made its way to the United States—the religion of **Baha'i**. Its history began with a Shiite Muslim, **Siyyid Ali Muhammad** (1819–1850), later called the Bab, or the "Gate." Combining Shiite beliefs about the return of the Mahdi with Persian Zoroastrianism, with its belief that a prophet would bring in a new age of final justice, he founded **Babism**. The Bab was killed in 1850, but he left among his followers **Husayn Ali** (1817–1892), later to be known as **Baha'u'llah** (the Glory of God). Ali came to see himself as the manifestation of God for the present age, the greatest in a long line of prophets. Thereafter, as Baha'u'llah, he spent the rest of his life, mostly in prison or in exile from Persia, proclaiming his religious vision.

Baha'u'llah taught that just as Islam fulfilled Judaism and Christianity, Baha'i completed Islam and all previous religions. Now, he announced, the world stood at the threshold of an age of universal unity and peace in which its one religion would follow the principles of Baha'i. He taught, too, the equality of all human beings, encouraged interracial marriage, and called for a reverence for all living things. Amid the universalism, he gave Baha'is a sense of distinctiveness through religious practice. So in a special solar calendar, Baha'is divide the year into nineteen months of nineteen days each, with days added at the end of the year to keep it in time with the sun. Each month begins with a feast day, while nine holy days throughout the year honor specific events in the history and revelation of Baha'i. During the nineteenth month, from 2 to 20 March, Baha'is fast, accepting the Islamic Pillar of the fast and transforming it. In another transformation of Islamic practice, Baha'is have retained the custom of prescribed daily prayers. However, they do not pray five times in a day and do not use the Qur'an—superseded in their view by the writings of the Bab and especially of Baha'u'llah. Meanwhile, at "firesides" Baha'is gather to discuss their religion with non-Baha'is.

From 1894, classes in Baha'i came to Chicago, and the city continued to offer a home to a thriving Baha'i movement—the Baha'i Mother Temple built close to it in Wilmette. With economic justice and peace issues joined to education, especially for peace and interracial unity, Baha'i has found an American niche. In the early twenty-first century, some 1,400 local spiritual assemblies can, in fact, be counted. Baha'i forbids participation in partisan politics as an offense against unity but encourages efforts on behalf of the United Nations as a concrete way to advance that unity. Its strong organization, missionary effort, and distinctive sense of identity turn ordinary concerns into extraordinary religion. Baha'i contracts itself through religious practices that mark its difference; it expands in its universal vision of peace and justice.

Farther East: Hinduism

The religious culture of India, known to the West as **Hinduism**, came late to the United States. Until after 1965 and the change in immigration law, few Indian immigrants arrived. So export (not ethnic) Hinduism first caught the eye of Americans and then grew through a series of missionary movements. After the World's Parliament of Religions, **Vivekananda** (1863–1902) began to spread the Indian religious philosophy of **Vedanta** in the United States. Vedanta Societies sprang up in various places as "churches" to bring the message of the East to Americans who were religious seekers. Then **Paramahansa Yogananda** (1893–1952) arrived, and his **Self-Realization Fellowship** became the first in a series of movements centered on yoga that American culture absorbed. By the 1960s and 1970s, Hindu devotionalism appealed to some among a new generation of Americans even as increasing numbers of Asian Indian immigrants were bringing ethnic Hinduism to the United States.

Religious Themes in Hinduism

Indian speculation about the cosmos formed the backdrop for Hindu religious expression. Over the centuries, many Hindus concluded that the world existed as one reality and the sense of separation was an illusion. Behind the material world, these Hindus posited a vast, impersonal power. They named it **Brahman** and thought of it as the fundamental reality in the universe. Moreover, they thought that within each individual lay the **Atman**, which linked the person to Brahman. According to their teaching, a person, when he or she became a realized being, would come to know experientially that Atman *was* Brahman.

This religious system, called **monism**, or the philosophy of oneness, met dispute from other Hindus, who taught **dualism**. Here the distinctiveness of spirit and matter, of God and individual souls, formed the basis for any further religious thought or practice. Dualism—the philosophy of twoness and manyness—encouraged Hindus in their fascination with the material world. The religious landscape that dualism encouraged was also peopled with numbers of Gods and Goddesses, each of them the center of a devoted religious following. **Polytheism**, or the worship of many Gods, brought a striking sacramentalism to Hindu religious expression, with the material world considered sacred.

Overall, for Hindus, three broad routes—called forms of **yoga**—have led to the divine. In the path of devotion and the ritual of **puja**, family members, led by the head of the household, have daily greeted, bathed, perfumed, clothed, and fed one of the Gods by means of a statue representing the deity. Through this practice and its extension in other heartfelt acts, Hindus believe they can find salvation. Called **bhakti**—an Indian word for devotion—this religious path stresses the importance of personal feeling in worship. Love, practitioners say, is all you need.

The second religious path for Hindus is the way of action. In traditional India, each person came into the world as a member of a caste, which prescribed proper actions and obligations. For example, the duty of a (male) member of the priestly caste lay in teaching, while a warrior's duty was to rule and defend society. Merchants and servants also had their assigned tasks, and in all of the castes, women served their husbands and other household members. The religious way of action taught that each must live according to caste law without regard to results or satisfaction gained. Performing faithfully the actions required, called **karma**, Hindus believed, would lead a person to be reborn—reincarnated—in a higher state. After the official end of the caste system, the idea of karma has continued. In modern Hinduism, right deeds signal a life well spent and point to a fortunate rebirth.

The third religious path for Hindus is the way of knowledge. Here, as in American metaphysics, knowledge means insight and illuminated perception. Called **jnana**, this knowledge has come, for Hindus, through cultivation of inner states of mind. Here religious teachers, called **gurus**, give others techniques for physical and mental control meant to lead them into higher states of awareness. The path of knowledge aims finally for mystical experience. Yet, whether seekers reach that goal or not, the discipline of the path directs a person in daily life.

Hinduism in the United States

When Vedanta came to the United States at the end of the nineteenth century, it brought India's most widespread form of monism to Americans. A devotee of the mystic and religious leader **Ramakrishna**, Vivekananda shaped the movement into an international declaration of Hinduism, committed to the mystical ideal of Ramakrishna but also to action in the world. Beginning in 1896 with the Vedanta Society he founded in New York, Vivekananda presented Hinduism to Americans in a form that he thought they would understand. He added **raja yoga** to the three traditional yogic paths of bhakti, karma, and jnana, and raja yoga offered a new attention to techniques for meditative and mystical practice. Meanwhile, more than any other export Hindu movement in the United States, Vedanta conformed to Christian customs, developing a religious service that included hymns, scripture, prayer, and sermon.

Vedanta appealed to upper- and middle-class Americans and people from other cultures who were drawn to South Asian spirituality. Later, Vedanta appealed to Asian Indian immigrants as well. Teaching that the real nature of people is divine and that it is each person's duty to develop the Godhead within, Vedanta has offered ideas that blend with liberal Protestant teachings about the inner presence of God and the goodness of human nature. Moreover, with its belief that truth is universal, it agrees with the mood of many Americans. It has continued as a small yet stable presence in the nation.

However, the future of export Hinduism lay with newer movements. In diffused form, the noncaste-oriented karma teaching of **Mohandas K. Gandhi**, the political and spiritual leader of India during its struggle with Great Britain, influenced the nonviolent resistance of blacks in the American civil rights movement. Thus karma became that form of social action demanded by ideas of justice and right and performed regardless of personal consequences. Most of the export Hinduism in the United States, though, facilitated the growth of a **guru culture** among non-Asian devotees. As early as 1920, Paramahansa Yogananda arrived to take part in the International Congress of Religious Liberals, held by the Unitarians in Boston. He remained in America for thirty years to become the first major guru after Vivekananda. More than Vivekananda, he used American publicity techniques, something that later Hindu gurus on mission to North America would also do.

The word *yoga* means union and the discipline to bring it. In the sense used here, it means teaching and practice to unify a person's inner being and facilitate an experience of the oneness of all in Brahman. In the Self-Realization Fellowship, Yogananda offered Americans a Vedanta religious philosophy based on yogic teachings. The basic principles of this classical yoga begin with the body. Through a series of physical exercises, called **hatha yoga**, a person assumes prescribed physical postures—the **asanas**—in order to shift energy from one part of the body to another. Practitioners believe that these will encourage inward quiet and open spiritual centers to receive divine energy. Controlled breathing, known as **pranayama**, has the same goals, with the intent to release the individual into a meditative state that leads to bliss. In fact, the highest forms of yoga have taught meditation techniques. A person may fix inwardly on a sacred sound—a **mantra**—or focus consciously on a point within the body such as the point between the eyes or below the abdomen, aiming to reach a state of uninterrupted concentration and, ultimately, the experience of oneness.

In his teaching on meditation, Yogananda promoted a variation called **kriya yoga**. This system, understood as a form of God-realization, places emphasis on awakening an energy—**kundalini**—thought to lie at the base of the spine and directing it upward to the crown. Such a process, Yogananda taught, would bring energy and integration to seven **chakras**, or energy centers, in the body. Through use of the mind in an attempted movement of energy and through coordinated forms of breathing and mantra repetition, the yogic practitioner hoped to reach a superconscious state. Yogananda himself spread both classical and kriya yoga, with adaptive modifications for an American audience. He told Americans that there was scientific precision to yogic philosophy, he used Western psychological concepts to explain it, and he also introduced Christian ideas. His teaching has endured among both lay devotees and monastics into the early twenty-first century.

From the 1960s on, however, hatha yoga groups and teachers have exploded onto the American cultural landscape in a visibility that has gone much beyond Yogananda. Church organizations and community centers have sponsored short courses in hatha yoga techniques, while television programs and videos enable people to learn at home. Drugstores and newsstands have blossomed with paperback books, and groups as diverse as college students, housewives, and working people have signed on. Networks and associations of yoga teachers thrive, and since the 1990s the glossy, San Francisco-based popular magazine *Yoga Journal* is easy to find. New hatha yoga gurus have dominated the American scene, among them B.K.S. Iyengar with Iyengar Yoga and Pattabhi Jois with his Ashtanga form. At the same time, interest in meditation yoga has grown as part of the guru culture and outside it, too. Again, popular books and pamphlets are plentiful, while many hatha yoga teachers also teach meditation techniques. But a new guru for the late twentieth century—the **Maharishi Mahesh Yogi** (b. 1911)—has reaped the seed that Vivekananda and, even more, Yogananda planted.

The Maharishi's **Transcendental Meditation** came to the West in 1959, capitalizing on publicity even more than Yogananda had done. Like Yogananda, too, the Maharishi underlined the scientific aspects of his teaching, providing data claiming Transcendental Meditation (TM) lowered blood pressure, relieved stress, increased intelligence, and even reduced crime in areas where enough people were meditating. And like Yogananda again, he taught a popularized form of monism. Transcendental Meditation was based squarely on the teachings of the Indian spiritual books, the Upanishads, as interpreted by the ninth-century Vedanta school (not to be confused with the Vedanta Society) of Shankara. But TM has stressed that it is a simple and natural technique that anyone can practice with striking results. In fact, in its public presentations it has frequently denied that it is a religion at all. In 1979, however, a United States Court of Appeals ruled TM to be a religion and therefore unlawful as part of a public-school curriculum. Still, Transcendental Meditation has continued to teach that it is a form of knowledge—"the science of creative intelligence"—and consequent practice. Its Maharishi International University, at the former site of Parsons College in Fairfield, Iowa, confers both bachelor's and master's degrees and is an American hub for a world movement.

Straddling a line between the guru culture of export Hinduism and the **temple culture** of ethnic Hinduism is the **International Society for Krishna Consciousness (ISKCON)**. Founded in 1965 by **A. C. Bhaktivedanta Swami Prabhupada** (1896–1977), Krishna Consciousness evolved from the teachings of a dualistic sixteenth-century sect established by Chaitanya Mahaprabhu. At the center of ISKCON is **Krishna**, a Hindu deity and supreme personal God for his followers. As Krishna monotheists, ISKCON members hail Chaitanya Mahaprabhu as an incarnation of Krishna. In its full form, Krishna Consciousness has emphasized boundaries, demanding a total surrender to Krishna made visible in a monastic life-style. Rising before 4:00 a.m. and eating vegetarian food, devotees from the 1960s became known for their "Hare Krishna" chant, which, they claimed, brought altered consciousness and bliss states.

After the death of its founder, however, ISKCON declined in its non-Asian convert membership. Then, conflict in its governing body and criminal court cases led to the expulsion of a major center at New Vrindaban, West Virginia, in 1987. But New Vrindaban had more reasons to be noticed. Its lavish and ornate temple, strikingly "other" in the West Virginia countryside, told of the rising importance of temples—and temple culture—for ISKCON. By the 1990s, more than sixty temples belonged to the group, most of them in cities. Increasingly, ethnic Hindus were frequenting them. So ISKCON moved from being an export form of Hinduism to one that incorporated both export and ethnic elements. Indeed, Asian Indians have provided the difference between mild decline and virtual extinction. They bring not only membership but also financial support, greater public respectability, and a more denomination-like religious style.

Other forms of export Hinduism—and guru culture—thrived in the congenial climate of the late-twentieth-century United States and after. Groups like the Divine Light Mission (Guru Maharaj Ji), the Siddhya Yoga movement (Swami Muktananda and later the female Gurumayi Chidvilasananda), Integral Yoga (Swami Satchidananda), the Rajneesh Foundation International (Bhagwan Rajneesh), and the Sri Aurobindo Society (Sri Aurobindo), to name but a few, persisted despite internal problems and even scandals in some of the movements. But after 1965, South Asian immigrants and their temple culture grew in striking ways, and a new ethnic Hindu story began unfolding. Despite the ISKCON example, amalgamation with export Hinduism gave way to other patterns. With a dramatic presence after centuries of virtual invisibility, Hindus now had the numbers and the means (they were overwhelmingly highly educated professionals) to make a religious difference in the nation. They also wanted to transmit Indian culture to their children, and they condemned American materialism and what they saw as decadent American values. Ethnic Hindus continued to practice puja in their homes, used astrology traditionally to determine the best times for staging important events, and preserved their celebrations of inherited feasts and holidays.

Especially, as the example of ISKCON already suggests, they began to build temples. There were problems, to be sure. With sixteen major languages in India

Dedication of the Rama Temple, Lemont, Illinois. Although the temple was not yet completed, the dedication of its tower was held, significantly, on July 4, 1986. Honoring the hero of the Indian epic *Ramayana* and two other deities, the Rama temple is the main shrine in a larger temple complex at Lemont and is especially favored by South Indians.

and a series of regional cultures and devotions, no one pattern of Hinduism could speak for all of the immigrants. Yet despite the differences and often because of them, Hindus turned to the new temples—often large and impressive—as religious homes for their many deities and local cultures. As early as 1986 forty Hindu temples existed, and by the early 1990s over 150, suggesting the rapidity with which the religious landscape was changing. Some of these have been small, but others represent massive building projects. Generally, architectural style, deities, ritual practice, and the like distinguish the temples as South Indian, North Indian, ecumenical (meant to have a broad appeal), or sectarian (dedicated to worship as carried on in one Hindu sect). Because building a major temple pulls members of the Asian Indian community, whatever their designation most Indian temples express some degree of ecumenicity.

Temples work as cultural centers as much as strictly ritual places. They preserve languages, arts, and practices from the ethnic past and provide an unusually clear example of how ordinary and extraordinary religion blend together in actual community affairs. They also express religious expansion and contraction at the same time. They enable these new Americans to bring their past into the present and so move out into the larger American community. Yet they also provide a place of refuge from American society. Often prosperous, the temples function as sources of pride and identity for Asian Indians. Depending on how mainstream Americans welcome or reject them, they signal a culture of religious expansion or contraction for the American host culture.

Farther East: Buddhism

Ethnic Buddhism came to this country with Chinese and, especially, Japanese immigrants of the late nineteenth century. The predominant form was a branch of **Pure Land Buddhism** that flourished in the regions from which the immigrants came. In the United States it became the preferred Buddhism of Japanese Americans, giving them a way of life that fused ordinary with extraordinary religion. However, the late nineteenth century saw wide publicity for export Buddhism in the nation with the World's Parliament of Religions and the appearance there of Japanese Zen master **Soyen Shaku**. **Zen** thrived among converts, giving them a way to seek an extraordinary experience of enlightenment. Buddhism, perhaps more than Hinduism, would emphasize methods for the practice of extraordinary religion in the United States.

In general, while the ethnic form of Buddhism led at first to a "church" religion, the second, mostly convert (export) form led to meditation. A third form, which enjoyed a spurt of growth from the 1960s and 1970s, has been **Nichiren Shoshu** and then **Soka Gakkai International–USA**. This form of Japanese Buddhism, missionary for most of its American history, flourishes today among both mainstream converts and Asian immigrants. If we compare these forms of Buddhism with American Hinduism, there are parallels. A predominantly "church" form of religion, supporting action in the world (one's karma in Hinduism), gives place to one stressing meditation (for Hindus, jnana) and, in turn, a mostly devotional and evangelical version (for Hindus, bhakti). Both guru culture (to borrow the Hindu term) and temple culture thread their way through American Buddhism.

The Religion of Buddhism

Buddhists think of their founder, **Siddhartha Gautama** (563?–483? BCE), not as a prophet but as an example of how to live. Called the **Buddha**, which means the "enlightened" or "awakened" one, according to tradition he left a prosperous life as a member of India's warrior (ruling) caste to seek an answer to the problems of suffering and death. Tradition has it, too, that he sought help from various spiritual masters without success, all the while practicing great austerities and becoming physically weak. Finally, he ended these practices, began to meditate, and then one night, sitting under a bo tree, became enlightened. From that time, accounts say, he preached and taught others how they, also, might come to this state.

So from the first, Buddhism has stressed religious knowledge as spiritual "insight." Buddhist enlightenment means an experiential grasp of seemingly simple ideas summarized as the **Four Noble Truths** of the **dharma** (the law or teaching). Human suffering has a cause; the cause of suffering is desire; there is a way to end suffering; and the way to end it is to end desire, living in nonattachment to any persons, places, or things. Realization of the Four Noble Truths takes devotees into the one moment when, in the earliest form of Buddhism, **nirvana**—or unconditioned reality—is unmistakably known. Yet even with this lofty goal, the Buddhist teaching is practical, and the Buddha gave his followers the **Noble Eightfold Path** on the way to enlightenment. Named the Middle Path, it avoids extremes of asceticism and self-indulgence as well as all one-sided views and acts. Instead it calls on Buddhists to practice "right" views and intentions, leading to "right" speech, action, livelihood, and effort, and ultimately "right" mindfulness and concentration. Thus, the Eightfold Path traces the pattern of a spiral. It begins in the mind at the level of ordinary knowledge, moves from mind to body through forms of speech and action, and then returns to the mind, this time at the level of meditation.

The Buddha's closest followers lived together in a religious order, or community, thus lessening the significance of the caste system and urging people to leave their ordinary way of life in pursuit of the extraordinary. Lay followers also joined this radical community of monks and nuns, and gradually Buddhism became a religion that supported the ordinary culture of India. Yet with expansive zeal, it became the missionary religion of Asia, spreading from India to China and Japan as well as to all of Southeast Asia. Furthermore, as the Buddhist community—the **sangha**—reflected on the Buddha's message, different understandings of the teaching arose, and different forms of Buddhism resulted.

By the third century BCE, two major schools had developed. **Theravada**, which became the Buddhism of Southeast Asia, taught that it continued the original instruction of the Buddha. It emphasized the individual, whose goal was to become a solitary spiritual hero. And it revered the historical Buddha as a teacher of priceless truth and an example of what each person might achieve. For the elite, Buddha remained always human, never divine; and no God at all existed. Everything led to an experience of pure nonattachment in nirvana.

The second major school of Buddhism, **Mahayana**, became the Buddhism of China and Japan. The larger of the two schools, Mahayana stressed the community. Instead of the solitary monk seeking personal enlightenment, its hero became the **bodhisattva**, who, on the verge of experiencing nirvana, postponed the time out of compassion for others and in order to serve them. Meanwhile, rather than emphasizing the one historical Buddha, the Mahayana school found Buddhas wherever persons became enlightened. In a doctrine of Buddha bodies, Mahayanists posited three expressions of the Buddha. The first was the "body of appearance," or the physical body of the Buddha. The second was the "body of bliss," surrounded by light, as the reported reward for extraordinary spiritual practice. The third Buddha body became the "body of essence," the true being of the Buddha as an absolute beyond space and time. In beliefs about the body of essence and to some extent the body of bliss, the Buddha functioned in certain ways like a God—and so did others who became Buddhas.

In time, a third large school of Buddhism developed. From the third or fourth century, **Vajrayana (Tantric)** Buddhism grew from Buddhist, Hindu, and other popular religious roots to become the Buddhism, most notably, of Tibet. This form of Buddhism saw the many Buddhas of Mahayana as visualizations of the passions within each human being. In a process of working with symbols, Vajrayana Buddhists aimed to transform the inner passional forces into visible and audible beings and then merge them into a oneness at the center of the self. In other words, Vajrayana sought the mystical goal of union with a divinity within. By dramatizing the inner labor in a series of secret, and often sexual, initiations and magical techniques, Vajrayana Buddhists tried to make the spiritual concrete and to achieve practical control over it.

Each of the three major forms of Buddhism gave rise to many differing sects and schools of interpretation. Many focused on a specific Buddhist sutra, or writing, making it central to their devotions and lives.

Buddhism in the United States

The American Transcendentalists knew something of Buddhism. However, Henry Olcott of the Theosophical Society more directly aided Buddhism both overseas and in the United States, writing a Buddhist catechism that went through forty editions in his lifetime. His associate, Helena Blavatsky, included Buddhist teaching in her metaphysical works, and her references to Mahatmas identified them as Tibetans familiar with the practices of Vajrayana Buddhism. Both Olcott and Blavatsky formally became Buddhists. Meanwhile, a series of other individuals became Buddhist sympathizers and in some cases converts even before the Theosophical Society appeared.

As early as the 1850s, temples arose in San Francisco's Chinatown that blended Buddhism with Daoism and Confucianism (both native Chinese religions). But the future of ethnic Buddhism lay with the more distinct "church" Buddhism of the Japanese after the Civil War. **Jodo Shinshu** missionaries brought their sectarian form of Pure Land Buddhism to Hawaii in 1889 and to California a decade later. Like all Mahayana Buddhism of the Pure Land type, Jodo Shinshu taught faith in a Buddha being called **Amida Buddha**. According to traditional accounts, Amida established the Western Kingdom, called the Pure Land, in fulfillment of his earlier vows. Now, believers said, through trust in Amida and devotion to him, believers could enter the Pure Land after death and there experience enlightenment. They only needed to call on Amida with gratitude in the formula "Hail to Amida Buddha." Pure Land Buddhism thus put the "other-power" of Amida in place of the "self-power" that Theravada and the other meditation forms of Buddhism taught. Of all the forms of Buddhism, it probably most resembled Christianity.

Perhaps because of this similarity or for other reasons, Pure Land adapted well. Known as the North American Buddhist Mission from 1899 to 1944, it then became the **Buddhist Churches of America** (BCA). Although its membership gradually declined, probably 20,000 people belonged to the BCA in the mid-1990s. Notably, its Japanese teachers adapted their language to the American situation. No Buddhist churches operate in Japan, and community worship only takes place on special occasions. Yet now Buddhists were speaking of their churches and also calling their overseers bishops. They began Sunday services and schools, believing that they must find a practice for themselves and their children that conformed with American customs. Many have felt that the Buddhist Churches of America represents a necessary compromise.

Japanese and Tibetan monks have promoted a second form of Buddhism in the United States, stressing meditation. Chinese Ch'an Buddhism spread to Japan in the late twelfth and early thirteenth centuries where, known as Zen, it flourished as a combination of Mahayana religious philosophy and Theravada meditation techniques to gain enlightenment. With a division into two separate schools, one of them, **Rinzai**, has taught that enlightenment is a sudden event, triggered by unusual circumstances that jolt a person out of ordinary consciousness. Hence, its practice centers on meditation using **koans**, riddles or verbal puzzles meant to baffle and deactivate the ordinary working mind—as, for example, in the koan-style question "What is the sound of one hand clapping?" The other school, **Soto**, has insisted that enlightenment is gradual. Soto Zen teaches "just sitting" to quiet the mind and empty it of thought.

Soyen Shaku introduced Rinzai Zen at the World's Parliament of Religions. But his disciple Daisetz Teitaro Suzuki more than any other person spread Rinzai in the United States. From 1897 to 1909, Suzuki worked as an editor for the Open Court Publishing Company in La Salle, Illinois. After returning to Japan, he wrote prolifically in English about Buddhism, and his many books were widely read in this country. When he came back to the United States in the 1950s, he spoke frequently at universities, including one series of lectures at Columbia. Suzuki aided the communication of Zen to non-Asian Americans by stressing themes that agreed with the contemporary Western philosophy of existentialism. At the same time, he downplayed the discipline and ritual of the Zen monastic tradition and disregarded its social setting in Japan.

In the late 1950s, a group of San Francisco artists and writers that included Allen Ginsberg, Jack Kerouac, and, with qualifications, Alan Watts and Gary Snyder combined the interpretations of Suzuki with other elements to form "Beat Zen." As a group, they drew on the side of Rinzai teaching that stressed the suddenness of enlightenment, and they made it into an exaltation of emotional release and freedom. So Beat Zen pursued liberation at the expense of the rigorous meditation practices of the Rinzai tradition. Still more, Watts wrote many books to popularize Zen, using Western scientific and psychological categories. Snyder—with a background in anthropology and literature, an extensive knowledge of Native American religions, and ecological concerns—wrote poetry that expressed themes of interdependence among all creatures and later traveled to Japan to study Zen firsthand in a monastery. More than the others, he brought the two sides of Zen—its meditative discipline and its spontaneity—together.

Zen centers arose in New York, San Francisco, and other places. Monasteries also appeared, where individuals might spend either short or extended periods away from society. Meanwhile Philip Kapleau's book *The Three Pillars of Zen* (1965) united the Rinzai and Soto lineages. Kapleau visited Japan as a reporter in 1946 and less than a decade later studied there under a teacher who sought the unification of Zen. In 1966 he opened the Zen Meditation Center in Rochester, New York, where he applied ideas from his book. He worked to make Zen American, using the English language, adapting rituals, and wearing Western clothes during meditation. More recently, the Vietnamese Zen master and Nobel Peace Prize nominee Thich Nhat Hanh has promoted mindfulness meditation in a series of books and even a calendar that are geared to American new spirituality.

Most American Zen adherents have been young, middle-class converts, well-educated and white. So Zen became part of the American culture of religious expansionism and an extraordinary religion as well. Tibetan Buddhism in the United States echoed these themes. Brought to this country by Buddhist monks fleeing after the Chinese Communist takeover of Tibet, it became noticeable here after 1965. Through Tibetans on university faculties and through the establishment of meditation centers, knowledge of Tibetan Buddhism has spread, and the Dalai Lama has become an American hero and Asian "pope." Tibetan Buddhist masters, called **rinpoches**, have found a language to express their Buddhist teaching in humanistic psychology, and they have taken their places as gurus for a generation of Americans. They communicate with mainstream converts and sympathizers by showing the continuities between Tibetan Vajrayana and modern American beliefs. Especially under Tarthang Tulku in Berkeley, California, and, until his death Chogyam Trungpa in Boulder, Colorado, Tibetan Buddhism has provided Americans still another type of Buddhism stressing meditation.

Meanwhile, other Americans have turned to Theravada tradition to support their mediation practice, as the twenty-first-century popularity of **Vipassana** meditation shows. Vipassana means "insight." As a meditation practice, it teaches attention to the moment-by-moment stream of thought and bodily sensations. Within the practice, the meditator pays attention and lets go, moment after moment. Americans who trained with Theravada teachers founded the **Insight Meditation Society** in Barre, Massachusetts, in 1975, and since then have gradually expanded their efforts. Books by Jack Kornfield and Joseph Goldstein have served as teaching tools, and centers have sprung up to spread the teaching, too. Insight meditators often do not understand their practice as religious but emphasize the qualities of focus, mental clarity, and psychological healing it brings them. Still, by the 1980s, Insight leaders were promoting Buddhist lovingkindness meditation. Significant in all of this—Zen, Tibetan, and Theravadan—is the fact that practices originally understood as monastic have become, in the United States, the work of lay people.

Lay leadership also characterized the evangelical Buddhism that came to the United States in the form of Nichiren Shoshu and then an independent Soka Gakkai. Its membership grew rapidly after its first appearance in 1960, and today Soka Gakkai International–USA claims between 100,000 and 300,000 members in the American version of what has become a global religion. At first, most adherents in the United States came from Japanese ancestry. The few mainstream Americans who joined tended to be men who married Japanese women, and membership was overwhelmingly middle class, with many of the people involved in small businesses. Yet by the 1980s, internal estimates suggested that only one quarter of the membership were Asian. Alongside them, 40 percent of the group were Caucasian, 19 percent African American, and 5 percent Latino. Converts were younger and less well established, and they ranged from working class to college educated.

Devotees look to a monk named Nichiren (1222–1282) who, according to the traditional account, began to preach the centrality of a particular Buddhist holy book, the Lotus Sutra of the Mystical Law. Instead of chanting "Hail to Amida Buddha," urged Nichiren, they should chant praise to the Lotus Sutra, which explained the fundamental laws of nature. He is said to have told them, too, that Japan had gone astray by turning to Amida and to other forms of Buddhism. By turning to the Lotus Sutra, people would find their Buddha-nature within and attain happiness, prosperity, and peace. Aggressive from the first, the Nichiren movement attracted an enthusiastic new membership in twentieth-century Japan in the Soka Gakkai organization, a lay group convinced that they should use "forceful persuasion" to convert the world. So Nichiren Shoshu came to the United States as a missionary movement—like many other Asian export groups but probably more zealous. It appealed because of its simplicity and its promise of material prosperity and happiness. Although a strong philosophical basis grounded its teaching, it emphasized the devotional practice of the chant "*Nam Myoho Renge Kyo*" ("Hail to the Lotus Sutra"), reverence toward a Gohonzon altarpiece inscribed to recall the Lotus Sutra, and a pilgrimage, if possible, to the headquarters of Nichiren Shoshu in Japan.

Tensions within the movement between the original priestly leaders of the Nichiren movement and the lay Soka Gakkai organization led to the split in 1991 that created Soka Gakkai International–USA. In recent years, too, the missionary side of the group has become more muted. Important here, the presence of Asians in Soka Gakkai suggests a new American climate in which ethnic Buddhism has been flourishing. By the late 1980s, the American immigration law of 1965 and a volatile political climate brought new waves of East Asian immigrants to the United States. The new immigrants increasingly changed the way mainstream Americans perceived their religion. The huge number of East Asians forced the culture of expansion to expand further to make room for traditional religions practiced not as extraordinary exports but as ordinary ways of life. Estimates suggested, for example, 600,000 Vietnamese, the majority of them Buddhists and many of them in Southern California; 220,000 Laotians, with temples in Los Angeles, Chicago, and Washington, D.C.; 160,000 Cambodians; and over 100,000 Thais, with 40,000 of them in Los Angeles alone. Later United States Census figures confirm the large-scale presence of Asians, and—while statistics on the number of Buddhists among them are hard to come by—there may be several million. One sign of the times came as early as 1987 with the appointment of the first Buddhist chaplain to the United States armed forces. The same year, the establishment of the American Buddhist Congress provided another sign. Formed to explain Buddhism and Buddhists to non-Asian Americans and to articulate a Buddhist community opinion on public policy issues, the congress has aimed to make Buddhism a noticeable presence in American society. Today, as the Buddhist communities—ethnic and export—explore their American situation, the shift from Buddhism in America to American Buddhism is visible.

East Is West: Expansion, Contraction, and Combination

Throughout American religious history, **combinativeness** has been a prominent feature on the religious landscape. In the late twentieth century and after, pluralism is only part of the story. The other part—**postpluralism**—is about religious hybrids. With options as available as the foods on a supermarket shelf, it seems inevitable that people easily bring together religious ingredients from different sources. In many such combinations, the East has set the pace for the West in terms of leadership, mood, theology, and practice.

A good example is the **Healthy-Happy-Holy Organization** (usually known as the **3HO**), as it existed in the 1970s. Founded in the United States in 1969 by the Indian **Yogi Bhajan** (Harbhajan Singh; 1929–2004), it taught under his charismatic leadership a form of kundalini yoga, blending it with Tantric elements and with the **Sikh** religion. The Sikh tradition arose in northern India when Nanak (1469–1539) tried to reconcile Muslim and Hindu teachings, speaking of one God in all religions who could be realized through meditative practices. In the United

States, the 3HO drew on this multiple background, combining it with millennial expectation of a new age and with American patriotism. Members of the organization led a rigorous communal life, rising early, maintaining silence, meditating before a picture of Yogi Bhajan, practicing a demanding form of hatha yoga, and following a vegetarian diet. Yet after dinner each evening a session of religious singing using guitars and a folk-rock style closed the day. At the time of its greatest popularity (the 3HO has gone through many changes and has declined), the movement aimed to create a new society in the United States under God. While conceived in visionary terms rather than in plans for direct political action, the goal of building a nation brought patriotism together with leftist critique.

If the 3HO blended Eastern and Western elements to respond to the times, combinativeness is today a mental habit for many mainstream Americans, too. Religious believers and practitioners in the nation have freely and easily borrowed from one another, sometimes consciously and sometimes not. Here, the presence of combinative religions in the United States leads back to the East and the model of religious "otherness" that it has given the West. The East has taught the West to stretch to incorporate what seems religiously very different, providing non-Asian Americans with a primary means to pursue the culture of religious expansion. For converts a great part of the attraction of Hindu, Buddhist, and new East-West combinative groups has lain in their emphasis on the importance of knowledge and the value of practice in changing a person's mindset. Enlightenment, meditation, and inner peace are by definition mental states, and they are also expansive. The East has also made some non-Asians wary of too much religious innovation and promoted counter-attempts at contraction and consolidation. For their part, those born into Eastern traditions see themselves often as communities apart and, also often, want to stay that way. Religious combinations grow up in the midst of these counter-energies of expansion and contraction. Religious combiners—like the members of the 3HO—can form strongly separate religious groups who, even with their expansive universalist ideas, function socially in contractive ways.

In Overview

The end of the nineteenth century brought the growing visibility of Eastern religions in the United States. As **ethnic**, these religions united ordinary and extraordinary in traditional religious practices. As **export**, they gave the extraordinary to Westerners seeking "otherness." Both in ethnic and export forms, Eastern religions worked **contractively** to strengthen the boundaries separating their adherents from mainstream Americans and at the same time contributed to a culture of religious **expansion**.

When we make Europe and the Atlantic coast the vantage point, from Nearer East came the religion of **Eastern Orthodoxy**, one of the three major branches of Christianity. Traditionally organized in self-governing local churches, the Orthodox have strived for "right" belief and worship, expressing their desire for both in their theology of **icons** and mystical spirituality. From the Middle East came **Islam** with Arab Muslims and other immigrants as well as converts from, especially, the African American community. Following the strict monotheism of Muhammad, Muslims have inherited a program of religious action in the **Five Pillars** of their faith. Meanwhile, the new religion of **Baha'i**, an outgrowth of Persian Muslim culture, has made its presence felt.

From Farther East came **Hinduism** and **Buddhism** in both traditional and newer versions. Both religions offered followers spiritual paths through specialized forms of knowledge (yoga, meditation), through "churches" supporting action in the world, and through devotion. Movements linked to Hinduism include the **Vedanta Society**, the **Self-Realization Fellowship**, **Transcendental Meditation**, the **International Society for Krishna Consciousness**, and many more. Buddhism found expression in organizations like the **Buddhist Churches of America** and **Soka Gakkai International–USA**, and it also took shape in **Japanese Zen** and **Tibetan** Buddhist forms, in **Theravada** meditation techniques, and in other movements as well. Finally, new East-West combinative religions, such as the **Healthy-Happy-Holy Organization**, brought together charismatic leaders and mystical techniques with a sense of an impending new age. We can learn from these religions of the Nearer, Middle, and Farther East. They enable us to see more clearly how numerous the many are and how expansive religious culture is. At the same time, they point to the counter-energy that leads religious people to consolidate their worlds and contract.

By the late twentieth and early twenty-first centuries, both of these tendencies—expansion and contraction—pushed and pulled against each other in new ways. Some have called this time an era of "culture wars." Others have thought of it as an age of American religion-as-usual—only with the sound turned up. The sounds of the war (and the peace), loud or softer, tell a tale of present-time American religion.

Chapter 10

Fundamentals of the New Age: Present-Time Pluralism and Postpluralism

Helen Cohn Schucman grew up in New York City with a Jewish background. Yet her father neither believed nor observed his religion, and her mother, an English rabbi's daughter, once explained that she was a Theosophist but still "searching." Schucman's Catholic governess prayed the rosary in the child's presence and attended Mass while her charge sat in the hall outside. Like her mother, Schucman became a seeker. She wore a Catholic medal, received a Protestant evangelical baptism, and claimed mystical experience during a subway ride. But she fought her attraction to religion and at the time of her subway experience regarded herself as an atheist. By 1957 she had earned a doctoral degree in psychology, and she subsequently assumed positions at Presbyterian Hospital in New York and Columbia University's College of Physicians and Surgeons. Then a stormy relationship with William Thetford, director of Presbyterian Hospital's Psychology Department and Schucman's colleague at Columbia, led to a startling sequence of events. Encouraged by Thetford, who wanted to improve their tense relationship, Schucman began to work with dream images and symbols. She claimed to hear an inner voice that grew increasingly insistent. "This is a course in miracles," it kept saying. "Please take notes." From 1965 to 1973 she wrote what became nearly 1,200 pages of material.

Published in 1976, **A Course in Miracles** consists of a text, a workbook, and a manual for teachers. It announces itself a "required course," with only the particular time a person takes it "voluntary." It explains, too, that it does not aim to teach "the meaning of love" but to remove "blocks to the awareness of love's presence." Dissolving such blocks means, for the *Course,* a shift in perception that leads to forgiveness of self and others, with the perceptual shift a "miracle" and the foundation of other miracles. Throughout, the *Course* acknowledges God as Father and Creator, the Holy Spirit, and a "Son of God" identified with the voice that dictated the *Course*. By the 1990s, the work sold 500,000 copies and more, and groups who used it were meeting across the United States. Called a contemporary form of Christian Science, a restatement of the New Testament, and Christianized Vedanta, the *Course* took on a life of its own. Although drawn to it, Schucman never accepted it completely and resented much of its message. She died in 1981 apparently still an atheist.

A Course in Miracles is one of the "channeled" documents that claim a place in the new spirituality of the present. Although many who share its mindset prefer to describe themselves as "spiritual" rather than "religious," the *Course* exhibits familiar patterns of *religious* **expansion** and **contraction**. The work of an atheistic Jew with a theosophical mother and others close to her who were Catholic or Protestant evangelical, it expresses an expansive universalist creed and ethical code. Yet *A Course in Miracles* contains strict limits of its own. Its male-oriented language and schoolbook format provide boundaries that echo the religious structuredness of the nation's past. The *Course* puts rigorous demands on its students and imposes a strong discipline on their lives; it functions in contractive and consolidating ways.

In its religious openness and, at the same time, its search for discipline, *A Course in Miracles* tells us something important about present-day American culture. If we think of the nation's culture as the work of the social body made up of all Americans, we understand it as a system. Expansion and contraction, then, become self-correcting devices for the culture. Each has its strengths, and each its weaknesses. Together they function better than either of them alone, and together they display aspects of religion under conditions of **pluralism** and **postpluralism**, when new religious combinations are made. In the late twentieth and early twenty-first centuries, religious manyness has grown more intense, and patterns of expansion and contraction have become stronger. While some have called the present an age of "culture wars," that description is only part of the story. As religious combiners, Americans have also in many cases made their peace with religious difference.

Patterns of Contemporary Expansion: The New Age and New Spirituality

The **New Age movement** that became noticeable from the late 1960s and on reveals how expansive contemporary culture can become. The term *new age* itself, without the capital letters, has been a favorite phrase in American history since at least the time of the Revolution. But use of the term became more self-conscious in the nineteenth-century Theosophical Society. Theosophists took many turns as they traveled through the twentieth century. For one, later spiritual seekers began to claim that Helena Blavatsky's mahatmas appeared to them, and meanwhile, the mahatmas came to be known as **ascended masters**. For another, when unidentified flying objects (UFOs) caught national attention around midcentury, some began to claim that spaceships were landing and to see their commanders as, also, ascended masters. The high-technology world of the space commanders/ascended masters gave rise to talk of channels, as on radios or television sets. Now, though, the **channels** became individuals who could receive the messages of the masters and, along with them, other "entities" from a nonphysical world. A new form of spiritualism was spreading.

In England, groups of spiritualists and Theosophists were welcoming Asian teachers after World War II, and a mood of millennial expectation filled the air. Some began to talk about spiritual "light" as they remembered theosophical teachings about a new age to come. They formed groups to "channel" the light for global transformation. Then the light groups spread from England to this country, and by the early 1970s they were part of an international network that expected the imminent arrival of a New Age. The American alternative press helped to spread the word. At the same time, changes in the American immigration law likewise brought numbers of Asian teachers and teachings to the nation, while a holistic health movement began to gain momentum and Native American spirituality became increasingly attractive. In this climate, many Americans—after the Vietnam War era—seemed less spiritually certain of themselves and more open to new and combinative teachings.

A movement grew, at first quietly and without mainstream media attention, through a mostly informal network of communication. Contact with space visitors and channeling were in, and so were crystals, which captured light and energy. Bulletin boards, word-of-mouth messages, local pulp-print directories, small periodicals—all helped to announce the New Age. Teachers appeared, and so did gatherings. Movement leaders began to attract followings, and New Age people increasingly found one another. Then when film actor Shirley MacLaine published her autobiographical *Out on a Limb* in 1983 and later produced a video version of her story, she attracted national media attention. Seemingly overnight, the New Age movement was in the spotlight, and at the same time it began to change. Increasingly, its message shifted to themes of healing and the need to find the God/Self within. As it did so, the people who called themselves New Age expected a New Age less and dug in to live in the present more. By the twenty-first century, the millennialism of the earlier New Age movement had petered out. The New Age itself was dissolving into a new spirituality.

Roots of the New Age

The New Age is a contemporary manifestation of the metaphysical religion present in Transcendentalism, spiritualism, Theosophy, and New Thought, and it is also even more combinative than these older movements. Ideas about correspondence, the power of mind, the need for healing, and the presence of a world of energy at their disposal have predominated among New Agers, as they did among earlier metaphysicians. The **Transcendentalists** popularized the idea of a correspondence between this world and a larger one throughout the country. Later, in **New Thought**, believers used the mind in attempts to change matter. Short, repeated New Thought statements, called **affirmations** (of what one desired) and **negations** (of what one did not want), were considered a form of prayer and provided tools that practitioners said could change material conditions with mental input. Moreover, New Thought believers were unashamed in their desire for the good life on earth. Health, healing, and prosperity concerned them, and in keeping with the teaching of correspondence, they found the sacred in the world.

Theosophists, like the earlier spiritualists, united metaphysics with what they regarded as the latest reports of science. They championed belief in a lost continent of Lemuria, the existence of which was supported for a time by some nineteenth-century biologists. Theosophists believed, too, in the existence of a literal lost continent of Atlantis, in agreement with some popular-science theorizing at the time. And they rewrote Charles Darwin's theory of evolution into a story of the evolution of seven "root" races, the fifth of which included the Aryans, or Indo-Europeans. Ideas of lost continents and human evolution found a continuing home among New Agers.

As important as the content of theosophical teaching for the future New Age movement, however, were the organizational lineages begun by Theosophists or former Theosophists. Chief among them were the **"I AM" movement** of **Guy Ballard** (1878–1939) and the **Arcane School** of **Alice Bailey** (1880–1949). Ballard claimed that an ascended master named Saint-Germain had contacted him at Mount Shasta to announce, as the master's designated messenger, the Seventh Golden Age (the "I AM" Age of Eternal Perfection on Earth). Bailey, a California Theosophist, in turn claimed that Ascended Master Djwhal Khul (D.K., or "The Tibetan") was sending material to humankind through her. Bailey—or D.K., from whom she said the material had come—told of a Great White Brotherhood who guided the human race and of the coming of a world teacher who would appear near the end of the century. Teachers in these lineages taught the teachers of the New Age.

Ballard and Bailey had both begun to "channel" in the contemporary sense, and their followers received their works as scripture. But new Theosophists also claimed experiences that led them to change the script. So they slid into talk of contacts with space commanders. In a leading example, from 1954 Englishman George King—a yogic practitioner long familiar with the theosophical tradition—began, according to his own report, to have a series of unusual experiences. He believed that he had been designated by the Venusian Master Aetherius as the "Primary Terrestrial Mental Channel." By 1956, King founded the Aetherius Society in London, and later he moved to Los Angeles, where his movement grew. Other flying saucer contactee groups reported similar experiences and, in a technological replay of shamanism, claimed at times to be taken aboard spaceships and to fly. In these reports and among these groups, the early New Age movement was coalescing.

New Agers turned to science, too, in **quantum physics**. In 1900, the German physicist Max Planck countered the then-orthodox scientific theory that light existed as a wave with evidence that was different. Planck described energy "packets" in which, he said, light was emitted and absorbed. He called the packets *quanta*, and in his work quantum mechanics, the "new physics" of the twentieth century, had its beginnings. At the subatomic level, many scientists were saying, matter was not the solid entity that appeared to commonplace observation. Since light acted both like a wave and like a particle, the line between matter and energy was fluid. New Age people now carried these scientific ideas out of the subatomic world and into their own, finding in quantum theory, as they understood it, evidence to support their views. With light central to the mystical tradition, the behavior of light fascinated them. But whereas the new physics did not, in theory, value energy more than matter, New Agers clearly did. Their task became to transform matter into energy, or spirit.

Psychology, too, provided material for the emerging movement. New Age people turned to the work of Carl G. Jung with its dream symbolism that aimed to map stages on the way to the discovery of the "Self." They explored **humanistic psychology** and its themes of self-actualization and self-fulfillment as taught at Esalen Institute in Big Sur, California. Here, combining material taken from comparative religion with mystical and meditation theory, small groups worked with psychotherapeutic language and techniques toward goals of emotional growth and consciousness expansion. Esalen became the prototype for other centers that functioned to offer education understood as "growth-oriented," "spiritual," or the like, and a wide self-help literature arose. Still others turned to the new field of transpersonal psychology, which aimed to study religious states of mind and to incorporate traditional spiritual disciplines as part of its research methods.

Parapsychology became another element in the New Age mix. In the tradition of William James and the American Society for Psychical Research, the Parapsychology Foundation from 1951 supported experiments, conferences, and publications on parapsychological themes. Later, the Parapsychology Society appeared, established by J. B. (Joseph Banks) Rhine for those who, like himself, did parapsychological research. When, in 1969, the American Association for the Advancement of Science admitted the Parapsychology Society to membership, some viewed the move as a sign of new respectability for parapsychology.

Holistic healers provided yet another source for New Age spirituality. With their concepts that disease is self-created and that individuals have the power to heal themselves, the new alternative healers offered habits of thought and action that resonated with the emerging New Age consensus. Likewise, they modeled New Age preferences in their natural remedies (herbs, special foods, homeopathics), in their techniques of healing touch and massage (bodywork), and in their mind–body therapies in general. Meanwhile, **astrologers** played an important role in the movement. They taught that the qualities molding human character and destiny and shaping the mood of an era were written large on the sky "map" formed by the stars. So the **Age of Aquarius**—an early name for the New Age—became a symbol for the consciousness that New Age people believed would replace old and outworn beliefs. Understood as the time when the sun would leave the constellation of Pisces and enter the constellation of Aquarius on the day of the spring equinox (predicted for some 300 years after the last decades of the twentieth century), early New Agers, especially, looked to the Aquarian Age as a dawning age of the spirit.

After the change in the national immigration law in 1965, **Asian teachers** had a significant impact on the New Age movement. Beliefs about karma and reincarnation, for example, already popularized through the Theosophical Society and its offshoots, received new legitimacy from Asian sources. So persuasive did these ideas become that today perhaps one-fifth to one-fourth of Americans hold reincarnational beliefs. Similarly, **American Indian teachers** communicated parts of their traditions to New Age seekers. For example, the (nonnative) Bear Tribe Medicine Society, which the Chippewa native teacher Sun Bear founded in 1966, regularly sponsored Medicine Wheel gatherings as weekend camp conferences where he and other native teachers spoke of their religious beliefs and practices. Oblivious to criticism by Indian traditionalists and others who warned of mainstream American cultural imperialism, New Agers appropriated Native American rituals like the sweat-lodge ceremony in various pan-Indian versions. They borrowed American Indian rattles and drums, wore and used feathers, beads, and gemstones, engaged in variants of native pipe ceremonies, made pilgrimages to Indian sacred sites, and worked to practice shamanism.

The theme of the earth as a living being and concern for the environment as a common heritage also fed into the New Age synthesis, carried by Native American and Asian traditions and the ecological movement. As environmental concerns entered their awareness, New Agers linked them to theories of earth changes and purifications appropriated from American Indians and to harmonial ideas derived from Asians. Together, these ideas and concerns helped give the New Age movement a social ethic.

The Religion of the New Age

As the New Age movement coalesced and matured, different types of followers and sympathizers emerged. Some tended to be **social thinkers** with environmental, transformational, and holistic-health agendas. Others have expressed their concerns more as **individually oriented actors** who have engaged in practices such as channeling and work with crystals. Social thinkers have leaned toward ordinary religion, since ideas about social reform and reorganization have attracted them. On their side, individually inclined actors have underlined extraordinary religion as spiritual seekers who want direct evidence of and contact

Sun Bear at California Medicine Wheel Gathering, 1982. Sun Bear, founder of the Bear Tribe Medicine Society, until his death in 1992 promoted Medicine Wheel gatherings nationally and internationally. The weekend meetings, held usually in outdoor settings, continue under Wind Daughter to combine Native American ceremonies with workshops or study classes.

with the extraordinary. The first group ends with an ethical religion that stresses a way of life shaped by theoretical reflection. The second favors a strongly ritualized religion that emphasizes symbolic behavior. Both groups—and people in between—have shared a contemporary spin on earlier metaphysical religion that is worth exploring.

In the New Age version of the theory of correspondence, talk of the "**universe**" is uppermost. Where more traditional believers would refer to God, New Agers fill in the blank with the "universe." So a typical New Ager might say something like "the universe decided that I would get the job" (or "meet my significant other," or "find the perfect roommate," or the like). Here the universe has become a source of life's many events and coincidences, and it also possesses an intelligence that guides and guards people. But the relationship of the universe to individuals is not the same for New Age religion as the traditional relationship between God and his creatures is for Judaism, Christianity, and Islam. Rather, the New Age universe contains all of life and is also expressed in each part of it. So New Agers not only believe that the microcosm of human society reflects the macrocosm of the universe; they especially emphasize their conviction that separateness is finally an illusion.

New Agers speak about "**energy**" probably even more than they talk about the universe. Even though they see matter and energy as interchangeable, they also see energy as a "higher" manifestation of the one universe than is matter. They often talk about lower rates of vibration (matter) and higher ones (energy), and generally, the greater the energy quotient, the greater the good they discover for people's lives. New Agers, in their energy talk, also refer to "**chakras**," affirming a Sanskrit term and idea about energy exchange centers, seven of them major, located along the human body. And since they like to equate energy with light, linking modern physics with mystical symbolism, they end in religious company even if they dislike the term *religion*. At the same time, New Agers end in environmentalist company with their talk of the "**planet**." For many, the earth is Gaia, the Earth Goddess or Earth Mother. And for all, the earth is a living being, capable of being violated by the rapacious instincts of humans but capable, also, of being regenerated by human efforts at planetary healing. Here the theory of correspondence means that the greater world that surrounds human society is the world of nature.

As in other versions of the theory of correspondence, if everything is everything else in New Age belief, then everything can also *act* on everything else. So New Agers see the universe and planet as places of magic and miracle. Such ideas of often sudden and beneficial transformation link the New Age movement to traditional forms of American Christianity. New Agers speak of such transformation as a work of **healing**. In other words, they think of the human situation as in some ways deficient. There is a millennial ring to this kind of thinking, even though as the New Age has matured the millennialism has largely declined. Still, New Agers see present-day people as existing in states that are metaphysical equivalents of sickness or sin. Sometimes, in New Age understanding, that sickness or sin finds material, physical expression. At other times, its expression is largely mental or "spiritual." In both cases, the description of the human situation—in need of healing—echoes, in another key, ideas of original sin. It also paves the way for practice in everyday living and ritual work.

In keeping with their ideas about the universe, the planet, and the energy that inhabits all things, New Agers seek to live in harmony with the laws of nature and the "natural." Yet they also champion ideas that agree with American belief in progress. They are interested in the cultivation of self and in personal transformation. So their ethic is an ethic of change. The **New Age ethic** asks for a kind of pilgrim's progress; it offers guidance for a journey that is conceived also as a healing. Meanwhile, the ethic emphasizes individual responsibility for one's life and choices. One of the preferred New Age ways of reflecting on life is to see it as a series of lessons to be learned. Here the pilgrim becomes a student, and the world a New Age schoolhouse. Any number of paths will do, so long as they lead to personal transformation, and New Agers typically welcome many different tools to help them on their journey or at their school. With strong preferences for **combining**, many follow several disciplines at the same time. For example, a person who seeks to practice the code of forgiveness specified in the *Course in Miracles* might also follow the recommendations of an astrologer and practice vegetarianism as part of a spiritual discipline.

Individual ethics fan out into the social ethic of the New Age. Clearly concerned about the environment, New Agers worry about human abuse of nature and, when they get involved, work to undo the damage they believe society has done to the earth. This ethic connects them to metaphysical theories about earth changes and purifications. Moreover, the ethic relates environmental healing to reforming action that leads to politics. New Agers have defended animal rights, fought food irradiation and genetic engineering, and demonstrated against nuclear power plants. They have lobbied against pesticides and airplane spraying of crops, promoted organic farming, and joined in grassroots businesses to supply "environmentally friendly" paper products. They have helped to promote Earth Days and have supported environmental organizations. They have also promoted feminism and world peace. Oftentimes, their approach here has been "spiritual." For example, New Age people have spoken for cooperation over competition and for the "feminine" aspect of male character. Yet they have championed equal rights for women, and they have objected to mutual funds that invest in military weapons systems.

Meanwhile, **ritual work** within the New Age provides symbolic statements that agree with beliefs and ethics. Without the presence of organized "churches," New Agers carry on their ritual life with numerous means. Using crystals and consulting channelers, while seeming to be faddish, have been, for many, purposeful actions. In general, some New Age rituals stress the material world. For example, ritual work seeks to "harmonize" the energies of the body so that they resonate with larger natural forces and laws. In contrast, other New Age rituals seek to facilitate mental journeying into nonmaterial worlds. In these rituals the goal is to stimulate forces of mind and imagination so that they assume control *over* matter. In both cases, New Agers seek to alter the human condition; they aim to heal, even as they act out symbolically their creed and code.

An example of the first, harmonial, type of ritual work is the Japanese method of palm healing known as **Reiki**. Gaining attention in the late 1970s and 1980s and continuing until today, Reiki masters teach the existence of "universal life-force energy" and its use through special "attunements" received from them. They say that these attunements enable a person to receive and transmit life-force energy in a clearer, purer, and more powerful state. Receiving the attunements means going through a series of initiatory rituals. Just as important, when the initiated Reiki practitioner begins the actual practice of palm healing, that work also possesses ritual elements. Performed in systematic fashion with specified hand positions and, for the higher degrees, other secret instructions, the practice may take an hour or more. During this time, the client and/or the practitioner may report sensations of heat, cold, or body tingling. Reiki can heal, they believe, because Reiki energy can transform bodily organs and functions. In that respect, the ritual acquires practicality and, for believers, provides material proof of the metaphysical system on which it is based.

A good example of the second type of ritual work that has featured the controlled use of imagination is **New Age shamanism**. Shamans take mental journeys to attempt both to acquire power and to use it. In traditional societies, their work has been social in its intent and goal, with curing illness a significant focus. Although far less steeped in symbolic lore and, mostly, far less disciplined, New Age shamans have sought similar goals. They have sometimes been encouraged by specific organizations, such as anthropologist Michael Harner's Foundation for Shamanic Studies or adopted Huichol Indian Brant Secunda's Dance of the Deer Foundation. And they sometimes have learned shamanic techniques less formally, through audiotapes or shared experience. Whatever their introduction to shamanic ritual, practitioners have aimed, typically, to "visit" several worlds where they can meet power animals, guardian spirits, and also dangers. Mentally journeying through these various regions with the use of drum, rattle, and/or hallucinogenic plants, the shamanic practitioner seeks to live through a story that symbolically expresses the concerns with which he or she began. This story may help a practitioner make sense of a problem situation in life, bring healing, or give advice for spiritual growth.

In addition to self-conscious rituals such as Reiki palm healing and shamanic journeying, New Agers have often used seemingly nonritualistic activity in ritual ways. The wearing of crystals and other forms of New Age jewelry is one example, with crystals and gemstones thought to possess powers to aid individuals, to protect them, or to develop aspects of their character. Yet even when ritual practice is the work of one individual, it is based on beliefs and lifeways that are shared. The cultus of the New Age, therefore, points toward the New Age community.

Sociologists and other scholars have described that community as often middle-aged, sometimes young, usually urban, and overwhelmingly female. They have also seen it as middle-class and upwardly mobile, as better educated than average, and as not particularly alienated from society. High-priced and fashionable weekend workshops and conferences provide evidence for these judgments. Still, a strong working-class component exists within the New Age movement, although its presence is quieter and less noticeable. Evidence suggests, too, representative participation by Protestants, Catholics, and Jews, as well as by diverse others. Geographically, New Agers appear to be well represented on both coasts, with California and the Northeast as bellwether regions. New Agers are also strong in parts of the Midwest and probably weakest in the South. The size of the community in the 1990s may have been well over 10 million, although it is difficult to estimate. In recent years, though, the size of the community has declined. Still, with surveys suggesting that perhaps 20 to 25 percent of Americans accept the idea of reincarnation, the New Age has made its mark.

New Age community, in general, is fluid more than fixed. The homesteads of the mind that characterized the older metaphysical tradition characterize the New Age synthesis, too. The goal of world community, of a metaphysical oneness with all people, is especially attractive for those whose existing community is fragile. Without the historic supports of traditional community, New Agers tend to be ready to move on when circumstance or desire prompts change. They often read the same books and subscribe to the same magazines. Their interests have spawned a series of businesses that cater to them and provide places for them to meet one another. New Age networking has been loose but generally effective in bringing people together. And the New Age has constructed a community that, for all its looseness, works for those involved. What the community works toward may be described as a sense of empowerment in a world that, for many, has grown too impersonal, too corporate and bureaucratic, and too resistant to personal leverage. In the small groups that coalesce and dissolve, New Agers have created ad hoc means to meet their felt needs and to give themselves hope for a future that is noticeably better. In short, New Age community has been as expansive as the New Age itself.

New Spirituality

Perhaps the greatest impact of the New Age movement has been its indirect influence on non–New Age Americans. In fact, as the twenty-first century has progressed and as New Age millennialism has declined, the New Age movement itself seems to be gradually dissolving. At the same time, a **new spirituality** appears to be growing in a much broader segment of American society. Just as the earlier New Thought movement influenced huge numbers of Americans when people like Norman Vincent Peale and others began talking about positive thinking, the New Age movement has in many ways altered mainstream American beliefs and values even as it has merged with them. So many Americans now say that they are "spiritual" but not "religious" that the statement is a commonplace. And religious people have talked about constructing their own religion from many sources. For example, sociologist Robert Bellah and his professional colleagues have written about the religion of "**Sheilaism.**" Sheila Larson (not her real name), a nurse whom they interviewed, talked about this personal religion of hers in which she did not attend church but tried to love and be gentle with herself and take care of other people. She clearly believed in God, and she as clearly cared about others—in fact, healing them in her job as a nurse—but much more than that she could not say. Still, for her it was enough.

New spirituality means different things to different people. For all, though, it seems to stress ideas of self-help and personal healing. For example, New Age ideas about energy have now become almost conventional in what is called "**energy healing.**" Energy healing may include various types of bodywork and massage, or the Therapeutic Touch technique employed by some nurses and health care professionals in hospitals, or acupuncture, or even yoga and various martial arts. Practitioners understand these **holistically**—as healing not only the body but also emotions and spirit. Similarly, talk of chakras often keeps company with conventional acupuncture references to energy meridians, which the needles are said to stimulate. Many who would not describe themselves as New Age pay attention to energy derived from astrological signs, to meaningful coincidences, to omens, and the like. They talk about interpersonal relationships as energy enhancers or energy drains, and they link successful relationships to the intuitive tools provided by astrology and coincidence. Meanwhile, dreams guide many who look to them for insight. Still others turn to guides for understanding their character and how to improve it, as in tools like the psychic Helen Palmer's enneagram—based on nine character types said to be part of Sufi tradition. Catholic nuns, for instance, have used the enneagram. In another example, self-help books—with psychological advice offered in the language of energy and healing—are plentiful even in evangelical bookstores.

Teachers and authors on the "spiritual" circuit—like Caroline Myss, Joan Borysenko, Deepak Chopra, and Eckhart Tolle, for instance—straddle a line between New Age and new spirituality. Meanwhile, sociologist Wade Clark Roof has noted that those in the baby boom generation (from the end of World War II until 1964) are a "generation of seekers," who search the spiritual marketplace for what they desire and often find it—like Sheila Larson—by combining different sources. Many are unchurched, and those who find a church do it on their own terms. So new spirituality means finding God and/or personal direction outside church buildings or synagogues or mosques, or finding God in them in unconventional ways.

In many liberal Protestant churches today, as in an example noted in Chapter 4, some champion a new sexual ethic in which same-sex relationships are positively valued both for pastors and people in the pew. Not all agree. So Lutherans and United Church of Christ members, Methodists, Presbyterians, Episcopalians, and other Protestants have struggled at official denominational levels about whether to welcome gays and lesbians into their congregations, whether to sacralize their relationships in holy unions or marriages, whether to ordain gay clergy, or whether to allow them to continue as clergy if they announce their sexual orientation. In a much-reported case in 2003, as a case in point, Episcopalians by a 62-45 vote made V. Gene Hamilton in New Hampshire the first openly gay bishop in the Episcopal church. Catholics, meanwhile, have increasingly acknowledged the gay culture that has characterized seminaries and the priesthood, and some of them, in the nonofficial Catholic organization Dignity, as we saw in Chapter 3, have found Catholic ways to spiritualize their same-sex life-styles. All of this suggests new models and a new sense of the possibilities of the human that challenge older ideas of what counts as right thinking and acting. This is not New Age, but it is new spirituality.

Patterns of Contemporary Contraction: Conservative Religion Come of Age

Conservatives, however, have seen the world and their place in it in different terms. While metaphysicians were reporting contacts with ascended masters in the 1930s, Protestant fundamentalists were quietly increasing their ranks and building organizational strength. By the early 1940s, led by Carl McIntire, the more separatist among them formed the **American Council of Christian Churches**. Then moderate fundamentalists established their own organization, the **National Association of Evangelicals**. The organizational division reflected a new self-consciousness within conservative circles. The heirs of the earlier fundamentalist movement found their ranks divided between the most militant, who kept the name **fundamentalists**, and the relatively moderate, now known as **evangelicals**. Before the decade ended, Harold John Ockenga, founding president of the National Association of Evangelicals and then-president of conservative **Fuller Theological Seminary**, was speaking of the "**new evangelicalism**." Conceived by Ockenga as "progressive fundamentalism with a social message," this new evangelicalism found other advocates among theologians such as Carl F. H. Henry and Edward J. Carnell. The movement found, too, a major print vehicle through its periodical ***Christianity Today***. In the mood of the times, new evangelicals championed the revival work of **Billy Graham** and formed other institutions such as Campus Crusade for Christ International (1951). Moving away from strict dispensational theology and promoting the idea of the kingdom of God as progressively present in the world, the new evangelicals became a major force within conservative ranks until the late 1960s. Militants—fundamentalists—expressed displeasure. They denounced Billy Graham and avoided institutions that fostered the new evangelical message. Nonetheless, new forces were rising and new times coming that prompted even militant fundamentalists to change.

Fundamentalist and Evangelical: The Search for Conservative Identity

Today a number of major groups command attention on the conservative Protestant landscape. Theologically, for example, premillennial dispensationalists are strong. On the other side, moderates hold to the inerrancy of scripture but interpret it more broadly and find sin in the world but also grace. Historically, some stand in the tradition of the fundamentalist-modernist controversy, but others come from the holiness-pentecostal wing of conservative Protestantism. Socially, a quiet conservatism exists in thousands of Bible-oriented congregations, and a noisier electronic church has brought widespread notice. Politically, the New Christian Right contrasts with the views of radical evangelicals who are left of center.

Premillennial dispensationalism, far from disappearing, is flourishing. With the publication of Hal Lindsey's *Late Great Planet Earth* (1970), the mood of mixed fear and anticipation surrounding expected millennial events grew more tangible. Then, beginning in 1995, the ***Left Behind* series**, the work of Tim LaHaye and Jerry Jenkins, used the novel form to spread prophecy beliefs. With fourteen novels published to date, the wildly successful series has sold 55 million copies for its first ten titles, and six of the books have topped the charts at the *New York Times* and other places. The books explore the lives of those "left behind" when the prophesied "**rapture**" comes—understood as the spiriting away of the saints into the air at the time of tribulation. In this endtime scenario, the Antichrist rules the world before the battle at Armageddon when Christ defeats Satan and the millennium begins.

These prophecy beliefs represent an active system of reading the Bible and conferring meaning on world events. Not the same as simply reading the Bible literally, **premillennial dispensationalism** provides a future-oriented way to read the Bible. The Book of Daniel in the Old Testament and the Book of Revelation in the New Testament become preferred texts. Moreover, believers have read the notes to the Scofield Reference Bible or the Ryrie Study Bible, with their premillennial commentary on scriptural passages. With this background, watching the television news each evening becomes an exercise in seeing prophecy unfold.

What is it that attracts so many to premillennial dispensationalist views? Along with literal belief in the Bible and a separatist tendency, premillennial dispensationalism speaks to a desire for cultural contraction and consolidation among contemporary Protestant conservatives. Those who seek such cultural contraction, in numerical terms, have grown a good deal—so in one way they are part of the culture of expansion. But their preference for contraction expresses a habit of mind and a response to complexity in today's world. Within the response of the dispensational message is the idea that the world is growing worse and that human beings cannot by themselves undo the damage and right the situation. Divine rescue is necessary for premillennial dispensationalists, and until it comes, flight from the world, at least metaphorically, becomes desirable.

Old and new mix in contemporary conservative quarters, and so do contraction and numerical expansion. For example, regional enclaves have sprung up as evangelical sanctuaries in places like Colorado Springs, Colorado, and Orange County, California. Here **regional religion** transforms public culture and insulates it, to some extent, from the outside world. In Colorado Springs, for example, Pastor Ted Haggard has founded the **megachurch** New Life with a membership of 11,000. (A megachurch is usually defined as a church with over 2,000 members, and New Life's membership is far exceeded by the largest megachurch, Saddleback, in southern California, with its 80,000 members.) Haggard also now leads the National Association of Evangelicals, which in 2005 included 45,000 member churches and 30 million individuals. Colorado Springs is home as well to Dr. James Dobson's **Focus on the Family**, a ministry that offers radio shows, videos, magazines, and books for some 200 million throughout the world. The local conservative culture in Colorado Springs is friendly toward **Christian Reconstructionism**. Also known as **dominion theology**, this view looks to the Kingdom of God realized on earth through a society controlled by Christians and regulated according to their beliefs. So religion easily moves into politics and becomes the politics of the **Christian Right**.

The contractive impulse has been softer among some conservatives. As early as the 1960s, theological liberalism entered "new evangelical" ranks when higher criticism of the Bible became more acceptable. Fuller Theological Seminary, earlier a strict fundamentalist school, began to use once-condemned methods of biblical interpretation. Yet at Fuller, if all of scripture was not inerrant, some parts of it were. When the Bible taught about faith and morality, it made no mistakes. Only history and cosmology in the scripture reflected a more limited perspective. Fuller's move prompted public debate on biblical inerrancy. The results included for one denomination, the Lutheran Church–Missouri Synod, an acrimonious division into two. But the changes in evangelical theology spread to major evangelical theological seminaries and college religion programs. Moreover, beliefs in premillennial dispensationalism waned, as evangelicals got interested in psychological study and social-scientific approaches to religion. They were seemingly making peace with the world, and the world began noticing them more kindly. Evangelical pluralism grew, as earlier divisions seemed to multiply.

By the turn of the twenty-first century and before, evangelicals no longer avoided dialogue with those who disagreed—Catholics, liberals among Protestants, persons from other religious traditions. Academic recognition came; magazines and periodicals grew more nuanced; national presidents had already professed to be evangelical. Still, evangelicalism is not the same as liberal mainstream Protestantism. If the theological range within the fundamentalist-evangelical movement has become broad, the movement also consciously accepts more diversity than it did in its early-twentieth-century version. A major component now comes from the holiness-pentecostal tradition.

Originally, holiness-pentecostalist and fundamentalist believers recognized each other's differences, and both movements kept their distance.

Holiness-pentecostal emphasis on the work of the Spirit, sanctification, prophetic gifts, and strong emotionalism countered fundamentalist emphases on the power of Jesus, conversion, biblical proficiency, and a qualified rationalism. By the late twentieth century, however, these differences melted away. United by a characteristic style of preaching, a focus on direct experience, championship of biblical authority, and attention to personal holiness, the two movements recognized their kinship in what seemed an increasingly alien world. Many in the holiness-pentecostal movement grew away from earlier material conditions of poverty, and, with fundamentalists, increasingly blended into general American society. At the same time, new groups—like the **Vineyard Christian Fellowship** with its 600 churches nationwide—further blurred the line between pentecostals and evangelicals. Clearly part of the evangelical family, the Vineyard also focuses on the Holy Spirit and versions of **charismatic experience** that are associated with older forms of pentecostalism.

Increasingly, electronic media have helped spread the new message of conservatives. The social style of the **electronic church** began almost with the twentieth century: the first religious radio broadcast came with the first broadcast of the human voice—at a Christmas service in 1906. By 1921, in Pittsburgh, Calvary Baptist Church was sending its Sunday evening worship service over the airwaves. Evangelists quickly understood the power of radio, and in 1925 perhaps 10 percent of American radio stations operated under religious auspices. The Federal Council of Churches soon got involved for liberals, but for their part, fundamentalists produced their own programs and more than stood their ground. Then, television offered a greater ability to reach mass audiences, and Christian church leaders recognized their opportunities. Mainstream Protestant clergy, joined by Catholics and Jews, received free air time. Conservative Protestants like Rex Humbard, Oral Roberts, and Billy Graham could be seen on television in the 1950s, but the networks mostly clung to their unofficial policy of giving free public air time to mainstream, more liberal denominations, thus fulfilling the federal government's requirement to produce public-service programs. Fundamentalists and other evangelicals, if they wanted time on television, had to operate independently and pay their way.

Pay their way they did, and, in fact, conservatives not only purchased air time but also acquired their own Christian television stations and set up distribution networks. But other changes altered the fundamentalist-evangelical future. The Federal Communications Commission ruled by the early 1980s that it would accept paid religious programming as fulfillment of the networks' public-service obligation. At the same time, local television stations, once dominated by network giants, acquired a measure of independence. They quickly discovered the profits of selling air time on Sunday morning to religious programmers. Long accustomed to receiving free time, mainstream and liberal religious leaders mostly turned away from the new order. They fought back by claiming that conservatives had relatively small audiences, that they were a minority within Protestantism, and that they were commercializing religion.

Meanwhile, new technologies increased communications possibilities for a growing evangelical empire. Cable networks, communications satellites from which signals could be bounced across huge distances, and ultrahigh-frequency (UHF) stations all transformed television and multiplied evangelical outreach. The work of the computer, too, aided the movement. Programmers could quickly and efficiently assemble audience mailing lists, implement direct-mail services, and personalize letters seeking financial support. **Televangelism** was becoming an important means of spreading the conservative gospel. Religious networks such as the Christian Broadcasting Network of Pat Robertson with its *700 Club*, the PTL ("Praise the Lord" and "People That Love") Network of Jim Bakker, and the Trinity Broadcasting Network brought religious television into millions of homes. The typical viewer, however, matched the profile of many in conservative Protestantism, and, so, what at first seems to show religious expansion on further scrutiny looks contractive and consolidating.

Moreover, after separate sex scandals involving pentecostals Jim Bakker and Jimmy Swaggart of the *Jimmy Swaggart* show in the late 1980s, televangelism began to lose support. National Religious Broadcasters (NRB), televangelism's major trade association, swiftly drafted new ethical directives. However, scandal was not the only reason for criticism. If liberals had from the first protested against the commercialization of religion in televangelism, conservatives themselves raised questions. Beyond that, the preaching within the televangelical empire shifted, as some evangelicals noticed. Premillennial dispensationalism, with its message of impending doom, is not an ingredient for television success. Entertainment—even "Christian" entertainment—eroded the self-conscious conservative boundary with the world. The culture of contraction has continued in the assumptions of the programming, in its preference for themes of family and domesticity and of personal (often sexual) holiness. But a less militant attitude toward the world has also become apparent. Still, untold numbers in the fundamentalist-evangelical community practice a quieter version of their faith than the preaching of televangelists would imply. Local churches and pastors have been more central for most; and if Christian booksellers and their sales are evidence, reading the Bible, biblical commentaries, and other devotional works occupies the time of millions. A more reflective spirituality exists side by side with the flamboyance of media-oriented religion.

Meanwhile, the electronic church has set the stage for the politics of the Christian Right, for—whatever else the televangelists preach—most preach a superpatriotism. **Pat Robertson** is a case in point. The highly visible founder of the CBN and talk-show host of its *700 Club* (named after his 1963 campaign to persuade 700 audience members to promise 10 dollars monthly in support of his budget), Robertson by the late 1970s was moving toward politics. He interviewed conservative political leaders and talked on television to financial analysts. Still more, he translated the dispensationalist message into a worldly language that warned of doom in Washington and a crumbling United States Capitol. In September 1986 Robertson announced himself a potential presidential candidate, and less than a

Fundamentalist Journal, September 1983. This front cover illustration from the (no-longer-published) *Fundamentalist Journal* evokes the image of an earlier, simpler time when, for editor Jerry Falwell and readers, virtue and education flourished together.

year later, with his goal of support from 3 million Americans met, he became an official candidate. Robertson later withdrew from the race when it became apparent that he could not win the Republican nomination. But his active participation until then signaled the power of the Christian Right and its link with televangelism. In recent years, Robertson has often spoken out nationally expressing militant and rightwing views.

Jerry Falwell, who reached a huge national audience through his *Old Time Gospel Hour,* also became a strong organizer for the Christian Right. His **Moral Majority**, founded in 1979, grew out of earlier overtures by Washington-based political organizers. But as early as 1975, Falwell had warned that the nation was scorning its heritage under God. Now his Moral Majority grew rapidly. At its height it numbered about 4 million members; with a name change to the Liberty Federation in 1986, the organization acted as a leader for the Christian Right until 1989. In an important sense, the **Christian Coalition** took the torch from Falwell. After Pat Robertson's unsuccessful bid for the presidency in 1988, he created the new organization as a lobbying group to elect conservative candidates and to promote conservative laws while defeating liberal initiatives. Under its executive director Ralph Reed, who steered the organization until 1997, the advocacy group grew by leaps and bounds. By 1996, Robertson claimed that the number of "members and supporters" had increased to 1.8 million. Significantly, it reached out to Catholics and Orthodox Jews as well as to blacks and Latinos. Coalition leaders issued congressional "report cards" and "voter guides." As they did so, they were taking active steps in the direction of a dominion theology that would transform the pluralist and postpluralist United States into a nation that was publicly Christian.

Today other organizations, like Dobson's Focus on the Family, are part of the Christian Right. These groups take aim against what they have called **secular humanism**, understanding it as the belief that human beings are ultimate and that earthly life on its own terms is of utmost importance. For the Christian Right, liberal politics supports secular humanism, eroding traditional values such as commitment to a strong family, prescribed gender roles, a devout and powerful nation, and an educational system that inculcates received knowledge and inherited ideas of virtue. So the Christian Right has crusaded against abortion and for school prayer, against homosexuality and feminism and for greater government support for religious education and faith-based charities, against "atheistic" communism and for a strong national defense. Employing sophisticated computer technology for direct-mail contacts and fund-raising, organizations in the movement network with one another. Political action committees (PACs), lobbies, and educational foundations work together, so that the PACs—neither tax exempt nor offering tax deductions for contributions—can take advantage of tax-exempt lobbies and tax-exempt and tax-deductible educational foundations.

One timely example of the Christian Right's political savvy has been its challenge to primary and secondary school biology curricula as they teach the theory of evolution. Earlier under the banner of **creationism** and more recently using the idea of **intelligent design**, conservatives have lobbied school boards and made their muscle felt, demanding discussion of alternatives to the Darwinian theory. Criticisms of creationism—the theory that taught the direct creation of the universe and the separate creation of humans and apes—cast doubts on its scientific credentials, and the theory did not withstand court challenges. So the broader and more philosophically oriented theory of intelligent design has mostly taken its place. Many raise questions regarding the presence of either theory in science classes, but the power and persuasiveness of the Christian Right are evident in its ability to mount a public campaign and force debate on the issue.

Despite its organizational expansiveness and power, however, the Christian Right evidences the religious culture of contraction and consolidation. With its strong tradition of religious privatism, conservative Protestantism is not finally at ease in a public world. The concerns that have mobilized a segment of the population not usually active in public life—the working class and lower middle class, both religiously separatist in the past—have largely touched areas of personal morality and life-style. Often, too, they have been single-issue concerns. Aside from support for a strong national defense, which fits the dispensational vision of a coming final battle with the forces of the Antichrist and evil, positions regarding abortion, pornography, homosexuality, feminism, school prayer, and the like speak to the ways in which intimate aspects of life impinge on society. In short, the strong organizing ability of the Christian Right in many ways supports a world looking inward more than outward, in order to promote the vision of an earlier, purer nation and to make it social reality.

Not all conservative Protestants, however, agree with the Christian Right. An important example of a counter **radical evangelicalism** is the **Sojourners Community** (now Sojourners Ministries) and the related ***Sojourners* magazine**. Sojourners began among Baptist seminarians at Trinity Evangelical Divinity School, outside of Chicago. There, in the Vietnam War era, a small group of students—all white, middle-class, and male—began to think of salvation as the redemption of society as a whole as well as the redemption of individuals. With **Jim Wallis** as their leader, they started a magazine and established a community. In 1975 they moved to the nation's capital. Thereafter they changed the name of their magazine and their community to reflect the self-conscious radicalism of their venture. The church, they thought, was an "alien society" of God's people, a body of "sojourners" present in the world but working for a totally different order.

This language of separation and otherness already suggests the contractive and consolidating nature of the politics of the left that the Sojourners have practiced. In keeping with the biblical image of sojourners as travelers or pilgrims who stay only for a time, members of Sojourners have understood their work as both priestly and prophetic. In priestly vein, they considered their intentional Christian community as a way to support one another on their journey, even as they have thought of their community as a model of the church of the future. In prophetic style, they have believed that people of conscience must participate in the political process. The church's mission, they have said, is to challenge the existing order, and they have criticized cultural conformism.

Instead, they have identified with the poor, in the 1980s engaging in community organizing, forming tenant unions and food cooperatives, and helping establish day-care centers in Washington, D.C. Beyond that, they moved into the more specifically political process through their challenges to government housing and welfare policies and, on the foreign front, to American support for governments they considered repressive. With peace and community reconciliation as stated commitments, the Sojourners have in the past been antinuclear publicists and activists. They have not hesitated to use *Sojourners* magazine to advance their political views. And as in the past, the Sojourners today include not only members of evangelical churches but also adherents to peace churches, mainstream Protestants, Catholics, and those with no church affiliation. With overlapping support groups and a fluidity to involvement, it is difficult to assign a size to the movement. One sure measure, however, is the paid circulation of *Sojourners* magazine, which in 1997 stood at 25,000. By this time, Wallis had taken a leadership role in a public declaration titled "The Cry for Renewal," the work of a broad new coalition—evangelically based but also strongly ecumenical. The declaration challenged the dominance of the Right and began to strike out on what it saw as a more "progressive" course. Out of coalition meetings emerged a new organization, Call to Renewal, administered out of *Sojourners'* offices. By the next year, the Sojourners Community had given way before Sojourners Ministries.

In the midst of its ecumenical diversity and outreach, the Sojourners message is the consolidating message of conservative Protestantism. Although it has gradually changed, it continues to condemn consumerism and greed. Preaching poverty instead of wealth and upholding "nuanced" pro-life values, the Sojourners count as traditionalist in many ways. Opposed to the policies of the Christian Right, radical evangelicals are hardly expansive social joiners. If a "radical" is one who returns to "roots," then these conservative Protestants condemn contemporary society and seek a return to biblical roots. For them, such a return has meant rejecting the arms race. But it has also meant repudiating even a Christian capitalism and rejecting what the Sojourners see as the corruption of a modern-day Babylon.

The Religion of the Fundamentalist-Evangelical Movement

Like New Agers, Protestant conservatives express their identity in their language. They are Bible-reading people, and their talk displays their intimacy with the text and also the beliefs and practices it makes uppermost for them. Unlike the impersonal universe of the New Age, the world of conservatives is inhabited by a personal God and his son Jesus. Believers speak of "**getting saved**" and "**coming to Jesus**." They talk of the "**sinner's prayer**" that precedes conversion and of asking Jesus into their heart. They witness to being "**born again**." For all, the **Bible** stands as the ultimate authority, inerrant in its revelation. Moreover, as close Bible readers, they accept in some form a set of Christian "fundamentals." The list varies depending on leanings to the right or left, and some accept its doctrinal statements more literally than others. But all agree on the centrality of Jesus. All acknowledge human sinfulness, divine grace, and a need for repentance. All believe in the importance of direct experience for assurance of salvation. And all hold firm to a sense of divine purpose in human history, so that in this sense all expect a second and final coming of Christ.

The biblical creed of conservatives reveals that, for them, sharp boundaries separate extraordinary from ordinary but divine initiative overcomes the separation. The code for living that is based on the creed also requires a sharp separation between the extraordinary life of the Christian and the ordinary proceedings of the world. For the individual Christian, the code demands **holiness**. This means strict and traditional morality, especially regarding sex, alcohol, and related issues. Depending on where one stands in the conservative world, these guidelines are more or less stern. But they are always enough to mark a difference, to set off the conservative Protestant from the world. For society, the code seeks good order and encourages missionary work. Ordered government, social services, conduct of foreign policy, and the like will, according to the conservative ethic, keep evil at bay and erect the safeguards that protect Christian life. This policy of containment also implies action to hold together a Christian society, and so political aims are built in.

Similarly, the directive to **mission**—the continuing expression of the mission mind—is also a boundary concern. Proclaiming the gospel forcefully can help conservatives keep what they see as evil outside their protected community. And it can help to keep the faithful within. Mission takes dramatic form not only in the electronic church but also in the pulpits of small churches and the revival tents of itinerant preachers. It takes world form in a vast foreign mission empire, expansive in the sense that it seeks to reach as many as possible but contractive in its goal of rescue and protection from evil. The directive to mission also means witnessing within daily life. And the ethic teaches, too, that personal behavior affects society. The example of personal holiness becomes a form of mission, as much as does the organized efforts of preachers and mission organizations.

Conservatives preach and witness to the **worship life** that for them provides divine assurance. The ideal for this life is direct experience. For fundamentalists and many others, conversion is primary, while for those with holiness and pentecostal roots, the quest for Spirit blessings and healings may be as significant. For all, the felt sense of the extraordinary—of Jesus or the Spirit—are the goals of activity in conservative cultus. So cultus takes place in the churches and in regular worship services in which sermons and prayers that foster devotion are central. It also takes place in mass revivals and rallies that marshal believers in demonstrations of heartfelt faith. More quietly and individually, cultus is expressed through regular biblical reading, study, and devotion, and through the practice of private prayer.

Studies of cultus often emphasize its formal and repeated character, and they underline a point. Despite their strong regard for experience, fundamentalists and evangelicals, like other religious people, practice their cultus in patterns of repetition and sameness. Fundamentalist and evangelical conversions are a lot like one another:

there are expected rules to follow. So, too, expected rules guide even the most spontaneous and emotional churches in contemporary holiness-pentecostalism. Some things are allowed and are considered—however disorderly they may look to outsiders—in good order. Other things are clearly beyond the pale. Similarly, reports of fundamentalist and evangelical prayer experiences, for all their emphasis on the spontaneity of emotion, display expected form. Conservative preachings and witnessings, even with their strongly emotional character, follow rhetorical patterns that can be mapped. So the quest for order in the conservative code is repeated in its ritual. Creed, code, and cultus are all expressions of a body of people with certain ideas about themselves and the nature of the world around them.

Members of this conservative Protestant community are today diverse and many-sided. Although their forebears may have numbered among the "disinherited," today's fundamentalist-evangelical movement encompasses working-class people with good job security, lower middle-class people, and many who have reached greater affluence. African Americans share in the community, as do, notably, Latinos (especially pentecostal and Southern Baptist), and Koreans. Even with the differences between fundamentalist separation and evangelical accommodation, conservatives form a community of the separated, of those who believe that they have been rescued from the sin and chaos of ordinary American society. Committed to maintain a pure community, they also seek to restore a perfect social order. All the same, just as the extraordinary is never fully removed from the ordinary, so the separate community acts in American society. Like the biblical God who interfered in history, fundamentalists and evangelicals are drawn toward the ordinary center of American society.

One good example of these generalizations is **Promise Keepers**. In 1990, former University of Colorado football coach Bill McCartney began to turn his men's Christian fellowship and prayer group into a major organization. For three summers after that the group held men's conferences in Boulder, with the third, in 1993, filling the 50,000-seat Folsom Field. The following year Promise Keepers began to travel, staging rallies throughout the country and drawing in nearly 300,000 men. Rallies and numbers increased by exponential factors, and by 1997 the organization announced that it had gone international, although more recently attendance at its events in this country has declined. Still, it is worth asking what it was that drew all of these men to the huge stadium settings. Certainly, the tempo of the times—in which a men's movement is an identifiable feature of the New Age and new spirituality movement—has had something to do with movement success. But at the heart of Promise Keepers is a distinctive set of seven promises that are clearly evangelical and that as clearly separate them from others. Promise Keepers solemnly affirm that they are committed to honoring Jesus Christ, cultivating a small community of other like-minded men to support one another spiritually, and practicing sexual purity. They affirm their intention to build strong marriages and families (commonly interpreted as meaning that men should be family leaders), support the mission of their local church, and move beyond racism and denominational bias. In their seventh commitment, Promise Keepers state their goal to influence the world, obeying both the "Great Commandment" of biblical love and the "Great Commission" to evangelize. Meanwhile, the organization's public face has been strongly expansionist, and so—even with their sense of difference—the men find themselves squarely in the midst of the world.

Promise Keepers, like other Protestant conservatives, reflect concerns about the amount and quality of separateness and accommodation to the world that Christian commitment demands. Creed, code, and cultus suggest that ambivalence about these matters is written into the conservative constitution, part of the religious structure of their world. At the same time, creed, code, cultus, and, finally, community tell us that the religious world of fundamentalists and evangelicals is a contractive and consolidating one. Marking and maintaining boundaries are exercises in clear definition. Separating extraordinary from ordinary, even if—from the side of the extraordinary—they are joined again, ensures purity. Teachings like premillennial dispensationalism and social forms like the electronic church, the Christian Right, and Promise Keepers erect walls to consolidate a community. That the contraction is strong, sometimes strident, and other times also irritating to outsiders suggests the strength of conservatives in the nation today.

Expansion and Contraction, Pluralism and Postpluralism

Religious expansion, whatever form it takes, will be with us for any predictable future. So will religious contraction and consolidation. Meanwhile, liberals and conservatives seem to be very different from each other, and many have talked about their "culture wars." This idea suggests that conflict multiplies as **pluralism** increases, and it would be hard to look at present-day religious America and not agree. But is there something else going on? Thinking in terms of **postpluralism** suggests that there is. Expansion and contraction need and require each other, and together they create a system that provides some cultural balance.

Openly hostile to each other, religious liberals and conservatives are also, in important ways, strikingly alike. First, for both, the presence of millennial themes and commitments is immediately noticeable—a "new age" dawning or to come; an imminent final age to unfold. Clearly, in both movements believers are drawn by the power of the future either beginning to unfold or about to do so. For both, too, direct experience and personal transformation are at the center of religion, and for both ongoing revelation is primary. God is with us, both groups seem to say; and, whether as the felt presence of Jesus, the words of a channeler, or the authoritative claims of a shamanic journey, the extraordinary world guides—and transfigures—everyday life for believers. Again, both new spirituality people and conservative Protestants find in the language of healing powerful metaphors to express their unease in contemporary society. Efforts toward holistic health, faith healing, and prayer for emotional recovery are ongoing concerns in a society that, for many, seems out of joint.

Ideas about language also join both camps, and both use special speech forms to distinguish their community. Moreover, New Age people are as likely as many conservative Protestants to insist on the literalism of their beliefs—Atlantis and Lemuria are places as real as the conservatives' Garden of Eden. Fundamentalists and evangelicals are as ready as New Agers to embrace a religious materialism in which miracles are evidence of the presence of the extraordinary. Finally, in both movements, spiritual democracy is key. In both groups, each believer is invited to create and authenticate religion on his or her own. Similarly, both have constructed religions of the nonelite, and both favor do-it-yourself thought and action. At the same time, both manage to create new kinds of network communities, fluid but also fixed in their ability to translate values into ever-new organizations; intimate in the bonding they produce but also distancing in the transient nature, many times, of the bonds themselves.

All of this suggests deeper connections between liberals and conservatives than many would acknowledge. It points to a **combinativeness** in which, in subtle ways, religious people copy one another and hold similar patterns of thought and value underneath apparent differences. Culture-systems theory argues that greater contraction is needed to balance greater expansiveness. More of one requires more of the other, and conflict is unlikely to disappear. Thus, pluralism itself helps religious people to define themselves. At the same time, the postplural situation invites scrutiny of the combinative ways in which religious Americans are alike. Ignoring the lines of connection means seeing only part of the picture.

In Overview

As religious **manyness** has intensified in the recent United States, religious cultures of expansion and contraction have also flourished. Leading examples of the contemporary religious culture of expansion are the **New Age movement** and **new spirituality**. With roots in mesmerism, Swedenborgianism, and spiritualism as well as Transcendentalism, New Thought, Christian Science, and Theosophy, the New Age has also drawn on quantum physics, psychology and parapsychology, and the environmental movement. The New Age reflects, too, forms of Asian and Native American religion, and it turns to alternative forms of healing even as it takes its name, in part, from its astrological beliefs. The early New Age movement focused on contact with **ascended masters** and **space commanders** related to them, and enjoined practices of contact with nonmaterial beings in the practice of **channeling**. The later movement turned more to therapy and healing. New spirituality shares some of these beliefs and practices of the later New Age in a looser way, but it involves people in many religious groups and outside of them, none particularly connected to the New Age.

Religious beliefs for New Agers center on the connection claimed by believers between the **universe** and themselves. Related ideas include the power of **mind**, the reality of an interchange between matter and **energy**, and the need for **healing**.

New Agers see right action for the individual as action conforming to the laws of nature and promoting healing. Similarly, right action for society becomes action according to principles of cooperation instead of competition. It also means what New Age people call "healing the planet," in causes ranging from environmentalism to antinuclearism and feminism. Meanwhile, New Age cultus has developed in a seeming kaleidoscope of ritual practices, all of them related to creed and code. Together creed, code, and cultus have helped to define a New Age community bound both by a common language and by the action that New Agers believe will empower individuals and transform society. With their many sources, diverse membership, and abundance of practices, New Agers are a prime example of a religious culture of **expansion**. A clear sign of the expansionism is that, even as the movement is growing weaker, its beliefs and practices have spread to many other Americans in the new spirituality movement.

By contrast, the **fundamentalist-evangelical movement** has, despite its numbers, expressed the religious culture of **contraction** and consolidation in contemporary American society. With the separation between strict and moderate fundamentalists, the stage was set for the present situation. Here strict **fundamentalists** retain the name, and moderates are known as **evangelical**. Others from the **holiness-pentecostal tradition** are also now considered evangelical. Together these groups, plural as they are, have found common ground.

Theologically, strict fundamentalists hold to **premillennial dispensationalism** with a sequence of endtime events that includes rapture for the saints, tribulation for the world, a final battle at Armageddon, and the victorious rule of Christ and the saints. More liberal evangelicals accept higher critical study of the Bible, modify beliefs in biblical literalness and inerrancy, and accommodate themselves to social-scientific approaches to religion and the like. In matters of social style, most visible has been the exuberance of the **electronic church**, with televangelists who have succeeded in building huge national followings. But there has been a quieter, more contemplative social style within the fundamentalist-evangelical movement, and its trail can be followed in the sale of millions of Bibles, the multiplication of biblical study groups, and other indicators of personal devotion. Meanwhile, fundamentalists and evangelicals have organized politically in the **Christian Right** in support of conservative causes. They have worked for a strong national defense and have paid attention to matters that touch domestic life, traditional sexual roles and morality, and the character of public education. Conversely, a small number have understood themselves as radical evangelicals and have worked for a view of the Bible that often translates for them into support for a politics of the left.

What unifies fundamentalists and evangelicals in the midst of these differences is their language of religious devotion to Jesus and a strong affirmation of the authority of the **Bible**. Conservatives take from it a traditional message regarding sin and grace, salvation and divine purpose in human history. They stress personal holiness for individuals and, in society, a quest for good order as well as missionary action. Related to creed and code, their cultus has emphasized preaching and prayer in community worship and has fostered, too, a concern for more intimate experiences understood as conversion and Spirit blessing. Biblical devotionalism is always central, and conservatives move between a sense of separation from the world and an impulse toward joining it.

Liberals and conservatives in America today show surprising points of **similarity**. Emphases on millennial themes, direct experience and personal transformation, ongoing revelation, the need for healing, common language, literalness in belief and expectation, and a democracy of believers and new forms of community characterize both groups. Thus, despite the intensity of present-day **pluralism**—which is reflected in the "culture wars"—an underlying connection exists. **Postplural** ways of combining and copying unconsciously from one another are evident, and they point toward a nation that is not only many but also, in some ways, one. In other words, for all the manyness within American religious history, there is a religious common ground, a **one religion**, if you will.

Washington Giving the Laws to America. In this anonymous engraving, George Washington's Caesar-like appearance, his seated posture giving commandments, and the presence of an angelic messenger combine to suggest the religious character of American law and society.

Part Four

ONENESS: AMERICAN RELIGION, AMERICAN IDENTITY

If Americans have been so many religiously, how—in any meaningful sense—can they be one? And did they not have to be one religiously to create a viable culture and nation-state? History demonstrates that some form of religion provides the most powerful source of unity for a nation, giving it the cultural cement or glue that it needs to survive and prosper. So were Americans, with their ideas of religious freedom and government neutrality about religion, risking their political experiment almost before it got off the ground? Were they gambling with the well-being of the people and the social peace of the country? The answer comes again from history. The nation did continue and did well. So the new question becomes why.

One answer is the presence of a **public Protestantism** that subtly transforms even non-Protestants in America. Another can be found in a religious nationalism that has been called **civil religion**. A third is a broad **cultural religion** that runs through much of public and private life in American society. Yet even with these sources of unity, religious conflict has thrived throughout American history and still does. If the one religious story of America can be discovered in these partial answers, Americans have still remained a contentious people on questions of religion. This is some of what **pluralism** is about. Moreover, Americans have also often borrowed and stolen religiously from one another and so have looked more like one another as time has passed. This is some of what **postpluralism** is about. Through all of these sources of common life, though challenged, a national culture succeeds in bringing together many Americans, some of the time.

Chapter 11

The Public, the Civil, and the Culture of the Center

In 1739 Benjamin Franklin stood in a crowd of Philadelphians listening to George Whitefield, the famous Methodist revival preacher. Whitefield was also raising money for an orphanage in Georgia, and Franklin, who had previously disapproved of parts of the plan, had refused to contribute. Now, though, he was so moved by the speaking gifts of Whitefield that, despite his best efforts to stop himself, he emptied his pocket—copper, silver, and gold—into the collector's plate. Franklin was a deist and rationalist—far different from the pious Whitefield. Yet, melted by the oratory, Franklin contributed. The golden-tongued Whitefield had persuaded him to join in a mass religious episode. In Franklin's case, the persuasion was temporary and minimal. Whitefield got Franklin's money but not his mind and heart. Yet thousands of others found the persuasion more lasting. These Americans were responding to a ritual that would continue until today as a feature of religion in the United States. Revivalism became a major element in the "**one religion**" of the nation.

In the midst of the religious manyness of America, different groups took on some of the characteristics of the Protestant mainstream. Reform Jews of the late nineteenth century moved their Sabbath services to Sunday morning and imitated the style of Protestant worship. Catholics after Vatican II adopted a leaner and simpler version of the Mass, closer to the worship style of the Protestant Reformers. Mormons and Adventists, who affirmed the good life in this world, resembled liberal Protestants in their optimism, while Japanese Buddhists in this country spoke of churches, acknowledged bishops, and initiated Sunday services. Meanwhile, middle-class African Americans often gravitated toward congregations that resembled the churches of white mainline Protestants. Pluralism was still thriving, but the boundaries of separate traditions were also overlapping the boundaries of Protestantism.

Protestants themselves, despite their liberal and conservative differences, often looked a lot alike. And the similarity *among* Protestants also became a similarity *with* other Americans. The majority tradition acted in subtle and not-so-subtle ways to wear away the sharp edges of separateness and to bring people toward itself. In some ways, then, Protestantism became the one religion of the country. **Public Protestantism** has meant acknowledged ways of thinking and acting supported by most institutions in society—by the government (though unofficially), the schools, the media, and countless churches and families. The chief extraordinary religion in the land was and is Protestantism, and similarly, the ordinary religion of mainstream American culture possesses characteristics that derive historically from the Protestant experience in the country. Although many times unaware, Catholics and Jews, Buddhists and Eastern Orthodox Christians could and did share in public Protestantism. So did countless others not formally Protestant.

Public Protestantism

Public Protestantism originated in the Calvinist Christianity of the early Puritan settlers. Their substantial numbers helped to shape public Protestantism, and so did their educational earnestness. With its opening lines, "In Adam's Fall/We sinned all," *The New England Primer* (1683?) was published in an estimated 7 million copies by 1840. The first printing press in the colonies operated in the Harvard College Yard from 1639, and the *Primer* as well as the famous *Bay Psalm Book* was printed there. Textbooks written for the schools, like the *Primer*, spread the message of Calvinist Christianity. As education became more common, it was no surprise that early New England textbooks provided models for the teaching material that came into use throughout the country. Clearly, New England had established a corner on the material that appeared in educational texts, and the effects can still be felt.

Similarly, the leadership class in the colonies helped to create public Protestantism. From the first, many of the people who governed were representatives of a committed elite of Calvinist Christians. Especially in New England and in Pennsylvania, a self-conscious moral and religious intent pervaded government. Political leaders shaped the civil life of their colonies to reflect their religion. The prestige of their positions lent added public importance to Protestantism. Moreover, Protestantism enjoyed legal privilege through an official and established Anglicanism in the southern colonies and through a Puritan establishment in New England. Such establishments fell away in the late eighteenth and early nineteenth centuries, but the religious imprint left by early colonial history was not easily erased. Finally, the usefulness of Calvinist Christianity in helping newcomers to meet the demands of their situation also enhanced its stature. Protestantism became dominant, in part, because there was a fit between its thisworldly ethic and the essentials of creating settlements. Protestantism seemed an ideal religion for those who wanted to "tame" a landscape and lead it out of its "wilderness" condition. Later, as the United States grew and prospered, Calvinist Christianity fitted a culture bent on material progress

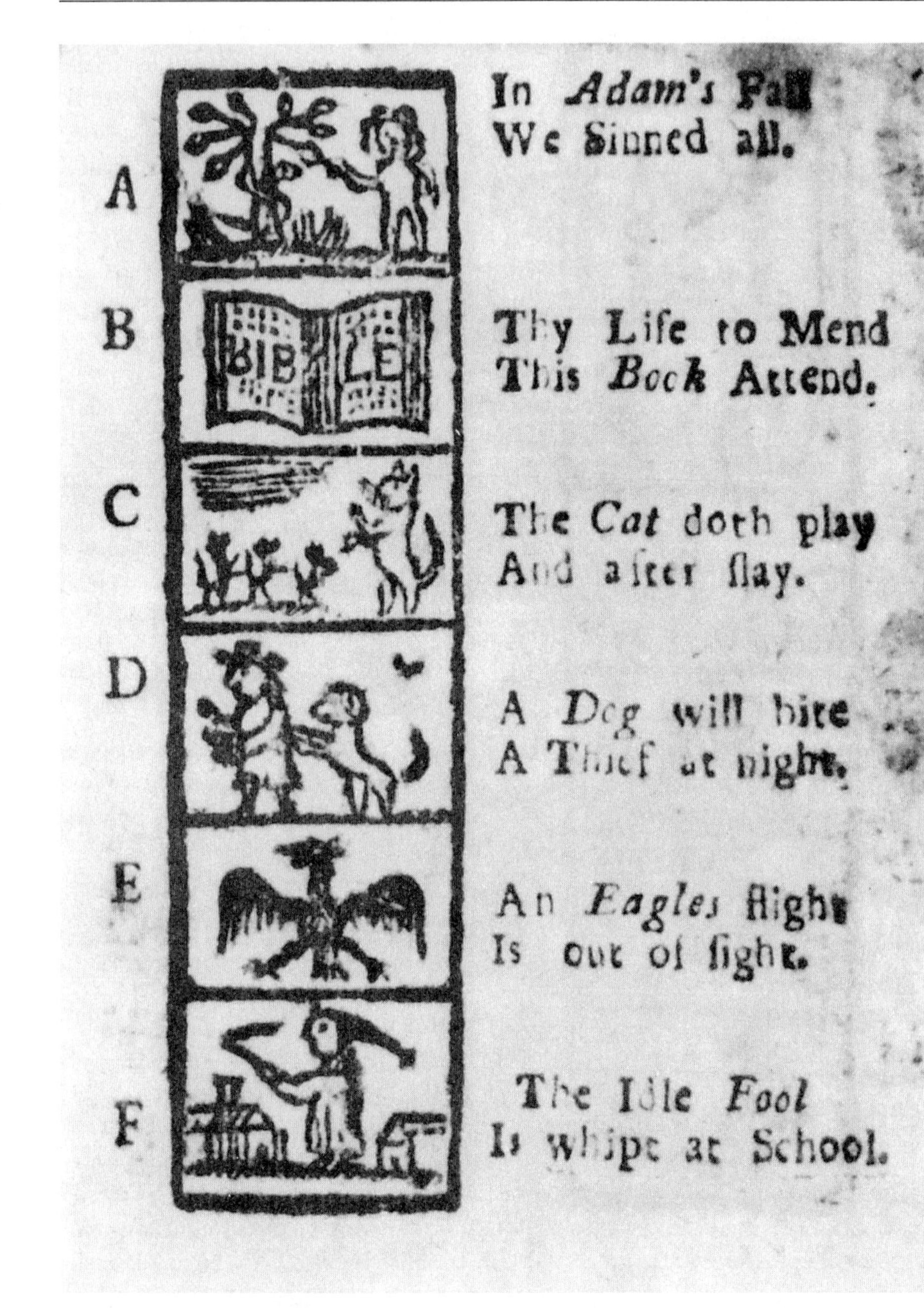

A In *Adam's* Fall
We Sinned all.

B Thy Life to Mend
This *Book* Attend.

C The *Cat* doth play
And after ſlay.

D A *Dog* will bite
A Thief at night.

E An *Eagles* flight
Is out of ſight.

F The Idle *Fool*
Is whipt at School.

The New England Primer. By the late seventeenth century, Massachusetts Bay was printing this text for young students, who would learn the alphabet and the Puritan vision of life at the same time. The primer became an influential model for later American textbooks.

and industrial efficiency. With its belief in a Word that led into the world and in the religious significance of success, it supported a developing nation.

The Protestant Code

Public Protestantism is marked by a group of related characteristics. Some are elements of a code of everyday behavior; some are aspects of its cultus; and some are parts of its belief system. Together these characteristics form a coherent whole. One characteristic leads logically and psychologically to the next, and the last characteristic leads back to the first. The **code** is perhaps easiest to see first—expressed as clear conditions, institutions, and underlying patterns for behavior within the mainstream. It begins with **religious liberty** and **democratic equality**, the social conditions that became a pattern of life, at first unevenly in the colonies and later with more consistency in the young republic. Religious liberty and democratic equality were important ideals for social life even in many colonies with religious establishments. When Americans adopted the Constitution in 1789, they legally specified religious liberty in **religious disestablishment**, or, as it came to be called, the **separation of church and state**. Congress could make no law either establishing a religion or prohibiting its "free exercise." Nor could the government require any religious affiliation for officeholding. Even though Americans understood themselves still as Christian and predominantly Protestant, separation of church and state created a radically new condition for religion.

This new condition led to the institutions of **denominationalism** and **voluntaryism**. Religious liberty, democratic equality, and church–state separation determined the ways in which religious communities could organize most effectively. Since religious associations could not count on state support, they could not hope to include all inhabitants. By the same token, because religious associations did not need to worry about state interference, they could loosen their boundaries. The preferred religious group became the denomination. Denominations thought their specific teachings important, and historically they many times denounced each other's teachings. Still, they came to see themselves as part of the larger spiritual organization of the Christian church, even as they embraced their separate ways. From the beginning, too, they existed as *voluntary* societies. In the new United States, however, they depended on voluntary support by their members instead of a public tax, and they fostered lay control. By the nineteenth century, they looked outward in their voluntaryism, cooperating in the formation of voluntary societies to spread the Christian message in the nation and the world. Despite their doctrinal differences, there were many points on which most of them agreed: the basic importance of the Bible, the use of Sunday schools to spread Christian teaching, the advantages of pamphlet literature about shared Christian ideas, plans for missionary efforts.

Members of voluntary societies had to be activists to accomplish anything, so **activism** became a noticeable pattern in public Protestant behavior. In a young nation that had to build and to plant to ensure the future, religious organizations had to do the same. Missionary work as well as the construction of churches, seminaries, and colleges expressed the public Protestant mood. Especially on the Anglo-American frontier, where institutions came after the first arrivals, Protestants saw their task as the advancement of Christian civilization. They thought that unless they provided the necessary structures to generate Christian influence, chaos and barbarism would thrive. Meanwhile, people who preferred to be religiously busy and active needed to keep things simple. So often they tended toward a pattern of **reductionism**—reducing matters to their simplest terms. In North America, it seemed, there was limitless space but limited time. So a "bare-bones" approach characterized the spread of Protestantism. People were uncomfortable with ambiguities, and they wanted precise rules for their deeds. They could live with "yes" or "no," but they were far less comfortable with "it depends."

In the area of ideas, reductionism became a more specific **nonintellectualism**. Active Americans tended to have limited intellectual opportunities and time for thought. Moreover, they were impatient with purely theoretical distinctions that could not be put to practical use. In a widely read nineteenth-century biography, George Washington was praised because he had not studied the impractical "dead" ancient languages of Latin and Greek. Later Americans followed in the path. In matters specifically religious, although European Protestantism had a strong theological tradition and New England Puritanism had encouraged the development of religious thought, nineteenth-century American Protestants seemed increasingly unwilling to encourage elites to engage in hard theological thinking. With democratic equality and voluntaryism as part of the atmosphere, many lay Protestants felt that theological thinking, as much of it as was necessary, was something they could do for themselves.

What nonintellectualism did for the mental "space" of ideas, **ahistoricism** did for time. Refusing to dwell on the past or to feel bound by the events of European history, Americans simplified history and tried to get outside it, especially in their love for returning to founding moments in their religions. Seventh-day Adventism claimed origins during the time of Enoch before the coming of Jesus. The Churches of Christ said they dated back to the time of Jesus. Christian Science announced it was restoring the healing practices of the early church. Fundamentalist churches zoomed ahead to the second coming of Jesus, turning the restoration into a millennium. All appealed to an era that skipped over the centuries of ordinary time. General American culture repeated the story. The original Henry Ford was reputed to have said that history was bunk, and today many Americans would agree.

If any one characteristic gave its overall shape to the Protestant code, however, that characteristic was **moralism**. The activism of Protestant Americans and their wish to simplify life led to a concern for the rules of action. Morality became the clearest test of Christian commitment and the key element in Christian life. Concern for morality combined with Puritan and Enlightenment influences as well as other cultural currents to produce an ordinary and extraordinary religion of moralism and reform. New England Puritans fostered pietism in their demand for an experience of conversion and continuing moral rectitude. Their sermons—called **jeremiads** by scholars—bewailed the sins of individuals and the community and predicted that these sins would force the divine hand in punishment. Later, Arminians encouraged

Family Temperance Pledge. American women organized together and actively promoted the temperance cause after the Civil War as well as before it, using domestically oriented aids like this one to exert moral pressure. The first reason given for signing the pledge is that "moderate drinking tends to drunkenness, while total abstinence directly from it."

moralism by stressing human freedom. Now no one's salvation was assured, and each person must strive earnestly to persevere in the Christian life. Enlightenment deists, too, taught an afterlife of future reward or punishment and so encouraged concern for upright behavior. The real test of religion for them was moral effort. Similarly, evangelical Protestants, stirred by the revivals, trod their own moral ground. Alcohol, gambling, sexual promiscuity, and even dancing, they thought, could corrupt people and separate them from Jesus. Besides, zeal for the gospel meant for evangelicals a need to labor for moral reform in society.

By the nineteenth century, all of these strands joined in general American culture in work for antislavery, for women's rights, for peace, or for other reform causes. One noticeable example, which stressed individual reform, was the pre–Civil War temperance crusade. The spread of the right to vote to men without property encouraged social leaders to push for a sober electorate. The existence of social problems such as poverty and crime also caught the attention of social leaders, who associated these evils with drunkenness. In this atmosphere, the clergy launched a vigorous campaign for moderation. Then after 1825 the focus of the movement shifted, and total abstinence from alcohol became the cry. The message was that drinking must end *now* as the code of moral purity required. Organizations sprang up to reform drunkards, and novelists did their share—like Timothy Shay Arthur, whose *Ten Nights in a Bar Room* became a best seller. Meanwhile, women staunchly supported the clergy, and prohibition legislation spread until a total of fourteen states and one territory had laws on their books. Only the tensions over slavery and the shadow of the coming Civil War distracted reformers and scattered the energies of temperance workers. By banishing drinking the body of society would also purge itself of crime, poverty, and an irresponsible citizenry. Women would be safe, and homes would be protected. So people rallied to the cause, moralism triumphed, and so did public Protestantism.

The Protestant Cultus

If moralism has been key to the public Protestant code, **revivalism** has been its cultus. As a ritual, it has offered a formal and repeated set of practices to bring conversion or encourage devotion. The revivals have marked off sacred space, either in a church, a public building, an open field, or a tent. Then during a sacred time created by the service, hymns, prayers, testimonies, and especially revival sermons would work to give to an individual a conviction of the burden of sin and, in earlier forms, of the torments of hell that would result. Alternately, hymns and testimonies evoked feelings of present joy in conversion and future bliss in heaven. Salvation hung on the sense of emotional liberation and peace that believers attributed to the grace of God. Therefore, older revival practices strived to produce for believers an unbearable tension between sin and possible grace, between the terrors of hell and the anticipated joys of heaven. When the tension became great enough, the conviction of sin sufficiently painful, in accord with revival theory the believing sinner might be jolted into an experience of conversion.

The connections between both the earlier and later, non-Calvinist ritual of the revival and the behavioral patterns of the Protestant code are not hard to find.

The activism of the Protestant style was satisfied in active congregations who sang, prayed, gave testimonies, and, more importantly, developed feelings of the burden of sin and the compassion of the Christian God. Individuals *worked through* or prayed through to conversion. Especially after the beginning of the nineteenth century, when Calvinism fell away, the active role of the seeker played an increasing part in the process. The revivals also supported the Protestant desire for simplification. Here preachers distilled religion to sin and grace, or hell and heaven. No need for an elaborate theology arose in this way of doing things.

Similarly, the practice of the revivals led away from concern for tradition and into a vivid concentration on the present—or on a future outside the time of history. Finally, the revivals served Protestant moralism. Authentic conversion and devotion, believers said, would be expressed in the reformed character of Christian lives. The private vices that moralism sought to cleanse—radically, instantly, and all at once—were the signs for believers of the need for revival, while their eradication demonstrated revival success. Meanwhile, the zeal of converts and devoted Christians often led to their involvement in reform work. In a situation of religious liberty, the revivals gave people a democratic God who might come to rich or poor, model citizen or town derelict. In the legal setting of separation of church and state, the revivals provided mission fields to be mined by denominations in search of new church members. The voluntaryism of the revival experience helped to fill congregations with volunteers who would work, in and out of official organizations, for the Christianization of the land.

The Protestant Creed

The ritual of the revival was connected to a religious conception of life. Here public Protestantism voiced a series of major belief commitments, among them ideas about the **importance of the individual**, the existence of a **higher law** that trumped human law, and **millennialism** and a related **perfectionism**. As religious experience, revivalism focused on individuals. In fact, American Protestant revivalism lived with a tension in which it at once *believed* in individualism and then immediately sought to change it. Revivalism tried to make community out of the material of many private experiences by establishing a common place and language in which these experiences could become public. Yet through it all, revival preachers were speaking out of the creed of individualism.

Circumstances in North America encouraged the growth of individualism, too. The presence of vast stretches of land, the clear business opportunities created by the absence of an economic establishment, and the necessity of self-reliance for people uprooted from traditional community ties combined to emphasize individual worth. Patterns of ever-greater mobility developed to increase the trend. Politics and government also promoted and expressed individualism. Under the loose Articles of Confederation and later the Constitution, the states functioned like so many separate and individual planets revolving around a federal "sun." In fact, the Civil War spoke not only to the issue of slavery but also to the other issue of how far the rights of individual states could extend. Meanwhile, the glorification of the "common man" and what that individual could do became part of the culture. Schoolbook texts like the McGuffey *Eclectic Readers* of the nineteenth century stressed individualistic virtues—like independence, thrift, industry, and perseverance—that would help a person succeed. By the late nineteenth century Horatio Alger's many novels became famous for their orphaned or fatherless boy heroes who, with luck and pluck, won out over obstacles.

Organized Protestantism provided a theological home for individualism. Denominationalism and voluntaryism supplied an institutional framework in which individual efforts were the bulwark of church organizations. The activist style relied for its success on the individual involvement of numbers of responsible church members, while the simplifications that Protestantism fostered arose precisely because, in a world in which every individual, however poor or uneducated, counted equally, material and intellectual subtleties had to be reduced to a minimum. Through the various programs for moral reform—many of them directed toward private behavior—individuals made their mark as individuals.

Self-reliant individuals also asked questions about the authority of others. In a nation of self-directed individuals, what law or authority could be the final court of appeal? Could equal individuals be submissive to a king, a president, or a written law? Could they be forced to obey the dictates of a pope, a bishop, a synod, or other religious leaders? Answers came through a public Protestant consensus that the authority of any written law rested on its agreement with a higher, unwritten one. If written and unwritten law were in conformity, then the written law should be respected and obeyed. But if there was a discrepancy, if the written law violated **higher law**, then free individuals owed allegiance to the higher order.

Sources for this belief include the heritage of the Reformation as well as Puritanism. Quakers especially—as radical Puritans—used their teaching of the Inner Light to urge believers to hear the voice of God in the voice of conscience. Baptists, too, felt compelled by conscience when they protested the Congregational church establishment. These sectarian believers found their message joined to the heritage of the Enlightenment with its glorification of reason and nature. Framed in the political rhetoric of the nation's foundation, higher law became the law under which a God of nature gave unalienable rights to individuals. But Americans could also put such beliefs to self-serving uses. Sometimes, for example, they justified taking land from Indians by calling on higher law. By the middle of the nineteenth century they talked about **manifest destiny** to spread their government and way of life across the continent. In all of this, it is difficult to say where the Protestant heritage ended and ordinary American culture began. Because belief in a higher law is so clearly tied to ideas about God or higher forces such as nature, it possesses an extraordinary quality. This is why the justification of Indian removal by appealing to higher law is especially repugnant.

Significantly, for many Americans, the higher law meant an unfailing law of progress—a clue to the millennialism that became a third belief in the American creed. **Millennialism** refers strictly to beliefs about the end of time generated by reading the Bible. American Bible believers have often been **premillennial**—expecting the return of Jesus *before* the millennium. Their belief has prompted pessimism about the world and urged them to rescue as many individuals as they can for Jesus. Often, too, they have been **postmillennial**—placing the return of Jesus at the end of the millennium. Here millennialism has led to optimism about human beings and society, inspiring a host of reform efforts to hasten the second coming.

In both cases, millennialism began in Protestantism, but non-Protestant religious movements came to share the millennial fervor. So, in a second and looser sense, the term means extraordinary religious beliefs in any tradition about the end of the present world being near. Common to these millennial beliefs is the faith that, whatever the suffering involved in getting there, an age of peace, prosperity, and the fulfillment of all hopes will come soon. For example, American Indian Ghost Dance religion expresses just such ideas. Millennialism, in still a third sense, can refer to beliefs outside of any extraordinary religion. Expectation of a new era of peace and plenty can take place in terms of ordinary culture. Optimism about an age of progress and amazement at cultural changes can give rise to popular beliefs that a new period in world history is dawning. Mainstream American culture, from the late eighteenth on, has reflected this kind of millennialism. Here, once again, public Protestantism and general American culture became intertwined.

In all of these forms, millennialism has fit seamlessly with the behavioral code, the cultus, and the remaining elements of the creed of public Protestantism. In both premillennial and postmillennial forms, it has been activist—either attempting to save and rescue souls or to bring about social reform. In both its forms, also, it has expressed the American Protestant search for simplicity. Millennial themes are cast in terms of clear alternatives of good and evil, of war between opposite factions, and of final triumph for good without the intrusion of any evil. Similarly, both forms of millennialism are moralistic. Premillennialists have sought to lead lives of private virtue in light of the approaching end. Postmillennialists have sought the radical reconstruction of society for the same reason. For both, the evangelical model of the relationship between God and the individual presented by revivalism has provided a ritual foundation. For premillennialists, a radical turn from evil is necessary for rescue before the tribulation of the endtime. For postmillennialists, the fervor of religious awakening is a sign of the nearness of the millennial kingdom. For both, with its pull toward the future, millennialism has echoed the message of the revival—that humans are estranged from God and from one another. For all of American millennialism, finally, religious liberty and democratic equality, guaranteed by separation of church and state and institutionalized in denominationalism and voluntaryism, have functioned as necessary background.

Civil Religion

Public Protestantism blended and overlapped easily with American patriotism to produce American civil religion. While various definitions exist, **civil religion** generally refers to a religious system that has existed alongside the churches, with a theology (creed), an ethic (code), and a set of rituals and other identifiable symbols (cultus) related to the state. Jean-Jacques Rousseau first used the term in eighteenth-century France, but the religious nationalism to which it refers is as old as Western culture, and two major models can be identified.

In the Hebrew model, ancient Israel understood its government as a **theocracy**, with God as its true king, ruling by law and under a covenant with his one people. In the later Roman imperial model, Romans believed that their emperor possessed a spiritual double called his **genius**. They considered the emperor's genius divine, and people were required to take part in an annual ceremony paying homage to the genius. In this way, the vast state composed of many ethnic and religious groups expressed a degree of unity. In the Hebrew model, one nation, bound by ties of blood, history, and language, expressed these bonds in combined religious and political language and actions. In the Roman, different peoples, with different ethnic heritages, came together from the top down through formal ceremonies and ideals. In the United States, civil religion took something from each of these models. Some of the major symbols of American civil religion rose out of Puritan experience, the expression of a people united by ethnic ties and traditions. But the history of civil religion made it increasingly a bond designed to unite *many* peoples from *many* different nations into one state.

The distinction is important. A political state such as the United States means a civil government that contains within its jurisdiction distinct ethnic and religious groups. A nation, in the strict sense, means a group of people bound by language, past history, and real or alleged kinship, like each American Indian culture. A nation-state means a nation that has taken on a formal and political expression so that government is identified with one nation. Modern Japan is a nation-state. Previous chapters have followed common usage in speaking loosely of the United States as a "nation." But here it is necessary to be careful in the choice of words. Civil religion in this country has been an attempt to create a nation and a nation-state, partially on the basis of the English Puritan national heritage, partially on the basis of more universal symbols derived from the Enlightenment, and partially through symbols that grew out of American political history. Yet as the years passed, more and more Americans did not share either the English Puritan national tradition or an American ancestry of any sort. At the same time, the Enlightenment, as a cultural event, receded into the past. Thus, civil religion grew less meaningful. At best, civil religion was never more than the expression of many American people some of the time. Still, with its overtones of extraordinary religion, it is an important example of the **religion of oneness** in this country, and it can surge up strongly during times of war, crisis, or confrontation, as the events of September 11 demonstrate.

Civil Religion in Historical Perspective

Civil religion grew and changed throughout American history, but its essentials came from the seventeenth and the eighteenth centuries. By the time George Washington took his oath of office as first president of the United States, its fundamentals were in place. They had arisen out of New England Puritanism, but especially out of the fusion of Puritanism with the actions of American patriots in the Revolutionary War. In this setting, Americans reinterpreted the Puritan past, linked it more strongly to the Enlightenment (it had already been so linked), and joined it to the tradition that Americans were creating by their own deeds in the war—deeds widely understood as the beginning of the millennium.

After Congress proclaimed independence from Great Britain, officials throughout the colonies solemnly read the Declaration of Independence. People fired cannons, raised cheers, made toasts, and consumed liquor. A year later came unofficial celebrations with bells and fireworks along with cannons, cheers, and toasts. In 1778 Congress gave official orders to honor the Fourth of July, and a year afterward it told its chaplains to prepare sermons suitable for the event. By the following decade, Americans were giving similar praise to the Constitution. Huge constitutional parades were staged in most of the new state capitals to pay tribute.

In Philadelphia, on the Fourth of July, 1788, after enough states had ratified the Constitution to make it the law of the land, it seemed as if the entire city was either participating in the parade or watching the eighty-eight divisions that extended for a mile and a half. Exhibits included the "new roof" of the Constitution, erected in a carriage pulled by ten white horses, and the federal ship of state on another float. Meanwhile, tradespeople walked to express their enthusiasm as workers in the new union. There were sacks of federal flour and signs for a federal cabinet shop and a federal printing press. Tellingly, in the clergy's division, members of different Christian denominations and the Jewish rabbi walked linking arms—eloquent testimony to the sermon that the parade was preaching. The real ground of unity in the United States was not any of the sects or denominations, said the parade, but the civil religion of the American Revolution that the Constitution summed up.

This attempt to make a new religious statement through the Revolution and to create a religion around it is strikingly expressed in the Great Seal of the United States. An eagle with an olive branch and thirteen arrows to represent the states announces, in Latin, *e pluribus unum;* that is, "one from many." On the back of the seal, a symbolic eye caps an uncompleted pyramid. Beneath the pyramid the message reads *novus ordo seclorum*, "the new order of the ages." The Americans who first approved the seal were saying that they had brought something new into the world and that they had inaugurated the millennium for which history waited.

By the time of the Civil War, millennial dating convinced Americans that the new order was about to dawn in earnest. Many thought that the Antichrist must fall in the year 1866, bringing on end-of-time events. In the North, even in religiously liberal Boston and far from literal millennial belief, Julia Ward Howe—who did not acknowledge miracles or a special revelation in the Bible—wrote "The Battle Hymn of the Republic." She had visited an army camp, and after the experience the words came to her, describing the coming of Jesus for the biblical final battle and linking it to the march of the Union army. Beneath the surface of liberal culture in the United States, themes of Armageddon lived on, able to shape the interpretation of events and to give them powerful meaning. Then, five days after the war ended, Abraham Lincoln was assassinated. He had just begun his second term in office, telling Americans that they should bear malice toward no one and have charity for all. As it happened, the president was shot on Good Friday, and that fact was not lost on others. He had been sacrificed, they said, as Jesus had been on the cross—one victim to redeem all the people. His blood had paid the price of liberty, mingling with the blood of the nameless soldiers who had given their lives for their country.

At other moments in American history, millennial chosenness became ordinary religion. For example, during the era of "**manifest destiny**," as we noticed earlier, expansionist ventures were justified as part of the country's divine destiny. The journalist John L. O'Sullivan used the term in 1845 to argue, regarding Texas, that it was America's manifest destiny to expand across the continent. After that, the phrase became a catchword to sum up a spirit and a time, but the ideas it expressed had been present in outline much earlier. Mainstream Americans still believed that they were a chosen people, whether they expressed that idea in the language of the Bible, of the Enlightenment, or of nineteenth-century ordinary culture. Likewise, they still believed that they must be an example to the nations and, even more, that they had a mission to perform. Whether they felt Providence, destiny, or the land commanded them, Americans believed that their mission was to establish a millennial age of empire. They were convinced that the natural right and providential plan for Americans was to hold more land.

The Structure of the Civil Religion

As the loose religious system that it is, American civil religion contains elements of creed, code, and cultus. The **creed** has rested on fundamental assumptions that the United States is a chosen and millennial nation. Both qualities can be understood either in Christian or in more general terms. Chosenness might come from God, from nature, or from historical events. Millennialism could mean the coming of the kingdom of God or of a golden age of peace and prosperity that Americans have created on their own. In either case, chosenness separates Americans from members of other societies. It burdens them with the twin tasks of being an example of democratic equality and fulfilling a mission to bring that democracy to others. Millennialism has split the world into simple alternatives of good and evil and at the same time encouraged both optimism and anxiety regarding the country's future. Both chosenness and millennialism have been attempts to create a nation out of a political state.

The **code** of the civil religion is already contained in its creed. Being an example and fulfilling a mission mean that citizens in the chosen nation must engage in public activity. Loyalty and patriotism as inner qualities are not enough. Rather, as in the majority religion of Protestantism, citizens need to *work* for the collective good. Voting in elections becomes a symbolic act to sum up the duty of the citizen. If the citizen is male, the ultimate action that may be required is service in the country's armed forces and even death in its defense. Here human sacrifice for

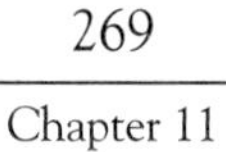

Apotheosis of George Washington, 1802. John James Barralet's stipple engraving reflects popular estimates of Washington's near-divinity in the years immediately following his death. The Washington cultus was one early republican expression of civil religion.

religious reasons is demanded in a new form. The code is also a statement about the political community and how it should behave toward the world. Being an example and having a mission are directives for foreign policy. So world leadership has been a self-fulfilling prophecy in American history. Similarly, Americans have often seen their wars as moral crusades.

Finally, a **cultus** for the civil religion grew up. Sacred space has included shrines and significant places like George Washington's home, Mount Vernon in Virginia, and Independence Hall in Philadelphia. A catalog of national "saints" has honored individuals who embody the ideals of the civil religion. George Washington is only the first among a community of founders who came to be venerated in the public life of the country—men like Thomas Jefferson, Benjamin Franklin, and John Adams. The nineteenth century brought new heroes and saints, like Andrew Jackson and Abraham Lincoln, while later history brought Franklin Delano Roosevelt, John F. Kennedy, and Martin Luther King, Jr., among others. The original copies of the Declaration of Independence and the Constitution became sacred objects to revere. Formal ritual practices commemorated the founders; Fourth of July fireworks flourished; other celebrations, like Memorial Day from after the Civil War, have expressed similar themes. Important in all of these rituals have been their attempts to unify people as a political community and a nation. Like all rituals, the rites of the civil religion are endeavors to change the many into one.

Creed, code, and cultus together form the visible structure of the civil religion. But at a deeper level, its meaning is more than the sum of its parts. Its meaning is also ambiguous, pulling in different directions at once. Rooted in the past, it urges Americans toward a millennial future. An ordinary religion linked to life within the human political community of one country, it has extraordinary aspirations and—based on Protestant Christianity and Christianity's Jewish background—contains the power of extraordinary religion. Rooted in ideas of chosenness and a special millennial destiny, it is shaped to create an exclusive community but intended to bind *all* Americans together. In other words, in a state beset with boundary questions between social groups, civil religion proposes a common inclusivity premised on a citizen-oriented natural-rights philosophy. If there is a central meaning, it lies in its millennialism. Whether looking to past or to future, under God or under the United States, deliberate or spontaneous, hypocritical or sincere, civil religion revolves around the memorable deeds that Americans have performed to begin an age unknown before in history. Here, actions have to "make history" to be meaningful. And for people who do not like to dwell in the past, Americans are exceedingly anxious to achieve a past on a grand scale.

Civil Religion into the Present

With World Wars I and II, making history preoccupied many Americans as they saw events unfold in what seemed to them millennial terms. In more peaceful times, the regular ceremonies of the Fourth of July, Memorial Day, the birthdays of Washington and Lincoln, Thanksgiving, and, later, Armistice Day recalled the national heritage. But as time passed and the events of the Revolution became mostly chapters in history books, the power of the civil religion to inspire Americans began to fail. Even more, the second half of the twentieth century brought wars in Korea and Vietnam that did not lend themselves easily to familiar millennial interpretations. Moral ambiguity clouded the domestic scene as well, so that civil religion grew to be the faith of fewer Americans, less of the time.

The slow decline did not go unheeded by thoughtful people. In fact, since at least the 1960s, a number of scholars have thought about the meaning of the United States in religious terms. One of these scholars, the sociologist **Robert N. Bellah** revived the term *civil religion* in 1967. For some sociologists, like Bellah, and for some historians, like **Sidney E. Mead,** scholarship about civil religion became an attempt to revitalize the tradition. Bellah saw the growing (at that time) conflict in Vietnam as a third time of trial for the country, a new crisis on the order of the American Revolution and the Civil War. Mead's many essays on the "**religion of the Republic**"—and later its theology—identified sectarianism as the cause of national disunity and praised the universal religion of the Enlightenment born in the Revolution. Meanwhile, another sociologist, Will Herberg, argued that Protestants, Catholics, and Jews had merged their differences in the **American Way of Life**, and he warned against its idolatry when it forsook the biblical God. So in their awareness of the lessening hold of the civil religion and their concerns for its evolving values, descriptive scholars became theologians and preachers. Their reflection and writing were in fact an attempt to boost the civil religion or warn of its dangers. Although scholars have been less interested in civil religion in recent years and the so-called civil-religion debate is largely over, there is much that can be learned from the decade and more of scholarly exchange.

As the past has become older, many Americans have trouble relating to the founders and their foundation. Still more, Americans who are people of color and immigrants who are newer and more diverse find the civil religion's ties with the past not especially meaningful. Civil religion can give Americans a creed, a code, and a cultus, but it cannot—save rarely in exceptional moments like wars and terrorist attacks—transform them into one community. Still, there is another side. From the first, civil religion has been a religious system in addition to the churches. It had brought ordinary American history into touch with extraordinary religion. Yet unlike being Methodist or Jewish or Muslim, being a believer in the national faith does not mean belonging to an organization or breaking ties with a previous one. A believer in the civil religion can even be an atheist, since a good part of the symbolism of the civil religion can be used without reference to a God. So despite its limitations, to some extent civil religion has functioned as an answer to the problem of manyness—an overarching religious system under which most denominations, sects, and other spiritual groups may find a place. Whatever its problems, civil religion is a "**one story**" created to form the many into one.

Cultural Religion

Besides civil religion, Americans have ordered their lives and searched for meaning within the everyday world using other aspects of their culture. Beyond civil religion, they have reached moments when, using ordinary culture, they have touched an "other" world. American **cultural religion**—the culture of the center seen in religious terms—began to assume the shape we know today in the late nineteenth century. In this era, the crisis of the Civil War had passed; industrialization was changing the face of the United States; cities were multiplying in number and in size; and the most massive waves of immigration to that date were flooding them. At the same time, such familiar features of American life as organized sports, expanding technologies, and, in literature, Western novels were becoming commonplace. Americans, as religious people, expressed their ideas and values in the mainstream culture that evolved. They re-internalized that culture, too, in their own lives. Meanwhile, they drew lines connecting contemporary American cultural religion to public Protestantism and civil religion. Here themes of millennialism continued to figure prominently. So did a search for authentic religious experience and a community of feeling, even as voluntaryism became the great given.

The American Ritual Calendar

Probably the most observable aspect of cultural religion is the American **ritual calendar** through which a series of holidays (holy days) bring people together. Halloween begins an early winter cycle that includes Veterans Day and Thanksgiving, and culminates in Christmas and New Year. Halloween was once All Hallows' Eve, the night before the Catholic feast of All Saints' Day, when people remembered all those considered hallowed—in other words, the saints in heaven. Veterans Day—created much later and more deliberately, acknowledges the formal public debt to veterans of America's wars. Thanksgiving, the harvest festival of the Pilgrims, originally expressed gratitude for divine blessing on the crops after a successful planting. Christmas commemorated the birth of Jesus Christ. In the twentieth century and after, though, the meanings associated with these feasts have changed. A number of Americans, like some observant Jews and Japanese American Buddhists, object to Christmas celebrations in American culture. Many other non-Christians, however, continue to observe the day and season without a Christian interpretation. Halloween has become a beggars' night for neighborhood children; Thanksgiving, a family feast of abundance centering on turkey and trimmings; and Christmas, with its Christian message muted, a winter feast of evergreens, department-store Santas, and community good feeling. New Year's Eve, in turn, resembles archetypal accounts of pagan festivals. The revelry of the night imitates ancient ways of perceiving—and coming to terms with—time's passage. With an old year running down and a new order rising, Americans break old patterns of action by their social release—and share in the creation of a new order in their New Year's resolutions.

In the first half of the new year, another series of holidays makes symbolic statements about the meaning of American life. Remembrances of the civil faith include the January commemoration of Martin Luther King, Jr., and the February commemoration of the birthdays of Washington and Lincoln, now joined as Presidents' Day. Memorial Day at the end of May and Flag Day in June provide later reminders of the message. In another set of holidays, Valentine's Day, Mother's Day, and Father's Day pay attention to the private sphere. By midsummer, Americans are ready for the Fourth of July, when picnic, fireworks, and patriotic displays bring family, friends, and community together. Then, as summer unofficially closes in time for school, Labor Day, with its September picnics, honors the role of work in the foundation and continuance of their society. Finally, as October returns, Americans commemorate the European "discovery" of the Americas in Columbus Day.

Four of the holidays—the Fourth of July, Memorial Day, Veterans Day, and Presidents' Day—are associated with millennial themes that recall catastrophic wars and sacrificial deeds on behalf of country. A fifth, dedicated to African American Martin Luther King, Jr., suggests the pluralism that American civil religion seeks to incorporate and continues the millennial theme in its acknowledgment of King's assassination and, so, his sacrifice. Also with the flavor of civil religion, Flag Day—observed legally only in Pennsylvania—honors the flag as a symbol of the nation; themes of millennialism and sacrifice are built in, since a flag is a war standard. Similarly, Columbus Day turns, like Martin Luther King Day, on millennial themes of promise and pluralistic ones of incorporating outsider groups. Still, the commemoration suggests the problems of memory in a pluralist society. Meant to appeal to Southern European ethnic groups, especially to Italian Americans, Columbus Day offends others, among them Native Americans, as a symbol of European conquest and oppression as well as of other social and environmental problems attributed to Western culture.

Different from these holidays, other occasions highlight family themes or related ones of social intimacy. Halloween and Christmas belong to children, and adults, when they participate, often use these times to renew general social ties, as at Halloween, or family ones, as at Christmas. Similarly, Valentine's Day, Mother's Day, and Father's Day show regard for one another within close relationships. What all of these occasions have in common is that they seek to honor innocence. There is the natural innocence of children on Halloween and Christmas and the more deliberate innocence of family and friends on all of the feasts. Interrupting, at least in theory, the economic cycle of the marketplace, the sanctity of their themes of intimacy is underlined—even if it is easy to see that they are heavily commercialized.

Thanksgiving strikes a middle position between public and private. The day incorporates millennial meanings, but here the millennium is one of peace and plenty rather than final battle; and here, too, the banquet theme signals the domestic setting of family and community. Labor Day echoes some of these ideas in different ways. Begun in 1882 by the Knights of Labor, this holiday with its union roots suggests a golden age of equality, when common people create a new society with their work. Like Thanksgiving, it points toward a millennium of peace and plenty and weaves domestic themes of innocence into the millennial cloth. Finally, New Year's Eve combines millennialism with innocence in its anticipation of the dawning of a new era when the mistakes and misfortunes of the past will be erased. Old

Father Time hobbles along on his cane, his white beard reaching almost to his ankles. Then, at midnight, the diapered infant of the new year appears, fresh and innocent to encounter the future.

American Sacred Stories

Traditional **sacred stories** tell people who they are, where they have come from, what their tasks ought to be, and what their world means. In other words, sacred stories are **creeds** in narrative form; they recount the basic beliefs people hold about their human condition. In the public culture of the United States, such narratives unite by providing a common fund of meaning for all to share. Television and film spread the creed, and so do popular literature and magazines as well as popular heroes and entertainment stars. More strongly than the teaching of any organized religion, which is heard perhaps once or twice in a week, the belief system embedded in American culture shapes Americans from cradle to grave.

Studies show that thousands of the plots on stage and in literature can be reduced to a very few. The names, personalities, and events change, but underlying patterns remain the same. As we follow a story, we frequently know how things will end. The good side will win; the captive will be rescued; the criminal will be caught and taken to jail. With this near certainty, the question becomes, Why bother to pay attention? Some may argue that the answer is that there are many plots providing novelty "just for entertainment," but others would say that powerful beliefs about life are being expressed and reinforced. Through the medium of the story, we are being told *what* the world means and *how* it means, and so we feel better able to go about our lives. Yet is there any "one story" that Americans learn? Again, the answer goes beyond the many plots of "just entertainment" to suggest that in television and film, one favorite plot, with variations, does dominate. This plot organizes a great many stories and underlies many of the all-time successes in the living room and at the box office. This plot echoes the millennial Puritan and revolutionary background of American culture and, in fact, is a modified version of it.

The plot might be summarized as trouble in paradise with eventual redemption for a hard-pressed community. Typically, the story turns on a wholesome and innocent society invaded from outside by overwhelming evil. Members of the society are caught off guard and unable to defend themselves. Just in the nick of time, a powerful stranger, also from outside, comes to save them. His past and background are impressive but unclear; and he seems to want nothing, not even sexual favors, from the community. Once he has conquered evil through righteous violence, he leaves members of the redeemed society to continue their lives as before. Classic characters like Superman, the Lone Ranger, and—with a change of gender—Wonder Woman, all figure in plots that conform to this basic plot. With some variations, the once-popular Rambo films fit the pattern. So, too, do science fiction films of the *Star Wars* variety, the many incarnations of *Star Trek*, *The Matrix*, and similar films.

One important reason for their appeal is that they tap mainstream Americans' fundamental understanding of themselves and their world. To the extent that people with vastly different backgrounds find themselves caught by the power of these productions, they have joined the mainstream and, in a loose way, the one religion of Americans as Americans. The plots turn on **millennial themes** of the conquest of evil and righteous innocence, as in old Puritan and revolutionary visions. The saving stranger, like Captain Kirk of *Star Trek* fame, is a transformed version of the messiah of the final battle, the Word riding forth for Armageddon. So violent destruction becomes warranted and right. As the stranger fades into the distance, a millennium of peace and justice can reign in the plot's redeemed, but notably passive, community, be it in the galaxy, in the hold of a spaceship, or on the earth.

Popular literature, especially science fiction and Western novels, repeats many of these themes. Meanwhile, tales of love and romance introduce a more intimate world, and popular magazines, written especially for men or for women, provide models for personal identity. Generally, millennial themes are far more subdued in this literature, but the **perfectionism** implicit in the millennial idea lives on as problems of sexuality and relationship are explored. It is worth noticing how much the American *ideal* of individualism provides a background for these books and magazines, even though in actual life they often foster conformity to media models of living.

If television, film, and print provide a web of fundamental beliefs for Americans, so does music, and so do popular singers who embody the themes they sing. Accounts of film idols mobbed by their admirers and spending hours to sign autographs are familiar. So, too, are fan mail and fan clubs, fan magazines and the paraphernalia that go with being a star. In fact, entertainment idols are one kind of American hero. Like political leaders, Western roughriders, and self-made men and women who rose from rags to riches, the stars of the entertainment empire demonstrate the qualities that Americans most admire. It is probably not a coincidence that they are called idols. In fact, fans revere them in ways similar to the worship offered to the avatars of India—living persons believed to be the incarnations of the Gods. Consider, for example, the career of Elvis Presley (1935–1977), the "king" of rock and roll who ruled musically for over twenty years. Even after his death, people continued to pay him homage. By the late 1980s, some had come to deny his death and believed he continued to live or, as in the gospel account of Jesus, had risen from the dead. For the millions who championed him, Presley spoke in powerful ways, assuring them that the values they cared about were real.

Presley grew out of the pentecostal evangelical tradition, and he took from his evangelical background the strong sentimentality that ran through his music and his personality. As a teenage rebel, he took the excitement of the revival into a new setting. He made of it sensual and sexual passion, giving people a "natural" freedom and the foretaste of a paradise in which liberty would be lasting. A symbolic reminder of the innocence of the 1950s, when the swivel of a singer's hips and the glance of his eye were thought risqué, Presley seemed to assure people in a later age that old truths were still true and that good and evil were clear. He stood for the golden age of the millennium that Americans recalled in the Eisenhower years, a time they identified with peace and plenty—without environmental crises, financial uncertainty, or public affairs that could not be settled by simple formulas. Yet

Presley was a victim of his own success. The symbol of spontaneity, he could not appear freely as he chose. The public for which he lived became his torture, and according to reports, he turned to drugs as stimulants and depressants. With his early death, he became for devotees a kind of martyr.

Presley is only one among the country's cultural icons, and his songs are only a small number among the ballads and tunes that tell people who they are and what their lives mean. Together, idols and songs, literature and magazines, films and television serials surround Americans with reminders to reassure and reinforce their systems of belief. Although the language is disguised and not often openly religious, the gospel that mass culture preaches through the media persuades powerfully because it builds on what people already believe. More than any organized religious denomination, it is able to capture the public eye and ear. Created by society, it also creates a society in its image.

American Codes of Living

Mainstream American culture offers the public not just a ritual calendar and sacred stories and models, but also **guidelines** for living. Sports, technology, popular psychology, and ideas about nature all provide behavioral codes for many. In the case of **sports**, historically, they originated in religious rituals. Ceremonial games functioned at the center of many Native American traditions in this country. In ancient Greece, funeral games honored slain heroes, and various Greek city-states held sacred games to offer reverence to one of the Gods. Today's Olympics descend from some of these. In an echo of these games, there are many ways in which even the sports of the contemporary United States are like (extraordinary) religious rituals. Like other deliberate religious rituals, sports events mark out a separate area for their activities—a "playground" or sacred space. Both also divide the time of their performance from the ordinary passage of minutes and hours. In both, people take on assigned roles, often wearing special symbolic clothing to distinguish them from nonparticipants. Sports and deliberate religious rituals, through their performances, create "other" worlds of meaning, complete with their own rules and boundaries, dangers and successes. Finally, in sports and deliberate religious rituals, the goal of the activity *is* the activity. Play or ritual is satisfying for its own sake.

From this perspective sports, with their ordinariness in our society, have provided a ritual-like setting for millions of Americans. By setting up boundaries and defining the space of the game, sports have helped Americans fit a grid to their own experience in order to define it and give it structure. So it is not surprising that public games have given people a code of conduct for everyday living. If the ball field is a miniature rehearsal for the game of life, the message is that life is a struggle between contesting forces in which there is a winning and a losing side. The message, too, is that success depends on teamwork in which members of the winning side conquer the opposing team by pulling together. In this contest, competition becomes a value in itself and generates a set of accompanying virtues that identify a good team player. Loyalty, fair play, and being a "good sport" in losing are all examples of these virtues. So are self-denial and hard work to achieve victory. Finally, as in the scriptural story of the final millennial battle, there is a good team (our side) and a bad one (the opposing side). Coaches urge the members of their team to pour all their efforts into winning—as if this were the last game they would play on earth.

The code that the games offer to Americans is one that subtly agrees with **millennial themes**. It is a code that promises to guarantee success in business, industry, or government, for in it individualism bows before the unity of an elect community. Corporate executives may have risen on their merits, but, according to the code, in the executive suite they must be good team players. Here life is seen as a game of winners and losers, and only those who compete are considered worthy and succeed. Rigorously prepared for the fight by their previous exercises in self-denial, those who compete to the end are expected to win the day—or, at the very least, to lose with the grace and dignity demanded by the code.

A second code for everyday living comes to Americans from **technology**. People often unconsciously adopt the machine as a model for their humanness. They see their bodies as complex machines, and in many aspects of their lives they pattern their behavior accordingly. So the technological code demands that Americans act like their machines. Corporate life is built in part on the image of the machine with well-oiled components, each properly performing its function. Bureaucracies are, implicitly, huge machines in which people are expected to do their jobs efficiently, without attracting undue attention to themselves or creating undue stress by forming time-consuming relationships with their co-workers. Meanwhile, the nuclear family—different from older-style extended families—is mobile. Like the automobile and the train, this family can move speedily, ready to pull up stakes and start again somewhere else if economic interests demand.

The technological code encourages Americans to be as cool and passionless in public as their machines. It likewise expects people to be uniform and standard. Like the interchangeable parts produced by the factories, they must be able to replace one another. Still more, the code defines no person as absolutely necessary. Because they can replace one another, people—like uniform parts in a machine—are expendable. The technological code has also altered the way in which Americans think of time. With the introduction of the machine came factory time, measured by the precise movements of the clock. In the nine-to-five day, each moment is defined like every other moment, qualitatively no different. Like people, time has been divided into interchangeable parts. Many jobs demand exactly the eight hours of the working day, no more or less. The technological code urges people, too, to be consumers. They need to purchase the products of the machine so that the economic wheels of society will turn. Often goods are deliberately planned to wear out quickly in order to be replaced, thus providing jobs and employment for workers. Advertising creates new needs, people keep buying, and the consumer society spends itself to own more and more. But the technological code gives Americans a return to a kind of innocence. No ambiguity troubles the world that the machine controls, for it is as precise and measured as interchangeable parts. Technology reinforces a view of the world in which it is complex on the surface but ultimately simple.

Much different from the behavioral code derived from the machine is the code that modern psychology provides Americans, especially in the **human potential movement**. Unlike older forms of psychology, the human potential movement from the 1960s and on has not so much sought to heal the mentally ill as to bring ordinary people to a greater capacity for happiness and creativity. While an authoritarian model predominated in the doctor-patient relationships of older psychologies, the new therapies stress community and peer relationships. Or they are self-help techniques that closely parallel the practices, like meditation, of a number of contemporary religious movements. And while traditional psychologies developed a technical scientific language, the new forms use a vocabulary that is, sometimes openly and sometimes more subtly, religious. Often the language is borrowed from Asian traditions, especially Buddhism, Hinduism, and Daoism. Also unlike the lengthy therapies of the past, which were still seen as temporary, the new psychologies aim to instruct people in a way of life. Lectures, seminars, and workshops teach techniques that, leaders claim, can be used for life. Encounter groups, dream diaries, various self-actualization techniques—all have become familiar examples of the new psychology.

For this **humanistic psychology**, control and organization—key for the technological ethic—are the enemy. Instead of machine-like behavior, the code that comes from humanistic psychology stresses the free expression of feeling and the formation of open communities to achieve health and happiness. At the same time, it turns people toward themselves or toward others in intimate relationships more than toward a public world. Some find this ethic alien to American culture, an import fed, perhaps, by Asian religious movements and the like. Yet the code of humanistic psychology is as American as the expectation of a millennial golden age of peace and plenty. From the point of view of numbers, the movement is far more widespread than a simple catalog of those who have participated in a group-process weekend. The psychological code shapes the millions who read self-improvement magazines and various self-help manuals or attend classes on effective parenting, making marriage work, codependency, and similar. Professional educators have adopted many awareness and encounter techniques. Radio and television talk shows feature guests who give popular psychological advice, while soap operas daily probe the inner workings of their characters' psyches in the language and style of humanistic psychology. Meanwhile, the New Age and new spirituality movements have made the language of the new therapies fundamental to their own expression.

A fourth behavioral code comes from American ideas about **nature**. Today nature has become a central symbol by which Americans orient themselves, expressed in everything from a preference for cereals advertised as "natural" to use of earth tones for room decoration and the practice of yoga and jogging for health. Nature has meant many things to Americans—a new birth to a millennial golden age of innocence, a place to be wild, a body to be befriended, an obstacle to be mastered, a resource to be used. In all of these expressions of meaning, nature has given Americans direction about how to live. The past offers numerous examples of how much Americans felt drawn to nature. The American Transcendentalists provide one expression, but so does the rise of environmentalism in the later nineteenth century and its continuance into our own time. For many, following nature can also show what kind of healthcare is best (alternative and low technology). Following nature can mean certain kinds of musical preferences, certain architectural choices, certain clothing styles, even certain ways at death to be buried.

Like humanistic psychology, the natural code stresses spontaneity and freedom. More than the new psychology, though, it promotes simplicity and a lack of complication. It also, in some forms, fosters strong individualism. The natural code may, for example, promote homesteading as a way of life, teach the importance of growing your own crops, and encourage survivalism and independence from the technological infrastructure of society. In all of these ways and others, too, nature guides mainstream Americans as they live in the ordinary world. But besides, because nature can inspire and provide the space for contemplation and a sense of the grandeur of the unbuilt world, it can lead Americans into deep and intense forms of religious experience. The code can become much more than a behavioral guide and can provide a means of touching an extraordinary world.

Afterthoughts on Cultural Religion

The complexity of the cultural processes studied here should not escape notice. Unlike organized religions, the religion associated with general American culture is partial and indistinct. It would not be fair to think of the two forms of religion as the same, but it is fair to see the two as, in some ways, similar. Identifying the religious dimension of culture can help us to understand the power of culture to knit many people together. It can also show why some stories, persons, and songs attract so strongly. Still more, the distinction between ordinary and extraordinary religion needs to be redrawn to take account of cultural religion. The introduction to this book describes ordinary religion as more or less synonymous with culture, while the book as a whole points to specific religious organizations as giving people the fundamentals of extraordinary religion. That distinction is, for the most part, useful. As people who are part of a culture, members of religious organizations easily blend ordinary and extraordinary concerns, or, seeking a sharper definition of their religious identity, they try in various ways to separate the two. In turn, the general culture goes its own way, giving people the means to make sense of the world in its everyday reality.

Yet sometimes the stories, behavioral codes, and rituals of culture push beyond the boundaries of daily routine. Just as people who practice extraordinary religion in one way or another express the ordinary religion of culture, so culture, too, has its moments when it becomes extraordinary. In our own time, when the role of organized religion has shrunk and when it cannot unify all Americans, it is not surprising to find culture expressing its share of transcendence. Still, it is necessary to be cautious about determining how effectively cultural religion unites Americans. Much of mainstream culture turns on the middle class. People of color and of markedly non-Anglo or European ancestry—as leaders and followers—are also often underrepresented. Like civil religion, cultural religion is the (mostly) ordinary religion of many Americans some of the time. In fact, civil religion is one expression of the larger presence of cultural religion; and to locate civil religion in this way gives clues about how to look at the many other aspects of cultural religion. They are all many smaller circles within the larger circle of culture.

With its long history among us, **millennialism** has repeatedly appeared in cultural religion in one of two forms. Sometimes it has been the **dominating millennialism** that takes its cue from visions of a final battle when good will triumph over evil. At other times it has been the **innocent millennialism** that seeks to make utopias in an uncorrupted landscape. Both kinds of millennialism provide Americans with an ordinary religion that yet contains extraordinary moments. Both direct them in the course of their lives, interpreting the meaning of things, offering occasions for ritual, and providing ways to seek empowerment for daily life. Furthermore, both kinds of millennialism share a dualistic way of looking at life. Good *or* evil, right *or* wrong, this *or* that provide a framework for thinking and acting.

The instincts of public Protestantism are at home here. Moralism, the search for simplicity, and the activism of doers and achievers are part of the millennial theme. Significantly, though, in many expressions of cultural religion, expressions of community counter American individualism. Ideologies of teamwork, cooperation, and harmony are as frequent as those of solitary achievement. While American cultural religion pays lip service to the nation's historic individualism, it also preaches a need to live and act together. And in its cultivation of union among the many, once again cultural religion has learned from the values taught by public Protestantism. Voluntaryism is to be encouraged, it suggests; but in a land of different peoples and different traditions, cultural religion teaches that the only way to be alike is to feel alike. So the community that cultural religion seeks to create is, finally, a **community of feeling**.

In Overview

Public Protestantism still dominates the United States, even despite loss of influence in the twentieth century and on. Present from colonial times in Calvinistic Christianity, sheer numbers, political and social prestige, economic power, and an early educational monopoly all contributed to public Protestant success as the "**one religion**" of Americans. Those who were not Protestant also contributed to its position of power by their acceptance of its influence and imitation of its ways. As both extraordinary and ordinary religion, public Protestantism shaped the country. It has offered a code, a cultus, and a creed to Americans, the three elements closely interlinked. The code begins in conditions of **democratic equality** and **religious liberty**, later expressed legally in **separation of church and state**. These conditions encouraged the growth of **denominationalism** and **voluntaryism** in public Protestantism. Within it, too, **activism**, a **search for simplicity (reductionism, nonintellectualism, ahistoricism)**, and—most prominently—**moralism** have flourished.

Related to the code, the public Protestant cultus of **revivalism** has stressed activism in working through to conversion, simplicity in its religion of bare essentials, and moralism in its emphasis on belief in sin and a need for purification. Historically, the revivals helped to deal with estrangement by creating a place and time in which private feelings could legitimately be expressed in public. In this way people could have a sense of community without confronting their lack of knowledge of one another or their absence of intellectual agreement. In its creed, public Protestantism in turn promoted beliefs about the **importance of the individual**, the existence of a **higher law**, and **millennialism**. Moralistic in code, revivalistic in cultus, and millennial in creed, public Protestantism acted as a solvent for the many religions in the country.

Civil religion—the religion of nationalism—has also weakened boundaries between people and bound them together. New England's Puritans laid its foundations, and, later, so did the patriots of the Revolution, who linked Puritan millennial themes to Enlightenment religion and the experience and remembrance of their own deeds in the war. By the time of George Washington's first inauguration, the creed, code, and cultus of the civil religion were firmly in place, linking the ordinary history of the country to extraordinary religion. The creed has proclaimed the United States as a chosen and millennial nation. The code has emphasized patriotic behavior by citizens and government. And the cultus has designated sacred space and time in national shrines and patriotic holy days. It offers national "saints," revered objects, and ritual practices to encourage Americans to keep their connection with creed and code. Although there are many ambiguities in the meaning of creed, code, and cultus, their central affirmation is the **millennial politics** of making history by deeds of greatness.

However, civil religion is only part of the religious landscape. Although they are many, Americans have created a mainstream culture—a **culture of the center**—that tells them who they are, advises them how to act, and provides them with rituals to express these meanings. As a religious system, a diffused **cultural religion** provides a mostly ordinary expression of American religion. The cultus of cultural religion centers on an annual **ritual calendar** that evokes millennial themes of dominance in patriotic holidays and innocence in family feasts. The creed of cultural religion unfolds in thematic popular stories spread, for example, by television, film, literature, and entertainment stars. Commitment to **millennial ideas** appears in recurring plot structures of violent redemption and triumph over evil coming to a passive people from outside, while **perfectionism** and innocence live on in the icons of screen and print. Finally, the code of cultural religion expresses norms of behavior guided by **sports**, **technology**, **humanistic psychology**, and **nature**, all of them expressing one or another side of millennial belief and commitment.

As public Protestantism, civil religion, and general cultural religion, the **one religion** seeks to dissolve the differences in American life. The power of the one religion is evident in that much of the time it works in public and part of the time it also works in private. So we are left on one side with many religions, each trying to maintain separate identity, and on the other, with one religion trying to unite them. In America, many religious centers meet, with the one religion competing, finding allies, and combining with the many in a variety of ways.

Chapter 12

Many Centers Meeting

In 1834 Ursuline nuns were conducting a convent school for girls in Charlestown, outside of Boston. The institution had attracted the daughters of some of Boston's first families and of wealthy families in the vicinity. Their Protestant and, specifically, Unitarian parents wanted the educational advantages that the nuns might provide. They felt little sympathy for what they regarded as the narrow Congregationalism of the public schools. By contrast, people who lived and worked near the Charlestown convent were poorer, suspicious of "papist superstition," and resentful of upper-class Unitarians. Writers at the time said that the Catholic church was trying to convert Protestant children, especially females, so that it could gain control. Supported by respected Congregational institutions and ministers, the fears of Catholicism and of education at the Charlestown convent spread. The well-known Lyman Beecher preached revival-style against Catholicism and warned of a link between the pope and despotism. In this emotionally charged atmosphere, with a series of circumstances driving tensions higher still, a working-class mob torched and burned the convent and a nearby farmhouse down.

Well organized and with hints of involvement by some of Boston's prominent citizens, the fire exposed dynamics of class and ideology intertwined with religion. On one side were the working people who came, many of them, from the brickyards at Charlestown. Fed by class jealousy and outrage at liberal ideology, they also upheld the extraordinary religious commitment of the Reformation. On the other side, the Unitarians reached out toward Catholic difference as an expression of their own sense of breadth and upper-class freedom from old prejudices. They also marked their disapproval of the rigorous legacy of Puritanism and of the classes who carried it.

The Charlestown incident underlined, once again, the boundary question. This time the question concerned the one religion of the dominant and public mainstream as it tried to determine its borders in the presence of outsiders. For some, like the strict Congregationalists, maintaining strong boundaries was important in a situation seen as threatening. Foreign religious ideas seemed a source of disorder that might lead to erosion of the Protestant heritage. For others, like the liberal Unitarians, being open for exchanges was a good thing. Liberals wanted to go out farther and absorb more inside.

American religious history became the staging ground for many encounters between and among people of faith who also were part of different social and cultural worlds. Some acts, like the torching of the convent, expressed culture wars. Other encounters displayed a greater sense of tolerance and cooperation. And still others demonstrated an underlying combinativeness in the religiosity of Americans. People who gravitated toward different religious centers—Protestant or part of the many—often reached toward others in exchanges that loosened boundaries.

Conflicts

Mainstream Protestants generally displayed anxiety toward the cultural "invaders" adopting the country as their new home. Convinced of Anglo-Saxon chosenness and superiority, they often barred gates more than opened them. Just as, instinctively, humans have experienced the boundaries of their bodies as charged with danger, they have viewed the social body in the same way. So, in America, the dominant Protestant population wanted to preserve the social body—to keep wrong substances from entering and corrupting it and to prevent its energies from being drained away. The social result became discrimination. To cite examples from the seventeenth century, American Indians felt the brunt of Protestant fears. Beneath the Puritan attitude toward Indians lay the fear that, far from the centers of European civilization, Euro-American Christians would revert to the "savagery" they imagined in Indians. Symbolic of this savagery, for Puritans, was the "heathen" worship that Indian cultures practiced and the moral codes associated with them. Similarly, Protestants generally feared informal social contacts with their black slaves. When the slaves got their freedom, the dominant culture continued to uphold, as much as it could, the tradition of separate societies.

The nineteenth-century influx of immigrants challenged Protestants with new contacts that they often preferred to keep at a minimum. Many Protestants thought foreigners were ready to overwhelm them, and so they felt they had to fight to maintain their moral superiority as the chosen nation. Some reform movements that Protestants led in the nineteenth century appear in a different light against this background. For example, beneath the surface, fear of immigrant drinking habits in part fueled the temperance crusade. Protestant fears thus became general cultural fears of the outsider, and nowhere was this more the case than in Protestant attitudes toward Catholics and Jews.

The Roman Catholic "Plot"

In keeping with their Reformation heritage, American Protestants thought of the pope as the Antichrist. They believed they stood on the side of the Lamb in the war between good and evil, while the pope and the Catholic church served Satan. For most colonial and nineteenth-century Protestants, Catholics were not even Christians. They thought Catholics were engaged in a secret plot to take over the world. More than that, Protestants ascribed to priests and nuns an immorality they feared would wreck the moral order of the country. Catholics were engaged in wild sexual promiscuity, many Protestants thought. Already in the seventeenth century, clear **anti-Catholicism** was evident, especially in Maryland and Massachusetts Bay. By the Revolutionary War era, Enlightenment thinkers influenced American attitudes. Suspicious of the Catholic church and its "superstitions," Enlightenment leaders condemned its priests for keeping ordinary people in intellectual darkness. The church's papal and authoritarian system, they believed, had deterred Catholics from acknowledging the sovereignty of reason.

It was in the 1840s, however, that old fears of Catholic power revived and intertwined with social welfare concerns, as Irish immigrants began to come in huge numbers. Fleeing a potato famine in Ireland, these migrants were very poor. They strained the social services that government and private agencies could provide, and Protestants complained that they blighted the cities with their slums, their diseases, their lack of cleanliness, and their foreign ways. According to Protestants, they brought unwelcome competition for jobs and so reduced the wages that the market would pay to all. At the same time, the trusteeship controversy within Catholicism—over the question of lay control of church property—generated unfavorable publicity. New Protestant converts, born of the zeal of the Finney revivals, spread anti-Catholicism in the various voluntary societies they joined. Religious newspapers began to warn their readers of the tyrannies of the pope and the dangers of the Catholic church. And by 1832 the New York Protestant Association was promoting the Reformation by public discussions that aimed to undercut Catholicism.

In this hostile climate, the burning of the Ursuline convent became the first act in a Protestant war against nunneries. Books appeared claiming to reveal the horrors of convent life, among them **Maria Monk**'s *Awful Disclosures of the Hotel Dieu Nunnery of Montreal.* Professing to be the work of an escaped nun, the book contained "awful disclosures" of secret sexual unions between priests and nuns. The children born of these relationships, according to Monk, were strangled in infancy after being baptized. Their bodies, she said, were hidden in a secret passage that linked the convent to the home of the priests. Actually written in New York at the urging of a group that included several Protestant ministers, the book, needless to say, got noticed. Although the Hotel Dieu was finally searched by trustworthy investigators who found no evidence to support even the floor plan of the convent as described by Monk, many still believed the allegations of her book.

Protestants regarded **celibacy** (living without sex) as an unnatural state. Moreover, Catholic **secrecy** about what took place behind the walls of a convent,

THE AIM OF POPE PIUS IX.

The Aim of Pope Pius IX, 1855. This titled cartoon from a Protestant nativist flyer advertised the Reverend Isaac Kelso's *Danger in the Dark*, an anti-Catholic novel. With the cartoon's depiction of the pope destroying the U.S. Constitution, note the irony of the caption's allusion to "Romish intolerance."

so different from the open social style promoted in a democratic republic, also disturbed Protestant Americans. At the same time, Protestants believed they had new cause for worry as rumors spread of a papal plot to take control of the Mississippi Valley with the aid of European despots. Lyman Beecher wrote his *Plea for the West,* warning of Catholic plans to use schools as a way to win converts and so win the country. For this reason, he urged, Protestant schools and colleges had to be established in the new territories. In the East, Catholicism became embroiled in other school-centered controversies as church leaders protested against the reading of the King James (Protestant) Version of the Bible in the public schools. Further, Catholics were upset by many of the textbooks that their children were required to use because they thought that the books presented an unfair and untrue picture of Catholicism. In Philadelphia, these and similar issues provoked a confrontation between Protestants and Irish Catholics that led in 1844 to the burning of two Catholic churches in the Kensington suburb of the city. The discontent between the two factions brought a state of civil riot to Philadelphia.

Protestants continued to form organizations to counter what they perceived as the Catholic threat. Many of the best-known voluntary societies—the American Tract Society, the American Home Missionary Society, and others—spread anti-Catholic attitudes. Then in the mid-1840s Protestant nativism assumed political form as the **Native American party**, which demanded that the naturalization law be changed to require a twenty-one-year wait before an immigrant could become a citizen. By the early 1850s, the secret **Order of the Star-Spangled Banner**, known in its public activities as the **Know-Nothing party**, used local, county, state, and national councils to fight Catholicism. Its members "knew nothing" when publicly questioned, but they succeeded in bringing their slates of candidates to office in local contests and later carried states—Massachusetts, Delaware, and Pennsylvania among them. So confident was the party that it hoped to capture the White House in 1856 (it failed).

The country experienced another strong resurgence of anti-Catholic sentiment in the 1870s and especially in the 1880s, when the heaviest immigration in American history began. When in 1886 a bomb exploded in the midst of the police officers called to Chicago's Haymarket Square during an anarchist meeting, the incident triggered renewed nativism. A year later, the American Protective Association formed, with members pledged never to vote for a Catholic or hire one if they could prevent it. Anti-Catholic feeling continued for roughly the next fifty years and has lingered in subdued form in some circles until the present. By 1915, the revived **Ku Klux Klan** made Catholicism one of its targets. Meanwhile, theories of "scientific" racism alleged that the Teutonic, or Northern European, "race" was superior and that therefore the Protestant peoples—the Germans and the English—were the lifeblood of the nation. It followed that the Mediterranean "race"—Southern European Catholic immigrants—would weaken the nation.

In the Prohibition era, when in 1928 New York's governor, **Alfred ("Al") Smith**, ran for the presidency on the "wet" (pro-drinking) Democratic ticket, his Catholicism became a key issue in his—and the wet—defeat. The United States did not elect a Catholic president until 1960 when, after successfully answering questions about his religion, **John F. Kennedy** won the office. Even after World War II, fears of Catholicism persisted, as when in 1945, for example, Carl McIntire warned that Catholicism threatened the nation more than Communism did. After 1948, Protestants and Other Americans United for the Separation of Church and State (POAU) warned of the growing authority of the Catholic church in the United States and found the possibility of federal aid to parochial schools especially disturbing. It was only after the election of Kennedy and Vatican Council II that a new era began for Catholics in the United States. More recently still, with the end-of-century growth of the Christian Right, Catholic traditionalists and "pro-life" advocates have made common cause with conservative Protestants. Still, in the early twenty-first century, residual pockets of anti-Catholicism remain.

The Jewish "Conspiracy"

Unlike anti-Catholicism, **anti-Semitism** did not become a serious factor in American life until the later nineteenth century. There were reasons. First, the Puritan belief in the covenant had fostered a strong identification with the biblical Israel. As chosen people and visible saints, Puritans believed, they had inherited the mantle of divine election that had formerly protected the Jews—who had played an honored role in a divine plan. Second, Jewish presence in the colonies was minimal—smaller even than the presence of Catholics. Moreover, no Jewish power, such as the Catholic powers of Spain and France, opposed English presence in North America. Finally, early Jewish immigrants did not drain public welfare programs. They were largely tradespeople able to earn their own living.

Still, there *were* reasons why Protestants might erect barriers against the Jews. The Christian gospels, and especially the gospel of John, portrayed the Jews as disobeying their God and rejecting his prophets. The ultimate rejection had come, according to Christian accounts, when Jews refused to recognize the messiah and crucified him. Throughout the Middle Ages and into the time of the Reformation, the charge that the Jews were Christ-killers stuck, often combining with other factors to lead to episodes of Jewish persecution. Meanwhile, because the medieval church prohibited **usury** (lending money with an interest charge), European Jews became identified with money lending and banking. Prominent members of the Jewish community lent money to their Christian neighbors, prospered materially, and frequently attracted their resentment. From the Christian point of view, there was something suspicious—even wrong—with wealth that was obtained from money. Seeds planted in the ground would grow and reproduce. But money could not be planted and, in its own form, could not be used. Therefore, according to this rationale, it must be an agent of the devil.

These ideas, the common possession of all Christians before the Reformation, continued among both Protestants and Catholics. So despite seeing themselves as the New Israel, American Protestants felt ambivalence toward Jews. Even in colonial times, prohibitions against atheists and non-Christians slowed Jewish immigration, while the Jews also suffered legal disabilities. Yet in comparison with the restrictions Jews experienced in Europe, America seemed like the promised land, and the Jewish community prospered. Not until the time of the Civil War did anti-Semitism become noticeable, as Jews in both the North and the South were blamed with profiteering from the war and with treason. Then, after 1880, a huge immigration of Eastern European Jews, poor and distinctly foreign, brought Jewish people increasingly to public attention. At the same time, the success of older Jewish Americans, sometimes greater than that of Protestant Christians, aroused hostility. Jews found themselves barred from prestigious social clubs and summer resorts. College fraternities began to exclude Jewish students at eastern schools, while Jews faced difficulties in obtaining housing.

By the 1890s, with the prominence of European Jewish banking families, such as the Rothschilds, anti-Semitic feeling crystallized around the suspicion that Jews were responsible for an international conspiracy to base the economy on a single gold standard. By contrast, American populists believed that the "free" coinage of silver would ease economic conditions, especially for farmers and working people, and so silver purchase became the law. Then, when a financial panic swept the country in 1893, the steady drain of gold from the treasury to purchase silver became a matter of serious concern. At a special session of Congress, silver legislation was repealed. Farmers and working people felt betrayed, and after President Grover Cleveland obtained a gold loan from the Rothschilds, anti-Semitism flared. At the Democratic convention in 1896, William Jennings Bryan gave the "Cross of Gold" speech that won him the presidential nomination. "You shall not crucify mankind upon a cross of gold," he declared in a long-remembered statement.

Whether or not he was consciously aware of it, Bryan's rhetoric was anti-Semitic even as it defended Protestant cultural boundaries. He had combined the old charges—that the Jews were Christ-killers and that they were banking conspirators—with the populist cry for free silver and widespread images of rural Protestant strength. Bryan had not named the Jews, but most people knew that he meant them. During these years anti-Semitic rhetoric and literature became an open part of American life, a pattern that continued until after World War II.

An often-cited example is the **Leo Frank case** in Atlanta in 1913. There, new city dwellers from rural areas felt tense and uncomfortable, and violence erupted periodically. The Jew, historically identified with cities, came to stand as a symbol of all that these Americans hated and feared. So when thirteen-year-old Mary Phagan was murdered one night at the National Pencil Factory, her employer, Leo M. Frank, was immediately suspected. Although Frank had witnesses to his whereabouts, he was placed on trial. He admitted having seen the Phagan girl alive on the day before the night of the crime, and strands of her hair as well as bloodstains were found in a workroom opposite his office. Furthermore, he possessed something of a reputation for making advances toward his female employees. Thus, although many years later his name was cleared, Frank was railroaded through a trial in the midst of public outrage. It was no surprise when the jury found him guilty. Public oratory and newspaper editorials made identifications between the northern Jew, the evils of the city, and the death of the "little factory girl." Stories circulated that Frank's Jewish friends had tried to bribe the jury, while his lawyers received anonymous threats. After fruitless appeals all the way to the United States Supreme Court, the governor of Georgia commuted Frank's death sentence to life imprisonment. But shortly after the decision, the prison was stormed, and Frank was kidnapped and lynched.

Meanwhile, a revived Ku Klux Klan began directing its attacks against Catholics and Jews, as well as blacks. Identifiably Protestant, the new Klan had its own chaplains and hymns. By 1923 it had grown to nearly 3 million members, a militant reminder of the threat felt by many Protestants in a mixed society. During this decade, too, Henry Ford in 1920 championed the American publication of the *Protocols of the Elders of Zion*, the fabricated account of a conference of nineteenth-century Jews planning to overthrow Christianity and to gain control of the world. Significantly, in the *Protocols* the gold standard was to be the Jewish weapon in the attempted subversion.

Now a "polite" form of anti-Semitism spread, as Harvard and other universities introduced quota systems because they feared that Jews would alter the traditional character of their institutions. A decade later, in the 1930s, the Great Depression and the growth of European Fascism stimulated American fears of the Jews. Many Catholics as well as Protestants became openly anti-Semitic—that fact a pointed reminder that "Protestant" identity often included non-Protestants. In this blend of ordinary and extraordinary religion, Jews had come to stand for many of the ills that troubled the republic. For numbers of Americans, Jewish unbelief challenged Christianity, Jewish wealth wrongly outstripped that of the leaders of the New Israel, and Jewish identification with cities helped to corrupt the wholesome rural flavor of the United States.

Nor was mainstream Protestantism alone in its anti-Semitism. In a culture in which many centers were meeting and interacting, it is no surprise that prejudice could be shared. For example, Catholics, too, inherited ideas of Jews as Christ-killers and conspiratorial moneylenders. The medieval church emphasized these views, and until the aftermath of Vatican Council II the Catholic liturgy for Good Friday spoke of the "perfidious Jews." In a notorious American case, during the 1930s, especially late in the decade, **Father Charles E. Coughlin** influenced millions through his anti-Semitic radio sermons. The Jews had been key leaders in the Communist movement in Russia, he said, and during the Spanish Civil War, they had spread Communist propaganda, opposing the Catholic General Francisco Franco. In an old argument, Coughlin complained that most of those who controlled the world's wealth were Jewish and that with their money they dominated the press and shaped public opinion. Coughlin added insult to injury by calling on Jews to accept Christ as a way to banish the "Jewish problem." He reprinted the *Protocols of the Elders of Zion* in his weekly newspaper and, in general, continued to spread his ideas until his religious superiors silenced him.

The Pluralist Struggle

The people who believed and practiced the many religions of America countered intolerance and scapegoating in different ways. In one response—**separation**—they turned inward to their own communities, attempting to keep their identities intact. To do so, they maintained and created distinctive rituals. For example, African Americans preserved remnants of the African past during their years in slavery. When they began to use Christian religious language, they evolved their own form of Christianity that sought to express an authentic black religiosity. In the style of their preaching, in spirituals, in marriage and funeral customs, and in the blend of idea and emotion that characterized their worship, blacks spoke and acted their own ordinary and extraordinary religion. In root work and voodoo and later in religious movements that made blackness central, they created a religious culture that drew a line between themselves and white society.

Native Americans had a similar story, although in their case they fought to maintain boundaries in spite of mainstream culture. Christian missionaries and government agents tried to break down Indian nations' ways and to replace tradition with Christianity and modernity. Still, in response to these developments, many deliberately sought to preserve their religious and ethnic identity. In the later twentieth century and after, a movement for return to tradition grew in reservation cultures. For the Hopi and the Oglala, for instance, ordinary and extraordinary religion worked together to create newly self-conscious and interlinked worlds of belief, behavior, and ritual drama. In other cases, Native Americans reinterpreted Christian elements combinatively to maintain boundaries between Indian and white society. For example, the Rio Grande Pueblos of New Mexico added Catholic ritual to their already full ceremonial life. More radically, the Paiutes who created the Ghost Dance transformed Christian millennialism into an expression of Indian renewal.

Among whites, non-Protestant believers also used boundary markers to tell themselves and their Protestant neighbors that they were different. Jewish dietary laws expressed a commitment to the religion of Israel and likewise distinguished Jews in a public way from Gentiles. Similarly, the growth of the parochial school system among Catholics demonstrated their refusal to be assimilated to mainstream Protestantism through the culture of the public schools. Jews and Catholics also strongly rejected Protestant missionizing in their midst. And in a related response, different ethnic groups within the Catholic church struggled to maintain their religious traditions in the face of dominant Irish power—closer, for them, to the Protestant mainstream. Germans and Poles fought to keep their native languages in religious services. Italians steadfastly continued their devotions to their favorite saints. Mexican American Catholics cherished home altars and turned to the Virgin of Guadalupe. Meanwhile, members of new religious movements also adopted badges of identity. Seventh-day Adventists maintained their dietary laws, and Christian Scientists avoided medical doctors. Mormons participated in temple ceremonies forbidden to outsiders. Shakers lived apart in celibacy, and spiritualists met at séances to contact the spirits of the dead. Later, Anglo-American followers of Krishna wore saffron robes and sandals and chanted publicly in honor of their God.

The desire for separation from the one religion could provoke emotions of fear, anger, and even **revolutionary resistance**. The Nat Turner rebellion among blacks in the nineteenth century is a good example. In the later twentieth century, the story of Jim Jones and his Peoples Temple provides a case as clear. Jones began his ministerial career in the Disciples of Christ denomination and countered Protestant racial exclusionism with interracial work. He admired Father Divine, was influenced by Divine's inclination for religious combining, and subsequently evolved a combinative religion of his own that functioned, also, as a counterreligion to mainstream Protestantism. In the late 1970s, he and his group relocated to Guyana. Here Jones hoped to build a model socialist society in an agricultural community that he named Jonestown. He came to see himself as a messiah to liberate poor people and black people from the one religion with its entanglement with capitalism and nuclear power. In 1978, when Congressman Leo Ryan and others were murdered while visiting Jonestown, Jones led more than 900 followers to his version of a revolutionary religious suicide. Members of the group made a ritual of their own demise as they drank prepared poison.

In Jim Jones and Jonestown, alienation from mainstream religion and culture reached a final limit, as the Jonestown devotees overcame the Protestant world through the ultimate separation of death. Others, however, had a different strategy for overcoming mainstream religious culture. They missionized. Catholics are a major example of this strategy with their self-understanding as a universal church and their long history of **mission involvement**. Many Catholic parishes held inquiry classes for members of other denominations. Moreover, the Catholic mission movement of the nineteenth century had as its secondary goal making Protestants better acquainted with the Catholic church. Catholic schools, which in the nineteenth century sometimes catered to Protestants, hoped to influence their charges in the direction of the Catholic faith. Meanwhile, bishops who debated Protestant preachers, either in person or through the press, wanted to convince them of the truth of Catholicism. Similarly, when the Transcendentalist Isaac Hecker became a Catholic convert and priest, he founded the Paulist order in 1858 dedicated to domestic missionary work; Catholicism was the religion best suited to democratic America, he wrote and said, and his press energetically spread the word. In the twentieth century, radio and television helped Catholics to make their message known. In an often-cited example, the millions who watched Bishop Fulton J. Sheen's *Life Is Worth Living* series in the 1950s learned how Catholics saw the world.

However, it is the small religious groups—the sects and even smaller spiritual practice groups—who have often expended the most noticeable efforts on missions. This work has been part of the identity of many of these movements, so that using missions to counter the Protestant mainstream came for them almost without thought. For instance, Shaker preachers followed the revivals to gain converts. Later it became customary for young Mormon men to work two years as missionaries. In a more subdued example, Christian Scientists have established reading rooms in the business districts of cities and towns across the country to attract shoppers. At the other end of the religious spectrum, Jehovah's Witnesses, called "publishers," spend hours in weekly door-to-door visitation. Among newer movements, devotees in the International Society for Krishna Consciousness initially drew attention for selling flowers in airport terminals and missionizing mainstream Americans as they did. Members of Sun Myung Moon's Unification Church have gone from door to door for similar purposes. Followers of Eckankar, a group that teaches soul travel, or astral projection, continue to distribute literature on college campuses and to advertise in national publications, while members of the International Meditation Society lecture widely in order to introduce people to Transcendental Meditation.

While the many non-Protestants jockeyed for space in American society and struggled to find their voice, mainstream Protestants increasingly exhibited a pluralism that eroded their central consensus. Beginning after the Civil War, liberals and conservatives grew more noticeable, and so began what Martin E. Marty has called the "two-party system" in American Protestantism. After World War II, the rifts between Protestants only increased, and after the 1960s, with liberals hemorrhaging and conservatives gaining, the battle for the center went into full swing. A series of social and political issues became touchstones of liberal or conservative identity. Should abortions be permitted, as the Supreme Court decided in *Roe v. Wade* in 1973, because citizens had a constitutional right to privacy? Or should they be legally banned because, as evangelicals said, abortion was murder? Should same-sex couples have the same legal rights as heterosexual ones—and, by the twenty-first century, could they marry? Was feminism good or bad? Was the teaching of evolution corrupting the minds of the young? Should they also be hearing, in biology classes, about creationism and, later, intelligent design? Should affirmative action be supported? What should the government do about illegal immigration, and should amnesty be granted to some immigrants? Should there be free trade or fair trade? What could the Social Gospel mean, if anything? Did Providence expect America to lead the way in wars to support and spread democracy? Or should religious people be protesting against the nation's wars as arrogant, imperialistic, and death-dealing? Was capital punishment the just hand of God administered by society, or was it vengeful and evil? Could medical uses of marijuana be permitted, or would they start society down a slippery slope to drug use? What were proper end-of-life decisions? Could life support systems be turned off? Could food and water be withheld from dying patients? Could euthanasia be permitted under the law?

Coalitions

Religious people stood on both sides of these issues, and they fought for their views as strongly. Meanwhile, **coalitions** formed between unlikely partners. Protestant evangelicals counted conservative Catholics, Mormons, and Orthodox Jews among their allies. Liberal Protestants joined with humanists of many stripes and with new spirituality enthusiasts. Linked together for mutual goals, people from different faith traditions and no faith tradition found that they had more in common than they had thought. Still more, the two parties in American Protestantism were hardly alone in seeking common cause with others. Protestants aside, American Catholics, for example—despite the historic anti-Semitism that long lingered in their church—began to forge alliances with Jews.

Vatican Council II set the stage for a new era in **Roman Catholic–Jewish relations**. In a formal document, the **Declaration on the Relationship of the Church to Non-Christian Religions** (1965), the council addressed the ancient charge that the Jews were Christ-killers. It explicitly rejected the notions that all Jews or the Jews of its day were responsible for the death of Jesus. Further, it warned against characterizing Jews as "cursed by God," and it spoke of a common heritage shared by Catholics and Jews. Some Jews thought that the language of the document did not go far enough, since it did not condemn the accusation that the Jews were guilty of **deicide** (the murder of God) and did not express contrition for the church's anti-Semitism. Moreover, some were disappointed because the document did not flatly reject attempts to convert the Jews. Still, it was clear that the council had taken a major step.

In the years after the council, some Jews and Catholics—like other Christians—self-consciously engaged in **Jewish-Christian dialogue**. Today, at the grassroots level, interested Catholics participate in the Passover seder with Jews in home settings. Likewise, Jews have attended Catholic services and learned about Christian theology, even as Catholics have discovered the importance of the Law in Jewish life.

While Jewish-Catholic relations have developed as part of extraordinary religion, in another example, **Jewish-black relations** have expressed connections developed as part of ordinary culture. Jews and African Americans have had much in common, for both experienced years of suffering and persecution at the hands of white Christians. Both have thought of themselves as separate nations, and both have combined ordinary and extraordinary religion with their nationhood in distinctive identities. During the civil rights struggle of the 1960s, Jews prominently supported the black effort. They contributed substantial funds, and they marched beside blacks in demonstrations and protests. On the whole, they have expressed more concern than other whites about racism and have been more willing, as employers, to hire blacks. Jews took an active role in the foundation of the **National Association for the Advancement of Colored People (NAACP)**, an organization begun to win black equality through court contests. They have also made efforts on behalf of black education. Although blacks have had neither the wealth nor the occasion to return the gestures in kind, they have at times formed social and political alliances with Jews for mutual goals. The dialogue between the two groups has been characterized by frankness and honesty.

For the many in general, coalitions have been key. Just by sharing the status of "otherness," the many in the long run have made it more acceptable to be different. In fact, if historian R. Laurence Moore is right, the best way to be an "insider" in the United States has been to be an outsider. Moreover, the example of one group has sometimes provided a model for others. For instance, the black-power movement of the 1960s spurred the expression of a more militant ethnic and religious awareness among American Indians, Latinos, and even the descendants of various Catholic immigrant groups—the "white ethnics." Here the coalitions seem more inspirational than political, as these groups simply borrowed strategies from one another to make their voices heard. But politics did offer a vehicle for alliance, too. The Democrats, historically, have been identified as the party of the poor and the immigrant, the African American and the Jew. Through a coalition of these groups, the party often successfully challenged a dominant elite, obtaining social programs and policies intended to benefit the many. Banding together politically, in fact, has been for religious "outsiders" a step in becoming like the established culture by learning to be seen and heard—to "make history" in a way similar to mainstream insiders. When each could witness to all and each could listen to all, in ordinary and extraordinary terms, the many learned what they shared and deployed it for mutual goals. This was one result of **pluralism**.

Combinations

So coalitions meant that pluralism was coexisting with the one religion—sometimes in the midst of conflict and sometimes with a place and program as part of religious America. However, **postpluralism** became a feature of American society, too. **Religious combinations** flourished, and they told a story of Americans borrowing from one another, often without even being aware of what they were doing. The combinations told a story of subtle changes over the years that made each religion in America an increasingly American religion. In these religious combinations, the one religion of public Protestantism often took the upper hand, but not always. In fact, American religious combinativeness suggests a culture exploring ways to unify itself in terms that incorporate all peoples and their practices. It suggests a way that a distinctive American identity is being created.

For example, the Reform movement that spread through the nineteenth-century Jewish community brought changes that made it more "American." Protestant "decorum" became a feature of worship, and for a period Sunday services and Protestant-style hymns came into use. Theological liberals reinterpreted the meaning of Israel, so that the ethics of the biblical prophets provided support for the voluntaryism and activism of the American religious style. Jewish scholarship, traditionally focused on the Torah and the Talmud, transformed itself both in the United States and abroad to mean achievement at the university and in Gentile society. Meanwhile, Reform, Conservatism, and Orthodoxy took shape as forms of American Judaism that in many ways have paralleled mainstream Protestant denominations.

Lay Catholics early identified with the host culture as, in the nineteenth century, they struggled with their bishops to control church property through a system of democratic lay trustees. Later, a series of liberal bishops sought to "Americanize" the church until a message from Rome put a stop to the most open attempts. At the same time, Irish clerical leadership showed in its activism, moralism, and search for simple, nonintellectual answers how close to the mainstream it was. When, in the twentieth century, a new generation of Catholic scholars, both in this country and abroad, looked more kindly toward the era of the Reformation, they fostered ecumenical dialogue with Protestants. Then, after Vatican Council II, American Catholics quickly displayed signs of moving toward a dominant Protestant culture. The English Mass became an appeal to the biblical Word of God, with a corresponding deemphasis on the more elaborate aspects of sacramentalism. Many of the symbolic badges of Catholicism, such as Friday abstinence from meat and old-style paraliturgical devotions, began to disappear. The Catholic mission movement of the nineteenth century gave way to the charismatic movement that brought pentecostal tongues and revivalistic fervor to many members of the church. Individuals and groups, such as the radical Berrigan brothers and conservative pro-lifers, engaged in prophetic-style "Protestant" moral crusades. Democracy reinforced belief in the rights of private conscience as many priests and nuns left their religious orders and many laypeople made decisions about moral issues like birth control that countered traditional Catholic teaching. Meanwhile, gay Catholics defied their church in the Dignity movement. After the pederasty scandal broke, the Catholic lay organization called the Voice of the Faithful followed Protestant and democratic models in challenging the Catholic hierarchy.

For African Americans, emancipation from slavery brought a social revolution with accompanying religious changes. Holiness and pentecostal churches became havens in the cities for many African Americans, encouraging religious experience and a perfectionist behavioral code shared by many mainstream Protestants. Meanwhile, Baptist and Methodist churches affiliated with white denominations and introduced middle-class blacks to the more formal worship preferred by other Protestants. Black religious leadership in the civil rights era of the 1960s drew on traditional resources but also on the mainstream Protestant theological tradition, as reflected in the seminary education of church and social leaders like Martin Luther King, Jr. Blacks gained political power and socioeconomic success in white society to the extent that they learned to speak the cultural language.

Among Native Americans, some followed the strong suggestion of church and government, leaving reservations and adopting white ways and white society. Others, while they remained at home, became Christian. They substituted beliefs in the universal God of Christianity and his son, Jesus, for inherited religious beliefs and expressed their sentiments in Christian worship instead of traditional ritual. Meanwhile, they evolved their own combinative cultural style of being Christian, as the Kateri Conferences and Kateri Circles demonstrate. Acceptance of Christianity frequently came with willingness to be educated in government programs and to live in new housing, even on reservations. Indian traditionalists have often found themselves in conflict with many aspects of reservation life.

Sects follow a typical pattern in which, frequently, they become denominations. By the same token, in their attempts to create separate and exclusive religious societies, they have often ended by reflecting the dominant religion and culture they have tried to escape. For example, America became a central symbol for the Mormons, who, in their millennialism, shared the expectation of Zion that has linked many members of the Protestant mainstream. Likewise, Mormon theology has affirmed material abundance. It carries Arminian doctrines of free will to their logical conclusion, seeing unlimited possibilities for human beings to become "as Gods." Like mainstream Protestants, too, Mormons have made theology second to the moralism and activism of their lives, preferring to act their religion more than to think it.

Other new religious movements have reflected the general cultural millennialism, sometimes in specific teachings about the end of the world, as among Shakers and Seventh-day Adventists. They have also displayed the pragmatic American quality that makes religion a means to success in the world. Like Mormons, Seventh-day Adventists affirm the material abundance they find in American culture. Christian Science and the New Thought movement fulfill mainstream culture more than they depart from it, while spiritualism and Theosophy have also paid their respects to modern science. The mental homesteads provided by metaphysical religion are only prominent examples of the general tendency in the postindustrial United States to create private havens where personal relationships and interests are primary. This, in fact, is what new spirituality is about. Similarly, the evangelical desire for a private relationship with Jesus and the revivalistic quest for right personal feeling are not too different in style from metaphysical religion.

On another front, alienation is the common bond that has linked members of many sects and smaller spiritual practice groups with the mainstream. In recent times, the new religious movements that have turned to Eastern and Western forms of mysticism often try to leave American society. Yet time and again, they come to imitate it. Their use of various techniques, such as meditation, yoga, or chanting, reflects the general American search for tools that work. New Age people, as we have seen, in many ways resemble the fundamentalists and evangelicals they reject. More deliberately, many from Eastern traditions have sought to "Americanize" their religions. Japanese Buddhists speak of their churches and bishops. Muslims attend their mosques on Sunday, instead of the traditional Friday. Eastern Orthodox Christians have introduced the English language into the Divine Liturgy and placed Western-style pews in their churches. In all of these instances, various forms of religious combining have flourished. Creeds, codes, and cultuses became expressions of new powers, meanings, and values. Americans were forming a new people. Every American faith, in a sense, became a new—and combinative—religion.

Summing Up the Present

As the many centers meet, the old responses are still there. The one religion is anxious about its dominance, while the many seek to challenge it in the preservation of their separate identities. Patterns of housing, job, and educational discrimination still exist for African Americans, American Indians, and other groups. Christian Scientists come off slightly worse than others in some books and small groups are vulnerable to condemnation as "cults," even as mainstream Protestants still dominate on Capitol Hill despite a strong evangelical contingent and evangelical presence in the White House. In their desire to remain apart, Asian Indians erect lavish temples, suggesting by the character of the architecture their wish to separate themselves. Arab Muslims sometimes live in ethnic neighborhoods. Pueblo Indians often prefer their adobe villages, laid out with central plazas for the performance of sacred dances.

Although some among the many retreat from the mainstream, others seek greater assimilation and their coalitions become combinations with Protestant culture. Some Catholic Poles and Jews still change their surnames to blend into the "melting pot," even as other ethnics have proclaimed their religious and cultural origins loudly. Seventh-day Adventists discuss whether or not they have become a denomination, while numbers of fundamentalists edge closer to the mainstream. Blacks move to the suburbs, and Catholics, with their own colleges, attend major public universities. Jews, to the disappointment of rabbis, frequently intermarry and drift away from affiliation with a synagogue.

When the many meet the many, they often find reason to be hostile to one another. Native Americans and Latino Catholics in Santa Fe, New Mexico, have resented each other and lived in mutual suspicion as well as anger toward the often-Protestant Anglo-American inhabitants of the city. Because of white community feeling, Afro-Cuban Santerı́ans in Hialeah, Florida, were forbidden by law to slaughter animals for ritual sacrifices until, in 1993, the Supreme Court decided otherwise. American Arabs and Jews continue to face each other tensely in view of their different stances regarding the Middle East.

Throughout American religious history, Protestant attitudes toward the many have been ambivalent, ranging from a defensive fear and hostility, on the one hand, to, on the other, conversion attempts, qualified openness, and the expansive fascination that has led to some forms of cultural combining. The attitudes of the many toward public Protestantism have divided mainly between those who wish to preserve their old ways in the new land and those others who want to become more American and—it follows—more Protestant. At the same time, representatives of some groups have tried to win converts from the one (mainstream) religion. Finally, as the many have encountered one another, they have frequently exchanged insecurities by voicing mutual suspicions and accusations. Still, some have found common worlds to share and have made alliances, while others have expressed their social and religious commitments in missionary work directed toward different groups and persons among the many.

The United States is among the most pluralistic religious and social experiments in history. Its people live in a social situation complicated by great diversity. Religions abound, and so do peoples, their beliefs, styles of worship, and moral codes. Community is fragile and temporary, and alienation is probably the one thing that many have in common. While the vast machinery of government and of the corporate industrial complex continues, the frictions that face Americans are a recurring feature of life. The manyness of groups and movements heightens impulses for everyone to mark boundaries carefully. At the same time, the one religion of millennial chosenness, innocence, and hidden guilt fosters anxiety regarding the boundaries to the cultural mainstream.

Living with so many boundaries has proved a difficult task for Americans. There is a tremendous gap between the millennial goal of community and the realities of alienation that are often thinly veiled. Faced with the problems of impersonality that accompany the large-scale organization of any modern urban and industrial society, Americans have been beset with the serious *religious* problem of crossing the human boundaries that hinder community. That problem has had a long history: it began with the first collision between Native American ways of seeing and European interpretations of Indian life. It grew, too, with the political realities of a power situation in which, though insecure and fearful, Puritans could dissolve their fright in a millennial fervor that divided the world between separate good and evil sides. The balance of political power has always complicated the picture of religion in the United States.

To live without a public center—a one religion—seems humanly impossible. Shared sources of power, meaning, and value, however loosely expressed, must provide some kind of bonding, or society would lose all cohesion and fall apart. To live without the many who form so significant a part of American religious culture seems equally impossible. Although sometimes less fully organized and less visible, the many have deeply affected American life—which would not be American without them. So American religious reality is a dialectic between the one and the many. The one religion suits active and energetic people who desire clear and simple directives for their work. Its sense of certainty seeks to provide solace for Americans uprooted by a society on the move. Huge numbers, strong institutionalization, wealth, and political prestige have given it a clear role of leadership. Meanwhile, the many possess ordinary and extraordinary religious capital of their own. Their ways of living within boundaries and learning how to cross them tell us many things about human possibility and realization that the story of the one religion cannot tell. In a word, both American culture and American religious history would be diminished without the many. Their stories need to be told with a sense of texture and a feel for detail that hints of who they are and what material and spiritual resources they have acquired.

The coexistence through several centuries of one religion and many religions is, of course, a fact of American life. But it is also a significant ordinary and extraordinary religious achievement, an achievement that suggests a potential to be tapped and a basic fund of regard and respect to be counted. Still more, the tension between the one and the many is not simply a burdensome condition with which American religious history has been saddled and with which it has dealt in a successful way. Rather, the tension created by point and counterpoint is an asset. The tension has meant a more complex, more ambiguous, and finally more "live" religious situation for all Americans, one in which, as a next step, forms of religious combination have flourished in new and exciting ways.

Over the years, as pluralism grew stronger, postpluralism developed alongside it. Religious people who lived side by side began to take their cues from one another. The combinations are easier to spot among the many who acculturated to the

Protestant mainstream. But they worked the other way as well. In other words, Protestants began to look at what non-Protestants were doing and incorporate some elements from these other worlds into their own. Even in early America, some Puritans ran away to live with the Indians, and others who had been captured in Indian raids refused the ransoms that Anglo-American colonists raised for them. As time passed, whites learned, too, to consult Indian healers who used combined herbal and ritual means to make them well. White Southerners, in turn, often subtly changed their religious style in the presence of their black slaves. It is an open question whether the presence of blacks increased the emotionalism and the bodily "exercises" of the revivals. Black spirituals taught Americans a new way of singing, and in our own time it is religion as usual to find white congregations singing African American spiritual songs from slavery times. Meanwhile, Protestants have borrowed from Catholics in recent times in their increasing interest in liturgical forms of religion and in their embrace of mystical techniques nurtured within the medieval church. The labyrinth—a maze with intricate pathways and blind alleys that symbolizes the soul's quest to reach God in the center—can now be found in some mainstream Protestant churches. In our own time, also, new spirituality exists as a composite religious form from which many Protestants and other Christians borrow.

Despite the combinative instinct with regard to religious forms, the problem of creating community remains. Often, the "chosen" representatives of the one religion, as if in a fortress surrounded by a moat, cannot consciously let down the bridge to others. To do so might lessen the monopoly of the dominant center. The many, if they feel out of power, also have a hard time beginning an honest conversation. They need to define and maintain their boundaries—their side of the territory. So behind the problem of community in the United States is another one. The ordinary and extraordinary religious problem of the nation is a pronounced culture of contraction in the present (avoiding real contact) and an overexpansive millennial vision for the future. In short, caught between boundaries and dreams of what lies beyond them, the one and the many have found it difficult to maintain balance. The numerous forms of religious combination that have grown up have so far not been strong enough to do away with fears and conflicts.

Dreams, we know, are not reality. Although they can be a source of creativity and vital energy, they can also weave illusions that leave people ill-prepared to cope with daytime problems. Dreams can also mask fears that harm the waking lives of dreamers. In the case of millennialism, the irony of the dream is large. Bound to the vision of an expansive new heaven and earth, millennialism is an *old* dream from an *old* world. Although it has thrived in North America and has lent itself to many forms of religious combination, millennialism is largely a product of the European heritage and imagination. So even with the Americanness of American religions and religion, millennialism is not a fresh response to a new situation. Millennial time is not *lived-through* time; and it takes attention away from the present and the religious possibilities of the moment. Americans have not yet fully awakened from their dream, and a completely American religion has not yet come to be. People in the New World are still learning to do something really new.

SUGGESTIONS FOR FURTHER READING

Defining Religion in America

Bell, Catherine. *Ritual Theory, Ritual Practice*. New York: Oxford University Press, 1992.

Berger, Peter L., and Luckmann, Thomas. *The Social Construction of Reality: A Treatise in the Sociology of Knowledge*. Garden City, NY: Doubleday Anchor, 1967.

Eliade, Mircea. *The Sacred and the Profane*. New York: Harcourt, Brace & World, Harvest Books, 1959.

McGuire, Meredith. *Religion: The Social Context*. 4th ed. Belmont, CA: Wadsworth, 1997.

Mead, Sidney E. *The Lively Experiment: The Shaping of Christianity in America*. New York: Harper & Row, 1963.

Niebuhr, H. Richard. *The Social Sources of Denominationalism* (1929). New York: New American Library, Meridian Books, 1975.

Tweed, Thomas A. *Crossing and Dwelling: A Theory of Religion*. Cambridge, MA: Harvard University Press, 2006.

Van Gennep, Arnold. *The Rites of Passage* (1909). Trans. Monika B. Vizedom and Gabrielle L. Caffee. Chicago: University of Chicago Press, 1960.

Wach, Joachim. *Sociology of Religion* (1944). Chicago: University of Chicago Press, Phoenix Books, 1962.

American Indian Religions

Brown, Joseph Epes. *The Sacred Pipe*. Baltimore: Penguin Books, 1971.

Deloria, Philip J. *Indians in Unexpected Places*. Lawrence: University Press of Kansas, 2004.

Deloria, Vine, Jr. *God Is Red: A Native View of Religion*. 2d ed. Golden, CO: Fulcrum Publishing, 1992.

———, **and Parks, Douglas R., eds.** *Sioux Indian Religion: Tradition and Innovation*. Norman: University of Oklahoma Press, 1987.

Geertz, Armin W. *The Invention of Prophecy: Continuity and Meaning in Hopi Indian Religion*. Berkeley: University of California Press, 1994.

Gill, Sam D. *Native American Religions: An Introduction*. Belmont, CA: Wadsworth, 1982.

Holler, Clyde. *Black Elk's Religion: The Sun Dance and Lakota Catholicism*. Syracuse, NY: Syracuse University Press, 1995.

Loftin, John D. *Religion and Hopi Life in the Twentieth Century*. Bloomington: Indiana University Press, 1991.

Treat, James, ed. *Native and Christian: Indigenous Voices on Religious Identity in the United States and Canada*. New York: Routledge, 1996.

Vecsey, Christopher. *On the Padres' Trail*. Notre Dame, IN: University of Notre Dame Press, 1996.

———. *The Paths of Kateri's Kin*. Notre Dame, IN: University of Notre Dame Press, 1997.

———. *Where the Two Roads Meet*. Notre Dame, IN: University of Notre Dame Press, 1999.

Warrior, Robert Allen. *Tribal Secrets: Recovering American Indian Intellectual Traditions*. Minneapolis: University of Minnesota Press, 1995.

Weaver, Jace. *Other Words: American Indian Literature, Law, and Culture*. Norman: University of Oklahoma Press, 2001.

Judaism

Blau, Joseph L. *Judaism in America: From Curiosity to Third Faith*. Chicago: University of Chicago Press, 1976.

Diner, Hasia. *The Jews of the United States, 1645 to 2000*. Berkeley: University of California Press, 2004.

Frankiel, Tamar. *The Voice of Sarah: Feminine Spirituality and Traditional Judaism*. San Francisco: Harper, 1990.

Gaster, Theodor H. *Festivals of the Jewish Year*. New York: William Sloane Associates, 1953.

Glazer, Nathan. *American Judaism*. Chicago: University of Chicago Press, 1957.

Greenberg, Irving. *The Jewish Way: Living the Holidays*. New York: Simon & Schuster, 1993.

Heilman, Samuel C. *Portrait of American Jews: The Last Half of the Twentieth Century*. Seattle: University of Washington Press, 1995.

Hertzberg, Arthur. *The Jews in America: Four Centuries of an Uneasy Encounter*. New York: Simon & Schuster, 1989.

Heschel, Abraham J. *The Sabbath: Its Meaning for Modern Man*. New York: Farrar, Straus, and Young, 1951.

Nadell, Pamela S., and Sarna, Jonathan D., eds. *Women and American Judaism: Historical Perspectives*. Hanover, NH: Brandeis University Press, 2001.

Neuhaus, Richard John, ed. *The Chosen People in an Almost Chosen Nation: Jews and Judaism in America.* Grand Rapids, MI: William B. Eerdmans, 2002.

Raphael, Marc Lee. *Judaism in America.* New York: Columbia University Press, 2003.

Sarna, Jonathan D. *American Judaism: A History.* New Haven: Yale University Press, 2004.

Roman Catholicism

Cross, Robert D. *The Emergence of Liberal Catholicism in America.* Cambridge, MA: Harvard University Press, 1958.

Cuneo, Michael W. *The Smoke of Satan: Conservative and Traditionalist Dissent in Contemporary American Catholicism.* New York: Oxford University Press, 1997.

Dolan, Jay P. *The American Catholic Experience: A History from Colonial Times to the Present.* Garden City, NY: Doubleday, 1985.

———, and Deck, Allan Figueroa, eds. *Hispanic Catholic Culture in the U.S.: Issues and Concerns.* Notre Dame, IN: University of Notre Dame Press, 1994.

Fisher, James T. *Communion of Immigrants: A History of Catholics in America.* New York: Oxford University Press, 2002.

Gillis, Chester. *Roman Catholicism in America.* New York: Columbia University Press, 1999.

Greeley, Andrew. *The Catholic Revolution: New Wine, Old Wineskins, and the Second Vatican Council.* Berkeley: University of California Press, 2004.

Matovina, Timothy, and Riebe-Estrella, Gary, eds. *Horizons of the Sacred: Mexican Traditions in U.S. Catholicism.* Ithaca, NY: Cornell University Press, 2002.

McGreevy, John T. *Catholicism and American Freedom: A History.* New York: W. W. Norton, 2003.

———. *Parish Boundaries: The Catholic Encounter with Race in the Twentieth-Century Urban North.* Chicago: University of Chicago Press, 1996.

Nabhan-Warren, Kristy. *The Virgin of El Barrio: Marian Apparitions, Catholic Evangelizing, and Mexican American Activism.* New York: New York University Press, 2005.

Orsi, Robert Anthony. *Between Heaven and Earth: The Religious Worlds People Make and the Scholars Who Study Them.* Princeton: Princeton University Press, 2004.

———. *Thank You, St. Jude: Women's Devotion to the Patron Saint of Hopeless Causes.* New Haven: Yale University Press, 1996.

American Protestant Origins and the Liberal Tradition

Balmer, Randall. *Grant Us Courage: Travels along the Mainline of American Protestantism.* New York: Oxford University Press, 1996.

———, and Winner, Lauren F. *Protestantism in America.* New York: Columbia University Press, 2002.

Holifield, E. Brooks. *Theology in America: Christian Thought from the Age of the Puritans to the Civil War*. New Haven: Yale University Press, 2003.

Hutchison, William R. *The Modernist Impulse in American Protestantism* (1976). Reprint. New York: Oxford University Press, 1982.

———. *Religious Pluralism in America: The Contentious History of a Founding Ideal*. New Haven: Yale University Press, 2003.

———, ed. *Between the Times: The Travail of the Protestant Establishment in America, 1900–1960*. Cambridge: Cambridge University Press, 1989.

Juster, Susan, and MacFarlane, Lisa, eds. *A Mighty Baptism: Race, Gender, and the Creation of American Protestantism*. Ithaca, NY: Cornell University Press, 1996.

Marty, Martin E. *Protestantism in the United States: Righteous Empire*. 2d ed. New York: Scribner's, 1986.

Morgan, Edmund S. *Visible Saints: The History of a Puritan Idea*. New York: New York University Press, 1963.

Porterfield, Amanda. *Female Piety in Puritan New England: The Emergence of Religious Humanism*. New York: Oxford University Press, 1992.

Reardon, Bernard M. G. *Religious Thought in the Reformation*. 2d ed. New York: Longman, 1995.

Roberts, Jon H. *Darwinism and the Divine in America: Protestant Intellectuals and Organic Evolution, 1859–1900*. Madison: University of Wisconsin Press, 1988.

White, Ronald C., Jr., and Hopkins, C. Howard. *The Social Gospel: Religion and Reform in Changing America*. Philadelphia: Temple University Press, 1976.

The Protestant Churches and the Mission Mind

Anderson, Robert M. *Vision of the Disinherited: The Making of American Pentecostalism*. New York: Oxford University Press, 1979.

Blumhofer, Edith L. *Restoring the Faith: The Assemblies of God, Pentecostalism, and American Culture*. Urbana: University of Illinois Press, 1993.

Bowden, Henry Warner. *American Indians and Christian Missions: Studies in Cultural Conflict*. Chicago: University of Chicago Press, 1981.

Butler, Jon. *Awash in a Sea of Faith: Christianizing the American People*. Cambridge, MA: Harvard University Press, 1990.

Carpenter, Joel A., and Shenk, Wilbert R., eds. *Earthen Vessels: American Evangelicals and Foreign Missions, 1880–1980*. Grand Rapids, MI: William B. Eerdmans, 1990.

Emerson, Michael O., and Smith, Christian. *Divided by Faith: Evangelical Religion and the Problem of Race in America*. New York: Oxford University Press, 2000.

Hart, D. G. *That Old-Time Religion in Modern America: Evangelical Protestantism in the Twentieth Century*. Chicago: Ivan R. Dee, 2002.

Hughes, Richard T., ed. *The American Quest for the Primitive Church*. Urbana: University of Illinois Press, 1988.

———, **and Allen, C. Leonard.** *Illusions of Innocence: Protestant Primitivism in America, 1630–1875*. Chicago: University of Chicago Press, 1988.

Hutchison, William R. *Errand to the World: American Protestant Thought and Foreign Missions*. Chicago: University of Chicago Press, 1987.

Marsden, George M. *Fundamentalism and American Culture: The Shaping of Twentieth-Century Evangelicalism, 1870–1925*. 2d ed. New York: Oxford University Press, 2006.

McLoughlin, William G., Jr. *Revivals, Awakenings, and Reform*. Chicago: University of Chicago Press, 1978.

Noll, Mark A. *America's God: From Jonathan Edwards to Abraham Lincoln*. New York: Oxford University Press, 2002.

Sandeen, Ernest R. *The Roots of Fundamentalism: British and American Millenarianism, 1800–1930*. Chicago: University of Chicago Press, 1970.

African American Religion

Brown, Karen McCarthy. *Mama Lola: A Vodou Priestess in Brooklyn*. Berkeley: University of California Press, 1991.

Chireau, Yvonne P. *Black Magic: Religion and the African American Conjuring Tradition*. Berkeley: University of California Press, 2003.

Diouf, Sylviane A. *Servants of Allah: African Muslims Enslaved in the Americas*. New York: New York University Press, 1998.

Gomez, Michael A. *Exchanging Our Country Marks: The Transformation of African Identities in the Colonial and Antebellum South*. Chapel Hill: University of North Carolina Press, 1998.

Levine, Lawrence W. *Black Culture and Black Consciousness: Afro-American Folk Thought from Slavery to Freedom*. New York: Oxford University Press, 1977.

Lincoln, C. Eric, and Mamiya, Lawrence H. *The Black Church in the African American Experience*. Durham, NC: Duke University Press, 1990.

Long, Charles H. *Significations: Signs, Symbols, and Images in the Interpretation of Religion*. Philadelphia: Fortress Press, 1986.

Murphy, Joseph M. *Santería: An African Religion in America*. Boston: Beacon Press, 1988.

Raboteau, Albert J. *Canaan Land: A Religious History of African Americans*. New York: Oxford University Press, 2001.

———. *Slave Religion: The "Invisible Institution" in the Antebellum South*. New York: Oxford University Press, 1978.

Ray, Benjamin C. *African Religions: Symbol, Ritual, and Community*. Englewood Cliffs, NJ: Prentice-Hall, 1976.

Sanders, Cheryl J. *Saints in Exile: The Holiness-Pentecostal Experience in African American Religion and Culture*. New York: Oxford University Press, 1996.

Thompson, Robert Farris. *Flash of the Spirit: African and Afro-American Art and Philosophy*. New York: Random House, 1983.

Nineteenth-Century New Religions

Bull, Malcolm, and Lockhart, Keith. *Seeking a Sanctuary: Seventh-day Adventism and the American Dream.* San Francisco: Harper & Row, 1989.

Bushman, Claudia Lauper, and Bushman, Richard. *Building the Kingdom: A History of Mormons in America.* New York: Oxford University Press, 2001.

Carden, Maren Lockwood. *Oneida: Utopian Community to Modern Corporation.* Baltimore: Johns Hopkins Press, 1969.

Doan, Ruth Alden. *The Miller Heresy, Millennialism, and American Culture.* Philadelphia: Temple University Press, 1987.

Foster, Lawrence. *Religion and Sexuality: Three American Communal Experiments of the Nineteenth Century.* New York: Oxford University Press, 1981.

Gottschalk, Stephen. *The Emergence of Christian Science in American Religious Life.* Berkeley: University of California Press, 1973.

———. *Rolling Away the Stone: Mary Baker Eddy's Challenge to Materialism.* Bloomington: Indiana University Press, 2006.

Penton, M. James. *Apocalypse Delayed: The Story of Jehovah's Witnesses.* Toronto: University of Toronto Press, 1985.

Schoepflin, Rennie B. *Christian Science on Trial: Religious Healing in America.* Baltimore: Johns Hopkins University Press, 2002.

Shipps, Jan. *Mormonism: The Story of a New Religious Tradition.* Urbana: University of Illinois Press, 1985.

Stein, Stephen J. *Communities of Dissent: A History of Alternative Religions in America.* New York: Oxford University Press, 2003.

———. *The Shaker Experience in America: A History of the United Society of Believers.* New Haven: Yale University Press, 1992.

Tabor, James D., and Gallagher, Eugene V. *Why Waco? Cults and the Battle for Religious Freedom in America.* Berkeley: University of California Press, 1995.

Troeltsch, Ernst. *The Social Teaching of the Christian Churches* (1911). 2 vols. Trans. Olive Wyon. Reprint. Chicago: University of Chicago Press, 1976.

Metaphysical Religion

Albanese, Catherine L. *A Republic of Mind and Spirit: A Cultural History of American Metaphysical Religion.* New Haven: Yale University Press, 2006.

Braden, Charles S. *Spirits in Rebellion: The Rise and Development of New Thought.* Dallas: Southern Methodist University Press, 1963.

Campbell, Bruce F. *Ancient Wisdom Revived: A History of the Theosophical Movement.* Berkeley: University of California Press, 1980.

Carroll, Bret E. *Spiritualism in Antebellum America.* Bloomington: Indiana University Press, 1997.

Cox, Robert S. *Body and Soul: A Sympathetic History of American Spiritualism.* Charlottesville: University Press of Virginia, 2003.

Ellwood, Robert S., Jr. *Alternative Altars: Unconventional and Eastern Spirituality in America.* Chicago: University of Chicago Press, 1979.

———, and Partin, Harry B. *Religious and Spiritual Groups in Modern America.* 2d ed. Englewood Cliffs, NJ: Prentice-Hall, 1988.

Fuller, Robert C. *Mesmerism and the American Cure of Souls.* Philadelphia: University of Pennsylvania Press, 1982.

Godbeer, Richard. *The Devil's Dominion: Magic and Religion in Early New England.* Cambridge: Cambridge University Press, 1992.

Harvey, Graham. *Contemporary Paganism: Listening People, Speaking Earth.* New York: New York University Press, 1997.

Judah, J. Stillson. *The History and Philosophy of the Metaphysical Movements in America.* Philadelphia: Westminster Press, 1967.

Leventhal, Herbert. *In the Shadow of the Enlightenment: Occultism and Renaissance Science in Eighteenth-Century America.* New York: New York University Press, 1976.

Satter, Beryl. *Each Mind a Kingdom: American Women, Sexual Purity, and the New Thought Movement, 1875–1920.* Berkeley: University of California Press, 1999.

Eastern Peoples and Eastern Religions

Binns, John. *An Introduction to the Christian Orthodox Churches.* Cambridge: Cambridge University Press, 2002.

Coleman, James William. *The New Buddhism: The Western Transformation of an Ancient Tradition.* New York: Oxford University Press, 2001.

Coward, Harold, et al., eds. *The South Asian Religious Diaspora in Britain, Canada, and the United States.* Albany: State University of New York Press, 2000.

Eck, Diana L. *A New Religious America: How a "Christian Country" Has Now Become the World's Most Religiously Diverse Nation.* San Francisco: HarperSanFrancisco, 2001.

Erickson, John H. *Orthodox Christians in America.* New York: Oxford University Press, 1999.

Esposito, John L. *Islam: The Straight Path.* 3d ed. New York: Oxford University Press, 2005.

Fitzgerald, Thomas E. *The Orthodox Church.* Westport, CT: Greenwood, 1995.

Haddad, Yvonne Yazbeck, ed. *The Muslims of America.* New York: Oxford University Press, 1993.

———, and Esposito, John L., eds. *Muslims on the Americanization Path?* New York: Oxford University Press, 2000.

Mann, Gurinder Singh, Numrich, Paul David, and Williams, Raymond B. *Buddhists, Hindus, and Sikhs in America.* New York: Oxford University Press, 2001.

McCloud, Aminah Beverly. *African American Islam.* New York: Routledge, 1995.

Morgan, Diane. *The Buddhist Experience in America.* Westport, CT: Greenwood, 2004.

Narayanan, Vasudha. *Hinduism.* New York: Oxford University Press, 2004.

Neusner, Jacob, ed. *World Religions in America: An Introduction.* 3d ed. Louisville: Westminster/John Knox Press, 2003.

Nyang, Sulayman S. *Islam in the United States of America.* Chicago: ABC International Group, 1999.

Seager, Richard Hughes. *Buddhism in America.* New York: Columbia University Press, 1999.

Smith, Jane I. *Islam in America.* New York: Columbia University Press, 1999.

Stockman, Robert H. *The Baha'i Faith in America: Origins, 1892–1900.* Wilmette, IL: Baha'i Publishing Trust, 1985.

Williams, Raymond Brady. *Religions of Immigrants from India and Pakistan: New Threads in the American Tapestry.* Cambridge: Cambridge University Press, 1988.

New Age, New Spirituality, and Recent Conservative Protestantism

Balmer, Randall. *Mine Eyes Have Seen the Glory: A Journey into the Evangelical Subculture in America.* 4th ed. New York: Oxford University Press, 2006.

Bellah, Robert N., et al. *Habits of the Heart: Individualism and Commitment in American Life.* Berkeley: University of California Press, 1985.

Boyer, Paul. *When Time Shall Be No More: Prophecy Belief in Modern American Culture.* Cambridge, MA: Harvard University Press, Belknap Press, 1992.

Brasher, Brenda. *Godly Women: Fundamentalism and Female Power.* New Brunswick, NJ: Rutgers University Press, 1998.

Frykholm, Amy Johnson. *Rapture Culture: Left Behind in Evangelical America.* New York: Oxford University Press, 2004.

Fuller, Robert C. *Spiritual but Not Religious: Understanding Unchurched America.* New York: Oxford University Press, 2001.

Hadden, Jeffrey K., and Shupe, Anson. *Televangelism: Power and Politics on God's Frontier.* New York: Henry Holt, 1988.

Hanegraaff, Wouter J. *New Age Religion and Western Culture: Esotericism in the Mirror of Secular Thought.* Albany: State University of New York Press, 1998.

Hunter, James Davison. *Culture Wars: The Struggle to Define America.* New York: BasicBooks, 1991.

Marsden, George. *Reforming Fundamentalism: Fuller Seminary and the New Evangelicalism.* Grand Rapids, MI: William B. Eerdmans, 1987.

Pike, Sarah M. *New Age and Neopagan Religions in America.* New York: Columbia University Press, 2004.

Roof, Wade Clark. *Spiritual Marketplace: Baby Boomers and the Remaking of American Religion.* Princeton: Princeton University Press, 1999.

Schmidt, Leigh Eric. *Restless Souls: The Making of American Spirituality.* San Francisco: HarperSanFrancisco, 2005.

Wilcox, Clyde, and Larson, Carin. *Onward Christian Soldiers: The Religious Right in American Politics.* 3d ed. Boulder, CO: Westview Press, 2006.

Wuthnow, Robert. *After Heaven: Spirituality in America since the 1950s*. Berkeley: University of California Press, 1998.

Public Religion, Civil Religion, and Cultural Religion

Albanese, Catherine L. *Nature Religion in America: From the Algonkian Indians to the New Age*. Chicago: University of Chicago Press, 1990.

———. *Sons of the Fathers: The Civil Religion of the American Revolution*. Philadelphia: Temple University Press, 1976.

Bellah, Robert N. *The Broken Covenant: American Civil Religion in Time of Trial*. New York: Seabury Press, 1975.

Cherry, Conrad, ed. *God's New Israel: Religious Interpretations of American Destiny*. 2d ed. Chapel Hill: University of North Carolina Press, 1998.

Herberg, Will. *Protestant, Catholic, Jew*. Rev. ed. Garden City, NY: Doubleday Anchor, 1960.

Jewett, Robert, and Lawrence, John Shelton. *Captain America and the Crusade against Evil*. Grand Rapids, MI: William B. Eerdmans, 2003.

Lawrence, John Shelton, and Jewett, Robert. *The Myth of the American Superhero*. Grand Rapids, MI: William B. Eerdmans, 2002.

McLuhan, Marshall. *The Mechanical Bride: Folklore of Industrial Man* (1951). Reprint. Boston: Beacon Press, 1967.

Mead, Sidney E. *The Nation with the Soul of a Church*. New York: Harper & Row, 1975.

Novak, Michael. *The Joy of Sports: End Zones, Bases, Baskets, Balls, and the Consecration of the American Spirit*. New York: Basic Books, 1976.

Richey, Russell E., and Jones, Donald G., eds. *American Civil Religion*. New York: Harper & Row, 1974.

Schmidt, Leigh Eric. *Consumer Rites: The Buying and Selling of American Holidays*. Princeton: Princeton University Press, 1995.

Williams, Peter W. *Popular Religion in America: Symbolic Change and the Modernization Process in Historical Perspective*. Rev. ed. Urbana: University of Illinois Press, 1989.

Many Centers Meeting

Ahlstrom, Sydney E. *A Religious History of the American People* (1972). Rev. ed., David D. Hall. New Haven: Yale University Press, 2004.

Butler, Jon, Wacker, Grant, and Balmer, Randall. *Religion in American Life: A Short History*. New York: Oxford University Press, 2003.

Corrigan, John, and Hudson, Winthrop S. *Religion in America: An Historical Account of the Development of American Religious Life*. 7th ed. Upper Saddle River, NJ: Pearson/Prentice Hall, 2004.

Dinnerstein, Leonard, ed. *Antisemitism in the United States*. New York: Holt, Rinehart & Winston, 1961.

Franchot, Jenny. *Roads to Rome: The Antebellum Protestant Encounter with Catholicism*. Berkeley: University of California Press, 1994.

Higham, John. *Strangers in the Land: Patterns of American Nativism, 1860–1925*. 2d ed. New Brunswick, NJ: Rutgers University Press, 1988.

Marty, Martin E. *The One and the Many: America's Struggle for the Common Good*. Cambridge, MA: Harvard University Press, 1997.

———. *Pilgrims in Their Own Land: 500 Years of Religion in America*. Boston: Little, Brown, 1984.

Moore, R. Laurence. *Religious Outsiders and the Making of Americans*. New York: Oxford University Press, 1986.

Williams, Peter W. *America's Religions: Traditions and Cultures*. New York: Macmillan, 1990.

Wuthnow, Robert. *The Restructuring of American Religion: Society and Faith since World War II*. Princeton: Princeton University Press, 1988.

NAME INDEX

Note: Page numbers in bold type indicate an important reference to this individual. Page numbers in italic type indicate illustrations.

SUBJECT INDEX

Note: Page numbers in bold type indicate an important reference to this item. Page numbers in italic type indicate illustrations.

ILLUSTRATION CREDITS

This page constitutes an extension of the copyright page. We have made every effort to trace the ownership of all copyrighted material and to secure permission from copyright holders. In the event of any question arising as to the use of any material, we will be pleased to make the necessary corrections in future printings. Thanks are due to the following authors, publishers, and agents for permission to use the material indicated.

Introduction. 8: Museum of the City of New York, The Harry T. Peters Collection

Chapter 1. 16: California Museum of Photography, Keystone-Mast Collection, University of California, Riverside **32:** Courtesy of Museum of Northern Arizona Photo Archives

Chapter 2. 42, top and bottom: John Hoph

Chapter 3. 69: Arnold Zann/ Black Star

Chapter 4. 89: Steve Rosenthal

Chapter 5. 117: Library of Congress **122:** Catherine L. Albanese, Aaron Gross, and Bartay Studio

Chapter 6. 141: Bequest of Maxim Karolik, Museum of Fine Arts, Boston

Chapter 7. 158: First published by William E. Smythe, *The Conquest of Arid America*, 1900 **172:** The Western Reserve Historical Society, Cleveland, Ohio

Chapter 8. 186: Wellcome Institute Library, London **192:** Catherine L. Albanese and Aaron Gross

Chapter 9. 202: California Museum of Photography, Keystone-Mast Collection, University of California, Riverside **217:** Raymond B. Williams

Chapter 10. 233: Photo by Marti Kranzberg, 1982, Courtesy Bear Tribe Medicine Society **244:** *Fundamentalist Journal*, September 1983

Chapter 11. 254, 258: Library of Congress **261:** Courtesy of Billy Graham Center Museum **269:** The Metropolitan Museum of Art, New York, gift of William H. Huntington

Chapter 12. 285: Library of Congress